Y0-BDI-813

PEOPLE
and
PLACE

Society for the Protection of New Hampshire Forests

THE FIRST 100 YEARS

Editors:
ROSEMARY G. CONROY ❧ RICHARD OBER

Acknowledgment

The most difficult task in compiling a book like this one is making the difficult decisions about what not to include. Care was taken to include as many major events and acknowledge as many key people and places as possible. However, it was simply not possible to cover every campaign and event and program. We extend our regrets for any glaring omissions or errors.

Background material for this book came from many sources: Especially useful were Forest Notes, 1937 - 2000; the Society's archives, which are located at Special Collections, Dimond Library, University of New Hampshire; the book *A Greener Earth*, written by Evan Hill and published by the Society in 1977; numerous personal interviews conducted by the authors of many chapters; and an earlier history, *New Hampshire Everlasting and Unfallen*, written by UNH historian Paul Bruns (shown here with longtime Society leader Edgar Hirst) and published by the Society in 1967.

The editors

ISBN 0-9712102-0-9

Designed and printed by Imperial Company, Inc., West Lebanon, New Hampshire.

Society for the Protection of New Hampshire Forests
54 Portsmouth Street
Concord, New Hampshire 03301
(603) 224-9945
www.spnhf.org

This book is dedicated to
the members and volunteers of the
Society for the Protection of New Hampshire Forests.

Contributed Support

The Society is grateful to the following generous supporters who contributed to the publication of this book.

Eric Aldrich

Public Service of New Hampshire

As a fellow statewide organization with deep roots in New Hampshire, we share the Society's goals of preserving the state's rural heritage and enhancing its quality of life. Our alliance to protect nearly 50 acres along the Androscoggin River in Dummer is one demonstration of our shared commitment. Like other Society projects, the Paul O. Bofinger Conservation Area ensures that New Hampshire citizens will have the opportunity to enjoy the state's pristine beauty for generations to come. We congratulate the Society on this milestone and look forward to another century of working together to preserve the character and living landscape of New Hampshire.

Gary A. Long
President

George Barker

Country Woods Unfinished Furniture

We are proud to be part of an organization that early on recognized the myriad pressures on our woodlands and has made enormous contributions in preserving and protecting them. Trees are New Hampshire's renewable resource, but every resource needs skilled stewardship and the Society provides this in abundance.

Marilyn and Bill Cavanaugh
Owners

COUNTRY WOODS

Table of Contents

Places

Voices

Our Second Century

Appendix

Preface

IMAGINE LIFE WITHOUT the Society for the Protection of New Hampshire Forests. What would our landscape look like? Would more than one-fifth of the state be protected for people and plants and animals? Would New Hampshire's land conservation ethic have served as a model of collaborative problem solving for the rest of the country? Would the rivers run clean? Would the paths be hiked? Would the tourists visit?

I have been honored to work with the trustees and staff on the Trust for New Hampshire Lands, the Living Landscape agenda, growth management, the Land and Community Heritage Investment Program, and so much more. One hundred years of programs and projects have proven that a healthy economy, vibrant communities, and a protected environment are inextricably linked.

The Forest Society exhibits all the qualities of an organization that lives its mission and encourages individuals to build bonds and bridges for strong civic involvement. Ten thousand members tell a powerful story — a story about how to grow social capital and engage in our communities.

I have also felt the shade of the trees, smelled the balsam, and admired the views — preserved and protected by 100 years of dedication and extraordinary stewardship.

Imagine life without the Forest Society? No thank you.

Lew Feldstein
President
New Hampshire Charitable Foundation

Foreword

Jim Collins

We heard the coyotes last night. Their barking rose from the back field, very close to the house. Kristen and I went to the window, strained to see their dark shapes against the snow. Pale silver moonlight flooded the night, lit up the field beyond the spidery maples and oaks. A few weeks ago they had come right into the yard. Their barking had turned the air electric, set our hair on end. Tonight, after only a minute or two, the air was still again. Nothing stirred.

Before getting back into bed, I paused at the room's other window. In the distance the long wooded ridge that falls off to the south of Cardigan's summit stretched black in the moonlight, framing the flat wide expanse of Orange Pond. North of the pond, the blocky hump of Hoyt Hill wrapped around back home, impossibly close.

It was just this mixing of curve and flat expanse, of wild topography and open land, that drew us to this place.

I'd lived my whole life in New Hampshire, almost all of it in the watery, woodsy towns that ring Mount Monadnock in the southwestern part of the state. I'd fallen in love with the outdoors in the Dartmouth Outing Club, had worked for a glorious summer and fall in the White Mountains with the Appalachian Mountain Club's trail crew. Kristen had lived in the Pacific Northwest and responded to vertical landscapes and big sky.

Still, when we first came to this high bench of land in the shadow of Mount Cardigan, we felt a connection that went deeper than landscape. As in so many places in New Hampshire, something almost tangible seemed to rise from the history that lies so close to the surface here. This has been working land. The land along this dirt road has been farmed and logged and lived on. The farms blinked out one by one — ours in 1908 — but pockets of the land have stayed open; some

Crawford Notch, White Mountains. Protected in 1913. Photo: Harry Lichtman.

of it is still being hayed. Stone walls, of course, run everywhere, even up steep, wooded hillsides. Most of the woods are third-growth. A cabin on our property was used by mica miners in the 1910s. We have snowshoed up the old woods roads to the overgrown mines on Hoyt Hill. During the four decades our property ran as a summer camp, that same cabin was used by city kids who came here in search of nature. We've found remnants of their trails, of their tent clearings. So much life lived close to the land. So many reminders. And then there's Cardigan itself, whose bald, granite, fire-towered summit dominates this little hill town. It was the first mountain my grandmother climbed, and my mother, and I. In 2000, at two years old, my daughter made her first ascent. This kind of long family linkage is not uncommon around here.

New Hampshire's forested and working land is part of a subtle alchemy that creates our sense of place. The alchemy has a lot to do with continuity of land use and landscape. Our spot lies in the central part of the state: below the wilder, sparsely populated land north of us in the White Mountains and beyond the notches, and upstate from the flatter communities sprawling out from the seacoast and Massachusetts border country. The pressures from growth and a changing economy have affected all of the state to varying degrees, but no town has been immune.

That subtle alchemy no longer happens as a matter of course or by accident. We know, for instance, that much of the land along this road is taxed under current use assessment so its owners can afford to keep it undeveloped. We know that our view across Orange Pond — out to that lovely long ridge coming down off Cardigan's summit — is entirely within the 5,655-acre Cardigan State Park, which spreads all the way to the back shore of the pond. We know the view from Cardigan, itself, spreads out over a patchwork of protected forests and peaks, in every direction: north to Bald Knob and the Cockermouth Forest; west to Smarts Mountain and Cummins Pond, out across the protected shoreline of the Mascoma River and over the forever-wild fingery bays and coves of Grafton Pond; and farther south to more protected land: to Ragged Mountain and Mount Kearsarge and, on the far horizon, the familiar, triangular summit of Monadnock, reminding me how far I've come and how close I still I am. The views from Cardigan startle me, always. They are wilder now than when my mother climbed the mountain as a girl.

We feel blessed to live in a state where these wild and working lands have been protected. Where the past is not so divorced from the present that it's lost all historic meaning. Where an ethic of living close to the land, in and with the land, survives. Where there are citizen groups like the Society for the Protection of New Hampshire Forests watching over that land, and therefore over us.

"There's no backcountry here," Kristen observed once, thinking of the huge roadless wildernesses of the West. "It's all front country." But around much of the state, a surprising amount of that front country is rugged, filled with lives our parents and grandparents would recognize. We are living in a particular place, and are being formed by it. As we get to know it better — bushwhacking on skis, hiking the public trails, clearing our own, discovering high meadows and blueberries — our relationship with it grows intimate.

With continued stewardship and luck, in a generation or two someone living here will hear coyotes at night and feel a visceral, unspoken connection. He or she might read these words and feel a shock of recognition.

Introduction

RICHARD OBER

IN SPRING 1999, a newspaper published two letters to the editor criticizing the Society for its position on a policy affecting the White Mountain National Forest. One letter came from Ted and the other from John. Each author sternly took the organization to task for not standing up to the bad guys. Each warned that the Society's policy would alienate the public. Each predicted dire circumstances if the course were not corrected. They were the kind of letters that generally merit a firm response.

They didn't get one.

Ted and John, you see, were arguing diametrically opposed views. Ted said the Society was siding too heavily with big environmental groups; John said the organization was too cozy with loggers and foresters. Ted said we should advocate clearcutting in the White Mountains; John implored us to oppose all forestry there. Ted wanted us to listen only to people who lived in communities near the national forest. John wanted us to join a national campaign to force top-down changes in Forest Service rules.

The letters, in essence, canceled each other out. A formal response would have been redundant.

To those who prefer to choose up sides on environmental issues, this organization has remained an enigma. Is the Society a land trust that cuts trees or a forestry association that preserves biological diversity? Does it advocate for the environment or for traditional land uses? Are its allies bird-watchers or lumberjacks? Can it really promote with equal vigor both the wise use *and* the reservation of natural resources?

Answers: Both. Both. Both. And yes.

Filling these multiple roles has not been the easier path. To the contrary, it would have been much simpler to push only for land conservation or only for good forestry or only for strong environmental policy. Many fine organizations here and around the country have made great advances by sticking to just one of these goals. They

Lost River Gorge, North Woodstock. Protected in 1912. Photo: Ralph Morang.

may have had their critics, but at least the broadsides came from only one direction. Ted or John might be upset with them, but probably not Ted *and* John.

No, the Society balances these things for one reason: the mission. In 1904, three years after the organization was founded, the directors resolved: "The Society is a forestry association seeking to perpetuate the forests of New Hampshire through their wise use and their complete reservation in places of special scenic beauty." Much, of course, changed between 1904 and 2001. Scientific understanding evolved, population pressures increased, new conservation tools emerged. The interpretation of "special scenic beauty" expanded to include many other attributes that made land deserving of formal protection, and the term "wise use" was usurped for a short while by property-rights ideologues. The spirit of the mission, however, remained intact.

In this dual role people could find their own place — literally and figuratively. They could see that real progress took place not on the fringes of public debate but in the middle, where people were willing to roll up their sleeves and find practical solutions. They could visit Society reservations where forestry and environmental protection coexisted. They could learn to be stewards of the land in a way that honored all of its values — intrinsic, natural, spiritual, aesthetic, economic, social. They did not have to choose sides. And they could find the best of themselves in a realistic, collaborative relationship with the land and with others.

The founders included a former governor, a hotelier, a suffragette, a journalist. It was a prominent industrialist — T. Jefferson Coolidge of the Amoskeag Manufacturing Company — who helped break a congressional deadlock over legislation establishing the eastern national forests. A Boston financier allied with garden clubs and progressive women's groups to make possible the acquisition of Franconia Notch in the 1920s. The campaigns for timber tax reform, conservation commissions, current use, the Trust for New Hampshire Lands, and the Land and Community Heritage Investment Program united in common cause snowmobilers and backcountry skiers, suburban commuters and dirt foresters, wilderness advocates and loggers. After president/forester Paul Bofinger successfully mediated the process that led to the White Mountain Wilderness Act of 1984, Sierra Club activist Abigail Avery and North Country woodsman Burm Garland signed their names side-by-side on a plaque honoring the Society's leadership. On the membership rolls were scions of both Republican and Democratic politics: Adamses and Kings, Greggs and Dunfeys, Shaheens and Basses, Rauhs and Thomsons. By housing multiple tenant organizations with diverse missions, the Society's Conservation Center in Concord became a physical icon of this inclusiveness. In the meeting rooms and around the coffeepot, alliances were built and differences resolved.

More than any other one factor, this nearly genetic impulse to collaboration over confrontation has distinguished conservation in the Granite State and informed the Society's first century. Paul Bofinger always called it the "New Hampshire way;" Judd Gregg used the term "conservation ethic." Richard Moore, president of the Audubon Society of New Hampshire, has written, "It is a culture that includes many viewpoints, that values dialogue, and that expects creativity. It is thoroughly Yankee. It is a culture that is literally rooted in the land. . . New Hampshire's culture of conservation will always go back to the unquantifiable lay of the land, the sound of leaves underfoot, the shape of the canopy. It is not a matter of theory. It is a matter of calloused palms and well-worn boots."

As Richard distilled New Hampshire's conservation style down to its essence, in these pages we have tried to distill the essence of the Society's first 100 years. Here are the astonishing stories of campaigns to pass the Weeks Act and save the Old Man of the Mountain, the drives to protect the peaks, the struggles for current use and clean water, the never-ending imperative to educate, the commitment to sustaining forestry as a core value and land use. Included are a detailed timeline, lists of lands protected, rosters of trustees and staff and volunteers, quotes from partners in business and government and conservation. We have tried to compile a book that is at once appealing and informative.

In that content lies the what, who, where, and how of the Society's work. But we also asked New Hampshire photographers and writers to explore the *why*. With the help of Peter Randall, thirty-six members of the New Hampshire Society of Photographic Artists — professionals and gifted amateurs alike — volunteered to visit Society-protected lands over many seasons. Through their eyes and their lenses is revealed the power of place: a shimmering pitcher plant, a young girl's exuberance on reaching a mountaintop, a boat aloft in Lake Solitude, Mount Kearsarge shrouded in rose clouds.

Guest writers scratch a little deeper into the duff. Novelist Ernest Hebert becomes more a part of his little woodlot in Keene when he befriends a spoon maker. Activist Peter Forbes introduces us to a Laotian woman who helped him understand why land protection matters. From a rugged hollow in the shadow of Mount Cardigan, *Yankee* editor Jim Collins marvels at a landscape that is wilder for his daughter than it was for his mother. The late Donella Meadows implores us to consider appropriateness and quality as we shape our communities. Donald Hall speaks to his beloved Kearsarge, and John Hay takes us to the source of a brook.

These essays and images and historical accounts reflect relationships with land that are complicated, seminal, powerful, dynamic. They speak not of right and wrong but of calloused palms and well-worn boots. Of use and reservation.

They speak — and the Society's first century speaks — of people and place. ❧

MILESTONES

"*I*N MY MIND, NO ENVIRONMENTAL ORGANIZATION *has contributed more to the wise stewardship and conservation of our state's natural resources than the Society for the Protection of New Hampshire Forests. Since the campaign for the passage of the Weeks Act in 1911, to the establishment of the Land and Community Heritage Investment Program, the Forest Society has defined the New Hampshire conservation ethic, an ethic based on a deep and abiding reverence for the natural environment, informed dialogue and mutual respect, and a clear understanding of the human relationship to the traditional uses of New Hampshire's living landscape.*"

Senator Judd Gregg

Conservation Center, Concord. Protected in 1978. Photo: Duane Bailey.

The Weeks Act

How the White Mountain National Forest came to be.

Martha Carlson and Richard Ober

When the White Mountains were burning, it was said, laundry hanging on lines in Manchester would turn gray with ash. Wealthy tourists traveling north to the grand hotels found the mountains stripped of timber and smoldering from slash fires.

"Instead of cutting only timber that is matured, everything is cut to the size of five or six inches in diameter, and what remains is cut into firewood or burned at once, leaving a dreary waste," the New Hampshire Forest Commission reported in 1885. "In Lancaster, the timber and wood are nearly all gone and the mountains are being stripped to their summits. Originally a dense forest covered our state. This magnificent forest has long since disappeared."

In the second half of the nineteenth century, with most of southern and central New England cleared for farming, timber companies were looking ever farther north to satisfy the nation's appetite for wood. The White Mountains were particularly attractive, for they held large stands of mature softwood and hardwood trees. Timber companies bought large tracts of land in the mountains, stripped the forest, and shipped the wood south by train. Left behind were eroded hillsides and silted streams. Massive slash piles were sparked into conflagrations, often by cinders spewed by passing locomotives.

The forest, the commission declared, was a public resource. Perhaps the state should regulate forestry more stringently and encourage farmers and loggers to reforest their land. These ideas were bold for the times. State government had virtually no control over private timberland. Indeed, the state had spent the previous seventy years selling off its forests to settlers, including the summits of the White Mountains.

Two decades after the commission's report, however, concern over New Hampshire's forested mountains had sparked a seminal conservation law — the Weeks Act of 1911. Authorizing Congress to buy private timberland for national forests,

The White Mountains. Protected following passage of the Weeks Act, 1911. Photo: Jerry and Marcy Monkman.

the act enabled the creation of forty-nine national forests in the East, including the Green Mountain and White Mountain National Forests of New England.

A Spark

To ignite public interest, sweeping changes in land use policy, like the great fires that swept across the White Mountains, need fuel and the right conditions. In the 1880s those conditions started to develop. First, in 1885, the state of New York set aside a million acres of timberland in the Catskills and the Adirondacks as a public forest reserve to protect drinking water downstream. Six years later Congress passed the Forest Reserve Act, setting aside millions of acres of western land the federal government had never sold to private settlers.

In New Hampshire, meanwhile, fire scorched the Zealand Valley at the headwaters of the Pemigewasset River in the late 1880s. Crawford Notch was stripped of timber and left barren from the resulting erosion.

In 1889 the Forest Commission warned that deforestation had a direct economic impact on the White Mountain region's 1,100 summer inns and hotels and the $5 million their visitors spent each year; the region was New England's most popular mountain retreat, and the tourism industry relied on the scenery. The New York and Boston press called on the state of New Hampshire to save the forests.

Still the commission remained hesitant: "All the mountain forests in New Hampshire are private property, and we have no more control over their owners' treatment of them than we have over the condition of life on the moons of Mars."

The pressure to change that situation mounted in 1896 when T. Jefferson Coolidge, treasurer of the all-powerful Amoskeag Manufacturing Company in Manchester, produced an alarming annual report. The Merrimack River was drying up in summer and flooding in spring, Coolidge reported. Floods in the springs of 1895 and 1896 had shut down the Amoskeag mill, the nation's largest, and thrown 6,000 workers out of work. Coolidge blamed the floods on heavy logging at the headwaters of the Merrimack River in the White Mountains.

Even with this indictment from an industrial giant, the tinder of public outrage smoldered slowly. Then a small scrap of paper fluttered into the embers. It was a pamphlet entitled "The Boa Constrictor of the White Mountains."

Rev. John E. Johnson, an Episcopal missionary, ignored the statistics on the amount of timber cut, acres burned, and dollars lost to the hotels and mills. He focused instead on what deforestation meant in human terms. And he gave the public a clear and simple villain.

"What is it? The New Hampshire Land Company," his incendiary pamphlet began. "Where is it? Up among the granite hills of that state. What is its object? To deforest and depopulate the region lying around the headwaters of the Merrimack River in the heart of the White Mountains."

The New Hampshire Land Company had been organized in Hartford, Connecticut, to purchase land in New Hampshire. Speculating on a future demand for timber, the company's 250 shareholders bought cheap farm lots and tax sale lands, merged them into lots 10,000 acres and larger, and refused to sell anything smaller to farmers, hotels, or even local towns. Their sole customers were the "timber barons" — George Van Dyke, J. E. Henry, the Saunders brothers.

Johnson pulled no punches, accusing the Land

Company of a policy of "refrigeration." "The method adopted was a very simple one: [The farmers] were starved out. The company refused to sell them any land. The farmers, exhausting their limited tracts of woodland and unable to buy more at any price, gradually found themselves without logs for their local mills. Their sons, robbed of their winter employment, took no longer to the woods but to the cities, leaving the old folks to fall slowly but surely into the clutches of the company which took their farms from them or their heirs, in most cases for a dollar or two an acre."

Hill farmers were not the only victims of the Land Company. Tightening its hold on North Woodstock, for example, the firm refused to sell lots to hotel keepers, a physician hoping to start up a sanitarium, and even the town, for a public waterworks. He talked of selling the whole town to a pulp mill, "as though they were so many serfs or slaves and went with the land as a matter of course like a Southern plantation before the war," Johnson railed.

In the second half of the nineteenth century, timber barons were clearing whole mountainsides, leaving behind huge piles of slash and debris. This debris often caught fire, creating huge fires all over the White Mountains. People in Concord, 75 miles to the south, often complained about the smoke and ash fallout. Photo: SPNHF archives.

Stoking the Flame

Johnson's pamphlet enflamed the public. In October 1899 Governor Frank West Rollins called on legislators to use state funds to buy the White Mountains as a public park. The next month the popular weekly *New England Homestead* fanned the flames when it published three cover photographs of dilapidated wood slab homes in Thornton Gore. The New Hampshire Land Company, the newspaper reported, had squeezed out the residents, and the settlement had become a ghost town. The editors called for a White Mountain Forestry Association to address the crisis: "Instant action is imperative. This White Mountain Association should be perfected instantly so as to present the whole matter effectively to the incoming legislature."

F. W. Rollins, President. Joseph T. Walker, Secretary. George T. Cruft, Treasurer. Philip W. Ayres, Forester.

The Society FOR THE PROTECTION OF New Hampshire Forests

SAVE THE FORESTS

The Society for the Protection of New Hampshire Forests prepared a bill which was passed by the New Hampshire Legislature last winter inviting the Bureau of Forestry at Washington to make a thorough examination of the White Mountain region. This examination is now well under way. The Society desires to use the knowledge thus gained in making an appeal to Congress next winter for a National Forest Reservation in the White Mountains and asks your aid in so doing. The plan has the emphatic endorsement of President Roosevelt, Secretary John Hay, and members of Congress from New Hampshire and other states.

Memberships in the Society are as follows:

Patron Member, - -	$100.00
Life Member, - - - -	25.00
Sustaining Member, annually,	10.00
Contributing Member, - -	5.00
Annual Member, - - -	1.00

Checks may be made payable to George T. Cruft, Treasurer, and sent to Bethlehem, N. H., or to 5 Tremont Street, Boston, Mass.

Over the next few weeks, letters poured in from farmers, businessmen, outing clubs, women's groups, bankers, and legislators. Johnson himself kept at it, sitting at his writing desk late into the night "for the chance of hitting the devil with an ink bottle."

On February 6, 1901, shortly after finishing his second term, Governor Rollins organized a small meeting at the Board of Agriculture office in Concord. Among the luminaries present were Ellen McRoberts Mason, chairwoman of the Forestry Committee of the New Hampshire Federated Women's Clubs; Nahum Batchelder of Concord, editor, secretary of agriculture, and soon to be governor; George Cruft, legislator, hotel owner, and benefactor of Bethlehem; George Moses, editor of the *Concord Monitor*, secretary of the New Hampshire Forestry Commission, and later to be U.S. senator; and Joseph T. Walker, assistant secretary of state. Those in attendance resolved to form a citizens' advocacy group, and Mason suggested a name: the Society for the Protection of New Hampshire Forests. Frank Rollins was elected president of the executive committee.

Going National

To keep the fires burning for change, the Society hired Philip Ayres, forty-one, a historian who had worked as a reporter and charity organizer before finding his true calling: forestry and political action.

Ayres took the job as the Society's first staff leader on the condition that he be allowed to take the White Mountain campaign beyond Concord to promote the idea of protecting the region as a national resource. The executive committee agreed.

Ayres spent his first year traveling the White Mountains to see firsthand the devastation of the forests. In the high country he found loggers cutting two-thirds of the spruce trees and leaving them on the ground so that the largest trees could roll unimpeded to the logging roads, rail sidings, and rivers.

Ayres calculated that many of the spruce being skinned from the high mountain ridges were 200 years old. A public relations master, the forester hit the road, taking his story and lantern slides to dozens of women's clubs, Grange halls, and teachers' meetings throughout New England.

Initiating a tradition of working with all parties on forest debates, Ayres also interviewed tim-

Today the White Mountains have recovered from the devastation of the late nineteenth century. Thanks to the persistence of the fledgling Society and many other dedicated supporters, the White Mountain National Forest is a model for the nation. Photos: Ned Therrien (left); USFS archives (top).

By 1919 the White Mountain National Forest had grown to more than half its current size of 780,000 acres. In that year, forestry pioneers gathered on Mt. Carrigain to study five-year old slash. From left: Henry S. Graves, chief of the U.S. Forest Service and Society leader; J.J. Fritz, forest supervisor; Franklin Reed, district forester; Philip Ayres, Society forester; Allen Chamberlain, journalist and later to become president of the Appalachian Mountain Club; and C.B. Schiffer, district ranger. Photo: USFS archives.

ber companies. Orton B. Brown, general manager of the Berlin Mills Company, explained to him that the company hated to cut the timber in the Presidential Range but could not keep the mills running without more wood: "Our company is interested in preserving the scenic beauty of the state, and will contribute toward it, but cannot alone afford to maintain this tract as a park."

Only the national government could do that, Ayres concluded. The next year he addressed Congress, arguing that New Hampshire had too small a population and tax base to solve the state's deforestation problem alone.

Drought that spring of 1903 fueled the Society's argument for immediate action. Ayres kept a journal of forest fires reported across the state:

"May 15. Whitefield Town encircled by forest fires."

"June 3. Groveton Mills closed and all men gone to fight fire."

"June 5. Grange Pilot Range in a cloud of smoke so thick that it cannot be seen from the valley below; buildings cannot be seen 50 rods away. Showers of fine ash constantly falling."

In all, 200,000 acres of New Hampshire timberland burned before the rains came on June 9. That fall Senator Jacob H. Gallinger of New Hampshire introduced a bill in Congress. The intent? To purchase a national forest reserve in the White Mountains.

Now the real legislative battle began. "Not one cent for scenery," thundered House Speaker Joseph "Uncle Joe" Cannon. Rocky Mountain congressional leaders, bridling at the proliferation of Teddy Roosevelt's federal parks in the West, were outraged at the idea of actually using taxpayers' money to buy timberland for federal control in the East. The House Judiciary Committee declared that such a policy would be unconstitutional. Other lawmakers challenged Gallinger to prove that there was any scientific relationship between timber cutting in the White Mountains and the floods and droughts in the valleys downstream.

Gallinger's bill stalled in session after session of Congress. Ayres lobbied from afar, gaining endorsements from politicians, hotel owners, and journalists. The Appalachian Mountain Club became a major partner in the effort, as did women's, forestry, and civic groups from across the nation. Ayres traveled south to meet with southern politicians and citizens who were petitioning for national forest reserves in the southern Appalachians. In 1906 the two bills were combined into one proposal and funds were squeaked out of Congress for a study.

The Streams Converge

As the debate raged in Congress, the timber barons continued to strip the forests, and fires swept through the mountains. In 1909 nearly 12,000 acres of timber in Crawford Notch went up for sale. The Society convinced the legislature to buy the land for a state park.

Representative John Weeks of Massachusetts joined the battle late. Weeks was born in Lancaster, New Hampshire, and summered each year at his family home atop Mount Prospect. He could see the devastation caused by overcutting and fires, and he warned speaker Cannon that forestry and the White Mountain Forest Reserve were pet interests. Cannon respected Weeks as a businessman. The speaker told Weeks that if he would sit on the Agriculture Committee and could develop a forest bill acceptable to a businessman, he would support the legislation.

The next year Gallinger again filed his bill to acquire forest reserves in the Appalachians and the White Mountains. This time the bill was amended on the Senate floor to read, "for the purpose of preserving the navigability of navigable streams."

The conservationists had found a common cause with industry: reliable flow of water to power the mills. Four days later Weeks proposed a new bill in the House, one that did not mention the Appalachians or the White Mountains at all. It simply said that Congress would appropriate funds to purchase lands and forest reserves for "the conservation and improvement of the navigability of a river."

After filibusters and committee amendments delayed Weeks's bill for another two years, a voice vote passed the House on June 24, 1910. Cannon kept his word and cast one of the deciding votes. The Senate approved the same bill seven months later. On March 1, 1911, President William Howard Taft signed the Weeks Act into law.

The first land purchases established North Carolina's Pisgah National Forest in 1913. Later that year the federal government bought more than 100,000 acres in the Presidentials. Weeks's broadly worded bill would eventually authorize federal purchases of forestland in forty-eight national forests across the nation. The spark ignited in the White Mountains had roared into a national conservation revolution.

A decade after the Weeks Act was passed, a young journalist named Brooks Atkinson would hike the Sandwich Range, across barren summits and valleys tangled with blowdowns, burns, and young brush, to the summit of Mount Washington. The forest primeval was largely gone, he wrote in his journal. But the reckless destruction of the White Mountains had been halted, and the public's forest would heal its scars and grow green again.

Atkinson wrote, "No matter how unscrupulously the lumber kings have ravished their domains, the contours of the mountains still remain: the smooth brow of Lafayette, the burly bulk of Cardigan, the jagged teeth of Tripyramid. New England has nothing else so beautiful to offer." ❧

Franconia Notch: Sawed or Saved?

A dollar and a tree at a time, the Society raised the money to save the Old Man of the Mountain.

HOWARD MANSFIELD

The editorials and reports had the urgency of a ransom note. The Old Man of the Mountain, the Great Stone Face, hallmark of New Hampshire and presiding spirit of New England, was being held hostage.

"King of the Mountains: Save His Kingdom!" read the headline from the editorial page of the *Boston American*, December 27, 1927: "The money must be in hand before next March 1st. Otherwise, the lumberman's axe will smash, destroy and lay desolate one of New England's greatest natural attractions. If everyone who means one day to pay another visit to the Profile will give but ONE DOLLAR to the cause, the Old Man and the timbered hills across which he has been staring for centuries will be saved from the axe."

The Manchester newspapers, the *Union* and the *Leader,* were more direct: "SEND IN YOUR DOLLARS! BUY AS MANY TREES AS YOUR PATRIOTISM ALLOWS!"

It was the 1920s, and Franconia Notch was for sale. The "little Yosemite" was drawing more than 100,000 visitors a year to see the Old Man, the deep gorge and waterfalls of the Flume, Echo and Profile Lakes, and the dramatic prospect of the great mountain pass. A 1916 travel guide called the narrow pass a "huge museum of curiosities." On some holidays cars were spotted from forty-three states and five Canadian provinces.

It was a road that had brought about the discovery of the Old Man. In 1805

Franconia Notch. Protected in 1928. Photo: Alan Briere.

This specially created composite photo was part of Phil Ayres's campaign to stir people to action to save the Old Man of the Mountain. Photo: SPNHF archives.

two men from a crew building a state road through the notch first saw the profile on the side of Cannon Mountain. Luke Brooks and Francis Whitcomb had camped out at the edge of Profile Lake, and while retrieving water for breakfast looked up and beheld the stone likeness of President Thomas Jefferson, and so it was named for a time. Nathaniel Hall, who was out hunting partridges for the road crew's breakfast, was sometimes given credit for the discovery instead.

Word spread. Senator Daniel Webster paid the Old Man a visit in 1831 and proclaimed that "God Almighty has hung out a Sign to show that in New England He Makes Men!" Nathaniel Hawthorne followed the next year, later writing his popular piece "The Great Stone Face." And so the Old Man was certified as a wonder of the New World.

By the 1920s, Frank H. Abbott and Son owned the 6,000 acres of the notch, which spread out for 7 miles along both sides of the Daniel Webster Highway. The Abbott Company also owned the popular Profile House. When the hotel burned in 1923, the company decided not to rebuild. Lumber companies bid for the standing timber. The Abbotts were asking $400,000.

That's when the Society for the Protection of New Hampshire Forests stepped in. Leading the campaign to save the notch, forester Philip Ayres left little to the imagination. He circulated a composite photo that showed the horrors to come if the notch were logged: The Great Stone Face looking out on ruined "earth-brown mountainsides" of "broken saplings and tangled brush heaps left by lumbermen." "Franconia Notch, Sawed or Saved?" asked a Society brochure. The photo was widely reprinted, sometimes creating the mistaken notion that the notch had already been logged.

The indefatigable Ayres was determined to save the notch. With the approval of the Society's executive committee, he first tried to get the state of New Hampshire to buy the land outright. Governor John G. Winant, aghast at the asking price, resigned from the executive committee in protest. But still Ayres pressed for a "crusade" to raise the money. He reconciled with Governor Winant. The governor asked the state legislature for half the price, $200,000, a huge sum amounting to nearly 50 cents for every man, woman, and child in the state. The legislature unanimously approved the appropriation. James J. Storrow, who had served as Society treasurer, offered another $100,000.

This still left $100,000 to be raised in a few short months. While some urged the Society to solicit a small circle of wealthy donors, Ayres crusaded to save the notch by popular subscription, "selling" trees for a dollar each. Donors would receive a "Certificate of Purchase" that read, "This certifies that (bearer) has purchased _____ tree(s) at one dollar each, in Franconia Notch, to help save the Notch from destructive lumbering. These trees may be identified and cared for by the owners, but may not be cut or mutilated in any way."

The tactic proved to be brilliant, especially when Ayres added a final touch. The notch, he proposed, would be a memorial to the "men and women who have served the nation in times of war" and the profile "the sentinel eternally on duty to watch over them."

A Campaign for Birthright

The State Federation of Women's Clubs in New Hampshire took up the challenge. The club set goals for its more than 12,000 members in 151 New Hampshire towns and cities. "We said in war time 'give until it hurts,' we say now give until your heart overflows with joy!" urged the *Nashua Telegraph* in the spirit of the campaign organized by the Nashaway Women's Club. "What man or woman is there who would not gladly purchase not one but many trees, to save the notch from the woodman's axe, the hawker's raucous call, the hot dog vendor's station, and the curio dealer's stand," asked the *New Hampshire Federation Bulletin*, the magazine of the women's clubs. "We of New Hampshire will not sell our birthright for a mess of pottage."

The women's clubs helped New Hampshire celebrate Old Man of the Mountain Day on January 18, 1928. On the same day, the state's schools observed a Franconia Notch Day. With contributions as small as a nickel, the schools had raised $1,000. "Children have to be led to beauty," it was observed, and the Old Man would show them the way. "If parents give dollars where their children have given nickels, the fund will be completed without delay," Ayres said one month before the deadline. Some money walked in the door. "One of the first contributors to personally present their gift to James J. Storrow, Jr., treasurer of the fund," according to Ayres, "was a three-year-old youngster who came into the original Joy Street office with his mother to lisp, 'here's 15 cents – is it too little?'"

In Dover, retired newsman John Scales, age ninety-two, made the first donation. "I do not claim to be as old as 'The Old Man of Franconia Notch,'" he wrote. "Fifty years ago, I rode down through the Notch on the top of a large coach; I have never forgotten his face. Will you have a good healthy tree marked for me, to which he can look down and see my name?" Scales was not the oldest donor. Mary "Granny" Whitcher of Whitefield, at age 105, took that honor.

College students supported the cause as well. The Dartmouth Outing Club bought 100 trees to honor the college's war heroes. The weekly newspaper of the University of New Hampshire rallied students at the state college to aid the Old Man: "To 19th century New England he was the Emersonian 'oversoul' of the White Mountains."

Trees were in demand. The *Manchester Union* reported a "bull market" for trees in January 1928, "with several contributors offering as high as $2.50 for ordinary trees and one special tree, a birch bringing $5."

The Old Man had a national following. "They are about to slay the Old Man's friends, the trees where the sweet birds sing," read an editorial printed in newspapers in Ithaca, New York; Lima, Ohio; Augusta, Georgia; Pine Bluff, Arkansas; and Salt Lake City, Utah. What would result? "Stumps!

Here they would be like the blackened butts of cigars strewn upon a priceless Oriental rug!"

Other publications supported the effort, among them *Field & Stream, Nature Magazine, The Automobilist, Landscape Architecture,* and the *New York Times.* A Texas banker bought trees, as did the Paterson, New Jersey, Rambling Club. An Amherst, Massachusetts, real estate broker bought a small grove in memory of Henry David Thoreau. Money came from France and Panama. A midwestern lawyer bought twelve trees, one for each member of the family, including the family dog. The lawyer requested that his donation be returned if dogs would not be allowed to visit the Great Stone Face.

Your Dollar Will Stop This

FIFTEEN or twenty miles this side of Fabyans and Bretton Woods, the White Mountain tourist who has motored northward over the Daniel Webster Highway comes upon an enchanting little tarn known as Profile Lake, or "The Old Man's Washbowl." Close at hand is a signpost marking the spot which commands the finest view of the Profile, or "Old Man of the Mountains." The Profile is formed by granite ledges on the upper cliffs of Mt. Cannon, or Profile. The face, which looks toward the southeast, is 80 feet in height and 1200 feet above the lake. It was discovered in 1805 by two men who were working on the Notch road. They were washing their hands in the lake and happened to glance up and see the Profile.

The 6,000 acres of woodland which in part make up the realm of the Great Stone Face are seriously threatened by the lumberman and his axe. Unless $82,800 can be collected in One Dollar gifts before March 1, 1928, campers and tourists may expect to see Franconia Notch given over to saw mills. All who love nature and find inspiration in the mountains will be glad to co-operate in saving this world-famous scenic shrine.

Boston American Dec. 27, 1927

This poster was typical of the Society's ardent campaign to save the Old Man and the forests he watched over.

The Profile was "a poem wrought in stone among the eternal hills," long celebrated in literature. People responded to the appeal with poetry. "Buying a tree! What a thought that inspires" began a poem that Joseph P. Flynn sent in with his $2 donation. The *Sharon (Massachusetts) Advocate* ran this typical poem:

> It's our dollars against the sawmills
> Which say you shall win in the race?
> Come, Sons of New England, awaken!
> Keep faith with the Old Stone Face.

Nathaniel Hawthorne's story "The Great Stone Face," written in 1850, was part of the popular imagination. In the tale the people of the valley await the coming of a prophet who would look just like the Stone Face. The Old Man never speaks but is an abiding presence, a benevolent spirit looking down upon human folly. As people were inspired by that story, the poems poured forth: Schoolchildren wrote acrostics, the first letter of each line spelling out "Franconia Notch" or "Great Stone Face;" there were poems in a Franco-American dialect; a Littleton grammar school teacher, Frances Ann Johnson, won first prize in a national "America Beautiful" poetry contest; former governor John H. Bartlett composed verse at the request of the *Manchester Union.*

Poems were sent to the Society years after the notch was saved (one arriving by Western Union telegram). This was a place — "the very heart of New Hampshire" — that moved people. As Ozora S. Davis, president of the Chicago Theological Seminary, wrote of the notch: "I dreamed of it as a boy in Vermont, as a student at Dartmouth, in foreign lands, and here in my home on the prairies."

The publicity director for the campaign, Paul Hannah, was tireless, sending out daily news updates in the heat of the drive in January 1928. He sought support and endorsements. Only a few denied him: a prominent lumberman, a federal judge wishing to maintain his neutrality, and the American Automobile Association. He shot the auto club a note reminding them of the number of tourists who drove to the notch each year.

When some of the photographs predicting the potential devastation were incorrectly identified, Hannah quickly sent letters to more than thirty newspapers, saying: "Through a slip in this office, we did not label the composite picture showing how Franconia Notch will look should the New England drive fail and lumbermen take possession. We hope that if you use these pictures, you will point out that the Notch as yet is not cut, and nature lovers are asked to save it."

A Hawthornesque Ending

Still, with the March deadline closing in, the fund fell short. The Abbotts granted a ninety-day reprieve, and the drive was boosted when Edward Tuck, benefactor of Dartmouth, sent a check for $10,000 from Paris. Closer to home, the Appalachian Mountain Club, which maintained the Franconia Sky-Line Trail and was supporting a Georgia-to-Maine trail to run through the notch, gave $7,000.

The women's clubs raised $65,000, aided by the Granges, the Izaak Walton League, Kiwanis and Rotary Clubs, chambers of commerce, and Girl Scouts. Children at the Orphans' Home raised $20 from their pennies. One hundred and forty-three New Hampshire towns exceeded their quotas. The Society met the new June 1 deadline.

But the Society wasn't done with the notch yet. From the start, the plan was to give the forest to the state. But the state refused part of the gift, the Flume. The Flume was a moneymaker; 100,000 visitors paid 25 cents each to view the "wonderful chasm" in 1924. Governor Spaulding, who had made a personal donation of $1,000, said the State Forestry Department was too small to run it and there was no parks division. The Society's executive committee, in "shock," asked the governor to reconsider. He replied: "Your Society wanted this thing done. All right you run it." So for two decades, the Society ran the Flume at a profit, finally turning it over to the state in 1947.

On September 15, 1928, a gray, windy Saturday, Franconia Notch was dedicated as a war memorial. The ceremony was held on the shore of Profile Lake, its surface riffled with whitecaps. The Old Man of the Mountain, the speakers noted, was "an approving witness." "New Hampshire here and now gives to all the world the best she has in scenic beauty," said W. R. Brown, chairman of the State Forestry Commission, in his opening speech.

After leading the campaign to save Franconia Notch, the Society remained a vigilant steward. The Society ran the Flume from 1928 to 1947, and participated closely in the planning of the Cannon Mountain Aerial Tramway, the first in the nation. Photos: SPNHF archives.

Later in the ceremony, Frances Ann Johnson, whose poem had won the national contest, led her Kilburn School students in song. One song was from her pageant "Woodland," which depicted the saving of the notch; another was her song "Old Man of the Mountains."

"As the children stood at the edge of Profile Lake, singing and looking up at the mostly hidden Profile, I felt keen disappointment that he had not fully appeared," Johnson recalled. "Suddenly, as they began the chorus 'Old Man of the Mountains, Proud, noble supreme' a miracle happened. The wind swept aside the tumbling clouds, and the Old Man came into full, clear view. Then, as the song ended, clouds again veiled the Great Stone Face. It was as though he had recognized the tribute of little children... My eyes were blurred with tears, and my heart was full of gratitude." An ending right out of Hawthorne's story. ❧

The Second Campaign to Save the Notch

In 1956 the U.S. Congress decided to build an interstate highway system. After years of poking along on Route 3, New Hampshire citizens welcomed the idea of a north-south highway. But when the engineers encountered a significant obstacle in the shape of the White Mountains, they concluded that the only route was straight through the heart of Franconia Notch.

To make the original winding road conform with the rest of the interstate system, it would have to become a four-lane, divided superhighway, with cleared shoulders 30 to 65 feet wide. And, in order to maintain consistent highway speeds, this section would need to be as straight and level as possible. This meant significant blasting, filling, and grading in Franconia Notch State Park, and even some filling in of Echo and Profile lakes. Many people, including the Society and the Appalachian Mountain Club (AMC), expressed serious concern about the impacts all this "improving" would have on the notch. Other citizens were equally disturbed by the notion that the federal government had selected this option as the cheapest available — because the state already owned the land. With the notch's public fund-raising campaign and its subsequent dedication as a World War I memorial a proud memory, their sense of ownership seemed belittled.

It seemed beloved, historic, and supposedly protected Franconia Notch was about to be sacrificed just so cars and trucks could get from Boston to Montreal more swiftly.

And so the second campaign to save the notch began. After strident protests to Secretary of Commerce Sinclair Weeks by the Society and AMC, a more modest road design was proposed: a two-lane parkway that better fit the natural contours of the landscape. The state legislature initially approved the idea but later shelved it when a major landslide buried the designated location. Over the next seven years, the Society and AMC — backed by the now-retired Weeks and former governor Sherman Adams — fought the state's various plans for a bigger four-lane highway. The coalition hired a lobbyist, Henry McPhee, who successfully persuaded Congress to pass legislation blocking highways from running through public parks unless there was "no feasible alternative."

In 1968, after much study, Governor John King's Citizen Advisory Committee concluded a "cut and cover" four-lane tunnel beneath Eagle Cliff was the only possible solution. This idea was not well-received, but it managed to persist.

Under intense political pressure, Secretary of Transportation John Volpe "indefinitely" postponed construction of Interstate 93 through Franconia Notch in 1970. The reason: "The comparative low vehicle count and the other problems unresolved in the use of the Notch for interstate highway purposes." Despite this, the state highway department would not back down from their plans for a larger highway. In response, the Society and its growing number of allies formed the White Mountain Environment Committee. Paul Bofinger, the Society's president/forester, became the WMEC chairman.

In 1973, Senator Norris Cotton got federal legislation passed officially authorizing and funding a parkway, instead of the superhighway. The tunnel plan died a well-deserved death. The state highway department, nevertheless, still continued construction of the interstate north of the notch. Protracted legal battles ensued with the WMEC arguing that the on-going roadwork basically guaranteed that alternate routes could not be considered. Governor Meldrim Thompson further fueled the fire by threatening to sell the Cannon and Sunapee ski areas to private developers and having casinos installed at both sites. In 1975, a federal judge issued an injunction to stop the building and demanded an environmental impact statement (EIS) to consider alternatives. A new EIS was released a year later offering nine different options — including the two-lane parkway at the heart of the notch.

In 1977, fifty years after Ayres's initial campaign to save the notch, the state finally abandoned its superhighway plans. Construction of the parkway through the notch began in 1978 and was completed nine years later. In the end, the intensive letter-writing, testifying, and lobbying by the Society and others that saved the notch the first time, rescued it once again. ♣

ROSEMARY CONROY,
WITH HELP FROM PAUL DOSCHER.

Three Mountains

How Monadnock, Sunapee, and Kearsarge came to be saved.

Rosemary Conroy

In 1911, the Society for the Protection of New Hampshire Forests published its tenth annual report. In those pages the early members set a particularly lofty goal: "The Society will strive earnestly to protect permanently the many points of special interest and scenic beauty in New Hampshire. It seeks to protect every prominent mountain in the state."

Indeed, it was a time for thinking big. The early decades of the twentieth century were marked by a rapid influx of new ideas. Just about every aspect of everyday life was being radically transformed by inventions such as electric lights, motorcars, telephones, telegraphs, moving pictures, and even standardized time. Until the Standard Time Act of 1918 — just three years after the Society would protect its first 406 acres on Monadnock — every town in every state ran on its own time. New ideas like women's suffrage, fair labor laws, advertising, health reform, mass production, and even indoor plumbing swept across America like the waves of immigrants flooding its shores. Protecting land for permanent reservation — and long-term stewardship — was perhaps one of the most radical ideas of all.

Most people in New Hampshire at the turn of the century were working in mills or on exhausted farmland. Spending money to buy up more rocky land was, to put it mildly, a hard sell. In 1914, Philip Ayres wrote to a supporter that he was having trouble "getting money from the natives," who already felt they paid too much in the way of taking care of the needs of the summer residents. They would support his efforts to protect Mount Monadnock, but not monetarily. Lucky for Ayres and the early conservationists, the summer folk felt differently.

In the next few pages are accounts of how the Society came to save three of New Hampshire's most beloved peaks — Monadnock, Sunapee, and Kearsarge — and how Ayres's vision translated into these places remaining as icons of open space. Tree species may have come and gone, and pastures regrown, but the essence of these peaks remains untrammeled.

Mount Monadnock. Protected in 1915. Photo: Paul Spezzaferri.

The Grand Monadnock

Conservationists started protecting the great mountain in 1904.

"The White Mountains may be the soul of the Society, but Monadnock is her heart," was a favorite quote of former president/forester Paul Bofinger. Residents and visitors alike regarded Monadnock with something near reverence; saving it was Phil Ayres's first land acquisition project.

In the late nineteenth century, ownership of the many lots covering Monadnock was murky, a fact that speculators sought to exploit. The town of Jaffrey, for example, narrowly escaped losing part of the summit and main access road in 1884 because no one knew who rightfully owned it. Hotel owners on the mountain, who hoped to profit on the burgeoning horde of tourists, came close to sneaking off with the title. It must have been a shock to the town fathers, who had always considered Monadnock's slopes and rocky summit a no-man's-land. Luckily, they were able to save it for everyone.

A similar scenario played out again twenty years later. In 1904 a sawmill operator set up shop smack in the middle of the south slope, ready to liquidate 500 acres of timber he claimed to own. Alarmed citizens of Jaffrey and Dublin formed the Monadnock Forestry Association and petitioned the state to do something. Empowered by a never-before-tested 1893 law allowing it to buy land for "park and forest purchases," the state condemned the property. (The petitioners did raise $8,000 to compensate the landowner and the sawmill operator.) Thus, the state came to own one of its very first state parks. A concerted drive to save the mountain had begun.

In 1913, ownership of yet another large tract of land ringing the summit came into question. Abbott Thayer, an eminent landscape painter and nearby resident, pleaded with Ayres for his help. It seemed that the tracts had never been sold by the original colonial grantees, people who probably had never even set eyes on their gift from the British Crown. Ayres took on the task of tracking down their heirs — more than seventy-seven different people spread across the United States and Europe — to secure their signatures on quitclaim deeds. Even though it would take two years and a couple of lawsuits, he succeeded in getting the heirs (many of whom had no idea that they had any right to a mountain in New England) to sign over their claims to the Society. In 1915 the

Society received the deed to 406 acres on the upper slope, subject to certain conditions: "The Society for the Protection of New Hampshire Forests shall forever hold this part of Monadnock Mountain ... in trust, to maintain forever its wild and primeval conditions, where the forest and rock shall remain undisturbed in their wild state, where birds and game shall find natural refuge. That the forest shall remain unmolested and free to grow and decay as for untold ages past."

In the following two years landowners would donate 336 more acres, and the Society's commitment to the landmark mountain was solidified. Between 1925 and 1989, the Society would accumulate nineteen more parcels on the mountain; several hundred more acres were protected through conservation easements. The town of Jaffrey added 150 more acres to its holdings, and the state received nearly 250 acres in gifts.

Over the years, Monadnock's prominence in the landscape attracted its share of attention. Allen Chamberlain, a member of the Society's executive committee and longtime president of the Appalachian Mountain Club, penned the first definitive guide to the mountain in 1936. Many other books, poems, photographs, and paintings would follow.

Still, development threatened. The Society fended off several ill-advised ideas, like the one in 1940 proposing to build a road to the top of the mountain and another, five years later, to set up a transmitter tower on the peak. Outrage against the latter scheme, which was approved by Jaffrey officials without citizen input, prompted the quick formation of yet another group — the Association for the Protection of Mount Monadnock. The association persuaded the selectboard to cancel the tower lease and, to ward off future intrusions, purchased the Old Toll Road and the remains of the Halfway House, a historic inn perched on the southern slope. The group pledged to run the rustic resort "just as it was in the '60s" — the 1860s, that was. They did, until the wooden structure burned to the ground in 1954. Upon its dissolution in 1974, the association donated the site and the road to the Society.

The last decades of the twentieth century found the Society ever more involved in Monadnock's continued stewardship, working with the state, the towns, local activists, and fellow conservation groups such as the Harris Center for Conservation Education. Paramount in these later efforts was the obligation to protect the mountain against its new primary threat — overuse by recreationists.

A plaque placed on Monadnock many years ago and dedicated to Phil Ayres and Allen Chamberlain expressed this hope: "May it always remain as it is today, free and wild and beautiful, the unspoiled heritage of the past, a haven of refuge for those who seek its peace in years to come."

Turn-of-the century visitors to Mount Monadnock posed for their souvenir portrait. Photo: SPNHF archives.

"For a More Glorious Sunapee"

Mount Sunapee was the focus of the Society's first fund-raising campaign, which protected 638 acres on the summit as outlined in this 1910 photograph. Photo: SPNHF archives.

In 1930 Otto Schneib and John McCrillis went looking for a patch of late winter snow that might have survived the early April sunshine. Their search led them to Mount Sunapee, rising out of its namesake lake for some 2,700 feet. So reported a 1935 *Manchester Union* feature on the newly formed and rapidly growing Newport Ski Club. The two men thought Sunapee "presented untold opportunities" for ski trails. To implement their grand vision, the club sought permission to continue its trails over land owned by the Society for the Protection of New Hampshire Forests. The Society, which had already invested many hours and dollars in the trails on the mountain, saw this as an opportunity to further public enjoyment of Sunapee. The club built its trails and began to operate a small ski school, thereby establishing alpine skiing as a part of the New Hampshire winter experience.

When Schneib and McCrillis came to the Society with their plans, the organization owned nearly 1,000 acres on Sunapee, including the bulk of the summit. It was the result of over twenty years of effort by a few dedicated people who, in the words of one resident, had found "peace, freshness, and energy" from regarding and climbing this most picturesque New Hampshire peak. At the start of the twenty-first century, it was hard to picture the slopes of the Mount Sunapee Ski Area as once wild and untrammeled. But 100 years earlier, this long, bulky mountain was still considered a fairly remote place, a backdrop for the first summer residents who set up their cottages around the equally pristine lake.

Herbert Welsh was one of those summer colonists who looked up one day in 1909 and saw a huge gash on the slopes. Welsh investigated and quickly took action. He learned that two paper companies owned the land and were about to clearcut it. Recent upsurge in demand for pulp and lumber had made cutting Sunapee's once inaccessible trees suddenly more profitable. Welsh polled his neighbors and, assured of financial backing, asked Philip Ayres of the young Society for the Protection of New Hampshire Forests to intervene.

Ayres was able to persuade the paper companies to cease operations while negotiations were underway. He convinced the first, International Paper, to sell the Society 256 acres along the crest of the mountain, including much of Sunapee's rambling skyline. The second company, Emerson Paper, agreed to sell 382 acres that covered the slopes seen from the lake. The only sticking point was that Emerson had already sold the timber rights to the Draper Company, a bobbin mill in Newport, New Hampshire. Draper, clearly with nothing to lose, drove up the price to $8,000. Undeterred, Welsh and Ayres raised the princely sum, successfully testing untried tactics of all-out public education and direct appeal to area residents. In 1911 Sunapee became the Society's first reservation.

But Welsh, by then crowned head of the Sunapee branch of the Society, was not content with mere protection. He continuously raised money to clear and maintain trails, create firebreaks, and even build a small shelter. Lake Solitude crowned the now-protected summit and became a draw for the ever-increasing number of summer hikers. In 1915 the Society's Sunapee branch published the *Manual of Mount Sunapee*, which sold for 50 cents a copy, with "proceeds used for maintaining the trails on Mount Sunapee." Edited by Ayres, the manual described the geological history, flora, and birds to be found along the newly opened trails. Archie Gove was hired as summer superintendent of the reservation and would later become its full-time, salaried caretaker.

Welsh was also not content to stop at 638 acres. Over the next two decades, he oversaw the purchase of several more parcels. In order to help the Society handle the expenditures for what was rapidly becoming a large tract of land, he helped negotiate a deal with the state. It exempted the Society from property taxes on the mountain tracts "until their value was greater than $15,000 or more than 1,000 acres in size."

Welsh was a dedicated campaigner until the end. At age seventy-seven, he was still garnering publicity — this time for his thirteenth annual trek from his hometown of Germantown, Pennsylvania, to his summer cottage on Lake Sunapee. By the time he retired in 1929, Welsh had seen much of his beloved mountain permanently protected. Was he satisfied? One can only hope, but his sights had always been set high, as witnessed by the sign-off "Yours for a more glorious Sunapee" that ended all his correspondences.

In the post-Welsh decades of the 1930s and 1940s, the Society made its way through the Great Depression, Ayres's 1935 retirement, the hurricane of 1938, the fires of 1941, and World War II. Keeping Society lands well maintained had always been a budgetary strain. By the time newly prosperous Americans started increasing their leisure time after World War II, the Society was ready for a change. The state had been eyeing Sunapee, by then a small but popular ski area, as the perfect tourist development opportunity. The locals looked around at their handful of rough-cut trails and decided that a ski area with gondolas and groomed slopes would be good for business. The Society concurred: After all, the state had come a long way since the early days. It now had well-established forestry and parks departments, several thousand acres under public stewardship, and the finances to run a "real" ski resort. So in 1948 and 1949, the Society transferred all its land on Sunapee to the state.

By 2000, much had changed on the mountain, but much also remained the same. More ski runs were cut, the snow was more artificial than natural, and the Newport Ski Club had become all but a quaint memory. But primeval woods still rode Sunapee's mighty shoulders, hikers still wandered Herbert Welsh's trails to Lake Solitude, and the Society still contended with how glorious Sunapee could be.

"A Great Mountain for All Time"

This shows the very first "tower" to be erected on Kearsarge's summit. The next structure, which was vital in fighting fires across the state, was slightly larger — at 30 feet. Photo: SPNHF archives.

On an unseasonably warm December morning in 1998, the Society held a somber press conference. Standing before an array of microphones and video cameras, president/forester Jane Difley made an announcement that had been made only a handful of times in the Society's ninety-seven-year history: The Society was suing the state of New Hampshire.

The lawsuit disputed the placement of a telecommunications tower on the summit of Mount Kearsarge in Wilmot. The 180-foot structure had been erected on a parcel of land that the Society gave to the state in 1949 with the express requirement that it be maintained "as a forestry and recreation reservation for public use and benefit." Declaring that the tower clearly violated that deed, Difley said, "Our members need to know that we take our role as protector of open space seriously — especially with the land we once owned."

A Merrimack County Superior Court judge ultimately ruled against the Society, and the tower, aptly described by poet Donald Hall as an "excrescence" on his beloved peak, stood. Nonetheless, the Society's efforts to have the tower removed reflected its multidecade dedication to the mountain.

In 1918 the Society purchased its first 521 acres of what would become over the years nearly 4,000 on Mount Kearsarge; the goal was to preserve "a great mountain for all time" to be held in public trust. After Frank West Rollins, the founder of the Society, died in 1915, Society supporters chose their first purchase on Kearsarge as the memorial to honor him. "No more appropriate spot, I believe," wrote Philip Ayres to Rollins's widow, "could be secured than the summit of Kearsarge Mountain." Over the years, whenever land on Kearsarge was threatened by development, the Society acquired the endangered tract for later transfer to the state. These transactions include 1,500 acres in 1935, 585 acres in 1963, and 900 acres in 1971, plus a handful of smaller parcels. The state also independently acquired 839 acres.

The 1971 transaction was typical. A Massachusetts developer bought a large tract on the Andover side, planning to subdivide it for vacation homes. The Society purchased the land and turned it over to the state Fish and Game Department for a wildlife refuge. The same thing happened in 1973 and again in 1975, until everyone assumed the mountain would always remain open and undeveloped. A *Concord Monitor* article on the 1973 land protection deal ran a photo of the mountain with a bold caption, "Mount Kearsarge: Protected."

Perhaps that was why everyone was so shocked when in 1985 the development firm Patten Corporation Northeast bought a 316-acre inholding surrounded by protected parklands. Residents thought the state had long ago acquired those acres, but budget cutbacks had prevented it. Townspeople were split between pro-development forces who saw the sale as good for the tax base and those who had believed the mountain would always remain untouched. Despite claims by Dick Patten, owner of the company, "that we don't fragment beautiful pieces of land," the company was planning to do just that with the sale of its Mountain View Properties. Again, the state and the Society worked together and convinced the Warner Planning Board to turn down the application. The land would eventually be protected through the Land Conservation Investment Program.

Despite the tower controversy of the 1990s, the state and the Society had a history of working cooperatively on structures placed on Kearsarge as well. In 1923 Ayres received a letter from John Foster, the state forester, about erecting a fire lookout tower on the summit. The carefully worded letter sought the Society's permission to place a tower "20, or possibly 30," feet high partially on the Society's side of the peak. Foster very much wanted to avoid any criticism by the public. Ayres responded by sending a letter to Society members in the vicinity of Kearsarge, seeking opinions. He wrote, "The Society desires that as far as possible the structure should harmonize with the topography and be unobtrusive as possible at the top of the mountain." Since the tower was specifically for forestry purposes, the membership approved — then.

At the beginning of the twenty-first century, towers on mountaintops remained a controversial subject. However, there was unanimous agreement that the beloved Kearsarge remained a proud icon for the Society — a memorial to its founder and to all the members who considered it "a great mountain for all time." ❧

This view showed the fire tower dwarfed by the controversial 180-foot telecommunications tower the state erected in 1998. Photo: courtesy of Save Our Mountain.

PROFILE

Philip Wheelock Ayres

Forester, 1901–1935

At the beginning of the twentieth century, America was a very different land. Just a generation before, the state of New Hampshire had disposed of all of its "wild lands" — the last of which was in the White Mountains. One hundred seventy-two thousand acres, including Mount Washington, were sold for $25,000 in 1867 — less than 15 cents an acre.

The politicians who freed themselves of their "burden" of public land did not foresee that these wild places would attract eager logging companies. By the time the Society for the Protection of New Hampshire Forests was formed in 1901, many people had begun seriously to regret the giveaway of the state's land. A movement was stirring to protect the scenic state and take back some control — a radical shift in consciousness.

The man who would help create that shift was born in 1861 and grew up on a humble Illinois farm. Those early years helped shaped Philip Wheelock Ayres' abiding love of the land. In his memoir written just before his death in 1945, he could still clearly recall the type of trees that surrounded his childhood home and how they could be used.

During his youth, Ayres earned money for college teaching sharecroppers' children and reporting for the *Baltimore Sun.* After earning a Ph.D. from Johns Hopkins University he moved to New York City where he administered several charitable organizations. His sixteen years working with "the unfortunate poor" affected him deeply. He organized the first school for social work in the city, which later became a department of Columbia University.

When his health wavered at age forty, Ayres's wife Alice suggested he cash in his life insurance policies to study forestry. Subsequently he earned one of the first forestry degrees from Cornell University. Soon after, a fateful telegraph arrived from Governor Frank West Rollins. Ayres later wrote, "There were six great lumber companies, stripping the White Mountains with the most scientific efficiency that Yankee ingenuity could invent. He wanted to save at least a portion of it, and needed a forester."

Ayres took to running the fledgling Society with gusto. His past job experience served him well in rousing public sympathy for the national forest campaign. In the ten-year crusade, Ayres left no stone unturned, making numerous trips to Washington D.C., authoring rousing pamphlets, and even organizing delegations of school teachers to lobby recalcitrant members of Congress. Once the Weeks Act finally passed, enabling the creation of an eastern national forest system, Ayres began immediately to lobby for adequate funding to buy land for the WMNF. By 1914, 106,000 acres had been purchased by the federal government with another 150,000 approved. A *New York Times* editorial that year declared, "To the New Hampshire Society and its Forester, Mr. Philip Ayres, who fought weary years for the plan of a National Forest Preserve, New England and the country are in debt."

Besides the White Mountain National Forest victory, Ayres led the Society in protecting many of the great natural landmarks of New Hampshire, plus hundreds of acres of town and state forests and highway reservations. Along with other early leaders, he helped improve fire prevention techniques, established a state forester's office, and a state nursery. During the course of his thirty-four year Society tenure, Ayres also served as forester for Dartmouth College, as a director of the American Forestry Association, and as a one-term president of the Appalachian Mountain Club.

A bronze plaque on the shores of Echo Lake now commemorates Ayres's role in protecting Franconia Notch. But his most lasting monuments, of course, are the landscapes that are forever preserved for the public benefit. Ayres's grandson, Richard Givens, summed up his remarkable grandfather's legacy in a 1968 Littleton *Courier* article, "His life shows that the office of citizen in the United States is in itself one of the most powerful and responsible in the world." ❧

Rosemary Conroy

"This Forestry Work Must Not Stop"

A member's plea comes true.

Richard Ober

By the 1870s New Hampshire's agricultural heyday was long over, the victim of westward migration to better soils, the industrial revolution, and the Civil War. As farmers moved west or into the mill towns, logging companies bought large tracts of "unimproved land" — the woodlots farmers had used for fuelwood and lumber — and stripped the merchantable timber. The White Mountains were especially vulnerable, since the steep slopes that had not been cleared for farming still held virgin timber. Behind the loggers grew huge piles of slash that fueled destructive forest fires. Meanwhile, as the mature timberlands were harvested or burned, the second-growth forest quickly reclaimed pasture and farmland. Forest cover increased from 48 percent of the land base to 58 percent between the 1860s and the early 1880s.

In 1872 forestry pioneer Joseph B. Walker started speaking out against wasteful logging and calling for public controls. The legislature responded in 1881 by appointing Walker and seven other men to assess "the extent to which the forests of New Hampshire are being destroyed by the indiscriminate cutting of wood ... and ... the wisdom or necessity for the adoption of forest laws." Four years later the commission submitted the first official New Hampshire forest report. The members estimated the acres believed to be in forest (3.44 million, or 58 percent of the land area), tallied the annual value of forest products ($4.63 million), and inventoried dominant trees and shrubs.

The bulk of the report was given over to two problems: the woeful inattention to even rudimentary forestry principles and the devastating effects of fires. "There is as yet no system of caring for the forests of America, as has been in vogue for

Mixed hardwood forest. Photo: Ned Therrien.

Heavy logging in the White Mountains and elsewhere fueled the outcry for scientific forestry and fire protection measures. In 1909, after nearly a decade of advocacy by the Society, the legislature created the post of state forester and appointed Edgar Hirst. Hirst went on to be a Society officer from 1925-1965. Photos: SPHNF archives.

centuries in European countries, and the process of educating the landowner to recognize the importance of such a system of forest culture will be a slow one."

Over the next few years, the extent of forest destruction came into sharper focus. As the timber industry, and especially the pulp mills, grew, the forestry commission openly decried logging practices as wasteful, crude, ruthless: "The removal of our forest cover is felt ... upon our timber supply which is vanishing, upon our water-power which is rendered variable and uncertain, upon our scenery which is defaced, and upon our climate which is made less inviting."

The large spruce and pine trees were long gone, and pulp mills were cutting smaller and smaller trees, denuding large swaths of forest. In 1894 the commission called for "an early, radical, and complete change" in logging methods and suggested eminent domain or drastic tax changes to compel reform. Calls for public reserves to preserve scenery increased, especially in the heavily logged White Mountains. Forest protection was becoming a popular cause, but still the mountains burned and the trees fell.

A Forestry Agenda Emerges

The commission's 1902 report was a bit more upbeat. The industry was growing (total value had increased fourfold, to over $16 million, since 1885), and the commission detailed the extent of denuded woodlands in a region-by-region inventory. But it also reported that many larger timber firms had begun to employ trained foresters and were experimenting with more careful logging methods. Clearly, however, the commissioners were most buoyed by the emergence of a fierce new advocate: "The most directly active of all the forces now at work upon this problem in New Hampshire is the Society for the Protection of New Hampshire Forests which was formed [in 1901]."

In founding the Society, former governor Frank West Rollins and eight other concerned citizens had adopted seven goals, six of which were forestry-related. The goals were, to quote from the first annual report:

- To encourage forest growth throughout the state;
- To disseminate knowledge upon planting, managing and harvesting the forest crop;
- To establish a nursery for distributing

to farmers and other property owners within the state seedling forest trees and seeds at cost;

- To establish a demonstration forest where the soil capacity and commercial value of different species may be shown to the people;
- To preserve intact the scenic beauty in selected places throughout the state where the forest is an essential element, particularly upon the high and steep slopes in the mountains;
- To apply to the forests the principle of continuous yield, thereby protecting the future of the lumber mills and wood-working factories, upon which thousands of families depend; and
- To urge the passage of forest laws based upon the best experience.

As a private group, the Society could move much more quickly than a public agency. Although the young Society and its tireless leader, Philip Ayres, attracted a lot of attention for leading the push for a White Mountain public reserve, they were also doing the persistent work necessary to promote good forestry. The early conservationists believed, as the Society continued to believe 100 years later, that good forestry and land preservation were two sides of the same coin; that all conservation begins with good forestry. And so while lobbying for the Weeks Act, the Society convinced the state to create the state forester position, pass forest fire prevention laws, build forest fire towers, and establish the state nursery. It also sponsored major forestry conferences.

Ayres wrote for national publications and carried his lantern slides and lecture notes to Grange halls and women's clubs. Ayres was tireless not only as an advocate for change but also as a practitioner. He drew up management plans for dozens of landowners, including Dartmouth College.

In 1911 Ayres wrote that "the Society takes much satisfaction in the results of its ten years' work," and noted that all the initial legislative goals had been reached. "It is possible to believe that the time may not be far distant when the annual harvest of timber in New Hampshire will not exceed the annual growth, and when large areas of timber, valuable for scenic beauty and for protecting the flow of streams, are permanently safe from ordinary destructive lumbering and from the ravages of soil-consuming fires."

The Society had become a leader in the national conservation movement that equated good forestry with patriotism. "Forestry is a matter of immediate interest to every household in the land," wrote Agriculture Secretary James Wilson in 1906. "Forest destruction is no imaginary danger of a distant future. If it is not speedily checked its effect will sooner or later be felt in every industry and every home."

Such rhetoric from respected politicians ensured that forestry would remain a priority even in the most trying of times. When Society member John Wister enlisted to fight the Germans in World War I, he made arrangements for his annual membership dues to continue in case he didn't return. "This forestry work," he wrote, "must not stop."

Wister needn't have worried. Over the years, the Society advanced good forestry through three central means: Policy and collaboration; promotion and education; and practice of exemplary stewardship on its own lands. ❧

Policy and Collaboration

Governor Sherman Adams signs timber tax reform legislation in 1949. Photo: SPNHF archives.

It's hard to imagine a public policy less friendly to good forestry than New Hampshire's timber tax in the first half of this century.

Prior to 1949, timberland owners paid an annual tax of 2 percent of the value of their standing timber — as trees grew and log prices inflated, taxes increased. In short, the state penalized people who left their trees in the ground and awarded those who cut them down. If the same logic were applied to agriculture, state forester and erstwhile Society leader Edgar Hirst once quipped, "The inevitable result would be the picking of apples while still green, the gathering of corn in the silk, the cutting of hay before it is ripe."

Common sense, however, does not always prevail in New Hampshire's tax debate, and meaningful reform took nearly forty years of intense work. The Society first introduced legislation to change the timber tax in 1912. Encouraged by a very narrow defeat, it tried again. And again. And again. Indeed, the Society pushed for change in virtually every legislative session until 1938.

That year the legislature approved a constitutional amendment allowing timberland to be taxed differently than other land. Voters approved the amendment in 1942, and the yield tax, levied only when timber is actually harvested, was signed into law by Governor Sherman Adams in 1949. That system stands today. Of timber tax reform Hirst would later say, "That was a cause for which we died four or five times." ❧

Legislation prepared by the Society in 1903 and passed in 1909 called for a state forester to establish a system of forest protection, including measures to reduce forest fires. This fire tower was erected on Black Mountain in Cambridge in 1921. Above: The Society participated in the salvage of some 500 million board feet of timber following the devastating 1938 hurricane.

New Hampshire and the Society have been blessed with scores of prominent forestry leaders. A few of these from the 1950s were: Oliver Wallace, UNH professor; Burm Garland; J. Willcox Brown, assistant forester, trustee, and activist; Robert Wilson, Jr., of the U.S. Forest Service; Henry I. Baldwin, state forest researcher; Hugh Tuttle, soil scientist; William P. House, consulting forester; and Lawrance W. Rathbun, Society forester. All photos: SPNHF archives.

Forestry programs emphasized collaboration with others. Panelists at the 1959 annual conference included: Top: Wilbur Thompson, Merrimack County forester; Clark Stevens, UNH wildlife professor; Don Burbank, work unit conservationist; Paul Hooper, fisheries biologist; Perley Colby, Hillsborough County agricultural agent. Bottom: Theodore Natti, chief of lands and forest operations, state of New Hampshire; Fred Courtsal, animal control officer; Win Robinson, fisheries biologist; and Anthony Hamilton, soil scientist.

Right: In the energy-conscious 1970s, the Society advocated increased use of wood as fuel for heating and producing electricity. Improved markets for pellets, chips, and cordwood helped encourage good forestry. Above: In 1997, policy director Tammara Van Ryn was a leader, along with Tom Miner of the N.H. Division of Forests and Lands, in producing "Good Forestry in the Granite State," the definitive guide to sustainable forest management practices. All photos: SPNHF archives.

Forestry Promotion & Education

The Tree Farm program began in Washington state in 1941; the Society started the New Hampshire program in 1950. The idea was simple: to recognize those timberland owners who demonstrated a commitment to stewardship in their woods.

From the initial group of twenty-four charter members, the program by 2001 counted 1,677 tree farmers managing 857,310 acres of land in all corners of the state. To be certified, the landowner had to meet certain requirements to care for the wildlife, water, timber, and other resources. A team of more than 100 volunteers made up of private and public foresters reinspected each tree farm every five years. New Hampshire's program, cosponsored by the Society, the NH Timberland Owners Association, and UNH Cooperative Extension, began the twenty-first century considered one of the most rigorous and successful in the nation.

Top: Paul Bofinger's first job with the Society was promoting the Tree Farm program. New Hampshire governors, including Hugh Gregg, above, and John Sununu, left, strongly supported the program. With Sununu are an unidentified attendee; Phil Bryce, later to become state forester; and Karen Bennett, forestry educator with UNH Cooperative Extension. All photos: SPNHF archives.

Society forester Larry Rathbun, above, was a tireless advocate for forestry. Under his leadership, the Society taught forestry to adults and young people, helped fight outbreaks of pathogens, participated in hurricane salvage, and promoted high quality private stewardship. Rockingham County forester Roger Sloan, right, taught high school students how to use a Biltmore stick during a 1952 forestry short course. Photos: SPNHF archives.

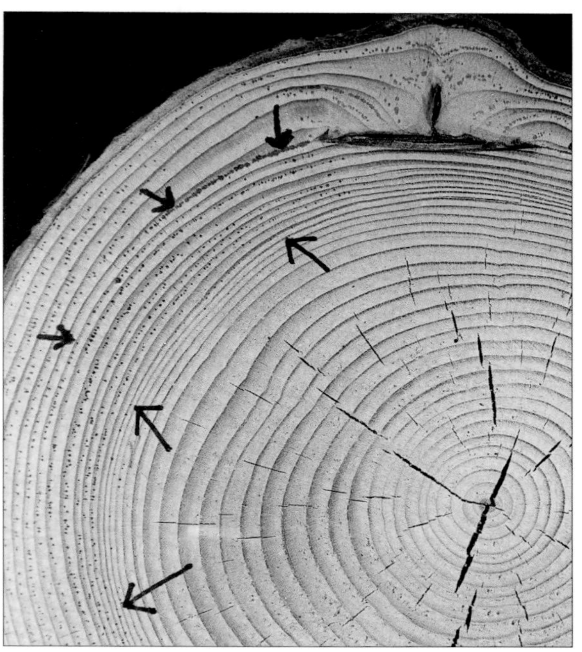

"What Quality of Pine Timber Are You Growing?" Forest Notes *asked readers in 1956. Through workshops and articles, the Society demonstrated that clearer lumber could come from pruned trees (horizontal plank) as opposed to unpruned. Substantial efforts were also put into fighting pests and blight, such as the disease that affected the pine at right. Photos: SPNHF archives.*

In the early 1990s the Society supported the creation of the Timber Harvesting Council, the state's professional logger program. Jeff Putnam taught this safe felling workshop on a Society reservation. Photo: Geoffrey Jones.

Practicing Exemplary Stewardship

One of the Society's original goals was "to establish a demonstration forest." That goal was met in spades as the Society's landholdings exceeded 30,000 acres in 2001. These lands have always been used to demonstrate new forestry techniques, experiment with new equipment, monitor forest growth, and teach other landowners.

The standard for good forestry has changed as scientists have learned more about how forests function. At the beginning of the twentieth century, there was simple "sustained yield": making sure that cutting did not exceed growth. By mid-century, "multiple use" gained favor, in recognition that wildlife, water, and other resources are affected by timber harvesting and management.

By the end of the twentieth century, the objective of model forestry had evolved again: The goal was not just to sustain timber but to sustain the intricate ecological processes of the forest itself. Toward that end, the Society was testing and applying innovative forestry techniques, including intensive biological inventories, computerized mapping and analysis, and "ecosystem-based" forest management plans. All of the Society's operations conformed to "Good Forestry in the Granite State," a guide to sustainable forestry practices developed by a team of biologists, ecologists, foresters, loggers, and other professionals.

This commitment to exemplary forestry was recognized in fall 1998 when the Society became New Hampshire's first green-certified landowner. The designation came after a comprehensive review by SmartWood, which is a part of the international Forest Stewardship Council (FSC).

Volunteers Terry Frost and Bill Luti planted trees at the Conservation Center in 1990. Photo: SPNHF archives.

When land acquisition increased dramatically in the 1970s, the Society hired veteran forester Sarge Goodhue, above, to help manage the growing acreage for forest products, recreation, wildlife, aesthetics, and clean water. Land management director Geoffrey Jones, left, discussed a timber sale in 1994 with logging contractor Don Hardwick. Photos: SPNHF archives; Alan Briere.

In 1994, the Society launched its nationally recognized land stewards program. By century's end, more than sixty highly trained volunteers had been placed as stewards on nearly half the Society's reservation. Based on its experience conducting timber harvests on high visibility reservations, including Mount Monadnock, the Society published the popular book A Guide to Logging Aesthetics *and the companion video, "The Careful Timber Harvest." Geoffrey Jones developed the concept and material for the book and video. Photos: Alan Briere, Geoffrey Jones.*

Green Certified Forestry

In the winter of 2000-2001, the Society conducted its first official "green-certified" timber harvest. Every step in the process – from planning to contracting with certified professional loggers to selling the wood – followed rigorous standards established by the SmartWood program of the Forest Stewardship Council (FSC). Consumers buying certified wood are assured that it came from a sustainably managed forest. Here is how the process worked:

1. First, Lionel Chute and other Society staff conducted a "biological-timber inventory" of the Wilkins-Campbell Forest in Deering. They used sophisticated equipment and a customized database to catalogue plants, soils, animal signs, trees, and dozens of other observations. The staff then wrote an extensive management plan, which included detailed recommendations for each acre of land.

2. Society foresters marked the trees to be cut, flagged skid roads, the landing, and buffer areas, and contracted with professional logger Aaron Sterling.

3. One of the best signs of high-quality forestry is what is left behind. In this case, the Society left thousands of dollars worth of quality timber to protect riparian areas, maintain genetic diversity, and offer corridors for wildlife.

4. To protect the "chain of custody" from woodlot to consumer, all the wood from the harvest went to a certified mill as well – Granite State Forest Products in Henniker, where it was stamped, stored, and processed separately.

Photos: 1: Richard Ober. 2, 3, 4: Ned Therrien.

1

2

3

4

"Once You Learn to Read the Land"

Aldo Leopold's hopeful quote defined the essence of Society education programs.

FRED TAYLOR

When the Society for the Protection of New Hampshire Forests was founded in 1901, two national figures embodied the young conservation movement. Gifford Pinchot, founding father of modern forestry, advocated the "highest use" of forest land with the principle "the greatest good for the greatest number for the longest time." John Muir, bearded prophet of wilderness preservation, quipped in response that "the greatest number is too often found to be number one." Regrettably, this schism widened through the twentieth century, and most groups chose one side or the other. From its beginnings, the Society has bridged this divide by adhering to a two-part mission: "to perpetuate the forests of New Hampshire by insuring their wise use and their complete reservation in places of special scenic beauty."

During a 1999 trip to the Lovern's Mill cedar swamp in Antrim, New Hampshire, it was clear that this inclusiveness has shaped Society education programs. The trip was both a collaboration and a victory celebration: Three groups had worked together to protect a unique piece of land. The diverse but coordinated protection strategies embraced the best of both Muir and Pinchot. The new reserve included a preserved core area of Atlantic white cedar swamp surrounded by a buffer of well-managed and protected working forest. Walking the land, Meade Cadot of the Harris Center for Conservation Education explained the significance of large protected areas for ecosystem health and wildlife survival. Krista Hemboldt from the Nature Conservancy described the ecological significance of Atlantic white cedar swamps. Then Society educator Dave Anderson pointed out bob-

Creek Farm, Portsmouth. Protected in 2000. Photo: Tim Gaudreau.

cat and fisher tracks as he led us into the tall cedars to discuss forest succession.

Since the Society's founding, education programs like the Lovern's Mill trip have woven together land protection, forest management, and natural history into a rich tapestry of ideas and facts and concepts — for in organizations, as in ecosystems, diversity creates stability.

Teaching the Teachers

Education was a core value for the Society from the beginning. Early annual meetings featured presentations on topics ranging from insect pests to the educational value of summer school for boys and girls. Annual reports dutifully transcribed the keynote addresses, becoming extensive volumes on forestry averaging 80 to 100 pages. The first forester, Philip Ayres, unflaggingly spread the message of land protection and good forestry, advising private landowners and corporations and speaking to civic groups.

In the 1930s, when dramatic events like the Dust Bowl roused concern over natural resource depletion, many state universities developed teacher education programs. The Society modified this approach by sending the teachers to camp. Cofounded by the New England Wildflower Preservation Society in 1932, New Hampshire Nature Camp was a weeklong, intensive, hands-on program of nature study. Thirty teachers came to Lost River — a dramatic Society-owned landscape of gorges, waterfalls, and mountain forests — to study with natural resource professionals.

The curriculum covered soils, water, animal life, and forestry: SWAF for short. This integrative approach was novel for the time. Aldo Leopold lamented in 1944 that conventional land management philosophy still looked primarily at parts rather than wholes. By contrast, the camp curriculum from 1948 covered "the study of the interrelationships between all species of plants and animals and the soil and water on which their habitat depends."

The instructors were equally diverse. Tudor Richards, who went on to head up the Audubon Society of New Hampshire, led teachers through the woods to observe birds, look for animal sign, and study wildlife habitat. Ted Natti, who would become state forester, taught both the theory of forestry and the practical skills of pacing, compass work, and measuring tree height by triangulation. Natti recalled that most of the teachers didn't know much about forests. But once they started to learn, they were, as Natti put it, "gung ho" — not only about the forests but about how to integrate the information into whatever they taught. Richards remembered it as "a grand time, my most significant environmental education experience."

In 1947 the Society began taking the message directly to high schoolers through the Youth Conservation Camp at Spruce Pond in Bear Brook State Park. The first such camp in the state, Spruce Pond used the same SWAF curriculum and faculty as the teachers' camp. Campers collected water samples to analyze for quality, slogged through a local cedar swamp to learn about rare plants, dug pits to study soils, and explored habitat in the park's woods and wetlands.

The young campers were sponsored by local organizations and, as representatives of the town, pledged to report back to their communities. A number went on to work in environmental fields, including Jack Sargent, who became state forester, and Joe Quinn, who had a lifelong career in parks and conservation. Camp counselor Mary Beth Robinson later served three decades as the Society's bookkeeper and personnel administrator.

Under the guidance of Society forester Lawrance "Larry" Rathbun, the teachers' and students' camps filled a unique niche in conservation education in 1940s. Rathbun's next move would be to hire a man with a true passion for education.

Les Clark

Les Clark arrived on the scene in 1958, bringing his compass, his megaphone, and his Paul Bunyan stories. As the first full-time educator for any conservation group in the state, he ushered in a period of expansion for Society programs.

Clark brought with him an extensive background in the new field of outdoor education from previous positions in Michigan and at Boston University's Sargeant Camp. He had studied and worked with the leaders in this new field, who drew on John Dewey's philosophy of "object learning," or learning by doing. Clark embraced the philosophy of an early mentor, "Captain" Bill Vinal, who employed a Socratic, question-posing method and insisted on process. "He had an almost complete dedication to the idea that a person must find out for himself most of the things he needs to know," Clark once wrote.

That aptly describes Clark as well. During his twenty-two years as education director, he directed both conservation camps, collaborated with schools and other organizations to develop curricula, set up nature trails, and organized new programs such as Project Learning Tree, Day Lab, and the EcoCenter at Mount Monadnock. He also saw publications as valuable educational tools. As editor, Clark guided the development of *Forest Notes* from a technical forestry journal into an award-winning magazine with wide audience appeal.

A teacher for all seasons: Les Clark and his ubiquitous megaphone. Photo: SPNHF archives.

One of his most popular projects was the Day Lab at Bear Brook State Park, where Clark took students tromping around, investigating glaciation, soil, natural history, erosion, and forest management. Clark's winter treks became legendary. "I have made a special point of winter, and had some 250 children during January and February," he wrote during the program's first season. "We had some wonderful experiences in the winter woods, tracking, finding animal homes, and learning to enjoy the winter beauty." The children responded warmly. Well-read and philosophical, Clark had a low-key approach to teaching characterized by humor, gentle persuasion, and the art of weaving together diverse perspectives through discussion.

Outdoor education pioneers: Ted Natti taught forestry to "gung ho" teachers at New Hampshire Nature Camp. Photo: SPNHF archives.

Following Clarke's death in 1992, Tudor Richards, Annette Cottrell, and other friends developed the memorial Les Clark Nature trail along the Merrimack River at the Conservation Center. The trail and kiosk were fine tributes to a man who, in Richards's words, was the "all-time leading conservation educator in New Hampshire."

New Challenges, New Solutions

In the years after Clark's retirement in 1981, Society educators wrestled with new challenges. During the early 1980s, under the leadership of Cleve Kapala and Jeff Wallner, the focus remained primarily on programs for young people. Youth Conservation Camp and Day Lab continued, and Project Conserve was founded in 1984 to train volunteer docents to teach six-month units on conservation in public schools. Wallner initiated nature walks at the Rocks in Bethlehem and was an adjunct teacher in the local school.

In the 1980s and 1990s, more and more field trips and workshops in land protection were geared to adults. Once the only group to offer youth conservation education, the Society had been joined by many others. A 1989 survey found that nearly a dozen groups were reaching most of the state's students with environmental education programs. Faced with this fact and confronted by a wave of unprecedented growth and loss of land in New Hampshire, the staff and trustees asked two basic questions: As important as it is to educate the next generation, what could be done to reach adults who were already making decisions about land? And how could education programs more directly advance the core Society goals of good forestry and land protection?

The trustees decided to cut back on programs for young people and devote attention to building a connection between adult decision-makers and the natural resources they control. John Hay, renowned nature writer and inspiring spirit for the Society, articulated the essence of this vision: "Our fundamental association with the land needs to be rediscovered. No land can provide us with insights into its real nature when we only maintain a distant relationship with it. If we learn to treat the land with respect, rather than thinking of it as an economic commodity under our control, its rewards will be inestimable. What we learn from living with the land, rather than apart from it, can encourage undiscovered possibilities in ourselves."

Through an internal research and development project called the Conservation Institute, education director Dan Sundquist and field educators David Anderson and Beth McGuinn developed multi-session courses for landowners, foresters, and volunteers. They included "Conservation Studies," a ten-week primer; "Taking Stock," which taught landowners how to inventory natural resources; "Working with Your Woodland," a forest management course; and "Portraits in Forest Ecology," which involved up-close studies of vernal pools, fungi, riparian zones, and other components of the forest. Courses ran at the Conservation Center, the Hay Reservation in Newbury, Shieling State Forest, the Rocks, and Society properties across the state. McGuinn coordinated a Land Stewards Training Program for people who wanted to become active volunteers in the care and maintenance of conservation land.

In the first two years, McGuinn recruited and trained forty-eight land stewards and put them to work on Society lands. Mike and Carol Andrews of Washington were attracted to this program as new landowners. "It gives you a broader approach to landownership," Carol Andrews observed. "We take care of land for the Forest Society, but we don't own it, and it makes us feel that way with our piece of land that we do own. We can't really own a piece of land. We are caretakers. It's something that belongs to everyone."

At the turn of the century, Society education programs were reaching more people than ever before. Building on and refining content developed under the Conservation Institute model, education director David Anderson and field educator Kristin Loomis were offering more than eighty programs annually. Programs ranged from forestry primers to mushroom hunts, botany walks on the Les Clark Trail to in-depth workshops on land protection options, the economics of conservation, mammal identification, and green-certified forestry. Mike Andrews, who was elected to the Board of Trustees in 1997, put it this way: "What these programs taught me was to see a little bit more. I walk through the woods now with a completely different view."

"We may be able to save New Hampshire so that it will be recognizable to us," David Anderson said. "There have to be black bears. There have to be pine martens. There have to be bobcats. I would like to think that we've become enlightened enough that we can sustain our forests and our forest economy, our clear drinking water, and all of the wildlife that lives here. I believe that education is a critical component of getting there." But as Les Clark showed us, Anderson said, realization is not enough: "You've got to feel that fire in your belly. You've got to feel like you're on a mission."

To this end, Aldo Leopold's hopeful statement has remained a guiding principle of Society programs: "Once you learn to read the land, I have no fear of what you will do to it."

Jeff Wallner teaching environmental education in Bethlehem Elementary School in the 1980s. Photo: SPNHF archives.

Profile

Lawrance W. Rathbun

Forester, 1935–1965

When the Society for the Protection of New Hampshire Forests's first forester, Philip Ayres, retired in 1935, America was in the middle of the Great Depression. By then, it had lost the innocence and optimism that marked the early days of the century. After one world war and the growing threat of another, the days of Ayres's great land campaigns seemed over.

Larry Rathbun was a forester who had been working in the woods around Dublin, in the shadow of Mount Monadnock. Invariably, he heard the name of the group who had protected the local landmark. Rathbun was hired first as assistant to Ayres and then took over as forester — the name for the sole employee, one-man show the Society was at the time.

Rathbun had a quieter, more restrained style than Ayres, but he perhaps better matched the times. Now that people had become generally supportive of conserving land, Rathbun was determined to educate them on how to take care of it. Forestry was still a new science, and Rathbun wanted to see it spread like religion.

Upon taking up the reins of the Society, he immediately moved its headquarters from Boston to Concord, New Hampshire. He started a periodical called *Forest Notes* as a means to talk to his audience, who appeared eager to listen. Rathbun initiated education programs for youth and adults alike.

Rathbun also picked up the torch for timber-tax reform, one of the Society's earliest but lesser-publicized efforts. Until reforms were finally passed in 1949, timber growing on private land was taxed annually. This dated back to times when the state was trying to encourage clearing of land, but now the policy was actively discouraging long-term forest stewardship.

Rathbun may have had big plans for the Society, but Mother Nature apparently had other ideas. In 1938 a severe low pressure system snuck up the East Coast and became an enormous, full-fledged hurricane. *The* hurricane. It barreled up the Connecticut River, flattening thousands of acres of forests. Regular operations were suspended at the Society, and Rathbun helped organize a timber-salvage campaign that would occupy him for several years.

Then came the "war to end all wars," and the Society once again switched gears to support the war effort. By the time the country emerged from the other side of World War II, Rathbun was ready for a less stressful period. He continued to work on landowner education, hired a few staffers, and revived Conservation Camp. In the 1950s and early 1960s, the Society's efforts included establishing town conservation committees — the forerunners of today's conservation commissions — and expanding the Tree Farm program it had brought to the state in 1950.

In 1961 Rathbun hired a young forester named Paul Bofinger to work with tree farmers and help out with land protection. Four years later, Bofinger would replace Rathbun as forester, and Rathbun became president of the executive committee. The country had changed yet again: Young people were loudly questioning the old ways, the environment was reemerging as a topic of concern, and rock 'n' roll, it seemed, was blaring from every radio.

Bofinger was named both president and forester at the Society's 1972 annual meeting, and Rathbun formally retired. Rathbun's goals of raising awareness for good forestry, expanding nature education across the state, and working to get local people taking care of local lands had been more than well met. But he also accomplished a crucial if less glamorous goal — keeping the Society alive and on track during some of the most difficult years this country has experienced.

Rosemary Conroy

Reclaiming New Hampshire's Waters

An undercurrent of water protection ran through Society programs from the beginning.

Suki Casanave

In the 1960s, Merrimack River fishermen sometimes found themselves thigh-deep in water coated with reddish scum — raw organic waste from toilets upriver. Hydrogen sulfide fumes from timber mills in Lincoln peeled paint off buildings in Bristol, 30-odd miles downstream. Textile dyes, dumped by the ton, left their stain on the river. Canoeists feared falling in. And the fish that survived smelled as appetizing as their environment. Efforts to sell riverfront property drew peals of laughter.

"It was so bad," said fisherman and lifelong water-quality professional Terry Frost, "you could plunge your hand into the river up to your wrist, and not be able to see your fist."

Given the statewide presence of the Society for the Protection of New Hampshire Forests and the seminal role water plays in ecological cycles, it was inevitable that the two would come together. In fact, water quality ultimately defined the Society's earliest campaign. The battle to pass the Weeks Act in 1911, which enabled the creation of the White Mountain National Forest and the eastern national forest system, was fought and won not simply because trees were being stripped from New Hampshire's mountains. The determining issue was that disrupted water flows caused by heavy logging near the headwaters of the Merrimack River were affecting textile mills as far south as Manchester and Lowell. The Weeks Act allowed the federal government to purchase public land to protect the navigability of rivers.

As early as 1912, a year after the passage of the Weeks Act, Society president

Crawford Notch, White Mountains. Protected in 1913. Photo: Harry Lichtman.

Frank W. Rollins wrote an open letter to the people of New Hampshire in the *Keene Sentinel*, making it clear that the war on water pollution was just beginning. "If there is one thing that is absolutely necessary to the state of New Hampshire," he wrote, "it is to have its water supplies pure and uncontaminated ... No state in the Union has so much at stake as New Hampshire in keeping the sources of water unpolluted, and yet pollution is rampant."

From the beginning, the Society promoted responsible logging as a practical means to help preserve water quality. "Problems cropped up all over the place because people just weren't aware of the issues," remembered Frost, the state's first director of permits and enforcement. He spent a lot of time cajoling and convincing, building relationships with loggers and sand and gravel pit operators, explaining the benefits of responsible resource management. With leadership from the Society and the New Hampshire Timberland Owners Association, New Hampshire became one of the first states in the country to adopt "Best Management Practices" — specific guidelines to prevent forestry-related water problems, including runoff and erosion.

The tumultuous 1960s: Granite Staters wake up to the fact that pollution has become a serious fact of life. Photo: SPNHF archives.

In the early 1960s, the pollution conversation took on a new urgency. A 1963 *Forest Notes* editorial declared water quality and quantity to be New Hampshire's number one conservation problem. "Like other renewable resources, water has heretofore, generation after generation, been in superabundance," wrote Society forester Lawrance Rathbun. "Now the population and water resources are approaching a balance which permits less and less margin for indifference."

When developers started eyeing the salt marshes on the seacoast in Hampton, Society leaders set out to acquire some key pieces to secure their water-cleansing qualities. But they also formed a coalition: the New Hampshire Better Water Committee (BWC). "We realized we'd never be able to afford to buy all the land necessary to help protect water supplies," recalled former Society head Paul Bofinger, who helped launch the BWC. "So we took a clue from Massachusetts and focused on legislation." New Hampshire's dredge-and-fill law was the second in the nation. A few years later, the BWC also helped push through the first legislation in the nation requiring statewide review of septic systems.

"The Better Water Committee shifted the perception that the Society was only interested in forest land and forestry issues," Bofinger said. "At the time, it seemed a stretch, especially with a name like ours. But water pollution was a big issue in the state. And for the most part our trustees understood that wetlands and water pollution were important and that we had a responsibility to these larger issues — partly because we were the only environmental organization in the state with staff."

With the passage of the Water Quality Act in 1965, federal dollars became available for sewage treatment plants, and the major focus of the BWC became convincing the legislature to increase matching state funds for these projects. "There was some serious opposition," Bofinger said. "It was the 'pickerel versus payroll' argument: Which is more important, fish or jobs?" Bofinger credited outstanding legislative leadership with the progress New Hampshire made. "At one time we had the highest percentage of state and federal aid of any state in the country." That was fortunate, considering that at one time two-thirds of New Hampshire's major rivers — aptly characterized as well-landscaped sewers — were considered unsafe for swimming or fishing.

The growing enthusiasm for environmental causes during the 1960s sparked the formation of two more coalitions in New Hampshire: first, the Statewide Program of Action to Conserve Our Environment (SPACE) and, later, the Environmental Coalition. "The Society was one of the driving forces in the formation of these groups," said Pat Jackson of the public relations firm Jackson, Jackson & Wagner, who worked with the Society as an adviser, member, and trustee. "Water quality issues were high on the agenda from the beginning."

When SPACE worked to pass the current use law in 1968, for example, water was a key selling point. "In trying to convince people to vote yes, we talked about saving open space as a way to help protect tourism, bring industry to New Hampshire, and protect the water supply in our rivers and aquifers by protecting space around them," Jackson said. "As with the Weeks Act early in the century, water was our selling point." An advocacy network of organizations and individuals, the Environmental Coalition was active for the next decade, helping to pass every major piece of water-related legislation in the state.

In the 1950s and 1960s, signs like these awaited visitors to many New Hampshire lakes and rivers. Photo: SPNHF archives.

With the celebration of the first Earth Day on April 22, 1970, water pollution secured its place as a major public issue. Once again, a *Forest Notes* editorial captured both the sense and the lingo of the times: "Pollution, environment, and ecology are magic IN words right now. Those of us who have struggled in the conservation battle for more years than we care to count welcome the new awareness and hope that the past apathy on the

"Save Our Saco!" These young activists from 1971 got their feet dirty so their river would be a bit cleaner. Photo: SPNHF archives.

part of the citizen majority will change to action-oriented concern."

Critical to the growth of "action-oriented concern" was the founding of local conservation commissions. The Society's Les Clark attended the very first New England Conservation Commission Conference held at Harvard University in 1960. Bofinger wrote letters to Society members and traveled the state to educate people about conservation commissions. With Society encouragement, the state passed legislation enabling towns to create conservation commissions; eighteen New Hampshire towns had formed conservation commissions by 1965. The Society housed and staffed the N.H. Association of Conservation Commissions for many years.

But it wasn't until 1973 that legislation, supported by the Society, was introduced to extend conservation commission authority to wetlands protection. "Conservation commissions played a very important role of holding selectmen's feet to the fire," Jackson said. "They were the ones who worked on the local level to convince towns of the need to put in sewers and sewage treatment plants."

With conservation commissions working as watchdogs at the local level and the Better Water Committee, followed by SPACE and the Environmental Coalition, working at the state level, the 1960s and 1970s saw a marked increase in public awareness of pollution issues. Consciousness changed. So did policies. And then practices. The results were dramatic. By the 1980s, Terry Frost was fishing and paddling in the Merrimack River.

In the last two decades of the twentieth century, the Society supported a slew of water-related initiatives through ad hoc coalitions and special projects. The Pontook Dam on the Androscoggin River north of Berlin, which threatened to drown out blue-ribbon white water and trout fishing, was downsized dramatically after the Society took the developer to court. In 1987 the Society helped found the New Hampshire Rivers Council, a network of local rivers advocacy groups; in the 1990s Society staff and members lobbied hard for the Rivers Management and Protection Program, through which nominated rivers get special state protection.

The Society also played an active role in water mitigation efforts during expansion projects at Loon Mountain Ski Area and along Route 101. And in 1987 the organization was instrumental in the creation of the state's Department of Environmental Services (NHDES), which consolidated all water-related bureaus and agencies into one department, guaranteeing better enforcement and efficiency. In 1999, after a decade of activism, the Shorelands Protection Program, requiring statewide minimum standards for setbacks along rivers and lakes, was finally put into place.

In 1998, an extensive report conducted by Society research director Sarah Thorne showed that nearly 90 percent of the land that surrounded public reservoirs or overlay public wells was unprotected from development and therefore vulnerable to contamination. Thorne and NHDES designed the Water Supply Protection Program to address the problem. In 2000 the legislature authorized and funded the program, making grants available to communities to acquire land and easements to protect their drinking water supplies. Land protection and water quality were once again married on the conservation agenda.

By the end of the twentieth century, the Merrimack River had rebounded to the point that Terry Frost characterized a canoe trip through Concord as nearly a wilderness experience. "The water is crystal clear. You can see the bottom. The salmon and shad are back to some extent. It's swimmable. We've come a long way."

Grassroots: In 1973, longtime Society members Annette Cottrell and Zenaide Bradley (left) and Richard Webb (far right) lobbied for legislation allowing conservation commissions to be local wetland watchdogs. Photo: SPNHF archives.

Current Use

The bedrock of conservation in the Granite State.

Richard Ober, Liz Lorvig, Isobel Parke

The cold November night in 1968 before New Hampshire voters would cast their ballots on current use taxation, Miriam Jackson called Paul Bofinger and told him to get out and distribute more leaflets.

Tired from months of heavy campaigning, Bofinger didn't jump at the suggestion. But Jackson's public relations firm, Jackson, Jackson & Wagner, had never led the Society for the Protection of New Hampshire Forests wrong before. So Bofinger, who led the Society from 1965 to 1996, pulled on his boots and went out to leaflet cars in a Concord shopping center. The next day, election day, voters approved the current use amendment by a slim margin. Years later Bofinger would still wonder if those 100 or so flyers helped change some minds.

That successful vote amended the state constitution to allow undeveloped land to be taxed at its much lower "current use" value rather than its potential development value. Five years later the legislature passed the set of specific laws to implement the program. By the year 2000, current use was the most important public policy affecting open space, with half the state's land enrolled.

Such a sweeping change in tax law did not come easily. The victory followed an intensive, multiyear campaign by a broad coalition called SPACE — Statewide Program of Action to Conserve Our Environment. The effort involved thousands of people in dozens of organizations, including the Society, the Audubon Society, the Farm Bureau, and the New Hampshire Timberland Owners Association.

As difficult as the campaign was, circumstances helped. In the 1960s, after decades of relatively low growth, demographic shifts were starting to alter the face of southern and central New Hampshire. Growth pressures from Boston and northern Massachusetts were making land in New Hampshire more profitable for development than for growing trees and crops. Real estate developers were buying large tracts relatively cheaply and building neighborhoods further and further from

Branch Hill Farm, Milton. Protected in 1990. Photo: Stephen Salniker.

town centers. The new households demanded new schools and other services, and towns raised property taxes to meet the need. Unable to keep up with the taxes, some landowners were forced to sell property that had been in their families for generations.

In the face of spiraling growth and rising property taxes, SPACE and the Society tried to show that current use taxation was the only fair way to slow the disappearance of open space and keep farmers and forest landowners in business. Once the voters approved the constitutional amendment, the coalition started lobbying the legislature to write the enabling laws. One tactic was taking a busload of lawmakers through the southern tier to see recent development for themselves. "Some couldn't believe their eyes," remembered Isobel Parke of the Jackson firm. The momentum grew.

Working with key legislators, including Howard C. Dickinson, Elizabeth Greene, Howard Townsend, and Marilyn Campbell, the coalition crafted a system of differential taxation that addressed many concerns and garnered broad bipartisan support. The program's 10-acre minimum meant smaller landowners could participate. A penalty charged when land was taken out of the program allowed towns to recoup lost revenues. The influential farm and forest industries backed the plan. Municipalities without planning or zoning ordinances saw they might get a little breathing room. Current use even ended up with the support of arch-conservative governor Meldrim Thomson, who signed the bill into law in 1973.

Support for current use remained strong, despite regular attempts from small factions to weaken or even eliminate the program. This support was based on the public's recognition of the value of open space and strong evidence of the economic benefits of keeping land open. A study conducted by the Society in 1998 showed that open space contributed $8.2 billion annually to the state's economy, which was one-fourth of all activity at that time. Other studies showed that towns with more open space have lower property taxes: Although open space land paid less in property taxes, it also required less in costly town services. The result was a net "profit."

Most important, however, current use remained vibrant because of the continuing partnership of conservationists, natural resource in-

The voters did say yes, thanks to the work of Dick Kelly, Paul Bofinger, Miriam Jackson, Tudor Richards, and many others. Question seven on the 1968 ballot enabled current use. Photo: SPNHF archives.

By 2001, half the state's land was enrolled under current use assessment. Photo: Bill Johnson.

dustries, landowners, and municipal officials who came together in the late 1960s to solve a common problem. The original victory was the work of many people from many walks of life, including Tudor Richards, Ray Connolly, Dick Kelly, Win Wadleigh, Phil Heald, Ross Heald, Jeff Smith, John Barto, Bob Norman, Isobel Parke, Patrick Jackson, and Miriam Jackson.

"Current use has worked well to achieve its original purpose," wrote former governor Walter Peterson, whose election in 1968 corresponded to the passage of the amendment. "The rural scenery — the farm vistas and forested country roads — appreciated by visitors and residents alike, is testament to the foresight of these leading citizens and lawmakers." ❧

A Landowner's View of Current Use

Martha and Bill Rotch on their land. Courtesy photo.

Some things we don't miss until they are gone. Some things we don't notice until they are on top of us — urban sprawl, for example: the fast-food restaurants, auto repair shops, and convenience stores that line so many of our highways. We seldom thought about them until suddenly they were there. At the other extreme is open space, the woods, fields, and meadows, the roadside views we take for granted until suddenly they are gone.

I think of this as I drive around Milford, Amherst, Hollis, and Merrimack. And I think of our own land that's in current use. In 1926 my father bought 80 acres or so of cut-over land just south of town. We planted 20,000 white pine and spent weekends for the next twenty years cutting sprouts, trimming pines, clearing paths.

As a boy I earned some 4-H forestry awards. My father died in 1955; he had asked that his ashes be scattered on the woodlot. The same with my mother a few years later. We chose an area under towering pines. We call it — not entirely in jest — the sacred grove.

During this time the lot was assessed as "sprout land." Taxes were modest. Then a number of years ago the town was reassessed. The value placed on the lot was $350,000. I questioned this, and the assessors agreed to take another look. This time they valued it at $475,000. How come? I asked. They pointed out that the lot had frontage on three roads and they had simply estimated the number of building lots and multiplied by the current value of a building lot in Milford.

There was a temptation to offer the land to the highest bidder and invest the money elsewhere. No one in the family wanted to do this. Nor, we agreed, did we want to pay taxes on a lot assessed for $475,000 while we watched the pine trees grow. So we applied for current use, the application was accepted as "managed woodland," and now we pay a modest tax bill each year.

The lot is managed by a professional forester, who ten years ago supervised a light cutting that improved the quality of the remaining trees. The lot has qualified as a Tree Farm and was recently recertified. Of more significance, the area all around the woodlot is being built up. Each month, it seems, there are new houses, new streets.

Am I being selfish? Some people have told me so. People need homes, and here is all this land, "just woods." Now and then the phone rings. Someone wants to buy a small piece, "just enough for a trailer." I say no and feel bad.

Would Milford be better off if I had sold the land to a developer for whatever the market would bear? I don't think so. Already schools are crowded, town services stretched to the limit. We have never posted the land. People are welcome to enjoy the laurel-lined paths and the hemlock-shaded brooks. What of its future? Mrs. Rotch and I have four children, and the decision may soon be theirs.

In the meantime, this Milford woodlot is a tiny portion of the land throughout New Hampshire that is taxed on its current use rather than its "fair market value." It would be shortsighted indeed for New Hampshire to ignore costs to the community of development and the value of open space in an effort to capture more real estate tax dollars. ❧

William T. Rotch

Land and Trust

The 1980s saw a huge increase in land protection efforts.

Rosemary Conroy

The building boom of the mid-1980s took New Hampshire by surprise. Development that had been seen as a way to build up the local tax base was dramatically transforming parts of New Hampshire. Towns that had always prided themselves on "home rule" found themselves at the mercy of developers and underequipped to keep up with the flow of subdivision and building permit applications. Responding partly to spiraling demand and partly to speculative desire, builders threw up condos on shorefronts, punched subdivisions into woodlots, and paved over cornfields with car dealerships. In one year, from 1982 to 1983, building permits increased by 72 percent. Single-family houses alone increased from 3,000 new units per year in 1982 to nearly 15,000 per year in 1986.

After decades of successfully campaigning to set aside the state's grand mountains and notches, the Society for the Protection of New Hampshire Forests found its services in high demand in the communities. As citizens scrambled to save cherished local places, and dedicated landowners looked for permanent conservation solutions for family lands, land protection activity increased dramatically. When the 1980s started, the Society owned 30 reservations with nearly 13,000 acres and held 38 conservation easements on another 6,413 acres. At the occasion of the 100th anniversary, in February 2001, the numbers had skyrocketed to 123 reservations with a total of 32,673 acres and 423 conservation easements on another 68,208 acres.

The bulk of these conservation areas were established by donations by families and individuals who entrusted their cherished lands to the Society. Every one of those projects and those families had remarkable stories of faith, commitment, and love of place. The following three stories are emblematic.

McCabe Forest, Antrim. Protected in 1982. Photo: Craig Blouin.

Phil Heald, Wilton

Phil Heald watched the superstores, fast-food chains, and car dealerships transforming Nashua, Milford, and Amherst — all less than 20 miles from his home in Wilton. He imagined how the land his family had lived on for over 100 years could change after he and his siblings were gone. He wondered what would become of the trails he had built and managed so well and the local schoolchildren who had come there to learn about the natural world. So beginning in 1984, Phil, his brother Ross, and his sister Helen Rader gave the Society several pieces of their beautiful land — a total of 927 acres of forest, wetland, fields, and trails.

"People say they'd rather come here than the White Mountains even though we don't have the peaks. But you don't have the crowds, either," Phil said, as he pulled out a trail map printed on orange paper and traced the dashed and dotted lines with his finger: Trails that snake through rolling forests ... down past the apple orchards his dad planted ... around the four wildlife ponds ... and out in three directions to his neighbors' woodlands. Almost every mile, he said, holds a personal connection for him. He recalled the pleasure of receiving the stacks of crayon-colored thank-you notes from school groups, praised the trail crew he had worked side by side with for more than a decade, named the local people who regularly wander his woods, and described the places where he and his late nephew "young Phil" cleared brush and blowdowns. Although he gave up taking his own chainsaw and pickax to the windthrows and water bars some years before, he still clearly envisioned more trails, more links — more places where one can roam unimpeded by crowds or concrete.

Phil Heald (shown here in a 1987 photo) along with his brother Ross and sister Helen Rader donated part of their family lands in Wilton to the Society, starting in 1986. Photo: SPNHF archives.

Phil had first connected with Society educator Les Clark and his colleague, "a young man named Paul Bofinger," back in 1974 when Phil served in the New Hampshire House of Representatives. It would take a dozen years of field trips and workshops on their land before the Healds decided to donate their first 410 acres to the Society. "That's just the way I am," said Phil with a laugh. Then he returned to his map.

Mary Lyn Ray, South Danbury

When Mary Lyn Ray was a little girl growing up in Little Rock, Arkansas, her mother read her a story about a farm below a mountain named "Kearsarge" in a faraway place called "New Hampshire." Perhaps that is why, many years later, when she found a white farmhouse tucked in a valley guarded by that very same mountain, it became her home. And when the 162 acres that lay between her and the mountain were about to be sold to a developer, she knew she had to save them, so that the former farmland and sloping forests could never be lost to condominiums. The only problem was: how?

As an academic writer and historian, Mary Lyn didn't have much disposable income. She spoke with her sister Linda about her financial dilemma. "Well," Linda suggested half-jokingly, "you could always plant pumpkins." If only something as simple as pumpkins could keep the fields from sprouting townhouses!

That night, the opening lines to a story came to Mary Lyn as she was drawing her bath. "I got a pencil and wrote it all down, while the water got cold," she recalled. She placed it — this first experiment with fiction — in a drawer, believing it was a story only for her, to give her the courage to go ahead and purchase the land.

By then, in 1987, Mary Lyn had been a member of the Society for some ten years and had followed with interest the increasing use of conservation easements. It sounded like a way one could keep the memories of a place alive — something that was very important to her. It would also allow her to save the 162 acres. With the Society's help, Mary Lyn worked out a complicated deal with a local bank: She would borrow the money for the purchase while simultaneously placing an easement on the property. She would pay back the money by mining the gravel that lay under the field and then reclaim

Mary Lyn Ray surveys her fields after they were reclaimed as part of her effort to protect them – and more. Photo: Randy Olson.

the land. It was an unusual move, but one the Society supported. "There was no other way I could do it," she recalled. "It was an enormous amount of money." But then disaster struck. The appraiser had been wrong — instead of 250,000 cubic yards of gravel, there were only 17,000 cubic yards. Determined to meet her huge monthly mortgage payments, she sold off most of her furniture and turned to a new line of work: writing picture-book stories for children.

This story didn't end there, however. With the Society's encouragement, Mary Lyn began to speak with her neighbors in the valley and convinced them to place their land under conservation easement, too. Inspired by her sacrifice, the poets Donald Hall and Jane Kenyon, then Mark Chamberlin, then Dr. and Mrs. Wood down the road, and Emily and Ted Hope placed easements on their land. More neighbors eventually followed. Mary Lyn even convinced her parents to move up the road to save an old farmstead that was about to be subdivided. Within a year, over 1,000 adjoining acres had been permanently protected. (Ted Hope went one step further and donated his land outright to the Society a few years later.)

There were more connections waiting to be made. Mary Lyn soon found herself engineering one of the most remarkable land protection projects of the decade. High on the flank of Ragged Mountain, which forms the eastern wall of this valley, 700 more acres had gone up for sale. Townspeople were shocked. The thought of houses being built overlooking their brand new conservation zone struck people as tragic. It was the last year of the five-year Land Conservation Investment Program, which had been set up to help people save special places in their communities. At her neighbors' behest, Mary Lyn applied for funds to protect this key tract. Competition for the funds was fierce, however, but if other landowners made matching donations of land, it would increase their chances.

Again, Mary Lyn Ray and the Society went to work. Piece by piece they connected parcels — through donations, bargain sales, conservation easements, and even a land swap — until they succeeded in protecting 2,000 acres on Ragged Mountain. "It was so satisfying to color each parcel green on the map as it was protected, watching them grow," she said. By the time the project was complete, just under 6,000 acres were protected in a nearly contiguous band stretching from South Danbury to Andover.

One day in 1999, Mary Lyn Ray sat on her front step and gazed across the valley. "All of this couldn't have happened without the Society being distinctly what it is — no other entity has such responsiveness to what is possible. When presented with a project, they don't say, 'Oh, that can't be done!' Instead they say, 'Let's see what is possible.' We must ensure that continues."

One way Mary Lyn continued that possibility was through her picture books. She eventually took that first story out of her drawer and sent it to a publisher; *Pumpkins*, the award-winning illustrated tale of how one man grew and sold pumpkins to raise money to protect his beloved field became her best-selling children's book. In the following years she has written thirty more stories — every one of them about people and their connection to the land. "Every story I write is informed by what I have learned living here," she said. ☙

Roger and Ann Sweet, Sullivan

Roger and Ann Sweet have always gardened. A lot. Herbs, corn, and beans grew behind their house; tomatoes, carrots, beets, asparagus, and squash to the south; potato hills up in the fields across the road. Not to mention apple, pear, and peach trees; raspberry patches; and high-bush blueberries scattered in between.

They bought their house with its lovely gardens from Roger's parents, who had purchased the farm in Sullivan sixty years before. It was a retreat from the Sweet family's busy life in Boston; Roger's mom came up on weekends to tend her vegetables. "We lived off the farm during World War II," Roger recalled proudly. The connection to the land was obviously passed down from mother to son. And shared by spouse. A "wistful longing for self-sufficiency," as Ann put it, led them to move to Sullivan full time in 1993 after years of weekend and summer visits.

Shortly after their move, Roger and Ann expanded their husbandry from their farm to the larger surrounding landscape of their town. Between them, they served on the local planning board, local music society, conservation commission, regional planning commission, and the Harris Center for Conservation Education. As master gardeners they worked at the Maplewood Demonstration Garden, where they sowed their message of the need to preserve agricultural lands.

Beginning in 1995, the Sweets lent their considerable knowledge and skill to the Society as land stewards of the Piper Forest Reservation just down the road. It was during their training in 1994, Ann said, that they first began to look seriously at maps of their area. By then, the Faulkner family had made their historic gift of an 11,000-acre conservation easement on their Andorra Forest in Stoddard. Roger wondered, "Could we connect Sullivan's Bear's Den and Potholes State Forest with the growing protected lands to the east?"

Being such do-it-yourselfers, the Sweets started by donating a conservation easement to the Society on their own 82 acres in 1998. The next day they invited to their home all neighbors who owned large tracts of land for an information meeting about conservation easements. As a direct result of that meeting, neighbors negotiated two more easements almost immediately, and by fall 2000 their goal of a protected corridor through Sullivan was achieved. "Roger and Ann are such a valuable resource for the Society," said land protection specialist Brian Hotz. "They are tireless in their efforts to save that area's open spaces."

Ann and Roger continued to work on those open spaces, too — leading walks for local people, clearing trails, and attending countless meetings. And of course, tending their own gardens and fields. "We like maintaining a landscape that you can live on," Ann said. ♣

The Sweets are master land stewards of the Society's Piper Forest, and beyond. Photo: Tim Gaudreu.

Right Time, Right Place

In the 1980s it was time for the Trust for New Hampshire Lands.

Ralph Jimenez

A generation can leave behind no better monument than unspoiled earth, ground from which plants will always rise and rain run clear. As more of us crowd the planet and land becomes more precious, that has become difficult to do. But sometimes those temporarily entrusted with the care of the earth today agree to bank some for tomorrow. That was the story of the Trust for New Hampshire Lands (TNHL) and the Land Conservation Investment Program (LCIP).

From 1987 to 1993, the partnership between the private TNHL and public LCIP protected 379 parcels covering 100,876 acres from Portsmouth to Pittsburg. Preserved for good were Canterbury's Shaker Village, the back 40,000 of Nash Stream Forest, the wild New Hampshire shores of Lake Umbagog, a chain of working farms on the Connecticut River, and stretches of Great Bay. State parks, forests, and wildlife areas were expanded and new reservations created. Community activists worked together to conserve scores of lesser-known places — riverbanks and sugar bushes and farms, quaking bogs and mountaintops, ponds, intervales, and open vistas.

By the time the LCIP funds ran out in March 1993, the equivalent of 1 New Hampshire acre in every 57 had been set aside. While many states — including Maine, Vermont, New York, and Massachusetts — had similar conservation programs in the 1980s, only Michigan's came close to New Hampshire's for efficiency and reach. Private contributions, the use of easements, landowner dona-

Great Bay, a focus of multiple protection efforts. Photo: George Barker.

LCIP funds helped secure a public access point on Webster Lake. Photo: Bill Johnson.

tions, and tough negotiating stretched the public's investment of $46.4 million into $83.3 million worth of protected land.

As important as the conservation victory was the renewed knowledge that a shared concern for New Hampshire's future could unite unlikely colleagues in an effort to make the future better.

A State with Its Seed Corn at Risk

For decades, growth had come with the steady rhythm of flycasting. People casting for the good life had slowly looped longer and longer arcs of line over the pool of New Hampshire and caught a piece of their dreams. But by the mid-1980s a run was on. Crowds lined the banks, spearing and snagging whatever could be landed quickly. Whooping men and women stepped back from the pool holding aloft shopping malls, condominiums, and waterfront homes. By 1987, New Hampshire was the second fastest growing state east of the Mississippi, its population increasing at 20,000 annually — twice the rate of neighboring New England states.

Although the growth brought much prosperity, the impact on the landscape was inescapable; forests and farms were disappearing at a rate of 20,000 acres a year. New Hampshire was eating its seed corn — its scenery, its natural resources, its way of life. "There was a lot of concern about what was happening to New Hampshire," said Stephen Taylor, the state's commissioner of agriculture. "A lot of people felt that the state was like a big truck rolling downhill with no brakes. You could steer the damn thing a little but you couldn't stop it."

Conservation and planning agencies were steering with all their might, trying to avoid hitting the goose that had laid such a brilliant golden egg. But applications to divide, dredge, fill, and build buried local planning boards. Towns in the southern tier saw building permit applications double from one year to the next and grappled with subdivisions of 100 lots when they had previously seen none bigger than a dozen. Many landowners were eager to leave their land as productive open space, but they simply couldn't afford it.

Paul Bofinger, longtime president/forester of the Society for the Protection of New Hampshire Forests, knew it was time for a new solution. In 1984 he took a sabbatical to find it. "I set out thinking that somebody else had the magic wand — the experience or technique that I could bring back to New Hampshire," Bofinger said. "But in the final analysis, I realized that wasn't going to work. Whatever would work would have to be something that fit the times and the New Hampshire scheme of things."

Bofinger figured that direct acquisition of land and rights to land, all on a willing-seller basis, was the only suitable response. He returned from sabbatical in 1985 with the germ of an idea: to offer cash to landowners to leave their land as open space. The concept wasn't new, but the scope was. To make a dent, Bofinger calculated it would take 100,000 acres and a whopping $50 million from the legislature. The Society Board of Trustees swallowed hard and endorsed the plan.

"The Society set aside its own immediate priorities to try something truly visionary," said George Hamilton, who would become chairman of the Land Conservation Investment Program board. "It was a financial, political, and organizational risk. But that's what it took to get the ball rolling."

Society trustees and staff approached leaders from all arenas — conservation, business, finance, tourism, government, philanthropy, and civic groups — with questions as well as answers. The Homebuilders Association and the Nature Conservancy alike were asked how the Society's plan could be accomplished.

Several elements quickly became clear. First, the times called for an all-out effort. No token project would meet the conservation needs of a burgeoning state that had not made a major commitment to land acquisition since 1963. Second, no single entity was big enough to pull it off. Despite missions that sometimes seemed at odds, groups would have to work in unprecedented harmony. And third, public money could do only part of the job.

"Even collectively there aren't enough public dollars to do the job. You have to move the public engine with private dollars," said Lewis Feldstein, president of the New Hampshire Charitable Foundation. A new nonprofit organization would have to be created to work in partnership with the state. In 1986 Feldstein and leaders of 150 other organizations became incorporators of the Trust for New Hampshire Lands.

With seed money from the Charitable Foundation, the Society set out to inventory the best of what was left of New Hampshire. A team of interns spent the summer of 1986 talking to state agencies, local officials, foresters, biologists, botanists, hunters, and anglers. They found universal enthusiasm and long wish lists, ending up with an inventory of more than 300,000 acres of land people wanted to save. It was time to see the governor.

"I sent John Sununu a four- or five-page draft of the proposal and made an appointment to see him," Bofinger said. "To his everlasting credit, he agreed with the proposal, suggesting only one change."

Rob Trowbridge and John Hardie led a $3.2 million fund-raising campaign for the Trust for New Hampshire Lands. Photo: SPNHF archives.

A Uniquely New Hampshire Solution

As nature abhors a vacuum, New Hampshire abhors bureaucracy. So the Trust for New Hampshire Lands didn't ask for one. Private donations would fund administrative costs; public money would fund acquisitions; the effort would have a six-year life span; and as much land as possible would be protected with conservation easements to minimize impact on local tax rolls.

Led by Rob Trowbridge, publisher of *Yankee* magazine, the trust's team of high-end volunteers raised $700,000 almost overnight; in two years an astounding $3.2 million came in from nine foundations, nearly 100 businesses, and 2,000 individuals.

Meanwhile, a sweeping grassroots public education campaign was under way to explain the concept and how donations of time, money, and sweat could make it a reality. Volunteers presented more than 100 separate slide shows wherever people were willing to gather: garden and gun clubs; church, school, and community groups; Rotary, Kiwanis, and Lions Clubs. Those who liked the idea were asked to sign a simple card saying so. Editorial support by the state's newspapers was unflagging.

When the legislation seeking public funds was drafted and filed in 1987, the idea had such broad support that Senate president Bill Bartlett assigned it the prestigious ranking of Senate Bill 1. At the

The Society's Sarah Thorne directed acquisition for the TNHL/LCIP partnership. At a ceremony completing the Lake Umbagog project were Phil Bryce and Brent Halsey of James River Corp., Paul Bofinger, George Hamilton, and then-Governor Judd Gregg. Photo: Richard Ober.

bill's first hearing, the leadoff witness was Congressman Judd Gregg, the man who would succeed Sununu as governor. He was followed by bankers, loggers, hunters, agency heads, and farmers. TNHL board member John Gemmill lugged a tub filled with cards signed by nearly 8,000 residents into the statehouse.

Senate Bill 1 overwhelmingly passed the legislature and was signed by Governor Sununu on May 2, 1987. The bill created the New Hampshire Land Conservation Investment Program and appropriated $20 million; subsequent allocations of $18 million and $7 million were made in 1989 and 1991. Including interest on the bonds, the state's contribution totaled $48.76 million.

Deerfield volunteers Al Jaeger, Kate Hartnett, and Frank Mitchell used LCIP funds to begin a greenbelt for conservation and recreation. Photo: Dan Habib.

Getting It Done

The legislation called for a state-appointed, fifteen-member LCIP board of directors to decide how to spend the public money. The Trust for New Hampshire Lands would work with towns and landowners to bring projects to this board, which would review applications and vote on which projects to fund.

The legislature had charged the LCIP board to focus on acquiring threatened land offering "aquifer recharge areas, forested watersheds, recreation lands, areas of special scenic beauty, plant and wildlife habitats, critical farmlands, undeveloped shorelines, wetlands, flood storage areas... and parcels contiguous to or enhancing land already protected from development." Aware that competition for funding would be fierce, organizers knew the selection process had to be ironclad. Building on the work of a task force chaired by Lew Feldstein, the LCIP adopted a point system for evaluating parcels: the more of these qualities a parcel embraced, and the more competitive the price, the higher its score. The application process was open to all landowners and towns in the state, whether or not a specific property had been included in the 1986 inventory. After lengthy debate, the board agreed that virtually all land protected by the program would have public access.

Things started to move quickly as four key professionals assumed leadership posts. Concord banker George Hamilton, a former state parks director and a graceful mediator, was chairman of the LCIP board. Will Abbott, Congressman Gregg's respected chief of staff, was hired as the LCIP's executive director. Forester Charles Levesque, the talented executive director of the New Hampshire Timberland Owners Association, was named program director of the Trust for New Hampshire Lands. Sarah Thorne, the Society's top land protection specialist and a skilled negotiator, organized and led the trust's team of six land agents. The agents fanned out across the state, meeting with owners of priority lands, responding to inquiries, and helping landowners and municipalities prepare applications for funding.

Bringing It All Back Home

Land conservation is usually thought of in terms of the spectacular — the efforts to save great national parks like Yosemite or grand state landmarks like Franconia Notch. But for most, dramatic, unspoiled vistas are the stuff of calendars, vacations, and memories. By definition, most people do not live where big chunks of land have been preserved.

The TNHL and the LCIP knew that if the ethic of stewardship was to last, at least a bit of nature must be set aside where people could make it a part of their daily lives. A child that grows up in the presence of butterflies values beauty and flight. Besides, it just made good political sense: something the program's rules recognized by requiring that at least one-third of the state's first two installments be awarded to towns on a matching basis to protect lands of local significance. The rest of the funds were used to protect lands of statewide significance to be managed or monitored by state agencies.

To receive state funding, municipalities had to contribute at least half the value of the properties proposed for protection. But the local match did not necessarily have to be in cash. It could be donations of land or conservation easements, a bargain sale in which the landowner sold at less than market value, private contributions or town appropriations, or any combination of the four options. This arrangement assured that not only wealthy towns would be able to afford to participate.

The Audubon Society of New Hampshire helped TNHL train community volunteers interested in the local program. Once a local task force or a few volunteers were in place, TNHL land agents provided assistance, guidance, and negotiation skills until the town's application was complete.

Ultimately, seventy-eight municipalities acquired 246 properties and easements. While only a one-to-one match was needed, landowners donated an astonishing $9.46 million worth of land and easements — 67 percent more than required. Sometimes a community identified a tract that was so important that it was considered to be of statewide significance, which required no match. The last undeveloped stretch of shoreline on Webster Lake in Franklin was on the block and ready to be carved into houselots when the TNHL and LCIP came into being.

"That part of Webster Lake means everything," said T. J. Slokum of Franklin's conservation commission. "The whole city was afraid that another developer with more power would come along and that would be the end of that. But the city had no funds to buy it." The LCIP ruled that it was in the whole state's interest to save the land, which will remain wildlife habitat and provide needed public access under Fish and Game management.

The story of Webster Lake was repeated on a far vaster scale in the North Country, where the last pristine lakes were being threatened with vacation homes. James River Corporation sold 7.3 miles of the shoreline of remote Lake Umbagog to the state for a bargain price and agreed to easements on 2,259 additional acres. Boise-Cascade Corporation and three other landowners got involved as well. The program also enabled the state to purchase Nash Stream Forest in the North Country — at 40,000 acres, the largest state-owned conservation area in New Hampshire.

The LCIP helped protect hundreds of acres of land around historic Canterbury Shaker Village in Canterbury. Photo: Bill Johnson.

A "Rare Positioning of the Stars"

The story of the TNHL/LCIP partnership was, in the words of dairy farmer and agriculture commissioner Steve Taylor, one of a "rare positioning of the stars." Not only were the will and talent there to make the dream come true, but money earned during the boom made that spending possible. Finally, once the money was in place, the swift decline in real estate values allowed the state to protect far more land than it otherwise could have.

In the end, the major legacy of the Trust for New Hampshire Lands and the LCIP was both invisible and the future's best hope. New Hampshire discovered a renewed commitment to conservation, an expanded sense of what is possible, and the knowledge and experience to make the possible a reality.

According to LCIP executive director Will Abbott, "We won a restored confidence in the ability of the public and private sectors to work together and actually accomplish something truly significant."

The TNHL and the LCIP kept their vow to expire. But hundreds of New Hampshire residents — who witnessed the impacts of overspeculation and runaway growth that left banks bankrupt and thousands of unneeded homes half built — were trained in the ways of stewardship.

"Behind every piece of land in the matching program might have been 50 or 100 local people who had a feeling of sharing and accomplishment," said Charlie MacVeagh of Marlborough, who sat on the boards of both the TNHL and the LCIP.

"There are a lot of great ideas out there that go nowhere — ideas every bit as smart as this one was," Lew Feldstein said. "This idea could have been nibbled to death if each person took a chunk out of it. But people worked together and in the end, we were all reminded that our collective actions can accomplish great things."

A Place Apart

Looking back, and ahead, at the Northern Forest.

RICHARD OBER

"In memory, the Northern Forest is like an intriguing stained glass: A soothing pattern of cool green spruce, rolling hills of birch and beech, riffled black rivers and deep lakes, moose-trodden bogs flat to the horizon. Recalling these patterns is as pleasant as speaking the place-names that give them shape: Umbagog, Penobscot, Baskahegan, Attean, Spednik, Parmachenee. In the Northern Forest, these remote and stunning landscapes are not decorations in the pattern; they are its base. From afar it seems that they alone make it a place apart.

But look a little closer and more intricate details emerge. Gravel roads begin to lace through the woods, smoky with dust from a passing log truck. A gray barn floats in the mist of a newly plowed field. Mobile homes and aluminum stove pipes glint through the trees. A chainsaw whines, a plume drifts out of the mill town, woodsmoke sharpens the air — and the full lure of the Northern Forest is revealed. It is not just the wonder of open space too vast to grasp; it is that here, unlike the places most of us know well, pieces shaped by humans are just a part of the pattern, but have not yet become the pattern itself. Nowhere in the northeast do people so live so close to the land, nor so sparsely on it. Nowhere are feelings for the land expressed with less pretension or artifice. And nowhere else is the sense of loss more complete when the cracks of over-use threaten the solder that holds the whole thing together."

I wrote these words for *Forest Notes*, the magazine of the Society for the Protection of New Hampshire Forests, in late winter 1994. By then the Society — and I — had been embroiled in the Northern Forest debate for six years. Society staff had held dozens of town hall and living room meetings in Coos County, worked to protect tens of thousands of acres north of the notches, helped found — and then resigned from — the Northern Forest Alliance, testified at hearings in places as

Percy Peaks, Nash Stream Forest, Stark. Protected in 1989. Photo: Bill Johnson.

diverse as Washington, D.C., and Berlin, New Hampshire, and developed positions on a wide range of topics. Former Society head Paul Bofinger served on both high-level committees formed to address the issue: the Governor's Task Force on Northern Forest Lands (1988–1990) and the Northern Forest Lands Council (1990–1994).

Why all the fuss? Because in these 26 million acres from Downeast Maine to New York's Adirondacks, the Society's core values of land protection and exemplary forestry were writ large. With intense national attention on the region, which includes a fifth of the state of New Hampshire, the Society and others hoped to moved beyond the polarized and damaging "loggers vs. owls" schism out West.

It all started in February 1988 when Diamond International announced it was selling a million acres of timberland up north. When a developer bought the New Hampshire and Vermont acreage, the news rocked the conservation community. Sprawling, remote lands held for generations by companies and families who kept them open for recreation even as they managed them for timber now seemed to be more valuable for speculative real estate than as working forest. With visions of runaway development parting the "granite curtain" of the White Mountains, the Society and the Nature Conservancy joined forces with public agencies to buy most of the New Hampshire land, including 40,000-acre Nash Stream, which remains the largest single conservation purchase in the state's history. Groups in Vermont, New York, and Maine also scrambled to find conservation solutions.

In 1989 Congress initiated the Northern Forest

Brake for moose: Sharing the roads and the woods in the Northern Forest. Photo: Bill Johnson.

Lands Study, a close examination of the trends that drove the Diamond sale. The study concluded that a wide range of economic and social factors would compel additional conversions of working and wild forests for development. An accompanying task force appointed by the region's governors suggested five conservation strategies: incentives for landowners to keep their property, public acquisition of land, better land planning, closer community involvement, and diversified economic development. Both study and task force called for a high-level Northern Forest Lands Council to recommend specific actions.

As the Northern Forest became the region's hottest environmental issue, it seemed for a while that our hope for a more thoughtful resolution was folly: At one far end of the debate were people calling for massive new national parks and draconian forestry laws; at the other were libertarian extremists who insisted there was nothing to worry about. Shouting matches and animal costumes were common at hearings on the issue, and in upstate New York property rights activists physically threatened public conservation agents.

Voices of the North Country

I covered these developments in some two dozen articles I wrote for *Forest Notes* in the late 1980s and early 1990s. From 1992 to 1994 I cowrote a book, *The Northern Forest*, with my friend David Dobbs of Vermont. In the introduction we explained our approach: "When we first conceived the book, we planned to bring some local perspective to the debate by profiling a few residents. Before we got very far, however, we realized that the relationship between people and land was more than a good way to tell this complex story of the Northern Forest — it *was* the story... The

Running from Downeast Maine to New York's Adirondacks, the Northern Forest includes 68,000 miles of rivers and streams, 2.5 million acres of wetlands, and some 250 species of vertebrate wildlife, including twenty-five unique to the region. It is also home to more than a million people, a population density one-sixth of the rest of the northeastern United States. Map: Jill Shaffer.

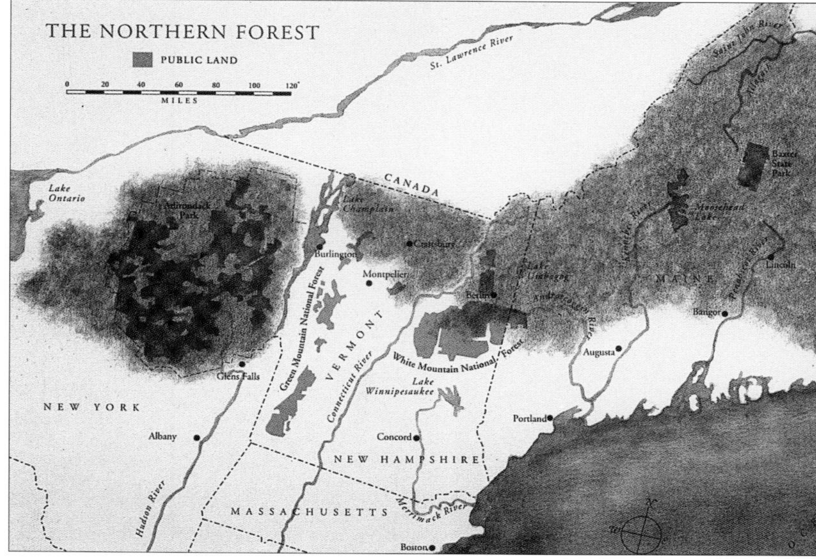

dilemma of the Northern Forest boils down to a single, vital question: Is it possible to protect a great forest without destroying the best parts of the resource-based economy and culture that both arise from and contribute to the land? This question resonates throughout the world; we've been given a unique opportunity to try to answer it here, in our country's first forest."

Rather than attempting a policy answer to this beguiling query, our book asked readers to come to their own conclusions as they read stories of loggers, hunters, biologists, farmers, mill workers, foresters, and others who live and work at the intersect of ecology and economy. This thesis melded well with the Society's own philosophy of working closely with the people who were affected most by the changes and any proposed

A young witness testifies to the Governor's Task Force on Northern Forest Lands in Lancaster. Former Society chairman Hank Swan is at left; longtime president/forester Paul Bofinger is at right. Photo: Richard Ober.

solutions. One of the Society's most gratifying projects was called "Voice of the Northern Communities," a listening tour organized by policy director Tammara Van Ryn that brought Society staff into personal contact with residents in every community in Coos County.

By 1994 virtually everyone involved agreed that three building blocks were needed to sustain both human and natural communities in the Northern Forest: healthy and productive forests, strong and diverse local economies, and protection of special places. When the Northern Forest Lands Council released its final report after four intense years, they called for thirty-seven actions at the private, local, state, and federal levels. Recommendations ranged from regulatory reform to bioreserves, from tax relief to logger education. "We believe urgent and sustained action is necessary for the long-term integrity, character, and productivity of the Northern Forest," the council reported. "Accomplishing this goal will demand new, imaginative thinking and doing."

The council left this menu of action for others to pick up. For several years, a coalition of groups attempted to codify much of the work in an omnibus congressional bill called the Northern Forest Stewardship Act. When that legislation met with resistance from western senators, advocates shifted strategies to push individual pieces. Predictably, some of these recommendations languished while others advanced. The Society focused its efforts on promoting the initiatives that most closely met its objectives and experiences. Specifically, the organization tried to help answer the Northern Forest Lands Council's call for:

* *Green certification*: A market incentive to encourage good forestry, whereby environmentally conscious consumers would choose wood products that are independently certified as coming from well-managed forests. The Society was an

advocate of both the concept and practice of certified forestry, promoting the idea through education and policy initiatives and in 1998 becoming the first New Hampshire timberland owner to meet the rigorous standards of the Forest Stewardship Council.

**Benchmarks for sustainable forestry:* The council urged states to set clear benchmarks for sustainable forest practices, a challenge the Society took up by coleading (with the New Hampshire Division of Forests and Lands) development of *Good Forestry in the Granite State* — a step-by-step practical guide to protecting ecological resources during forest management. The acclaimed guide was published in 1997.

**Land acquisition:* On the state level the Society was a leader of the Land and Community Heritage Investment Program, set up in 2000 to make grants to communities to purchase or protect key lands; on the federal level the Society joined coalition efforts to restore the Land and Water Conservation Fund and increase appropriations for land conservation in the late 1990s. North Country land projects included Lake Umbagog National Wildlife Refuge and additions to the White Mountain National Forest at Bretton Woods and Lake Tarleton.

Leo and Don Roberge of Berlin. Leo worked in the paper mill and was an avid outdoorsman. He supported conservation initiatives as long as they involved and respected local interests: "People, come up, enjoy the nature. But don't try to tell us what do. This is not a park. We were raised up here." Photo: David Dobbs.

**Conservation easements:* The council stressed the usefulness of conservation easements to keep lands open and productive. As one of the first statewide land trusts to negotiate working forest easements, the Society shared its expertise with other organizations and helped secure federal funding for Forest Legacy projects, a federal program that buys easements on working forests.

In the years after the Northern Forest Lands Council report, change continued to affect New Hampshire's North Country. The massive paper mill complex in Berlin changed owners twice, and employment there continued to fall; in 2000, International Paper bought Champion International, the state's largest landowner; pension funds and other timberland investment management organizations stepped up their purchases of timberland; tourists found their way ever further north; the state's population was the fastest growing in the northeast in 1998 and 1999; global demand for wood rose; some landowners continued to cut too hard or too often or both.

In the face of this, the Society remained committed to the three cornerstones of conservation in the Northern Forest: protected lands, healthy working forests, and strong local economies. And the organization continued to work with the people of the North Country — listening to their concerns and ideas, respecting their needs to work together on solutions to outside pressures. As a timberland owner from northern Vermont said in *The Northern Forest*, "For us to destroy our own forest would be like a farmer murdering his cows. We're going to be more protective of these forests than anyone. We earn our livings from them."

PROFILE

Paul O. Bofinger

President/forester, 1965 – 1996

Paul Bofinger was a lot of things to a lot of people — husband, father, friend, fisherman, and fellow conservationist — but to me Paul was the Great Facilitator, or maybe more accurately the Great Persuader. If he was on a mission of persuasion, he was harder to say no to than a shrill kid selling Girl Scout cookies. Paul accomplished a huge amount in his three-plus decades at the Society for the Protection of New Hampshire Forests. His work on the Northern Forest Lands Council was a good example of his style.

I well remember the day the telephone rang back in 1990. It was during a time when I was being mousetrapped into serving as one of the "New Hampshire four" on the Northern Forest Lands Council. I didn't want to do it and said so, citing various minor considerations such as three newspapers to publish, a printing plant to run, and a family still in the fledging-out phase.

Then Paul called with a classic Bofinger opener: "John, you've just gotta do this. We need you." If it were bottled and marketed like buck-lure, this intangible skill would be called "Essence of Bofinger." After I had been smooth-talked into the council I got used to the routine, which sort of reminded me of the Bataan Death

March. We spent most of that first year hunkering down in the trenches while the people who were sure we were commie land-grabbers and the people who were sure we were industry pawns fired endless salvos. Yet we had an agenda to move on and an enormously difficult task ahead. I was soon thoroughly sick and tired of all the time we were wasting defending ourselves. I was ready to quit.

But there was this guy in a plaid shirt, corduroys, and loafers, a guy with an upbeat attitude, a maddening ability to reason, and a smile that never quit. I stayed on, and I'm glad I did.

None of us will forget Paul, for he was the glue that held the council together. And it had to be some kind of glue. The council was, after all, made up of very strange bedfellows: ardent conservationists, government functionaries, capitalist-pig business owners (that's me), and people from the timber industry. Who should have been surprised that at several points we came within a whisker of falling apart? The public never knew it, but it happened — not once, but several times. Each time into the breach stepped Paul, with a conciliatory calm built on years and years of turning conflict into cohesion.

Paul's back bothered him, and during those long meetings there were often two empty chairs at the table — Paul's and mine, for Paul's back felt better when he stood, and I just plain couldn't sit still. The two of us would park ourselves somewhere on the periphery of the proceedings and listen, occasionally jumping in when we had something to say. I found that this behavior helped me see the big picture — the scope of what we were about and what we needed to do to work together and achieve it. I reached the conclusion that Paul was faking with this bad-back business. It just gave him an excuse to step back and take the wider look.

After many of the meetings, I'd emerge into the parking lot to find Paul getting into a vehicle attached to a boat. Paul always seemed to have a boat, and to be headed somewhere — Willoughby Lake, Memphremagog, Parmachenee, God knows. He told me stories about big fish, and flies that worked, and flies that might, and harrowing trips back to camp on lakes whipped to five-foot whitecaps by northwesterly gales.

"He's the very thing my mother told me to try to be," I thought. "He's the kid that refused to grow up, and he's done it." I'd bet, I thought, that he grins into the wind as he tries to steer the boat into the waves.

That's my enduring vision of Paul, the Great Persuader, heading up Parmachenee in a Force Five gale, grinning as he keeps his bow into the waves and telling the lake that it really ought to calm down — and of course it then goes flat as a pancake. ❧

John Harrigan

Photo: Pat Soule

PLACES

"When our children's children look back at twentieth-century New Hampshire, seeking significant milestones of centennial change, they will discover the remarkable story of the reforestation of the Granite State's landscape. And when they ask why it is that the landscape was so refreshed, they will learn that Mother Nature had a helping hand in this rebirth from the Society for the Protection of New Hampshire Forests. And if our children's children are to value the conservation of natural resources as an ethic they must pass on to their children, it will be because the Forest Society's second 100 years are even more progressive than the first."

Will Abbott, Executive Director
Squam Lakes Natural Science Center

Sharon Bog, Sharon. Protected in 1998. Photo: Don Johnson.

"YOU WILL FIND SOMETHING MORE *in woods than in books. Trees and stones teach you that which you can never learn from masters."*

Saint Bernard

The following pages showcase just a few of the special places that were protected by the Society during its first 100 years. Of course, none of these forests, meadows, shorefronts, and riversides could have been set aside without the generosity of their donors and the determination of members, friends, and partners. The Society is grateful for their support in helping save the lands that keep New Hampshire, *New Hampshire*. The photographs on pages 87-97, as well as many others throughout the book, were made by members of the New Hampshire Society of Photographic Artists. The Society is grateful to NHSPA for its participation.

For a complete list of every forest reservation and conservation easement protected by the Society from 1901 to 2001, please turn to pages 144 through 157. *Above photos: SPNHF archives; Alan Briere; Alan Briere.*

Grafton Pond, Grafton. Photo: Bill Finney.

Bear Island, Lake Winnipesaukee. Photo: Peggy Darnell.

Foster Conservancy, Henniker. Photo: Binney Wells.

Big Island in Lake Umbagog, Errol. Photo: Richard Sperry.

Franconia Notch. Photo: Robert Lawrence.

Cockermouth Forest, Groton and Hebron. Photo: Jim McDonough.

Devil's Slide, Kauffmann Forest, Stark Photo: Adrian Levesque, Jr.

George Smith Woodlot, Newfields. Photo: Tim Gaudreau.

Andorra Forest, Stoddard and Sullivan. Photo: Mark Fernald.

*Heald Tract,
Wilton.
Photo:
Alan Briere.*

*Indian Arrowhead Forest, Surry.
Photo: Barbara Henes.*

*Hoffman Conservation
Easement, Sullivan.
Photo: Alan Briere.*

High Watch Preserve, Freedom. Photo: George Barker.

Hope Forest, Danbury. Photo: Alan Briere.

Pierce Reservation, Stoddard. Photo: Roslyn Lawrence.

Lake Solitude, Mount Sunapee, Newbury. Photo: Chris Blais.

Hutchins Forest, Canterbury. Photo: Alan Briere.

Great Bay, Portsmouth. Photo: Chris McPhail.

Deering Preserve, Deering.
Photo: Alan Briere.

Elizabeth Simons Preserve, Weare.
Photo: Alan Briere.

Monson Village, Milford.
Photo: Walter Carlson.

Mount Kearsarge, Warner and Wilmot. Photo: Alison Forbes.

Madame Sherri Forest, Chesterfield. Photo: Claudia Rippee.

Cooper Cedar Woods, New Durham. Photo: Richard Carrier.

Hampton Salt Marshes, Hampton. Photo: Sheila Marr.

Yatsevitch Memorial Forest, Cornish and Plainfield. Photo: Alan Briere.

Sandwich Notch, Sandwich. Photo: Susan Nicolay.

*Sharon Bog,
Sharon.
Photo:
Don Johnson.*

*Woodland Associates Forest,
New Boston.
Photo: Arthur Rounds.*

*Conservation Easement, Dunbarton.
Photo: Althea Haropulos.*

Peirce Reservation, Stoddard. Photo: Alan Briere.

Jones Forest, Milton. Photo: Gary Samson.

Smith Conservation Easement, Ossipee. Photo: Tim Gaudreau.

The Conservation Center

The Society's headquarters in Concord demonstrates efficiency in both energy and collaboration.

Carol Cushing

High on a bluff overlooking the Merrimack River, the Conservation Center was built to face out over the river's forested floodplain, then beyond to the gleaming dome of New Hampshire's capitol building. More importantly, this southern exposure faced square into the low winter sun, which in the late 1970s helped to spawn a revolutionary idea.

The Society for the Protection of New Hampshire Forests was searching for a new home. Paul Bofinger, then president/forester, said the idea of a passive solar building gradually evolved from the convergence of several circumstances. The organization was feeling extremely pinched for space in its old State Street offices. "It felt like a rabbit warren there," Bofinger remembered. "There was never enough room for staff, for equipment, or for meetings." The environmental movement, then in full bloom and energized by the ongoing oil crunch, was also arguing forcibly for using alternative energy sources in any new construction.

Concord was also seeing its open spaces rapidly succumbing to development. So when longtime member Terry Frost and others offered to sell a large tract of floodplain to the Society at a bargain price, and acres on top of the bluff became available as well, Bofinger's dream inched closer to reality. Then generous donor Dorothy McCabe came forward with funds, and everything fell serendipitously into place. They broke ground in 1979.

Conservation Center, Concord. Protected in 1978. Photo: Duane Bailey.

The Conservation Center had become more than just an idea. It evolved into a plan that would conserve a diverse piece of floodplain for natural history education and recreation. It also offered a chance to construct a building that would demonstrate in concrete terms the concepts of solar energy and the use of renewable forest materials. Finally, it not only created living space for the Society and other conservation and forestry organizations, but it brought them together in less obvious ways as well.

The lobby at the Conservation Center. Photo: Carol Cushing

"When the question of a name for the structure arose," Bofinger said, "I liked the alliterative sound of the words 'Conservation Center.' But if we were going to call it a center, we needed more than just the Society to reside there. We already had a history of physical proximity with like-minded conservation organizations. In fact, several of these groups had actually been born within the Society, spearheaded by staff members there until they could get on their feet." When he approached groups like the New Hampshire Timberland Owners Association (NHTOA), and the Association of Conservation Commissions (NHACC), they were more than willing to move with the Society across the river and up onto that scenic bluff.

By sharing space and equipment, all the groups saved money. But it was more than that. "What really made the Conservation Center work was seeing each other at the coffee machine or chatting as we passed in the halls," he said. "This informal proximity may be why New Hampshire's environmental groups have always worked so well together. If you needed to speak with another organization's people, you just walked down the corridor and stuck your head in their door." This sharing of ideas about current projects and how they might impact each other's work, Bofinger said, removed many stumbling blocks and potential misunderstandings over the years. By 2001, tenant groups included NHTOA, NHACC, the N.H. Wildlife Federation, Project Learning Tree, the Rivers Council, the Appalachian Mountain Club, the Trust for Public Land, and the Statewide Program of Action to Conserve our Environment.

Aesthetically, the award-winning passive solar building designed by architect Stuart White of the firm Banwell, White, and Arnold is a feast for the eyes. On a bright winter afternoon inside the sun-lit lobby, the warmth reflects off the honey-colored walls and timbers made entirely of northeastern forest wood. These and the black slate floor soak up solar heat all day and, together with the thirty-two 64-gallon tubes of water, slowly release it back into the building at night.

Another example of the innovative yet practical features is the Conservation Center's conference room — actually a room within an air envelope. Sun-warmed air rises in the space between the south-facing windows and the conference room's wall, flows down the air passage between the roof and the ceiling, and then drops down the short, bermed north wall into a passage under the floor. This in-ground space retains a year-round temperature of around 55 degrees. This air, in turn, is pulled up the south side of the envelope by the rising sun-warmed air there. Consequently, the room never gets below 55 degrees. Additional heat, when needed, is provided by small wood pellet stove or by a roomful of humans having a meeting or a class.

In other portions of the building, solar technologies such as louvered blinds, photovoltaic cells, and heat-activated fans help keep the building warm in the winter and cool in the summer. In 1980 the added cost of these solar features was expected to be paid back in ten years. Engineers predicted the building would get 50 percent of its heat from the sun. Instead, the costs were recouped in nine years. In 2001 the building was getting an astounding 80 percent of its heat from solar energy.

Each year several thousand people visit the Conservation Center to attend a class, take a solar or a floodplain tour, or just amble down the forested bluff onto the biologically diverse floodplain. Instead of more development, these special 106 acres have become an oasis of open space.

Over the years the physical face of the Conservation Center has changed with the additions of the Weeks Wing in 1990 and the French Wing in 2001. But the award-winning features remain its centerpiece. Bermed into the earth on the north side and looking as though it's always been there, the center's south face, with its magnificent wall of glass, gazes out over the valley and soaks up the munificent bounty of the sun.

Amid the daily bustle of New Hampshire's capital city, there exists this quiet retreat — a deliciously open space to wander and explore, where a river continues its ancient and inexorable work, the sun sets over the capitol dome, and red-tailed hawks float high on the evening breeze. ☙

The Hay Forest Reservation

How abandoned hill farms became one of the Society's premier forest classrooms.

David Anderson

In 1923 New Hampshire poet laureate Robert Frost wrote:

> Just specimens is all New Hampshire has,
> One each of everything as in a showcase,
> Which naturally she doesn't care to sell.

The same may be said of the Society for the Protection of New Hampshire Forests's Hay Forest Reservation, with the addition: "but which she is more than willing to share."

The Society's Hay Reservation in Newbury has offered a little of everything. More than four miles of hiking trails wind through regenerating pine and oak forests on abandoned pastures and orchards, recrossing stone walls and the Old County Road. From the summit of Sunset Hill, sweeping views unfold to Lake Sunapee, Mount Sunapee, Mount Kearsarge, and the distant peaks of the White Mountains — icons of Society history. Interior farm roads access old cellar holes, some with lilacs and stone-lined wells. Stands of beech, sugar maple, and hemlock grow along the banks of crystal clear Beech Brook. Pockets of richer soil amidst granite outcrops support colorful wildflowers. Fern-clad springs feed the ever-flowing waters of Beech Brook, with its populations of tiny brook trout and spawning rainbow smelt. "Just specimens is all ..."

Sunset Hill, Hay Reservation. Protected in 1960. Photo: Alice Marzoli.

In summer, hikers discover ample evidence that chokecherries, blueberries, and mountain ash berries feed resident black bears. Winter snowshoe adventurers can follow tracks of moose, deer, coyote, bobcat, fox, fisher, mink, otter, and snowshoe hare, which range from shadowy spruce on the upper flanks of Sunset Hill to young pasture pines along Old County Road. In May dozens of species of colorful, migratory songbirds — warblers, vireos, tanagers, thrushes, and flycatchers — glean insects from the pastel buds of emerging hardwood flowers. "One each of everything as in a showcase ..."

By the 1990s, the Hay Forest Reservation had become the Society's premier outdoor classroom for natural history classes. Biological inventories and companion education workshops fueled a decade of discovery. Classes focused on topics ranging from mammals to mushrooms, from warblers to wildflowers. Students visited porcupine dens in a talus slope, bear-clawed beech trees along a ridge, hawk nests perched in ice-damaged yellow birches, and a hayfield-turned-beaver-meadow studded with dead hardwood snags and ringed with young softwoods.

A popular rite of spring has long been the annual field trip where students learned to identify wood frogs and salamanders breeding in a woodland vernal pool that was once a hog wallow of the Milton Clark farm.

Legend has it that Newbury hill farmers began the local tradition of real estate speculation while negotiating the sale of their farms to U.S. Secretary of State John Hay. Hay began construction of his summer home on Lake Sunapee in 1891, taking water from Beech Brook, whose purity would be compromised by wallowing hogs. He eventually purchased seven farms totaling nearly 1,000 acres and named it The Fells, after the rocky highlands of his ancestral Scotland. The Hay estate was a prominent example of the summer home movement that continues to fuel the economy of the Sunapee region.

John Hay died at The Fells in 1905, leaving the property to his son Clarence, an archeologist with the American Museum of Natural History. Clarence Hay and his wife, Alice Appleton Hay, transformed the rustic cottage overlooking the lake into a more formal dwelling, surrounding it with gardens, statuary, and fountains. Their children, John and Adele, spent long, idyllic summers on Lake Sunapee.

By 1960 the Hays were becoming concerned about the long-term protection of the property. They'd received offers to buy the 672-acre woodlot, crowned by the open ledges of Sunset Hill. Instead, they decided to donate the land to the Society in 1960. Clarence wrote, "I would like to think of the property as being useful, permanent, and in capable hands and not broken up into tiny house lots. I'm sure my father would have been pleased that the land would be managed for the public welfare." In 1987 the remaining 163 acres, with its buildings, gardens, and over one mile of undeveloped shoreline on Lake Sunapee, became the John Hay National Wildlife Refuge. The U.S. Fish and Wildlife Service has owned the refuge ever since and has managed it cooperatively with a local nonprofit group, the Friends of the John Hay National Wildlife Refuge. The friends have overseen maintenance and tours of the buildings and the gardens of the former Hay estate. The contemporary John Hay, son of Clarence and Alice, grew up to become an award-winning naturalist, author, and guiding spirit behind the property's educational focus.

In 1999 the purchase of a critical 37-acre missing piece of the Hay Reservation literally closed the circle of protected land around Sunset Hill. Called the Kidder Tract, the rugged parcel was dedicated to the memory of former Society trustee Bill Kidder, who was instrumental in its protection. Once slated as the site for an eighteen-unit condominium complex, the tract is now owned by the Society, "which naturally she doesn't care to sell ..."

Over the years the Society has hosted dozens of seasonal natural history and forest stewardship classes, workshops, and field trips, introducing hundreds of students of all ages to the natural and cultural resources of the Hay Reservation and the adjacent John Hay Wildlife Refuge. In the woods a camaraderie is developed among new and returning students learning to read the land. A magical convergence of landscape and legacies, people and nature, natural and built environments has defined the Hay experience. Naturalist John Hay's vision — that this forest and the stories it contains should inspire future generations — is being realized. A poetry of ecological relationships has been written in the woods of the Hay Reservation, poetry that the Society is more than willing to share. ❧

The Fells is the former summer home of John Hay and is contiguous to the Society's Hay Reservation. Photo: Nancy Horton.

The Rocks Estate

John Glessner's farm has become one of the North Country's best-loved places.

MIKE DICKERMAN

At the beginning of the twentieth century, the 1,300-acre Rocks Estate property in Bethlehem was a bustling, self-contained farm owned by successful Chicago industrialist John J. Glessner (1843–1936). Known for its hillside views looking east toward the peaks of the Presidentials and its miles of intricately constructed stone walls built from rocks extricated from the estate's fields, The Rocks "was a model working farm, without equal for its time in northern New Hampshire," according to White Mountain historian Bryant F. Tolles.

By the beginning of the twenty-first century, John Glessner's property had become one of the North Country's unique and best-loved parcels. And farming continued to be a mainstay of the Glessner estate, just one of many components that transformed The Rocks into one of the Society for the Protection of New Hampshire Forests' most popular properties.

The Society has owned and managed the former Glessner estate since January 20, 1978, when two of John J. Glessner's descendants donated The Rocks property. Included in the gift, which at the time was called "the largest Society acquisition in 40 years," were 100-plus acres of fields, 1,200 acres of productive woodland, and some twenty or so buildings scattered across the property.

The Rocks has served as the Society's North Country centerpiece. Among other things, The Rocks hosts the Society's North Country Conservation and Education Center, is home to The Rocks Christmas Tree Farm, and boasts seven miles of nature and hiking trails, and 1,300 acres of green-certified woodland managed for both wildlife habitat and quality timber production.

"The Rocks is a perfect example of open space being managed in a way that is in keeping with the way the land has always been," said Carlton Schaller of Lit-

The Rocks, Bethlehem. Protected in 1978. Photo: Kindra Clineff.

tleton, a longtime volunteer for the Society and an ardent conservationist. Schaller said the historic character of the property, combined with the Society's "wise use" of varying conservation practices, has made The Rocks an ideal setting for the many educational programs offered year-round on site.

"It has taken time, but we've reached the point where we are looked at as a true community resource, an asset," said Nigel Manley, property director of the Bethlehem tract since 1986. "We actively go into the local schools and offer a variety of educational programs. We also welcome area community members to help us care for and learn from what we have here."

It was during the first few years after the Society obtained the Glessner property that these community-rooted seeds were first sown. Even as the bulk of the property was being leased to the short-lived New Hampshire Farm and Forest Museum (an enterprise that lasted just a couple of years), former Society education specialist Jeff Wallner was regularly working with local students and establishing several annual community activities. These included the Wildflower Festival held every June and the wildly popular Halloween celebration in late October.

However, there was a period of uncertainty over what would become of The Rocks once the Farm and Forest Museum had departed. It wasn't until the decision was made in the late 1980s to establish a working Christmas tree farm on the property that the ties with the local community were truly solidified. As with the trees, this relationship began to grow shortly after the first seedlings were planted in the spring of 1989 on the sloping farm fields alongside Route 302.

"The tree farm really revitalized the property," said Manley. "Even though we only sold a couple dozen trees that first holiday season, it got people onto the property — some for the first time. Then we initiated a couple of school programs tied in with the tree farm, like our Christmas tree recycling (Treecycle) effort and the ForeverGreen program, in which kindergartners in Bethlehem plant their own trees and then watch and care for these same trees until they are ready for harvesting when the kids are in sixth grade."

As more people became familiar with the property, some through Society education programs and others from buying Rocks-grown Christmas trees, more and more people stepped forward to volunteer their time and services in whatever programs and chores Manley and his staff could conjure up.

"The whole historical perspective, along with the forest resources, and the great trail system, was a big part of the attraction of being here," said Karen Rosolen of Woodstock, who has volunteered at The Rocks for more than a decade. "It's a gem of a property, and I think it typifies what the Society stands for."

Rosolen's story is similar to that of so many of the volunteers who regularly lend a helping hand. She began as a docent with the Society's Project Conserve program, helped out with various other family-oriented programs, and now she and her husband, Dennis, are still regular participants in The Rocks's Halloween program and the many holiday-related events hosted by the Christmas tree operation.

"We have a core set of people who volunteer on almost all our activities, whether it be working in the schools, putting on programs at Bretzfelder Park [another Society-owned property in Bethlehem], or helping out with the tree farm during the holidays," said Manley. "And we have others who will work one particular event a year, such as the Halloween program, the Wildflower Festival, or our Autumn Fall Colors Festival. These volunteers have come back year after year. Without them, we wouldn't be able to do the kinds of things that we do. We just don't have the manpower."

Manley also has relied on community members to maintain and improve the sprawling property. For instance, students from the nearby White Mountain School (a private college preparatory boarding school) have fulfilled their mandatory community service requirements by raking leaves, planting and fertilizing trees, and helping maintain the various hiking and cross-country ski trails. Other area residents, including high school students from neighboring Littleton, have annually volunteered time in the spring for pruning apple trees as part of The Rocks's wildlife habitat improvement efforts.

It would not, however, be a stretch to compare The Rocks at the beginning of the twenty-first century to that of John J. Glessner's day. By all accounts, The Rocks has remained a model for others to emulate, only it's not just a farm anymore, but a true North Country jewel, unequaled in so many ways and very much a part of the White Mountain community. ❧

Choosing a tree at The Rocks has become a family tradition for residents and visitors. Photo: Tim Gaudreau.

VOICES

Mount Kearsarge

Great blue mountain! Ghost.
I look at you
from the porch of the farmhouse
where I watched you all summer
as a boy. Steep sides, narrow flat
patch on top —
you are clear to me
like the memory of one day.
Blue! Blue!
The top of the mountain floats in haze.
I will not rock on this porch
when I am old. I turn my back on you,
Kearsarge, I close
my eyes, and you rise inside me,
blue ghost.

Turkey tail fungi, Deering Preserve. Protected in 1999. Photo: Beatrice T. Hunter

Peter Forbes

Land conservation can make people and communities whole.

I spent a fall day ten years ago on my knees working the soil in a vacant lot the Trust for Public Land (TPL) had just bought on behalf of a local land trust in south Providence, Rhode Island. For most of the morning, I worked silently alongside a Laotian woman my age. We communicated mostly through laughs and nervous exclamations as a truck barreled too close through the narrow streets or when we found a piece of glass or jagged metal buried in the soil. By afternoon we had cleared almost a quarter acre, and we were comfortable enough with one another for her to try her broken English. Suke was twenty-eight, had arrived alone with her two daughters just four months before from a refugee camp on the Thai border, and was waiting for her husband to join her. While she waited, she gardened. Every day, she walked two miles through a city she didn't know to a place that had become very important to her. At the end of our time together, Suke held my hand for a moment and told me that these urban gardens had made her feel at home in America.

In the years since, I have thought often about Suke. I think about her whenever I consider my own rootlessness, and I am graced by the memory of how quickly she sought land and soil to affirm her place in America. I thought about Suke every time we completed a conservation project, because she asks of me, For whom have we conserved this piece of land? Whose life does this touch?

TPL's good work gave me the experience of Suke and gave Suke the experience of home. But it took an intervening ten years in the land trust trenches for me to better understand the great transformative power of land conservation to improve all of our lives. The story of Suke, and the stories of many people after her, allowed me to see that this power is possibly the greatest legacy of our good work. Each of us has seen land conservation change a community, has seen the impact far exceed the property boundary, where the resulting alchemy of human cooperation, activism, and the wild has led people to view themselves differently and to live better with one another.

Since Aldo Leopold wrote *A Sand County Almanac* in 1949 calling for an American land ethic that might "transform *Homo sapiens* from conqueror of the land community to plain member and citizen of it," a great deal has happened to elevate that debate. The number of environmental laws has quadrupled, and the number of conservation organizations has grown one hundredfold, but economic and social trends suggest that a shared land ethic still eludes us. To a large extent, even the conservation of land has been disconnected from personal practice and civic behavior.

The conservation movement has not fully accepted that the root problem spawning its crusade is not loss of species or decreasing air and water quality or dwindling wilderness or even relentless sprawl. These are the symptoms. The root problem is how we humans live each day, and from where we draw our values. Until conservation offers positive alternatives to people about how they might lead their daily lives, a land ethic will elude us.

Mahatma Gandhi, who was largely responsible for leading India's fight for independence and for starting South Africa's successful antiapartheid movement, spoke about "the dissonance between deed and creed" and how the separation between one's acts and one's ideals lead to a fractured individual. In one of history's great connections, Gandhi drew his inspiration for this thinking while in jail in 1908 reading the story of another jailed dissenter, Henry David Thoreau, who had written about fractured people in *Civil Disobedience*.

Thoreau's response to the need for healing in his own life was twofold: to seek nature on the banks of Walden Pond and to merge his creed and deed to such a point that he was even willing to go to jail for something he believed in. The fact that Thoreau's life story and the stories of his more modern torchbearers such as Helen and Scott Nearing remain such a source of fulfillment and interest is testament to our culture's thirst for what those lives teach us. It is worth pointing out that today we call these people environmentalists but that in their own day they would have called themselves social activists. It is only the modern conservation movement that has separated the imperative of social change from the needs of the earth.

Trying to live by land conservation's example of forbearance and equality may be today's civil disobedience. It may also be exactly what's required to begin to heal the dissonance and contradictions of modern society. Land conservation can help to make people and communities whole.

It may be useful to think of land conservation as a form of citizenship. David Suzuki, Canada's leading environmentalist, wrote recently that "consumerism has taken the place of citizenship as the chief way we contribute to the health of our society." Alternatively, the process of saving land takes us out of our private lives to realize something greater for ourselves and our neighbors. It is the chance to express our allegiance to ideals, to one another, and to the land, thereby enabling each one of us to become a citizen of a specific place. More emphatic and political than a sense of place, the act of land conservation offers us the choice of place. To say "this is my home and I care about it enough to protect it" is the essence of citizenship, and to act on such words begins to move us from isolation to community. ❧

Adopted with permission from Our Land, Our Selves, *edited by Peter Forbes. Trust for Public Land, 1999.*

Ernest Hebert

A Contoocook spoon maker helped the novelist understand his own little woodlot.

To get to know my forest — a little bit anyway — I bought a book to tell me the names of my trees, because without a name a thing is never known with any intimacy. It wasn't until I split some of the wood, however — looked at it, touched it, smelled it, and, when nobody was looking, tasted it — that I began to understand the forest that I loved so; I've spent a lifetime making my tiny 3-acre woodland a part of myself, or making myself a part of it — not sure which.

I started constructing things out of wood about three decades ago. I've whittled and carved and chopped wood during all that time, with an idea not to make anything straight. I whacked out a footstool from firewood, a number of bowed legs for not flat tabletops, and scores of wooden spoons, salad forks, and the like; I also made things that have no use whatsoever. Little abstract pieces, of worth only to the pleasure of my eye and the touch of my hand. I like to split wood along the grain, trim it, scrape it down, and finish it with whatever oil is lying around the shed.

My dilettante's attitude toward the woods has always bothered me. I've asked myself, "What's the value, other than self-satisfaction?" I thought that if I could find someone more skilled with woodworking tools, more committed to the enterprise, and more dedicated to this aesthetic ideal that has possessed me over the years, and if this person could also bring some practicality to the aesthetic ideal, why then I would have found the perfect New Hampshire artist, someone who could bring together nature and culture through art, and in that sublime action my question would be answered.

I believe I've met that person. He's about 6 feet tall, rangy, hazel-eyed, sharp-featured, with a full beard. His name is Dan Dustin. He lives in Contoocook not far from his family's farm, which was started in 1820 and which hung on into the 1960s without modernization. What Dustin makes is wooden spoons. In the simple object of the spoon, Dustin has found a living, a philosophy, and an art. Unlike some craftsmen who speak only through their tools and materials, Dustin is skilled with tongue and language as well. He has a lot to say about what it means to live in the New Hampshire woods.

He sees his spoons as the culmination of the knowledge of two cultures through more than a thousand years, European culture that brought metal woodworking tools to the New World along with know-how, and the native culture that provided an intimate knowledge of local woods along with another contribution, a subtle mix of technique, design, and necessity. The easiest way to understand this idea is to scrutinize a couple of Native American inventions, the birch bark canoe and the snowshoe. You look at these objects in their context of the northern woods and you know they belong here. A Dustin spoon has the same quality, but it is worked with tools developed in Europe — the hatchet, the froe, the spoke shave — and finished according to a family formula that includes walnut oil or olive oil and beeswax.

I think about such things, how the man who shapes the spoon is himself shaped by the spoon, how even a dilettante, as he walks his forest, becomes part of it by the quality of attention he pays to it.

He holds up a spoon whose beauty I have admired. "The fact that it's beautiful comes from its function," he says.

Dustin did not come to his art quickly or easily. When he left Bates College in Maine and struck out on his own as a woodworker, he put an ad in the *Christian Science Monitor:* "Useful Things, Hand Made of Wood." He was surprised to learn that people wanted wooden spoons. So he set to work, making spoons in what seemed like a logical way for production. He carved out spoons with a band saw. The results did not please him. "I got tired of making ugly stuff," he says. One day he was splitting firewood. The wood separated in such a way that a spoon was produced. He cleaned up around the split, and lo and behold was a spoon far more beautiful than any he'd made on the band saw. "After that I split wood like crazy, looking for spoons." Now he doesn't split wood like crazy; experience with thousands of trees and spoons has taught him how to see into the tree. "Now," he says, "I've got x-ray vision." What he sees is how a tree grows and moves, this way, then that. These stresses of natural movement responding to wind, soil, and light alternately make handles and bowls for spoons. "The tree doesn't know it's growing spoons, but I do," he says.

Dustin has experimented with every kind of wood available in the New Hampshire forest. Apple is excellent spoon wood, but it's hard to work. Good spoons can be made with just about any closed-grain hardwood such as maple or birch. But spoons of those woods nick over the years. Dustin didn't set out to fashion mere good spoons. He set out to create "the best spoons ever made."

For most of his art, Dustin has finally settled on two different woods that not only make excellent spoons, but also symbolize the two cultures that he credits with preparing the way for his magnificent creations. The second most used wood is lilac. Though the purple lilac is the state flower, the plant is not native to the region. It was brought here by the English colonists. The wood he uses the most is native to the region, mountain laurel, a small tree that grows in the southern, warmer parts of the state. "They say there's no old growth left in New England," says Dustin. "Not true. Old growth remains among trees that the white man did not value." Trees such as mountain laurel.

Some of that "old growth" remains in the character of our people, too. I think about such things, how the man who shapes the spoon is himself shaped by the spoon, how even a dilettante, as he walks his forest, becomes part of it by the quality of attention he pays to it. ☙

Donella Meadows

In her own inimitable way, the late columnist and activist exhorted us to cherish and protect beautiful places.

My work requires me to travel a lot. Wherever I have been in the world, no matter how nice it was, I feel, as the plane lowers over Grantham Mountain or the bus starts down the Enfield hill, overwhelming gratitude.

I am back home, in a place where Canadian highs bring in air so clean you take deep breaths just for the pleasure of breathing. A place where the streams and wells still carry mostly crystal-clear water. A place people come long distances to visit, just because it is so beautiful.

I appreciated this valley most of all during the first few months I lived here. I had spent the previous eight years in the scruffy edges of Boston where students can afford to live. For miles around me was a wasteland of industrial ugliness. I remember only one beautiful thing, a valiant wild cherry tree I passed on my way to work, surviving somehow, surrounded by asphalt, near a railroad crossing. That little tree was in bloom in May when I moved up north.

My soul had been conditioned to endure twenty blocks of red brick, neon, and shattered glass, waiting to drink in the sight of one cherry tree. Then I moved to an old farm in a green valley with thousands of blooming trees. Everywhere I looked there was beauty. I didn't have to wipe black grit off the windowsills every day. The water didn't taste like chemicals. The houses fit snugly on the hills, the people moved slowly enough to talk to.

I no longer had to hold myself in a state of internal tension, screening out ugly smells, sounds, and sights. I hadn't even been aware of that tension until I started letting it go, unfolding my senses again. I went around marveling at how full life can be, how alive one can feel, in a place that is simply beautiful.

But here, too, we are "developing." We have tangled arguments about this "development." Should we welcome it, regulate it, forbid it? Who has a right to do what? Is the Purity Supreme an improvement over the hayfield it replaced? If it is convenient to shop there, but its traffic adds an hour a week to my commuting time, plus a daily streak of ugliness, have I come out ahead? Does ugliness matter if there is a profit to be made?

These are difficult questions and we shouldn't give them knee-jerk answers, but we usually do. Some of us are just plain against development, all development, and some are for it, come what may. When we try to convince each other, we talk about jobs, profits, and taxes.

Jobs, profits, and taxes are important, but they are not really at the heart of the matter. The jobs are mostly for people we don't know, who don't live here, but who are expected to show up. Growth has yet to lower taxes noticeably in any place I know about. Profits in the new supermall replace the profits of the farms and the small stores the mall displaced; the profits tend to flow toward Connecticut or Boston now instead of staying in the valley.

I think we talk about jobs, profits, and taxes so much because they are countable things, quantities, and therefore legitimate considerations. Other considerations, such as cherry trees, grit on the windowsills, noise, neighbors, topsoil, and how it feels to be stuck in traffic by the supermall, seem not quite legitimate to talk about because they are qualities. It's tough to stand up in town meeting and talk about health, beauty, security, community, self-reliance, aliveness. It just isn't done, though in fact qualities are very real, and they are ultimately what count.

To make development decisions on behalf of the community, the land, and the future, we have to use a higher human faculty than the simple ability to count. We have to ask quality questions.

It is widely believed that "emotional stuff" is so uniquely individual that it can form no basis for public policy about development. I think that's true when the choice is trivial — should there be a KMart or a Dunkin' Donuts on the bank of this stream? But when the questions are serious and the answers taken seriously, a community can speak with one voice on issues of quality.

Once I helped out with a door-to-door survey in my town just before we passed our first zoning ordinance. An overwhelming majority favored no road upgrades ("would just make more traffic"), no shopping malls ("we can already buy everything we need"), no building at all on prime agricultural land, and no big developments that would drop hundreds of new families into the town at one time ("we wouldn't know everyone any more"). But the town was fiercely in favor of young folks being able to put up their own houses or to start their own businesses. There was great sympathy with low-income people, who should, the town thought, be able to have a place, even a trailer, "but not keep it junky." Everyone could name a favorite, beautiful part of town that should be protected from all development — and they all named the same places.

The only dissenters were the half-dozen people in town who had plans to sell to big developers and dollar signs in their eyes.

People were surprised, touched, and excited to be asked these questions. Most of them had never dared to express their feelings in public because they were sure no one else thought that way.

You could see this response as rural selfishness — we've got ours and we won't let anyone else in — or you could see it as an expression of love for a place, a plea for appropriateness, and a recognition that the kind of development that respects the land and the community's needs is more likely to come from within than from outsiders who arrive, build, and then leave the town to cope with the results.

To make development decisions on behalf of the community, the land, and the future, we have to use a higher human faculty than the simple ability to count. We have to ask quality questions. Will this project, which will affect our valley for decades to come, demean the lives of the people it touches? Is it motivated by someone whose senses are shut down, whose purpose is to substitute material stuff for the emptiness of a shut-down life? If so, it will have an unrelenting ugliness that will deaden all who are exposed to it. If not, if there is some care and commitment, some sensitivity to the land and community, a development project can uplift the builders, the owners, those who live or work or shop there, and everyone who passes by.

People can tell the difference, if you ask them. ❧

This excerpt comes from Donella Meadows's 1991 book, The Global Citizen, *a collection of her syndicated newspaper column of the same name. It was reprinted with permission from Island Press.*

John Hay

The award-winning naturalist rediscovers the forest's secrets at the source of the brook.

One fine day in early autumn, when the leaves of the swamp and sugar maples began to show tints of pink and red, David Anderson and I set out to climb up Sunset Hill and follow the brook to its source. Dave is the Society for the Protection of New Hampshire Forests's education director and has worked since 1990 at the Hay Reservation and John Hay National Wildlife Refuge. Both places were named for my grandfather, a poet and statesman who served as secretary of state during the administration of Theodore Roosevelt, the great originator of conservation law and the national park system.

We started up at the point where the "old county road" once led to the village at the south end of the lake; its wagon tracks are still visible. In the early 1960s, the Soil Conservation Service had built a small pond nearby, with water diverted from the brook, for use in case of a forest fire. A family of beaver moved in after that, and built a dam and a lodge on the downstream side. Four more dams followed, down the course of the brook, as the beaver used up the trees along the way. Their last effort was abandoned in 1994. When I last saw this dam, it seemed massive to me. It was about four feet high and thirty feet long, but the beaver had moved on, having used up their food supply. They had left a long, wide swathe of wet meadow behind them, where a few isolated trees stood out like skeletons. The beaver people, like human lake dwellers of long ago, who left traces of the pilings that held their dwelling above the water, never left a wasted and impoverished land behind them. The ancient waterways of a continent are in the minds of the beaver. They have a deep sense of the nature of water and how it moves. They could never destroy the very source of their well-being and their future; and some day, they will return. They leave new growth behind them when they press on. The wide opening made by the meadow has been of great benefit to other woodland dwellers, such as the mink, the otter and the wild turkey, deer and moose, as well as the black bear that move in to feed on the wild berries starting to flourish on the edges. Many species of birds have also been attracted to the beaver wetland; and it is a new source of nurture and protection for frogs and salamanders.

Along the old road above the meadow, tiny yellow gold frogs, the young of the year, jumped out of the grass. The spring peepers, or *Hyla crucifer,* so called because of the smudged black cross on their backs, and the wood frogs were the most visible. The peepers begin to sing in all healthy wetlands as the winter retreats, with a primal intensity that little else can equal. The frogs and salamanders in their courtship rituals and seasonal transformations have mysterious alliances with the medium of water itself, in its changing nature. We walk over a great underworld of knowing and sensuous relationships. On the surface, we may know the details of the shape-changing universe of frogs or butterflies, but fail to give it much connection with ourselves. Familiar, goggle-eyed frogs, once a favorite subject of country humor, are beginning to disappear, in many parts of the world. They are casualties of the poisons that we easily and idly let fall over the entire face of the earth, even when we are unable to predict the consequences of what we do. We have all become invisible destroyers who are incapable of identifying our victims. This can only be highly disturbing and frightening to those who are aware that their own, personal ties to the land are being frayed to the limit. It is as if we looked down into the surface of any stream and failed to find our own reflection there.

Dave and I trudged slowly uphill, following the course of the brook. We caught sight of a hole in the bank, occupant unknown, and passed under a tree where some raptor, probably a hawk had perched for a while, judging by the white droppings on the ground. Then we came on the raised mound of what was once the root mass of a big tree, probably a vestige of the 1938 hurricane, and saw a red eft lying there, as brilliantly colored as a devil dancer in some medieval painting, clearly outlined on the reddish brown form of the once living tree. It looked as supremely confident as a skunk, which knows that it is normally free from attack. The red eft is the juvenile phase of the eastern newt, which inhabits lakes, ponds, and slow-moving streams. It has a poisonous toxin in its skin. This enables the newt to swim at a depth of thirty feet in a lake without being devoured by fish. The eft wanders through moist woodlands for as long as seven years before returning to water to be transformed into an adult, aquatic salamander.

The charmed life once attributed to salamanders in less scientifically minded days probably owes as much to the nature of water as to fire, both partners in magic. Mercurial, chimerical water, flowing across the land and seeping through the soil, is the living agent of all transformations.

The tan, leaf-colored wood frog, with its black face mask, reverses the breeding cycle of the newts. Their eggs are laid in early spring in ponds or temporary vernal pools that may still be partially covered with ice. As they develop, the young move out onto the woodland floor. A wood frog, with its highly distinctive color and design, honors the environment of which it is a part. I remember picking one up out of another forest floor many years ago. As I held that perfect creature in my hand, so close to me, and still so far removed, I gave up all pretensions.

Farther uphill, the woods were increasingly full of the signs of travel. We met the great stout body of a yellow birch, probably 200 to 240 years old; it was hollowed out at the base of the trunk, a cavity full of wood shavings and dung. This was the home of a porcupine. In one of Richard K. Nelson's books about the Koyukon Indians, he quotes one of them as saying: "The porcupine knows Alaska like you know the palm of your hand." We walked past a line of young swamp maples, whose bark was stripped off by the lower incisors of a moose. The tracks of moose and deer appeared on the trail, their hoof prints clearly outlined in the dark mud, like some prehistoric markings on a rock. Because the brook's watershed is under conservation, it serves as a corridor for such travelers from the hills beyond it, a link between distance and space.

We can easily turn ourselves into outsiders, blinded by the tormented world we have made for ourselves, but we are incapable of replacing the truth. I once peered in at an early age and sensed the magic in that brook, but I was never fully aware of how much promise it carried with it.

The banks along the brook grew steeper. As I looked across it, I could see the understory of trees on the far side, so loaded with a rich flood of sunlight that they looked as if they carried its weight on their leaves. We had seen bear scat near the trail, and had looked for claw marks on a tree, which were reported to be numerous on the far side of Sunset Hill, where there is a grove of beech trees. During the autumn months, beechnuts are one of their favorite foods. One bear had been seen sitting in a big beech, breaking and bending down the branches so as to make a feeding platform, where it could eat nuts at its leisure. They are part of a domestic economy that we, busy in our narrow kitchen, are not aware of.

A solitary vireo was flying back and forth over the brook, working it for insects, that irrepressible tribe so essential to all life in a forest. Many more birds were traveling through the leaf canopy ahead of us, part of assemblies that precede outward migration. They included chickadees, as well as juncos, or "snowbirds," so familiar to New Englanders during the winter months. Various species of warblers flitted through the leaves. Among these were yellow-rumped warblers, black-throated greens, blackburnians, and chestnut-sided. The naturalist Edwin Way Teale called them "rainbow birds." With their sun-inspired colors, they carry the spirit of the rain forests north each year to blend with the northern trees.

Then we came on what we had set out to find. Under the brow of a steep slope not far from the summit, where the brook and its moss-covered rocks went no farther, was a wide, light green circle on the ground, covered with water-loving plants. The ever flowing waters seeped out of this spring to be carried down, century after century, trickling through a far-reaching network of roots and associated fungi, feeling their way through the soil to a great wilderness lake. The brook has guarded all the secrets of the forest, as well as its own origins, which lie at an unknown depth in the bedrock of this minor mountain. I once unconsciously drank of its waters, and for much of my life I had been far removed from it, but now I had come home, to the center, the waiting heart, which was not ours to claim alone.

We can easily turn ourselves into outsiders, blinded by the tormented world we have made for ourselves, but we are incapable of replacing the truth. I once peered in at an early age and sensed the magic in that brook, but I was never fully aware of how much promise it carried with it. This time, I remembered my father, a sensitive and generous man, who knew that we can never tell the land what it is meant to contain; you have to wait for it to tell you. ☙

OUR SECOND CENTURY

"I*N MY EXPERIENCE, THE SOCIETY HAS REACHED its greatest heights when it has identified a compelling need and responded with a vision that transcends current "political reality;" engaged the grassroots and public imagination as well as the ears of opinion leaders; and mustered the resources and energy of a wide range of partners to achieve the vision. Mounting a campaign of this sort is not easy. Few, if any, statewide conservation organizations have done so even once or twice, let alone time after time over the course of a century. But the greatest challenges are yet to come. New Hampshire forests are being destroyed on an unprecedented scale. All the cumulative vision, skill, and capacity of the past will be required to surmount this threat. I'm glad we have the Society to lead the effort. Onward!*"

Steve Blackmer, President
Northern Forest Center

Webster Wildlife and Natural Area, Kingston. Protected in 1972. Photo: Peter Randall.

Our Second Century

Jane A. Difley

What does New Hampshire mean to you?

For me, it means walking in the woods behind my house. The land isn't posted and my neighbors allow me to roam there. I rarely see anyone: occasionally a hunter, someone on snowshoes, or the family who owns the land. I can pretend the woods are my own.

My own in the human sense, that is. I share these woods with many others and I see their tracks: deer, turkey, small birds, fox, dog, and some that I can't identify. Each day the walk is different, although I travel the same trail. The slant of the light and its quality, the flowers as they emerge in the spring, the place where I sometimes smell fox, the color of the leaves, the wind, the songs of the frogs, the drift of the snow, the squishy spots in the trail, the gurgle of water in the seasonal streams — all these qualities, and more, change each day. My walk is tinged with the happy possibility that I could (despite the dog that accompanies me) catch sight of a deer, a turkey, even a bear or moose.

I walk knowing that both the ocean and the mountains are close at hand, and that the town where I live is, indeed, a community.

And I wonder, 'What will New Hampshire be like in the year 2101?'

Will we have places to roam freely, to experience wildness, to hear silence, to see the dark? Will farming, fishing, and forestry still thrive? Will our citizens know the out-of-doors? Will there be loons to awaken us with their eerie call? Will the possibility of encountering a moose or a great blue heron add a sense of anticipation to our ramblings? Or will today's picture postcards be the best reminders of something lost — a message to the future with a canceled stamp?

As the Society enters its second century, threats to this beloved landscape are well documented. About 13,000 acres of forest — the equivalent of half an average-sized New Hampshire town — are being gobbled up by development each year, eliminating wildlife habitat, productive forests, and open space. Not surprisingly, this is happening most rapidly in the southeastern part of the state. To make it worse, the best soils for growing trees are being developed faster than less productive soils. Even our most rare plants and animals in New Hampshire are not adequately protected from this onslaught. And nearly 90 percent of the forest land that protect public drinking water supplies from contamination are unprotected. There are economic threats, too. In 1999, open space directly or indirectly supported a quarter of the gross state product and 16% of the state's jobs. As we lose open space, bit by bit we lose one of the engines that drives our now thriving economy. It seems likely that trends in forest loss will mean that by 2050 we will consume more forest products that we can grow.

With a million new residents expected in the coming decades, it's hard to imagine what New Hampshire will look like twenty, fifty, one hundred years from now. Projections show that another million acres will be developed by 2050. Welcoming new citizens without giving up New Hampshire will challenge our creativity and our resolve. The conservation successes of our first century provide a rock-solid foundation, but do not assure New Hampshire's future. Only we can do that.

We do have reason to be hopeful, however. As we've rambled down the path of history in this book, certain strengths are evident, along with themes that have guided our first one hundred years and that will certainly guide us in the next.

The Society was founded on the notion that a small group of people could achieve big results if they applied themselves thoughtfully and persistently and with the right partners. Consider the Society's first big success: Along with the Appalachian Mountain Club (AMC) and others we worked hard for a decade to get the Weeks Act passed, creating not only New Hampshire's own crown jewel, the White Mountain National Forest, but also the entire system of eastern national forests. Partnerships and persistence also fueled early successes in protecting Franconia Notch, Mount Sunapee, and Mount Kearsarge, among others.

More recently, the Land Conservation Investment Program/Trust for New Hampshire Lands was a public/private partnership that protected 100,000 acres of land from development across the state. Building on that success, the new Land and Community Heritage Investment Program will help communities save their most cherished lands and cultural resources. These conservation accomplishments demonstrate that the partnership model — updated for the times — is timeless. Strong partners like AMC and the Audubon Society of New Hampshire, along with the critical dash of persistence, made these successes possible.

And in every campaign, at every bend in the road, there were individuals who dared to imagine success, who inspired and motivated others. These unsung heroines and heroes make it possible to feel hopeful about the future.

Mike and Carol Andrews were in the first class of Society land stewards — the volunteers who are trained and then "adopt" one or more of our reservations. Armed with knowledge of forestry, trail maintenance, and outreach skills, the Andrewses took on the Society's largest tract, the Peirce Reservation and the Williams Family Forest Reservation in Stoddard, as their own. They cleared and marked trails, enriched what they'd learned with experience, and got hooked on forestry. Soon, they bought land of their own and became proud tree farmers.

The conservation successes of our first century
provide a rock-solid foundation,
but do not assure New Hampshire's future.
Only we can do that.

Mike became a trustee in 1998 and chaired the committee that oversaw construction of the French Wing at the Conservation Center in Concord. Meanwhile, Carol joined the Friends of Pillsbury State Park. Both are now partners in a community-supported farm in Wilton, transferring skills they picked up as land stewards. This couple practices what they believe and gives back to their community and their native state.

Then there's Terry Frost and Win Robinson. Without Terry, there would be no Conservation Center in the first place. He was one of the owners who sold the land to the Society. I'm not sure these guys are inseparable, but you can usually find them together working to maintain trails, not just on Society reservations, but almost anywhere in the state. I am sure that they're practically tireless. They lead school groups on tours of the Merrimack River flood plain and show up at field trips and events as if they were staff.

Win was an instructor at the old conservation camp, and with his wife Mary Beth, a long time-staff member, and her sisters, accumulated 23 years as camp participants. Terry's been involved in almost anything there is about the state's water quality. His wife Marion is also a loyal supporter.

I'm not sure Sheila Weeks ever quite intended to become involved in forestry and conservation. She raised four children while volunteering for a range of social causes in the Lakes Region. Her husband Bob, however, loved the woods. In fact, Bob built their house from wood he cut on family land. When Bob died, his parents gave the woodlot in Gilford to the Society as a living tribute. Local schools take field trips there, as does the library. Visitors and local residents alike write to Sheila thanking her and expressing their appreciation for open land so close to the village.

Sheila and Bob's entire family love that land and think of it as a wonderful way to keep Bob's memory alive. At the Old Home Day parade the Weeks — three generations of them — created and rode a float dedicated to the Weeks Woods, complete with a tree farm sign. Meanwhile, Sheila became a Society trustee, bringing her experience and good thinking to statewide conservation concerns.

These are just a few of the people who bit by bit, in large ways and small, provide the energy for conservation in New Hampshire. They are what make the Society strong. And because of them and hundreds more who are equally dedicated, I can walk the path in "my" woods with confidence that my New Hampshire — and yours as well — will still be here long after we are gone. ☙

APPENDIX

"A T THE BEGINNING OF THE LAST CENTURY, *the beautiful forests and vistas we enjoy in New Hampshire today were almost completely decimated. In the last 100 years, we've breathed life back into our forests until now 83 percent of New Hampshire is again covered with trees. The Society for the Protection of New Hampshire Forests was then — as it continues to be now — the leader of the private effort to restore and protect what is special about our state."*

Governor Jeanne Shaheen

Heald Tract, Wilton. Protected in 1986. Photo: Michelle Duford.

A Century of Accomplishment by the Society for the Protection of New Hampshire Forests

1901

Governor Frank West Rollins and eight other concerned citizens form the Society for the Protection of New Hampshire Forests. Their mission: to protect the White Mountains, which are being devastated by indiscriminate logging and subsequent forest fires. The executive committee hires Philip Ayres as forester.

1908

The Society helps the state to buy Crawford Notch for a public park. It does three years later.

1909

As a result of Society urging, the state appoints a state forester and passes its first forest fire prevention laws.

1911

The Weeks Act is passed by Congress, after a decade-long campaign led by the Society and other conservation groups, creating the White Mountain National Forest and the rest of the eastern national forest system.

The Society buys 638 acres on Mount Sunapee to save the land from being clearcut.

1912

The Society buys 152 acres around Lost River Gorge. It still owns the land today.

1915

The Society acquires title to 406 acres on Mount Monadnock, beginning a process that would end up protecting more than 4,000 acres on the landmark mountain.

1918

The Society begins work to acquire 1,500 acres on Mount Kearsarge.

1920

The Society releases two breeding pairs of Minnesota beavers at Lost River. Prior to this, beaver had been extirpated from New Hampshire for thirty years.

1923

The Society begins a campaign to purchase 6,000 acres in Franconia Notch, including the Old Man of the Mountain, the Flume, the Basin, and two mountain lakes.

1925

The Society owns 1,029 acres of forest reservations.

1928

The Society and the state buy Franconia Notch for $400,000. The Society retains ownership of 913 acres, including the Flume, which it manages until 1947.

1932

The Society and the New England Wildflower Preservation Society open the first annual New Hampshire Nature Camp for teachers at Lost River.

1934

The Society helps defeat a proposal to build a "skyline drive" across the Presidential Range.

1935

Philip Ayres retires and is succeeded by Lawrance "Larry" W. Rathbun.

1937

The Society begins publication of its magazine, *Forest Notes*.

1938

The Society helps lead the effort to salvage more than 400 million board feet of timber following the Great Hurricane.

1942

The state passes a constitutional amendment to enable repeal of state taxation of growing timber.

1943

The Society helps protect land surrounding White Horse Ledge in North Conway.

1945

The Society helps form the New England Forestry Foundation to promote better forest practices.

1948

The Society transfers to the state all its lands on Mount Sunapee.

1949

Governor Sherman Adams signs legislation formally repealing the "timber tax," culminating a half century of Society advocacy on the issue.

1950

The Society brings the Tree Farm program to the state, which encourages landowners to manage their woodlands for the long term. The Society gives its final 520 acres on Mount Kearsarge to the state for the Frank Rollins Memorial Park, honoring its first president. The Society owns 2,995 acres of forest reservations.

1959

The Society makes its first formal opposition to a superhighway through Franconia Notch, beginning twenty-five years of opposition to the plan.

1960

Mr. and Mrs. Clarence L. Hay give the Society 672 acres of woodland on Lake Sunapee, the Society's first donation over 500 acres.

1962

The Society stops a plan to floodlight the Old Man of the Mountain. Working with the Audubon Society of New Hampshire and the state Fish and Game Department, the Society purchases land in the Hampton Salt Marshes to thwart a major development project.

1963

The Society leads the way on legislation that enables towns to create town conservation commissions.

1965

Larry Rathbun retires and is succeeded by Paul O. Bofinger as forester; the chief executive's title is later changed to president/forester. Eighteen towns have conservation commissions.

1967

Voters approve a constitutional amendment enabling current use assessment on undeveloped land.

1969

Plans for a nuclear power plant at Seabrook spurs the Society to lobby for extensive review of all major power installations.

1970

The federal government withdraws its plans for a tunnel and four-lane highway through Franconia Notch. The Society forms an interstate coalition to fight a proposed east-west superhighway across Vermont, New Hampshire, and Maine. The Society opens an EcoCenter at Mount Monadnock to teach the 75,000 annual visitors about the mountain's ecology.

1971

The Society negotiates its first conservation easement, which allows landowners to keep their land while preventing future development.

1972

The Society begins a campaign to protect Sandwich Notch — the last unprotected notch in the state.

1973

The legislature enacts current use taxation, allowing millions of acres of land to remain as open space. A plan for a smaller parkway through Franconia Notch wins Society support.

1975

The Society owns 6,958 acres of forest reservations.

1976

The Society celebrates the reopening of the Monadnock-Sunapee Greenway, first laid out in 1925 by Philip Ayres and his friend Allen Chamberlain of the Appalachian Mountain Club.

1980

The Society moves into its award-winning Conservation Center in Concord along with tenant organizations.

1983

The Society helps raise awareness about the impacts of acid rain on New England's forests, laying the groundwork for important amendments to the Clean Air Act.

1984

The Wilderness Act passes the U.S. Congress, designating 77,000 acres in the White Mountain

National Forest as wilderness. (Society head Paul Bofinger chaired the committee that reached consensus on the bill.) The Society creates the Forest Society of Maine to accept a conservation easement on the 23,000-acre Attean Township.

1986

The Society founds the Trust for New Hampshire Lands to advocate for a new public land acquisition program.

1987

The legislature creates the Land Conservation Investment Program and appropriates an initial $20 million. The first land and resource management plan is approved for the White Mountain National Forest. The Society plays a lead role in helping finalize the plan.

1988

63,000 acres of land in Coos County goes on the market; the Northern Forest debate begins.

1989

The Society, the state, the Nature Conservancy, and the U.S. Forest Service buy the 40,000-acre Nash Stream forest in northern New Hampshire.

1990

The Society serves on the Northern Forest Lands Council to find ways to sustain the four-state, 26-million-acre forest and its people.

1991

The Society negotiates a conservation easement protecting the 11,000-acre Andorra Forest in Stoddard and surrounding towns.

1993

The Society creates the New Hampshire Conservation Institute to enhance and streamline its education and research efforts. The Society produces its award-winning *Guide to Logging Aesthetics* and a companion video to promote low-impact forestry without high-impact costs.

1996

Paul Bofinger retires and is succeeded by Jane A. Difley as president/forester.

1997

The Society acquires it 100th reservation, the High Watch Preserve, in Ossipee.

1999

The Society becomes the first private landowner in New Hampshire to have its land green-certified under the international guidelines of the Forest Stewardship Council.

2000

Under the Society's leadership, the Land and Community Heritage Investment Program (LCHIP) is signed into law, creating a permanent statewide funding program to protect open space and cultural resources. The Society owns 32,673 acres in forest reservations and oversees 69,368 acres under conservation easements.

2001

The Society celebrates its 100th anniversary and opens the French Wing at the Conservation Center.

Society For The Protection Of New Hampshire Forests Executive Committee*, Trustees, and Officers

**Executive Committee evolved into Board of Trustees in 1973; leader changed from President to Chairman.*

Nahum J. Bachelder, Andover; 1901-1903

Albert E. Pillsbury, Boston, MA; 1901-1903

Joseph T. Walker, Concord; 1901-1909 (Secretary)

Frank W. Rollins, Concord, 1901-1915 (President)

Gen. George T. Cruft, Bethlehem; 1901-1929 (Treasurer 1901-1923)

Winston Churchill, Cornish; 1903-1923

Robert E. Faulkner, Keene, 1904-1915

Montgomery Rollins, Boston, MA; 1904-1915

Allen Hollis, Concord; 1907-1954 (Secretary 1907-1916) (President 1916-1950)

Robert P. Bass, Peterborough; 1909-1954

Allen Chamberlain, Winchester, MA; 1914-1938

Frank H. Foster, Claremont; 1916-1918

Sherman E. Burroughs, Manchester; 1916-1918 (Secretary 1918-1921)

Charles H. Porter, Tamworth; 1916-1950

Rolland H. Spaulding, Rochester; 1917-1942

William P. Wharton, Groton, MA; 1919-1938

Gen. Elbert Wheeler, Nashua; 1920-1924

John R. McLane, Manchester; 1921-1949

Robert L. Manning, Manchester; 1922-1923

James J. Storrow, Boston, MA; 1923-1925 (Treasurer 1923-1925)

John Winant, Concord; 1923-1925 (Secretary 1925-1950)

George E. Clement, Peterborough; 1923-1927

Edgar C. Hirst, Concord; 1925-1965 (Secretary (1925-1950) (President, 1950-1965)

James J. Storrow, Jr., Boston, MA; 1926-1965 (Treasurer 1926-1959)

Eaton D. Sargent, Sunapee; 1927-1929

Ashton Rollins, Rollinsford; 1928-1948

Karl W. Woodward, Durham; 1929-1958

Victor M. Cutter, New London; 1938-1946

Arthur S. Morris, Littleton; 1938-1954

Sherman Adams, Lincoln; 1942-1949

Laurence F. Whittemore, Pembroke; 1946-1960

Owen Johnson, Manchester; 1948-65; 1970-1973 (Treasurer 1965-1971)

Theodore L. Storer, Boston, MA; 1949-1965 (Treasurer 1959-1965)

Robert P. Burroughs, Manchester; 1950-1974 (Secretary 1969-74)

Richard F. Cooper, Rochester; 1951-1965; 1968-1974

Winthrop L. Carter, Jr., Hollis; 1954-1964

Lewis C. Swain, Durham; 1958-1959

Henry C. Waldo, Lincoln; 1958-1966

Ralph Wales, Sharon; 1958-1966

Sinclair Weeks, Lancaster; 1959-1966

Reginald M. Colby, Littleton; 1960-1966

Paul E. Bruns, Durham; 1963-1968

Percival S. Howe, Marlborough; 1964-1965

Gordon M. Tiffany, Weare; 1964-1974 (Treasurer 1971-1974)

Dr. James M. Faulkner, Stoddard, NH, Brookline, MA; 1965-1970

Robert S. Monahan, Hanover; 1965-1971

Lawrence W. Rathbun, Concord; 1965-1973 (President)

Frederick J. Harrigan, Colebrook; 1966-1970

Henry I. Baldwin, Hillsboro; 1966-1972

Carlton F. Heard, Center Sandwich; 1966-1972

Clarence S. Herr, Berlin; 1966-1972

Harlan Logan, Meriden; 1969-1975 (Chairman*, 1973-1975)

Richard H. Webb, Mt. Sunapee; 1969-1980; 1982-1988 (Chairman, 1978-1980)

Elizabeth Y. McGreal, Peterborough; 1970-1971

Robert P. Bass, Jr., Concord; 1970-1976

Jeffrey P. Smith, Hollis; 1970-1976

Gerald S. Wheeler, Laconia; 1970-1976

Stephen W. Smith, Plymouth; 1970-1977

Elizabeth A. Greene, Rye; 1971-1974

Zenaide V. Bradley, Whitefield; 1971-1977

Duncan Bruce, Durham; 1971-1978 (Chairman, 1975-1978)

Stephen H. Taylor, Meriden; 1972-1975

James Bork, Berlin; 1972-1978

John Hardie, Contoocook; 1972-1978; 1984-1993 (Chair, 1993-1995)

James R. Carter, Peterborough; 1973-1979

Sarah L. Hartwell, New London; 1973-1979

J. Willcox Brown, Dunbarton; 1974-1977

R. John Shortlidge, Keene; 1974-1977

Richard R. Weyrick, Lee; 1974-1979
Richard Gallant, Stratham; 1974-1982
David J. Bradley, Hanover; 1975-1981
Robert L. V. French, Hopkinton; 1975-1981
Eleanor H. Stark, Concord; 1975-1981
James P. Rogers, Laconia; 1976-1978
Marshall P. Hoke, Elkins; 1976-1982
William P. House, Chesham; 1976-1982 (Chairman, 1980-1982)
Susan W. Thoresen, Portsmouth; 1976-1984; 1987-1990
David S. Williams, Bristol; 1977-1980
John W. Barto, Pittfield; 1977-1983 (Chairman, 1982-1983)
Carl Siemon, Milton Mills; 1977-1983
E.H.B. Bartelink, Concord; 1977-1984 (Chairman, 1983-1984)
Mark E. Hamlin, Berlin; 1978-1984
C. Robertson Trowbridge, Dublin; 1978-1984; 1986-1992 (Secretary 1985) (Chairman, 1991-1992)
Howard C. Dickinson, Jr., North Conway; 1979-1980
David P. Olson, Durham; 1979-1985
Douglas A. Philbrook, Gorham; 1979-1985
John Skelton, Wolfeboro; 1979-1985
David F. Putnam, Keene; 1980-1986
Henry Swan, Lyme; 1980-1986 (Chairman, 1984-1986)
Janet Nixon, New Boston; 1980-1987
Lloyd W. Hawkensen, Plymouth; 1981-1987
Harold W. Janeway, Webster; 1981-1988 (Chairman, (1986-1988)
Anne D. Middleton, Bedford; 1982-1985
Charlton MacVeagh, Jr. Peterborough; 1982-1987; 1992-1994
Duncan S. McGowan, Concord, 1982-1990
B. Sharon Meeker, Lee; 1983-1986
Douglas Eldridge, Newmarket; 1983-1989
Carl B. Jacobs, Sr., Keene; 1983-1989
Chester B. Lucy, North Conway; 1983-1989
Warren Pearson, Dixville Notch; 1984-1985
Kenneth M. Brown, Nashua; 1984-1987
Malcolm McLane, Concord; 1984-1990 (Chairman 1988-1990)
Mary McKee, Dublin; 1985-1988
J. Bonnie Newman, Hampton; 1985-1988
George B. Foote, Contoocook; 1985-1990
Barry Kelley, Berlin; 1985-1991
Sydney Howe, Holderness; 1986-1992
Nancy Hayden, Marlborough; 1987-1995
Brian E. Rohde, Jaffrey; 1987-1992
Thaddeus Thorne, Center Conway; 1987-1992
Brendan Whittaker, Lancaster, Guildhall, VT; 1987-1992
William Dunlap, Bedford; 1988-1995; 1999-2005
Phyllis P. Folsom, Randolph; 1988-1991
Bruce McClellan, Dublin; 1988-1994
Robert Wells, Hopkinton; 1988-1994
Jane Blalock, Boston, MA; 1989-1991
Michael Harvell, Portsmouth; 1989-1995
Peter Stettenheim, Lebanon; 1989-1995
Diane Schott, Jaffrey; 1990-1997
Jameson French, Kingston; 1990-1996; (Chair, 1995- 1998), 1998-1999
Jennie Norman, Keene; 1991-1993
Ronald A. Wilber, Concord; 1991-1996
Elizabeth Hager, Concord; 1991-1997
Peter W. Powell, Lancaster; 1991-1997, 1997-1998
John Gemmill, Concord; 1992-1998
Willam F. Kidder, Jr., New London; 1992-1998
Lilla McLane-Bradley, Hanover; 1992-1995
Thomas N. Tillotson, Dixville Notch; 1992-1998
Sharon F. Francis, Charlestown; 1993-2000
Benjamin Gayman, Manchester; 1993-1999; 2001-2002 (Chair, 1999-2001)
Charles Watts, Freedom, NH, Boston, MA; 1993-1999; Secretary (1998-2001)
Lucia Kittredge, Canterbury; 1994-2000
Patrick Jackson, Exeter; 1994-2000
Merle W. Schotanus, Grantham; 1994-2000
Samual Adams, Lincoln; 1995-1999
Peter Burling, Cornish; 1995-1997
Sheila Weeks, Gilford; 1995-1999
Freda T. Swan, Lyme; 1995-2001
Powell Cabot, Walpole, 1996-2000
A. Bradford Wyman, Berlin; 1996-2002
Charles S. Faulkner, II, Hanover; 1997-2003
Michael Andrews, Washington, 1998-2004
Stuart (Mike) V. Smith, Jr., Lyme, 1998-2004
John E. Hoffman, Jr., Sullivan 1998-2004
Marilyn Kidder, New London 1999-2005
Ross D'Elia, Henniker 2000-2006
Katharine A. Eneguess, Peterborough, 2000-2006
Phyllis (Skye) Maher, Portsmouth 2000-2006
Kendra O'Donnell, Waterville Valley 2000-2006

Society For The Protection Of New Hampshire Forests
Permanent Staff Members

Name	Hire Date	End Date	Position Last Held
Ayres, Philip W.	1/21/02	7/11/35	Forester
Richards, Joseph L.	7/1/12	9/30/17	Assistant to Mr. Ayres, Lost River
McCarthy, Cora	5/31/15	5/31/45	Assistant to Manager, Lost River
McCarthy, Michael J.	5/31/15	5/31/45	Manager, Lost River
Bodwell, O. T.	6/1/30	11/24/42	Manager, The Flume and Lost River
Rathbun, Lawrence W.	8/1/35	10/12/73	Forester
House, William	12/1/37	10/4/41	Assistant Forester
Macauley, Austin	12/22/48	2/28/67	Manager, Lost River
Kimball, Charles	5/1/49	9/30/67	Caretaker, Lost River
Mendenhall, Howard	3/27/51	12/14/54	Assistant Forester
Ogden, Ruth	12/4/51	3/31/66	Administrative Assistant
Thom, Madeline	3/1/52	3/31/54	Administrative Assistant
Brown, J. Willcox	8/26/55	8/1/58	Assistant Forester
Young, Gail Crockett	9/4/56	8/26/59	Administrative Assistant
Clark, Leslie S.	10/1/58	5/1/81	Director, Education
Bofinger, Paul O.	9/1/61	8/31/96	President/Forester
Dodge, John	11/1/65	12/31/73	Education Specialist
Henderson, Sharon	3/1/66	8/31/74	Executive Assistant to President/Forester
Churchill, Patricia	3/1/67		Registrar/Volunteer Coordinator
Taylor, Malcolm "Tink"	4/1/67	5/31/78	Director, Assoc. of Conservation Commissions
Royce, Charles H. Jr.	6/16/67	8/31/78	Monadnock Crew
Carter, James	4/18/69	7/31/71	Wetlands Coordinator
Sheaff, Richard	9/1/69	6/30/73	Program Coordinator Upper Valley Studies
Mullins, Lee D.	1/1/71	4/30/77	Executive Assistant to President/Forester
King, Allen	2/3/71	5/31/81	Director, Land Protection
King, Geraldine	3/25/71	12/31/76	Special Projects Coordinator
Robinson, Mary Beth	12/1/72		Coordinator, Payroll/Benefits
Terrio, Sandra	1/1/73	5/31/93	Membership Assistant
McCabe, Beverly (Sieman)	7/17/73	10/31/81	Executive Assistant to President/Forester
Humm, William R.	9/10/73	8/31/77	Director, Finance/Administration
Redlich, Susan	1/1/74	12/31/74	Land Protection Specialist
Hallett, Ashton R.	5/1/75	5/1/89	Development/Land Protection Coordinator
Kapala, Cleve	1/19/76	10/30/84	Director, Education
Damman, Linda Cook	7/12/76	10/31/85	Executive Assistant to President/Forester
Hovland, Bruce	7/1/77	4/30/93	Director, Forestry and Lands
McClure, Jan Walker	11/21/77	4/30/84	Land Protection Specialist
Van Fleet, James	1/3/78	11/30/87	Director, Finance/Administration
Shirley, Ralph	1/20/78	9/30/85	Property Manager, The Rocks
MacMahan, Mary Lou	5/9/78	8/31/80	Administrative Assistant
Finnegan, Mark	8/14/78	9/30/84	Assistant Caretaker, The Rocks
Jones, Geoffrey	6/4/79		Director, Land Management
Morrill, Elizabeth	6/12/79	8/31/81	Wood Energy/Conservation Center
Lyman, Marcy West	11/13/79	8/31/85	Director, Policy
Peabody, Allan E.	10/27/80	10/31/85	Property Manager, Conservation Center
Winship, Stephen W.	2/23/81	10/31/81	Director, Communications
Quinn, Rita	3/31/81		Executive Assistant to President/Forester
Hills, David	4/7/81	3/31/83	Energy Education Coordinator
Gillespie, Margaret	9/8/81	9/30/85	Outreach Education
Soper, Diana K.	10/31/81	12/31/82	Administrative Assistant
Difley, Jane	1/25/82	4/30/84	Coordinator, Forest Awareness Program

Name	Hire Date	End Date	Position Last Held
Reno, Rebecca	2/10/82	7/31/83	Administrative Assistant, Wangan
Harrington, Barbara	5/17/82	7/31/83	Wood Energy Education Coordinator
Long, James	5/24/82	9/30/84	Property Manager, McCabe
Wallner, Jeffrey	8/9/82	5/31/93	North Country Education Coordinator
Morgan, Christopher	1/10/83	8/31/84	Director, Communications
Farber, Susan	2/7/83	8/31/85	Membership Assistant
Gillies, Jane	7/5/83		Manager Admin. Services/Gift Shop
Thorne, Sarah	7/5/83		Director, Research
Kimball, Deborah	9/12/83	5/31/84	Director, Development
Crane, David	5/31/84	7/31/85	Property Manager, McCabe
Pope, Ellen	6/6/84	11/30/98	Vice President, Development/Finance
Zicus, Sandra	8/24/84	8/31/91	Coordinator, Project Conserve
Burgess, Annette Morrill	9/4/84	8/31/92	Administrative Assistant
Carlson, Martha	10/15/84	4/30/85	Director, Communications
Hahn, Catherine	2/11/85	5/19/87	Land Protection Specialist
Ober, Richard	4/24/85	6/29/01	Senior Director, Outreach Programs
Parrott, Carolyn	9/10/85	6/30/87	Membership Coordinator
Johnson, Mark	10/15/85	1/31/92	Property Manager, Conservation Center
Ham, Kelly	12/4/85	2/6/87	Administrative Assistant
Blackmer, Stephen	1/2/86	11/30/89	Director, Policy
Fleury, Patricia (Chiasson)	6/2/86		Administrative Assistant
Campbell, Susan	6/9/86	9/30/86	T.N.H.L., Land Agent
Morrone, Michele	6/9/86	9/30/86	T.N.H.L., Land Agent
Smart, Melissa	6/9/86	9/30/86	T.N.H.L., Land Agent
Winneg, Nancy B.	7/7/86	5/31/87	T.N.H.L., Community Action Coordinator
Didio, Priscilla	9/3/86	9/30/93	North Country Education Coordinator
Brown, Nancy	9/4/86	9/16/87	T.N.H.L., Fund Raiser Assistant
Birchard, Susan	10/6/86	3/31/88	Land Protection Specialist
Doscher, Paul	10/20/86		Senior Director, Land Conservation
Sheehy, Carol	11/20/86	9/30/91	T.N.H.L., Data Assistant
Manley, Nigel	11/30/86		North Country Property Manager
McCullough, Anne	12/29/86		Receptionist
Ward, Leslie	1/26/87		Finance Director
Trowbridge, Cordelia	2/2/87	7/16/87	T.N.H.L., Outreach Assistant
Leland, Forbes	4/15/87	11/30/88	Land Protection Specialist
Charles, Robin	6/15/87	5/31/88	Administrative Assistant
Levesque, Charles	7/1/87	5/31/91	T.N.H.L., Executive Director
Chamberlin, Robert	7/5/87	8/31/92	T.N.H.L., Land Protection Specialist
Tumosa, Judy	7/6/87	12/31/89	T.N.H.L., Land Protection Specialist
Whittemore, Henry	7/6/87	6/30/90	T.N.H.L., Land Protection Specialist
Slown, Elizabeth	7/10/87	8/31/91	Membership Assistant
Mitman, Tammalene	7/13/87	2/29/88	T.N.H.L., Coordinator
Jordan, Roberta	8/17/87	8/31/91	T.N.H.L., Land Protection Specialist
Lind, Brenda	8/17/87	8/31/93	T.N.H.L., Land Protection Specialist
Freeman-Woolpert, David	2/22/88	1/31/92	Director, Finance and Administration
Fales, Barbara	2/29/88	6/30/91	T.N.H.L., Administrative Assistant
Harrigan, David	5/1/88	8/31/94	Staff Lawyer/Policy Director
Boelhower, Mary Ellen	7/15/88	5/31/97	Land Protection Specialist
Didier, Katharine	10/17/88	12/31/89	North Country Education Assistant
Bates, Sylvia K.	1/23/89	10/31/97	Director, Land Protection
Wadlegger, Robert Jr.	6/5/89	7/31/93	T.N.H.L., Data Assistant
McLaughlin, Diane	7/26/89	2/28/99	Administrative Assistant
Yorke, Diane E.	2/1/90	2/28/93	Coordinator, Project Conserve
Watkins, Margaret	5/23/90	5/31/92	Coordinator, Local Lands Protection Program

Name	Hire Date	End Date	Position Last Held
Anderson, David	7/2/90		Director, Education
Van Ryn, Tammara	8/21/90	7/31/97	Director, Policy
McGuinn, Beth	7/25/91	1/31/01	Director, Easement Stewardship
Schaefer, Diane	9/16/91	10/31/95	Director, Development
Leveille, Paul	1/8/92		Property Manager, Conservation Center
Conroy, Rosemary	9/8/92		Director, Communications
Soule, Patricia (Wells)	10/30/92	4/30/97	S.P.A.C.E. Administrative Assistant
Tebo, Mary	1/19/93	9/30/96	Community Tree Steward Program Coordinator
Williams, Deborah (Mitchell)	2/16/93		North Country Education Coordinator
Ferguson, Paul K.	5/24/93	5/31/98	Membership Assistant
Sundquist, Daniel	6/1/93		Director, Science
Perron, Stephen	6/7/93		Forestry Specialist
Purrington, Anne L.	7/6/93	6/30/95	Membership Coordinator
Tumosa, Judy	9/27/93	6/30/96	North Country Education Coordinator
Abdinoor, Claudia	6/26/95	3/31/98	Membership Assistant
Morse, Margaret	9/25/95	8/31/96	North Country Education Coordinator
Butson, Daniel	11/13/95	4/30/01	Field Hand/Foreman, The Rocks
Liszka, Margaret	1/22/96		Director, Member Relations
Amirault, Vernon J.	3/21/96	3/31/98	Assistant Caretaker, The Rocks
Wells, Matthew R.	5/14/96	7/31/99	Assistant Caretaker, The Rocks
Chute, Lionel	5/20/96		Field Forester
Howe, Thomas A.	8/1/96		Senior Director, Land Protection
Difley, Jane A.	8/12/96		President/Forester
Bodien, Marybeth	2/4/97	3/31/98	S.P.A.C.E. Administrative Assistant
Leveille, Penelope	5/1/97		Bookkeeper
Loomis, Kristen	9/8/97		Outreach Coordinator
Niebling, Charles	10/1/97		Senior Director, Policy/Land Management
Seegar, Michael	1/19/98	6/30/99	Policy Assistant
Hotz, Brian	2/9/98		Land Protection Specialist
Santaniello, Lindsey	2/21/98		S.P.A.C.E. Administrative Assistant
Harvey, Elizabeth	3/5/98		Special Projects Coordinator
Shadley, Beverly	7/13/98		Director, Corporate Giving
Hart, Brian	7/20/98		Policy Specialist
Chabot-Vogel, Amy	8/3/98	4/30/99	Easement Stewardship Assistant
Howard, Thomas	11/15/98		Land Protection Specialist
Kibler-Hacker, Susanne	3/22/99		Senior Director, Development
Ackerson, Judith	4/26/99	4/30/01	Administrative Assistant
Huckins, Nancy F.	5/4/99		Membership Assistant
Alderman, Andrea	5/18/99		Forestry Assistant
Kane, Christopher	5/19/99		Stewardship Assistant
Slack, Susan	8/30/99	10/31/00	Policy Specialist
Brochu, Gerard P.	11/1/99		Mail Clerk
Carlson, Judith	1/19/00		Membership Specialist
Stansfield, Gary	2/14/00		Land Steward Coordinator
Tillotson, Regina	8/7/00		Communications Coordinator
McGraw, David C.	8/8/00		G.I.S. Specialist
Moore, Peter R.	10/10/00		Business Membership Specialist
Hahn, Catherine E.	1/9/01		Land Protection Specialist
Stern, Kenneth	3/12/01		Director, Land Stewardship
Ritz, Kristen R.	3/26/01		Administrative Assistant
Taylor, Dorothy T.	6/4/01		Director, Ctr. for Land Conservation Assistance

Temporary Staff (Main Office)

Name	Hire date
Fowler, Robert E.	8/21/53
Quinn, Joseph	1/31/59
Enos, Lucinda	11/1/69
Blakeney, Gordon R. Jr.	11/15/71
Sheaff, Cheryl	1/2/72
Zellars, Jeffrey	4/24/72
Merriam, DeWolf	9/1/72
Vogel, Gary I.	12/20/74
Asselin, Alan	7/29/75
Shaw, Lee	8/8/76
Raymond, Darcy	12/1/76
Flamand, Patricia	12/1/76
Hemeon, Jeannette	12/1/76
Byrne, Mary P.	12/1/76
McCabe, Stephen A. Jr.	4/4/77
Ashton, Richard V.	5/1/77
Weinberg, Walter	10/1/77
Goodhue, Sargent	5/24/78
Bofinger, Lisa	6/3/81
Leonard, Ray E.	11/15/84
Steenbergen, Andrew H.	1/2/85
Richardson, Amanda	5/4/85
Emery, Harold	2/4/87
Osgood, Delbert	5/16/88
Bentley, Charles	5/21/91
Green, Mary	9/25/91
Pepin, Sally	12/8/91
Koppana, Imogene	5/31/93
Fyon, Johanna G.	9/1/93
Gillies, Kristine	11/24/95
Erikson, Will	4/30/97
Allen, Frank	7/21/97
Lurgio, Scott	11/26/97
Osmer, Thomas	6/27/00
Smith, Deborah	1/11/01

Temporary Staff: The Rocks

Name	Hire Date
Grilli, Daniel	11/15/82
Hicks, Kenneth	9/14/85
Manley, Ellen	9/12/88
Odell, Gregory J.	3/6/90
Huntington, William	4/1/91
Hard, Sean	5/1/95

Temporary Staff: Lost River Guides and Naturalists

Name	Hire Date
Hulbert, Henry W.	7/1/12
Hulbert, Chauncy	7/1/12
Hulbert, Woodward	7/1/12
Young, Roscoe	7/1/14
Grinnell, Edward R.	7/1/14
Abbe, Fred	7/1/14
Hodges, Hallett J.	7/1/14
Homer, Thomas J.	7/1/14
Kimball, Richard E.	7/1/15
Tewksbury, Donald O.	7/1/18
Knowles, Gilbert H.	7/1/18
Harrison, Parker	7/1/19
Roberts, Porter	7/1/19
Hollis, Franklin	7/1/20
Benton, Harold E.	7/1/20
Ashley, Rowland	7/1/21
Wilder, Howard B.	7/1/21
Hunt, Richard A.	7/1/22
Taylor, Dwight K.	7/1/22
Dewey, Charles S.	7/1/22
Morrison, Hugh S.	7/1/23
Guyol, Philip N.	7/1/23
Davis, Richard J.	7/1/23
Davis, Homer L.	7/1/24
Jeffrey, Allen C.	7/1/24
Lindsay, Roger	7/1/24
Nelson, Horace M.	7/1/24
Morrison, Robert D.	7/1/25
Woodbury, Scott	7/1/25
Wheeler, Arthur J.	7/1/25
Oatman, Frederick	7/1/25
Hunt, Frederick A.	7/1/25
Sears, Frederick E. Jr.	7/1/25
Hazzard, William G.	7/1/26
Bang, Eris	7/1/26
Shippen, E. Rodman	7/1/27
Webster, John Rowe	7/1/27
Williamson, Carleton H.	7/1/27
Ayers, Dwight T.	7/1/28
Taylor, Robert B.	7/1/28
Harrow, Dalton	7/1/28
Buck, Frederick M. Jr.	7/1/28
Jump, Ellis B.	7/1/28
Waterman, Arthur J.	7/1/29
Woodbury, Wallace	7/1/29
McCullum, John H.	7/1/29
Jeffrey, Robert L.	7/1/29
Street, Dana Morris	7/1/29
Miller, John B.	7/1/29
Clough, Samuel A.	7/1/29
Bradley, Prentice	7/1/30
Pinfold, Wallace K.	7/1/30
Wall, Robert A.	7/1/30
Vickerson, Harry J.	7/1/30
Choate, Malcolm C.	7/1/31
Pinfold, Russell W.	7/1/31
Millar, Melville	7/1/32
Murray, Frederic R.	7/1/32
Wells, Richard C.	7/1/32
Little, Carroll	7/1/32
Millar, Branford P.	7/1/32
Douglas, Samuel T. Jr.	7/1/32
Bampton, Robert F.	7/1/32
Ransmeier, John C. Jr.	7/1/32
Kimball, Richard N.	7/1/33
Reisner, Edward H.	7/1/33
Sharpe, Lawrence W.	7/1/34
Choate, Paul	7/1/34
Bassett, Roderick E.	7/1/34
Austin, John C.	7/1/34
Scott, Joseph W.	7/1/35
Angell, Gardiner	7/1/35
Foster, Robert Nelson	7/1/36
Grandin, Edward S.	7/1/36
Slocumb, John	7/1/36
Winslow, William Allen	7/1/36
Miller, William B.	7/1/37
Fletcher, John R.	7/1/37
Lawrence, Homer E.	7/1/37
Foster, Elliiott	7/1/37
Killele, Joseph	7/1/37
Angell, Richard	7/1/38
Collingwood, Thomas P.	7/1/38
Shipp, Harold	7/1/38
Powers, Ernest	7/1/39
Hughes, Owen K.	7/1/39
Miller, James B.	7/1/39
Bennett, Frank	7/1/39
Hardenorff, Victor	7/1/39
Fernald, Bartlett	7/1/40
Jenkins, Ward S.	7/1/40
Burbank, John	7/1/40
Wood, William	6/15/49
Avery, Sherwood	6/15/49
Macauley, Arthur	6/15/49
Jackson, Arlene B.	6/15/49
Shepard, Ernest	6/15/49
Welch, Robert	6/15/49
Kenney, Evelyn	6/15/49
Hutchins, Floyd	6/15/49
Nickerson, Henry A.	6/15/49
Jackson, Philip	6/15/49
Slason, Bruce	6/15/49
Carpenter, Alden	6/15/49
Staples, David	6/15/49
Keenan, Eugene	6/15/49
Pellitier, Wallace	6/15/50
Buchanan, Alden	6/15/50
Proper, Richard	6/15/50
Foley, Ralph	6/15/50
Foley, Dorothea	6/15/50
Sears, Fred	6/20/50
Blanchard, Jean	5/1/51
Leclair, Jeanette	6/15/51
Talbot, Wesley	6/15/51
Lavoie, Ronald	6/15/51
Butler, Rose	5/20/52
Butler, Richard	5/20/52
Doran, Francis	5/25/52
Jackson, Philip L.	6/15/52
Young, Kenton	6/15/52
Hornaday, Richard	6/20/52
Turner, Henry	6/20/52
Richardson, Patricia	6/25/52
LeClerc, Roland	5/1/53
Macauley, Myrtle	5/15/53
Rock, David	5/25/53
Walsh, Dan C.	6/15/53
Talbot, Wesley	7/1/53
Santy, Betty Ann	8/1/53
Leclare, Robert	5/15/54
Santy, William	5/25/54
Jackson, Philip	6/15/54
Walsh, Daniel	6/15/54
Durgin, Edward	6/15/54
Gauthier, Paul	7/15/54
Bean, Clayton	6/15/55
Walsh, Carolyn	6/20/55
Steele, Frank Everett	5/1/56
Willard, James	6/15/56
Rouillard, John	6/15/57

Hammond, Curtis	6/15/57
Erskine, Alan	7/1/57
Downing, Arthur	7/1/57
Kendall, Dale	6/15/58
Clark, Floyd	6/15/58
Huot, Jonathon	6/15/58
Bond, Richard	6/15/58
Raymond, Allan	6/15/58
Sharp, Philip	7/1/58
Nelson, David	6/15/59
Cobden, G.	6/15/59
Mellett, William	6/15/59
Mellett, Doris	6/15/59
Randall, Harold	6/15/59
Randall, Peter	6/15/59
Emerson, Betty Ann	6/15/60
Clapp, John C.	6/15/61
Willaid, Thomas	6/15/61
Bishoff, Courtney	6/15/61
Rowley, Craig	6/15/61
Emery, Floyd	6/15/61
Sawyer, Stephen	6/15/62
Frazer, Richard	6/15/63
Fuller, Robert	6/15/63
Gerhard, Robert	6/15/63
Johnson, Wayne	6/15/63
Woodward, Francis	7/1/63
Lipsey, Bruce	6/15/64
Garvey, Peter	6/15/64
Redmond, Gary	6/15/64
Willard, John	6/15/64
Cussik, Joseph	7/1/64
Brengle, Denis	7/1/64
Parker, Stephen	7/1/64
Coughlin, Francis	6/15/65
Downing, Charles	6/15/65
Freese, Christina	6/15/65
Langley, Stephen	6/15/65
Kaufman, Greggrey	6/15/65
Bilheimer, Mary	6/1/68
Wilson, Arlene	6/1/69
Phelan, Albert	9/1/69
Steele, Frederic L.	6/1/70
Dutton, Stanley	7/1/70
Hamblett, Robert	6/3/73
West, Arthur J. Jr.	6/12/75
Kelly, Carol	5/24/76
Parker, David S.	5/28/77
Hardy, William H.	6/12/78
McIntyre, Carol Gay	6/26/78
Fitzpatrick, Scott	5/21/79
Clark, Russell	5/21/79
Soule, Arlene	6/9/80
Matte, Susan	6/1/81
Strimbeck, Richard	6/1/82
Hayden, Sean	5/16/86
Martin, Craig	5/12/90
Tempest, Christopher	6/20/90
Mortz, Bernard	6/14/91
McNeill, William	5/24/93
Mattrick, Christopher	5/27/94
Davison, Scott	5/20/95

Temporary Staff: Mount Monadnock EcoCenter and Trail Crews

Name	Hire date
Burrage, Charles D.	12/1/50
Smith, Richard	5/1/60
Deschenes, Richard	5/1/62
Smith, John F.	5/18/66
Royce, Charles H. Jr	6/16/67
Given, Stephen	7/1/70
Vreeland, Robert	6/12/72
Hardy, Elizabeth	6/21/72
Morse, Randall	6/21/72
Crimp, Peter M.	10/10/73
Brackley, Frances	6/15/74
Dudziak, Stanley	6/23/74
Royce, Jennifer A.	7/13/76
Youst, Rick	8/6/77
Leary, Daniel John	6/30/79
Sumner, Deborah	6/30/79
Levin, Steven M.	7/23/79
Brown, Julian	7/11/81
Leary, Suzanne M.	9/5/81
Fish, Michael D.	9/6/81
Jenkins, James	5/12/83
Leary, Patrice	9/8/85

Temporary Staff: Christmas Trees Operation at The Rocks Estate

Name	Hire Date
Didio, Michael	4/24/90
Cabaup, Jean	7/29/91
Brodien, Daniel E.	10/30/92
Tuite, Hilary	5/31/93
Mitchell, Diane Amy	5/1/94
Jurado, Marcus	8/1/94
Andersen, Peter	6/19/95
Tupaj, Andrew	8/7/95
Francis, Vanessa	11/9/95
Driscoll, Mark, Jr.	6/12/96
Brodien, Nathan J.	6/24/96
Didio, Ryan	8/12/96
Butson, Joshua	6/2/97
Bresnahan, Kara	6/19/97
Daniels, Michael	6/23/97
Geiger, Debra	9/11/97
Mackay-Pearson, Kim	9/11/97
Geiger, Timothy	11/11/97
Andross, Elizabeth	11/6/98
Fearon, Wendy M.	11/23/98
Spaulding, Jason	12/5/98
Mitchell, Dennis	4/19/99
Anderson-Davidson, S.	6/22/99
Dickerman, Garth	11/14/99
Considine, Timothy T.	12/10/99
Stinehour, Meryl	6/26/00
Doyle, Robert	10/20/00
Parcell, Ryan	11/27/00

Society for the Protection of New Hampshire Forests Interns

Name	Hire Date
Little, Justin	6/1/74
Kittredge, Lucia	6/1/74
Kostcke, Diane	6/1/74
Crothers, Leah	6/1/74
Jones, Richard Jr.	6/4/74
Oakes, Stephen F.	6/18/74
Mazur, Peter	6/1/75
Corell, Elizabeth	6/1/75
Difley, Jane	6/1/75
Grossberg, Michael	6/1/75
French, Jameson	6/1/75
Goldman, Stephen	6/1/75
Yannotis, John	7/1/75
Gilrain, Paul	5/12/76
Doolittle, Patricia	6/1/76
Gerstein, Richard	6/1/76
Broad, Robin	6/14/76
Kofinas, Gary	6/15/76
Beale, C. Marshall	6/28/76
Donovan, Thomas	7/1/76
Bell, Janice	7/1/76
Levek, Amy	7/1/76
Williston, Stephanie	7/1/76
Smithers, P. Bradford	1/1/77
Taylor, Dorothy	4/20/77
Sherman, Amy P.	5/9/77
Mayer, Barton	5/22/78
Baghdoyan, William E.	6/4/79
Lorentzon, Karen A.	6/19/85
Blake, H. Emerson	6/1/92
Robinson, Morgan	6/14/93
Breth, James L.	6/22/93
Allen, Mark N.	6/22/93
Hogan, Scott	7/6/93
Bielski, Susan	3/28/94
Michaud, Steven V.	5/24/94
Glazebrook, Catriona	6/1/94
Chase, Victoria P.	5/1/95
Seth, William III	6/20/95
Calvin, Jane	7/5/95
Argue, Michael	6/1/95
Filiault, Andrew	9/1/95
Hadley, David A.	6/6/96
Hammer, Christopher	3/26/97
Gieseking, Jennifer	5/30/97
Mathews, Andrew S.	6/1/97
Corcoran, Clare	6/2/97
Walsh, Matthew	9/9/97
Miles, Sherri	6/1/97
Whitney, Sarah N.	6/1/98
Mulder, Jesse	6/1/98
Shindledecker, Erin	6/8/98
Spitze, Michael	12/12/98
Prausa, Christina	1/15/99
Cantara, Bryan	6/21/99
Moseley, James	6/21/99
Dubois, Garrett	12/1/99
Michaelides, Kristen V.	10/1/00

NOTE: *The preceding personnel lists include regular employees who worked for more than one year and temporary employees who worked for more than two seasons.*

Society for the Protection of New Hampshire Forests's Volunteers of the Year

Prior to 1979, the Society gave out medallions and carved mushrooms for special recognition. There were also special tributes for outgoing trustees and retiring staff which are not included here.

Special Recognitions 1972-1979

1972	Henry I. Baldwin and Wilbur Thompson
1974	Chet Ladd and Mary McKee
1975	Claire and Leon Batchelder
1976	Mark E. Kelley
1984	Robert P. Bass and H. Charles Royce
1991	David Allen

Volunteers of the Year 1979-2000

1979	James D. Abbott
1980	Charlotte Scripture
1982	Florence Harris
1983	Robert Tripp and Edwin H. Robinson
1984	H. Charles Royce
1985	Ian and Charlotte Gillespie
1986	Terry Frost
1987	Phyllis Stafford
1988	George Conrod
1989	Gertrude Smart
1990	Barbara Hayden
1991	Elmer Allen
1992	Weston McEvoy
1993	Jeanne Lewis
1994	Carleton Schaller
1995	Helen Arsenault
1996	Gladys Nicolls
1997	Velma Ide
1998	Ray McGrath
1999	Tanya Tellman
2000	Marjorie Tuttle

Society for the Protection of New Hampshire Forests Conservationists of the Year 1984 - 2000

1984	Buhrman Garland and Abigail Avery, representing the ad hoc WMNF Advisory Committee)
1985	Eleanor Briggs and Clotilde Straus
1986	J. Willcox Brown
1987	Rob Trowbridge
1988	George Hamilton
1989	Mary Lyn Ray
1990	Governor John and Anna King
1991	Charles Faulkner, representing the Andorra Forest Limited Partnership
1992	People for the Protection of Pickerel Cove
1993	John Hay
1994	John Harrigan and Beaton Marsh
1995	John Kauffmann
1996	Paul O. Bofinger
1997	City of Lebanon
1998	Robert L. V. French
1999	Michael Yatsevitch
2000	John Barto

Prior to 1984 and the initiation of the Conservationists of the Year, the Society regularly recognized members and volunteers for special achievement or occasions.

Lands Protected by the Society For The Protection Of New Hampshire Forests

Permanent Reservations as of 12/31/00

** = addition to existing reservation*

No.	Date Protected	Property Name	Town	Acres	Donation of
1	1912	Lost River Reservation	Woodstock	152	Matson Manufacturing Co.
2	1914	Sutton Pines	Sutton	3	G. Davis Clay and R. Davis
3	1915	Monadnock Reservation	Jaffrey/Dublin	406	Masonian Heirs
*	1916	Monadnock Reservation	Jaffrey	186	Louise Amory
*	1916	Monadnock Reservation	Jaffrey	25	George F. Weld
*	1917	Monadnock Reservation	Jaffrey	125	S.C. Derby
*	1925	Monadnock Reservation	Jaffrey	80	Eugene O. McCarthy
*	1925	Monadnock Reservation	Jaffrey	50	Maro S. Brooks
*	1925	Sutton Pines	Sutton	1	Moses B. Pillsbury
*	1927	Monadnock Reservation	Jaffrey	200	Annabell M.P. Bonney
*	1928	Monadnock Reservation	Dublin	364	D.J. Hart
*	1929	Monadnock Reservation	Jaffrey	293	Elizabeth Poole
*	1931	Monadnock Reservation	Jaffrey	90	E.J.H. Starbuck
*	1932	Monadnock Reservation	Jaffrey	2	W. Kimball
*	1933	Monadnock Reservation	Jaffrey	452	Abbie Cowen
*	1933	Monadnock Reservation	Jaffrey	160	Percy L. Cutter
*	1934	Monadnock Reservation	Jaffrey/Dublin	60	Helen A. Sprague
*	1935	Monadnock Reservation	Jaffrey	150	David H. Harling
4	1935	Gipson Forest	Greenfield	12	Emma Gipson
*	1947	Monadnock Reservation	Jaffrey	183	Assoc. to Protect Monadnock
5	1954	Wilton Forest	Wilton	51	Audubon Society of N.H.
6	1960	Hay Reservation	Newbury	672	Clarence L. Hay
7	1960	Peabody Forest	Shelburne	83	Ralph I. Peabody Estate
8	1961	Brewster Forest	Dublin	272	Margaret Brewster
9	1964	Catterall Forest	Bristol/Alexandria	215	Ralph T. Catterall
10	1966	Jelleme Forest	Warner	48	Mabel Briggs Jelleme
11	1967	Hampton Salt Marshes	Hampton	5	C. Rawding and M. Rawding
12	1967	Blaine Forest	Jaffrey	167	Graham Blaine
*	1967	Monadnock Reservation	Jaffrey	266	Edric A. Weld
*	1968	Hampton Salt Marshes	Hampton	10	D. Morris Lamprey
*	1968	Hampton Salt Marshes	Hampton	20	Marion L. Penniman
*	1968	Hampton Salt Marshes	Hampton	3	Marion L. Penniman
13	1968	Cooper Cedar Woods	New Durham	29	Can Ran Realty
*	1968	Monadnock Reservation	Jaffrey	50	Wilpas E. Saari
*	1968	Hampton Salt Marshes	Hampton	6	K. Langley and H. Pierson
14	1968	Dickinson Memorial Forest	Swanzey	71	Paul E. Dickinson
15	1968	McGreal Forest	Hancock	26	Elizabeth Y. McGreal
*	1968	Monadnock Reservation	Jaffrey	70	C.P. Beauregard
16	1971	Perry Reservation	N. Ipswich/Rindge/ Sharon	409	Lenna W. Perry
*	1971	Hampton Salt Marshes	Hampton	4	Frank E. Leavitt
17	1972	Webster Wildlife and Natural	Kingston	125	The Webster Heirs
*	1973	Perry Reservation	New Ipswich	12	Lenna W. Perry
18	1974	Gap Mountain Reservation	Troy/Jaffrey	636	Gap Mountain Corp.
*	1974	Gap Mountain Reservation	Jaffrey	11	Land Vest Properties
*	1974	Gap Mountain Reservation	Troy	48	Land Vest Properties
*	1974	Monadnock Reservation	Jaffrey	7	Assoc. to Protect Monadnock
*	1974	Monadnock Reservation	Jaffrey	238	Edric A. Weld
*	1974	Gap Mountain Reservation	Troy/Jaffrey	111	Jane Fiske
19	1975	Jones Forest	Milton	227	Elizabeth Jones' Estate
20	1975	Bockes Memorial Forest	Londonderry	71	Patricia Ingersoll

21	1976	George F. Smith Woodlot	Newfields	49	George E. Smith
*	1976	Gap Mountain Reservation	Jaffrey	165	Charles L.J. Noble
22	1977	Hurlbert Swamp	Clarksville	34	Almon Young
*	1977	Hampton Salt Marshes	Hampton	4	Elizabeth Smith
23	1977	Perry Forest I	Rindge	74	Lenna W. Perry
24	1978	The Rocks	Bethlehem	1,319	John Lee and Martha Batchelder
25	1978	Conservation Center	Concord	17	John O. Morton
*	1978	Gap Mountain Reservation	Jaffrey	30	Edith E. Forbes
26	1978	Peirce Wildlife and Forest Reservation	Stoddard/Windsor	3,461	Elisabeth T. Babcock
27	1979	Merrimack River Outdoor Education and Conservation Area	Concord	1	W. Cate and R. Latham, Sr.
28	1979	Patrick Woodlot	Colebrook	70	David K. and Barbara M. Patrick
29	1979	Bretzfelder Park	Bethlehem	17	Estate of Helen Bretzfelder
30	1979	Thurston V. Williams Family Forest	Stoddard	379	Thurston Williams
31	1980	Woodland Associates Forest	New Boston	174	Woodland Associates
32	1980	Sidney Butler Smith Woodland	Tuftonboro	59	Sidney Butler Smith
*	1980	Merrimack River Outdoor Education and Conservation Center	Concord	68	R. Grossman, T. Frost, and T. LaCava
*	1980	Perry Reservation	Sharon	83	Lenna W. Perry
*	1981	Gap Mountain Reservation	Jaffrey	12	Land Vest Properties
33	1981	Beulah Land	Rindge	66	Hope Haney West
*	1981	Merrimack River Outdoor Education and Conservation Center	Concord	9	Concord Lumber Co.
34	1981	Troy Mills Wetland	Jaffrey	4	Troy Mills Inc.
35	1981	Bruce Forest	Dublin	23	Larry Rathbun
36	1982	McCabe Forest	Antrim	192	Dorothy McCabe
37	1982	High Blue	Walpole	164	Stephen Warner Estate
38	1982	Taves Forest	Roxbury/Marlborough	83	Judith deForest
39	1982	Taves Reservation	Roxbury	571	E.H. Taves and J. deForest Taves
40	1982	Brundage Forest	Pittsburg	238	Brundage Foundation Trustees
41	1982	Perry Forest II	Jaffrey	28	Lenna W. Perry
42	1982	Sharp Forest	Sandwich	57	Huldah Cheek Sharp
*	1983	Bretzfelder Park	Bethlehem	5	Leslie and Alice Dreier
43	1983	Big Island	Errol	50	Oxford Paper Company
44	1983	Morgan Forest	Jaffrey	52	Joseph O. Morgan
*	1983	Bretzfelder Park	Bethlehem	55	Raymond and Rosalie Little
45	1983	Guy I. Burch Forest	Freedom	20	A. Wihelmine Gibboney
46	1984	Eastman Forest	Grantham	40	Controlled Environment Corp.
47	1984	Grafton Pond Reservation	Grafton	940	William and Virginia Risley
*	1984	The Rocks	Bethlehem	20	Laurance Herbert
48	1984	Chute Forest	Hillsboro	124	Lionel and Yura Chute
49	1985	Rachel Adams Memorial Forest	Lincoln	12	Sherman Adams
50	1985	Stearns-Lamont Forest	Rindge	121	Richard H. Stearns
*	1985	Gap Mountain Reservation	Troy/Jaffrey	57	Eleanor R. Snelling
51	1985	F.L. Hill Wetland	Francestown	24	Elizabeth Hill-Houlihan
*	1985	Foster Conservancy	Henniker	60	Winslow Foster
*	1985	Big Island	Errol	106	J.M. Huber Corporation
*	1985	Monadnock Reservation	Dublin	103	William W. L. Glenn
52	1985	Hidden Valley Wildlife Area	Lyme	64	Lloyd E. Wilmott Estate
53	1985	Foster Conservancy	Henniker	60	Winslow and Johanna M. Foster
54	1986	Wilson Land, David	Sharon	934	Lenna Perry
*	1986	Hampton Salt Marshes	Hampton	7	Marion L. Penniman
55	1986	Langenau Forest	Wilmot	165	Doris Langenau
56	1986	Daniel Upton Forest	Stoddard	157	Margaret B. Cline
57	1986	Heald Tract	Wilton/Temple	340	P. Heald Jr., R. Heald, H. Rader, C. Sullivan
58	1986	Jennings Forest	New Durham	376	Ellen Jennings
*	1986	Gap Mountain Reservation	Troy	40	Albert Gins
*	1987	Langenau Forest	Wilmot	3	Kearsarge Cable Comm. Inc.

*	1987	Gap Mountain Reservation	Troy	20	John T. and Joan B. Tyler
*	1987	Daniel Upton Forest	Stoddard	6	George F. Cahill Jr.
59	1988	Etta and Leon Tilton Memorial Forest	Gilmanton	203	Arthur A. Tilton
60	1988	Everett Forest	Wilton	37	Edward N. Everett
61	1988	Royal C. Nemiah Forest	Lyme	105	Elizabeth Ladd and John C. Nemiah
62	1988	Weeks Forest	Gilford	86	John and Esther Weeks
63	1988	John and Anna King Forest	Deering	311	Anna M. King
64	1988	King-Hibbard Forest	Lyndeborough	36	Anna M. King
65	1988	Woodland Associates — King	New Boston	17	Anna M. King
*	1989	Monadnock Reservation	Jaffrey	1	Wilma H. Jewell
66	1989	Stimson Forest	Ossipee	45	William and Barbara Stimson
67	1989	Hutchins Forest	Canterbury	88	Quentin and Mary Hutchins
*	1990	Foster Conservancy	Henniker	91	Winslow Foster
*	1990	Merrimack River Outdoor Education and Conservation Center	Concord	5	Harold S. and Cecil D. White
*	1990	George F. Smith Woodlot	Newfields	30	Triton Corp.
68	1990	French-Harris Memorial Forest	Surry	138	William C. Harris
69	1990	Bear Island Forest	Meredith	56	George and Rita Mayo
*	1990	Bear Island Forest	Meredith	56	East Bear Island Assoc. Inc.
70	1991	Madame Sherri Forest	Chesterfield	488	Ann R. Stokes
71	1991	Emily and Theodore Hope Forest	Danbury	373	Theodore S. Hope
*	1991	Stearns-Lamont Forest	Rindge	2	Alice C. Stearns
72	1991	Pickerel Cove	Stoddard	127	CSB Cambridge Crossings Corp.
*	1991	Heald Tract	Wilton/Temple	70	Philip C. Heald Jr.
*	1991	Heald Tract	Wilton/Temple	2	Philip C. Heald Jr.
*	1991	Heald Tract	Wilton/Temple	142	R. Heald Jr., R. Heald, H. Rader, C. Sullivan
*	1991	Heald Tract	Wilton/Temple	4	Philip C. Heald Jr.
73	1991	Prince Pasture	Webster/Boscawen	92	Ida J. Prince
74	1991	Cockermouth Forest	Groton/Hebron	1,002	William B. Wadsworth
75	1992	Richardson Forest	Stratford	14	Joseph C. and Virginia Richardson
76	1992	Sudrabin Forest	Orange	60	Dorothy and Leon Sudrabin
*	1992	Taves Forest	Roxbury	89	E.H. Taves and J. deForest Taves
*	1992	Taves Forest	Marlborough	35	H. V. Taves and J. deForest Taves
*	1992	Taves Forest	Roxbury	57	Judith deForest
77	1992	Sanborn Memorial Forest	Epping	27	Leland C. Sanborn
78	1992	Morgan Forest II	Jaffrey	106	Joseph O. Morgan
79	1992	James and Eleanor Crider Forest	Stoddard	70	Eleanor S. Crider
80	1992	Indian Arrowhead Forest Preserve	Surry	282	James and Ruth Ewing
81	1992	Zephaniah Breed Forest	Weare	52	Jessie Vint
82	1993	Cabot Memorial Forest	Boscawen	57	Thomas D. Cabot
83	1993	Colby Hill Forest	Henniker	107	Eva M. Goss
84	1993	Jewell Forest	Jaffrey	16	Wilma Jewell
85	1993	Milt Street Tract	Sharon	14	John M. Street
86	1993	Allison Nims Piper Memorial Forest	Sullivan	199	R. Piper, D.L. Piper, P. Hanrahan, N. Murray
87	1993	Highland Lake Island	Washington	1	Town of Washington
88	1993	Van Zandt Williams Family Preserve	Westmoreland	43	Mary B. Zehnder
89	1994	Marks Memorial Forest	Alton	236	Emily H. Marks
90	1994	Kauffmann Forest	Stark	801	John M. Kauffmann
91	1994	Blodgett Forest	Grafton	100	Gard D. Blodgett and Joyce Dole
92	1995	Merriman Forest	Sandwich	102	Frederika W. Merriman
93	1995	Michael M. and Claudia Yatsevitch Forest	Cornish/Plainfield	800	Michael M. Yatsevitch
94	1995	Stephens Forest	Wilton	120	Edna B. Stephens
*	1995	Bear Island Forest	Meredith	40	B. Smith; R. and A. Mosher; L. Drew
95	1995	Arthur S. Flint Memorial Forest	Hebron	79	Rodger Greig
*	1995	Sidney Butler Smith Woodland	Tuftonboro	5	Margaret E. Centola
*	1995	Kauffmann Forest	Stark	123	John M. Kauffmann
*	1995	Kauffmann Forest	Stark	72	John M. Kauffmann

*	1996	Kauffmann Forest	Stark	62	Gerard M. Damiani Sr.
*	1996	Hay Reservation	Newbury	2	Robert and Lynne Bell
*	1996	Hay Reservation	Newbury	1	Margaret A. Rasweiler
*	1996	Peirce Wildlife and Forest Reservation	Stoddard	115	Mr. and Mrs. Donald R. Holland Sr.
96	1996	Millicent Scott Gardner Memorial Forest	Hollis	150	George and Millicent Gardner
97	1996	Quint Preserve	Richmond	290	John D. Quint
*	1996	Kauffmann Forest	Stark	14	Raymond Farrar and Marianne Boss
98	1997	United Brotherhood Credit Union	Conway	80	United Brotherhood Credit Union
99	1997	Rumrill Family Forest	Stoddard	77	Freeport Development Inc.
100	1997	High Watch Preserve	Effingham	1,035	Charles H. Watts II
101	1997	Roger D. Whittemore Reservation	Lyndeborough	99	Estate of Roger D. Whittemore Jr.
102	1997	The Cottrell Place	Hillsboro	115	Annette and Bill Cottrell
103	1997	Estes Forest	Concord	43	Frank B. and Marjorie W. Estes
104	1997	Natt W. Emerson Tract	Candia	67	William Emerson
105	1997	Paul and Thelma Ambeau Memorial Forest	Canterbury	20	Paul Ambeau
*	1997	Heald Tract	Wilton	101	Philip C. Heald Jr.
*	1997	Heald Tract	Wilton	15	P. Heald Jr., R. Heald, H. Rader, C. Sullivan
106	1997	Woodman Forest	Boscawen/Webster	115	Timothy W. Woodman
*	1997	Taves Reservation	Roxbury	106	Peter Doyle
*	1997	Kauffmann Forest	Stark	600	John M. Kauffmann
*	1997	The Cottrell Place	Hillsboro	4	Julie Crooks
107	1998	Monson Village	Milford/Hollis	37	Red Mill Lane Assoc. Realty Trust
*	1998	Jennings Forest	New Durham	20	B.A.W. Realty Inc.
108	1998	Monson Village	Hollis	30	C. Kennedy and K. Gibbons
109	1998	Shea Reservation	Webster	122	Lucille F. Shea
110	1998	Sharon Bog	Sharon	72	Pike Industries, Inc.
*	1998	Monson Village	Hollis	30	Anonymous
*	1998	Monson Village	Milford/Hollis	125	Russell and Geraldine Dickerman
111	1998	Olsen Family Forest	Sullivan	775	Stanley C. Olsen
*	1998	Michael M. and Claudia Yatsevitch	Cornish/Plainfield	120	Stanley C. Olsen
*	1998	Heald Tract	Wilton/Temple	183	P.Heald Jr., R. Heald, H. Rader
*	1998	Cooper Cedar Woods	New Durham	107	R. Cooper and C. Walworth
112	1998	Rosemary's Woods	Danbury	250	Anonymous
113	1998	Victor's Woods	Danbury/Alexandria	255	Anonymous
*	1999	Hay Reservation	Newbury	37	Washington Street Realty Corp.
114	1999	Wilkins-Campbell Forest	Deering	215	United Church of Christ
*	1999	David Wilson Land	Sharon	12	Erazim Kohak
115	1999	Simons Preserve	Weare	118	Elizabeth Simons
*	1999	Beulah Land	Rindge	16	Louise T. Grummon
*	1999	Weeks Forest	Gilford	21	Robert and Mary Pomeroy
116	1999	Deering Preserve	Deering	210	Beatrice T. Hunter
117	1999	Natale and Willcox Brown Forest	Dunbarton	159	Natale and Willcox Brown
118	1999	Porter-Rogerson Forest	Tamworth	203	Jean P. Rogerson
*	1999	Wilkins-Campbell Forest	Deering	6	Jane N. Spragg
119	1999	Journey's End/Bell-Cofield Forest	Washington	202	Nancy D. Blasdell
120	1999	Haffenreffer Forest	Enfield	199	John Haffenreffer
121	2000	Welch Family Farm Forest	Hancock	243	Elizabeth Welch
*	2000	Conservation Center	Concord	6	Harold and Vera Morin
*	2000	Kauffmann Forest	Stark	23	George D. Reardon
122	2000	Creek Farm	Portsmouth	35	Lillian Noel
123	2000	Lamprey River Forest	Epping	108	Gail Chase
TOTAL RESERVATIONS:				**32,673**	

Society for the Protection of New Hampshire Forests
History of Land Transferred to Public Agencies and Non-Profits

Date Acquired	Date Transferred	Property Name	Town	Acreage	Transferred To
1911	1948	Welsh, H. (Sunapee State Park)	Newbury/Sunapee	256	State of N.H. (D.R.E.D.)
1911	1948	Emerson Paper/Draper (Sunapee)	Newbury/Sunapee	382	State of N.H. (D.R.E.D.)
1912	1979	International Paper Co.(Lost River)	Woodstock	577	W.M.N.F.
1917	1917	Emerson Paper Co. (Royal Arch)	Springfield	40	Town of Springfield
1918	1950	Champlain Realty (Kearsarge)	Warner	521	State of N.H. (D.R.E.D.)
1922	1948	Hollis, A. (Sunapee State Park)	Newbury	80	State of N.H. (D.R.E.D.)
1922	1962	Pearson, W. (City Hill)	Nelson	11	Town of Nelson
1924	1949	Emerson Paper Co.(Sunapee State Park)	Goshen	33	State of N.H. (D.R.E.D.)
1924	1948	Emerson Paper Co.(Sunapee State Park)	Newbury	184	State of N.H. (D.R.E.D.)
1925	1960	Littlefield, I. (Dutchman Pond)	Springfield	50	Town of Springfield
1927	1935	International Paper Co.(Lost River)	Woodstock	48	W.M.N.F.
1928	1947	Profile and Flume Hotels	Lincoln	913	State of N.H. (D.R.E.D.)
1931	1935	Bodwell	Franconia	50	Town of Franconia
1932	1932	Freeburn, M. (Meadow Pond State Forest)	Gilmanton	42	State of N.H. (D.R.E.D.)
1932	1932	Conant, S. (Binney Pond State Park	New Ipswich	77	State of N.H. (D.R.E.D.)
1933	1933	Allee, L. (Strawberry Hill State Forest)	Bethlehem	59	State of N.H. (D.R.E.D.)
1934	1948	Donigan (Sunapee State Park)	Newbury	250	State of N.H. (D.R.E.D.)
1935	1935	Davis (Carroll American Realty)	Sutton/Salisbury/Warner	1525	State of N.H. (D.R.E.D.)
1936	1936	White, G. (Chesterfield Gorge)	Chesterfield	13	State of N.H. (D.R.E.D.)
1937	1948	Chadbourne (Sunapee State Park)	Newbury	3	State of N.H. (D.R.E.D.)
1938	1938	Carroll, J. (Shadow Hill State Forest)	Sutton	19	State of N.H. (D.R.E.D.)
1939	1945	Whitford, R. (Ordway Woods)	Warner	4	Warner Conservation Commisson
1941	1942	Partridge, A.	Sutton	1	Sutton Conservation Commission
1961	1963	Morgan, W. (Kearsarge)	Wilmot	585	State of N.H. (D.R.E.D.)
1964	1964	Shaw, H.	Hampton	22	State of N.H. (F. and G. Dept.)
1966	1975	Rogers, K. (Bear Brook State Park)	Allenstown	90	State of N.H. (D.R.E.D.)
1967	1979	Fogg, J.	Hampton	10	Audubon Society of NH
1967	1970	Butterfield	Pembroke	28	Town of Pembroke
1967	1968	Edgerton, H.C. (Cole Pond)	Enfield and Grantham	1367	State of N.H. (F. and G. Dept.)
1968	1979	Fogg, R.	Hampton	6	Audubon Society of NH
1968	1979	Lamb, N.	Hampton	2	Audubon Society of NH
1969	1979	Palmer, A.	Hampton	7	Audubon Society of NH
1969	1975	Dodge, I. (Kearsarge)	Wilmot	78	State of N.H. (D.R.E.D.)
1970	1979	Garland, M.	Hampton	5	Audubon Society of NH
1971	1971	Churchill Real Estate /Douglass	Wilmot	5	State of N.H. (D.R.E.D.)
1973	1975	Tasker, V. (Kearsarge)	Wilmot	215	State of N.H. (D.R.E.D.)
1973	1979	Remick, E.	Tamworth	5	Town of Tamworth
1975	1975	Langley, F. (Gile State Forest)	Wilmot	37	State of N.H. (D.R.E.D.)
1975	1977	Peaslee, E.	Sandwich	70	Town of Sandwich
1975	1980	Jones	Milton	27	N.H. Farm Museum
1976	1976	Boies, D.	North Hampton	51	Town of North Hampton
1976	1979	Astles, R. (Bear Brook State Park)	Allenstown	27	State of N.H. (D.R.E.D.)
1976	1976	Loring, B. (Belknap Reservation)	Gilmanton/Gilford	805	State of N.H. (D.R.E.D.)
1976	1986	Dulac, R.	Andover	60	State of N.H. (F. and G. Dept.)

1976	1979	Hurlin, R.	Antrim	10	Town of Antrim
1976	1979	Smith, E.	Exeter	47	Town of Exeter
1976	1982	Orr, D.	Freemont	103	Town of Freemont
1976	1977	Paige, H.	Sandwich	16	Town of Sandwich
1977	1978	Cheney, W. (Kearsarge Wildlife Area)	Andover	108	State of N.H. (F. and G. Dept.)
1977	1979	Densmore/Methodist Church	Charlestown	10	State of N.H. (D.R.E.D.)
1977	1979	Dorland, F. (Cardigan)	Orange	146	State of N.H. (D.R.E.D.)
1977	1981	Wheeler, H. (Monadnock State Park)	Jaffrey	91	State of N.H. (D.R.E.D.)
1977	1978	Sawyer, R.	Atkinson	48	Town of Atkinson
1978	1979	Applecrest Farm Orchards	Hampton	16	Audubon Society of N.H.
1979	1989	Smith, O.C.	Sandwich	51	W.M.N.F.
1980	1982	Sanborn, H.	Sandwich	65	W.M.N.F.
1981	1982	Wood Farm Associates	Lebanon	820	City of Lebanon
1982	1984	Briggs 2/5 interest	Hancock	275	Harris Center for Conservation Education
1982	1983	McClellan, R.	Albany	1	W.M.N.F.
1985	1987	Boothman Forest	Randolph	243	W.M.N.F.
1986	1992	Heald Tract/Pack Monadnock	Temple	44	State of N.H. (D.R.E.D.)
1986	1987	Lovewell Mtn. (Pillsbury State Park)	Washington	490	State of N.H. (D.R.E.D.)
1986	1987	Moore (Gilson Pond) (Monadnock State Park)	Jaffrey	2	State of N.H. (D.R.E.D.)
1986	1992	Nichols Tract (Kearsarge)	Warner	30	State of N.H. (D.R.E.D.)
1986	1987	Goodwin #3	Plainfield	16	Town of Plainfield
1987	1989	Currier	Hampstead	32	Town of Hampstead
1988	1990	King Property	Lyndeborough	50	State of N.H. (F. and G. Dept.)
1988	1990	Goodwin Property	Enfield	96	State of N.H. (F. and G.)
1988	1989	King Property	Francestown	388	Town of Francestown
1988	1989	Marshall Property	Bethlehem	100	W.M.N.F.
1989	1990	Trinity House Camp, Inc.	Atkinson	59	Town of Atkinson
1990	1993	Warner Property	Hart's Location	10	W.M.N.F.
1990	1992	Stark Property	Stark	202	W.M.N.F.
1993	1998	Weeks	Durham	19	Town of Durham
1996	1998	Currier Property	Kingston/E. Kingston	104	State of N.H. (F. and G. Dept.)
1996	1998	Meserve Property	Fitzwilliam	74	State of N.H. - (D.R.E.D.)
1998	1998	Ct. River Driver's Trust	Colebrook	20	State of N.H. (F. and G. Dept.)
1998	1999	Olsen	Cornish	271	Town of Cornish

NOTE: *This list does not include over 60 transactions totalling over 100,000 acres for properties that the Society helped protect with other state, federal, and conservation agencies. These properties include Crawford Notch (5,925 acres) in 1913; the balance of Franconia Notch (5,244 acres) in 1928; Gile Forest (6,638 acres) in 1973; Pine River State Forest (3,300 acres) in 1977; Bretton Woods (6,576 acres) in 1979; Pine Mountain/Pilot Range (10,538 acres) in Gorham/North Umberland; and Nash Stream Forest (42,217 acres) in Stark/Odell/Columbia. For a complete list, contact the Society.*

Society for the Protection of New Hampshire Forests Conservation Easements (*Grantee Interest*) as of 1/01/01

Town	Grantor	Acreage	Date Acquired
Alexandria	J. Willcox Brown	110	1996.11.26
Alstead	Warren and Nancy Hall	219	1996.09.27
Alton	Jakob and Anna Mutzbauer	352	1987.11.11
Andover	Martin and Marianne Fairall	7	1992.09.04
Andover	Ragged Mountain Fish and Game Club	976	1995.01.23
Andover	Taunton Hill Realty Trust	210	1992.09.06
Andover	Barbara Wood	54	1987.12.31
Andover	Douglas Wood	96	1987.12.31
Andover	Douglas Wood	48	1990.11.26
Andover/Salisbury	Elliot and Catherine Reiner	849	1993.12.15
Antrim	Nancy and James Dennison	90	1991.09.09
Antrim	Herbert Nilson	47	1999.10.13
Antrim/Windsor	The Nature Conservancy	484	1999.11.05
Ashland/Holderness	Philip Preston	600	1999.12.29
Barrington	Stephen Jeffery	65	1984.10.23
Bartlett	David Armington	47	1997.12.08
Bartlett/Jackson	Bigelow and Jeanne Crocker	196	1989.12.15
Bedford	Frank Grogan and Helen Evans	160	1986.08.21
Belmont	Robert and Paul Breck	10	1987.09.08
Bethlehem	Suzannah Hatt	16	1993.06.08
Bethlehem	White Mountain School	120	1993.06.01
Boscawen	Timothy Woodman	93	1990.12.03
Bow	William and Cynthia Gunn	22	1999.06.16
Brentwood	Victor and Emily Schmalzer	64	1999.12.29
Bristol	Ann Giles	32	1992.09.24
Bristol	Samuel Worthen	118	1991.08.06
Campton/Rumney	Henry and Pauline Parker	600	2000.10.19
Canaan	Finn Caspersen	26	1971.12.28
Canterbury	Gerow Brill	61	1989.03.27
Canterbury	David Buten	20	1997.01.10
Canterbury	Town of Canterbury	22	1996.12.31
Canterbury	David Curtis	39	1989.10.17
Chatham/Conway NH and Fryeburg, ME	Douglas Burnell	794	1993.07.20
Clarksville	Joan Shatney and Kathleen McKinnon	49	2000.07.05
Colebrook/Dixville	Peter Johnson	105	1990.06.29
Concord	Lawrence Hale	60	2000.12.29
Concord	Lester Spear	71	1991.04.26
Concord	Spofford Farm Associates	33	1986.12.29
Concord	Timothy Woodman	178	1989.02.03
Conway	Carol Boynton	18	1990.12.27
Conway	Carol Boynton	76	1990.12.27
Conway	Highfields Farm Inc.	70	1993.03.12
Conway	Chester and Lydia Lucy	91	1988.12.06
Conway	Margaret Thorne, Thaddeus and Virginia Thorne, Lydia and Chester Lucy, Mary and Kingdon Gould, Harold and Evelyn Thorne	35	1990.04.27
Danbury	Mark Chamberlin	95	1987.12.30
Danbury	Theodore and Emily Hope	108	1987.12.23
Danbury	Mary Lyn Ray	80	1987.12.29

Danbury	Mary Lyn Ray	82	1987.12.29
Danbury	Olan and Artelia Ray	53	1991.04.09
Danbury	Walter and Judith Walker	196	1992.01.27
Danville	Charles Churchill Stafford	45	1992.12.23
Deerfield	Frances Menard	230	1994.09.23
Deering	Harriet Cope	132	1997.09.16
Deering	Robert L.V. French	267	1976.12.15
Deering	William and Patricia Thompson	120	1995.12.20
Deering	William and Patricia Thompson	13	1998.12.30
Deering	Beverly Yeaple	77	1998.09.28
Dorchester	Massachusetts Audubon Society Inc.	63	1991.03.12
Dover	Dennis and Nancy Quinlan	6	1998.10.20
Dover	Ruth Sousane	46	1998.10.20
Dublin	William Allis	190	1987.12.24
Dublin	Grenville Clark Jr.	51	1983.05.12
Dublin	Town of Dublin	151	1999.07.26
Dublin	William and Amory Glenn	197	1986.10.17
Dublin	William and Amory Glenn	148	1988.11.16
Dublin	William Glenn	42	1994.11.22
Dublin	Ellen Kennelly	52	1989.12.12
Dublin	Nancy Perkins	127	1986.12.30
Dublin	Louisa Spencer	134	1983.01.31
Dublin	Louisa Spencer	71	1992.12.02
Dublin	Samuel Spiker	43	1987.06.29
Dublin	Tula Stowell	222	1991.12.23
Dunbarton	Robert L.V. French	127	1985.12.10
Dunbarton	Frederic Greenhalge	50	1990.06.06
Dunbarton	Richard and Jane Hough	130	1986.12.31
Durham	The Nature Conservancy	18	1998.03.04
Eaton	Carol Boynton	48	1996.12.02
Enfield	John Haffenreffer	195	1999.12.30
Francestown	Harriet Cope	53	1990.12.31
Francestown	John and Anna King	79	1989.12.19
Francestown	John and Anna King	61	1989.12.19
Francestown	Kingsbury Timber Corp	35	1991.07.31
Francestown/Deering	Harriet Cope	14	1995.05.02
Franconia	John Coffin	96	1990.02.22
Freedom	Sara Kaplan	118	1991.12.23
Gilford	Thomas and Lucile Allen	18	1994.12.27
Gilford	Parkman and Helen Howe	23	1988.12.30
Gilford	Parkman and Helen Howe	25	1989.12.15
Gilford	Parkman and Helen Howe	36	1990.12.19
Gilford	Parkman Howe	188	1993.09.27
Gilford	Robert and Mary Pomeroy	10	1999.11.19
Gilford	Arthur Tilton	60	1987.12.30
Gilsum	Alexander Gardner	35	1991.12.13
Gilsum and Sullivan	John Calhoun	325	1999.12.21
Goffstown	Kingsbury Timber Corp	202	2000.01.12
Goffstown	Eileen Phinney	122	1989.11.08
Goshen/Lempster	Sylvan and Virginia Schendler	364	2000.11.29
Greenland	Rosamond Hughes	20	1988.05.05
Greenland	Rosamond Hughes	118	1996.12.31
Green's Grant	Glenn House/Mt. Washington Summit Road Co.	192	1994.03.10
Hampstead	Robert L.V. French	7	1979.12.18

Hampstead	Trust for Public Land	17	1998.09.29
Hampstead	Walworth and Mary Louise Williams	7	1982.03.20
Hampstead	Walworth and Mary Louise Williams	13	1982.03.20
Hampstead	Walworth and Mary Louise Williams	80	1986.11.10
Hampstead/Atkinson	Robert L.V. French	34	1978.12.27
Hampstead/Derry	Governors Island	207	1984.10.10
Hampton Falls	William and Claudine Ackroyd	63	1993.11.10
Hampton Falls and Kensington	Paul and Mary Avery	63	1996.12.23
Hancock	Eleanor Briggs	1978	1985.05.14
Hanover	Richard Karl	106	1997.12.24
Hanover	Allen and Nancy King	100	1977.04.12
Harrisville	Anne Howe	103	1998.12.09
Haverhill	John Rogers	139	1997.12.31
Haverhill	Trust for N.H. Lands	150	1991.07.30
Henniker	James Davis and Mary Polly Davis	83	1989.12.18
Hill	John Chandler	43	1993.08.18
Hill	James and Mae Quimby	316	1979.12.26
Hill	Mary Thompson	136	1993.06.08
Hillsborough	Edwina Czajkowski and Judith Pratt	146	1986.12.15
Holderness	Ellen Barry	21	1988.08.30
Holderness	Boulderwood Trust	14	1991.12.13
Holderness/Center Harbor	Gray Twombly	23	1986.10.30
Hollis	Hollis and Ellen Nichols	76	1986.03.12
Hopkinton	Meadowsend Saw Mill, Inc.	69	1999.12.22
Hopkinton	Meadowsend Timberlands	348	1999.09.03
Hopkinton	Meadowsend Timberlands	7	1999.09.03
Hopkinton	Meadowsend Timberlands	880	1999.12.22
Hopkinton	Binney Wells	115	1984.12.28
Hopkinton	Evermore Timberlands Corp.	230	1999.12.22
Hopkinton/Henniker/Weare	The Marshall Fund	283	2000.12.29
Jackson	Arthur Holcombe, Thomas Holcombe, Elizabeth Milliken	70	2000.05.23
Jaffrey	Harriet Hollister Andrews	179	1986.03.27
Jaffrey	Suzanne Pierce	50	1987.12.30
Jaffrey	Frederick Richardson	62	1976.02.23
Keene	Avril de la Cretaz	110	1994.12.28
Keene	James and Jean Henderson	302	1999.12.15
Keene	Michael Kidder (Stonewall Farm)	62	1999.03.25
Keene	George Kingsbury	100	1986.12.31
Keene	Stearns Hill Timber Watch, LLC	608	2000.12.19
Kensington	Charles Hodges	178	1987.02.04
Kensington and So. Hampton	Leslie and Martha Briggs	176	2000.06.27
Lancaster	John, William, Sinclair Weeks, Frances Lawrence, Beatrice Bast	479	2000.06.28
Lebanon	Connecticut River Watershed Council	20	1997.04.07
Lebanon	City of Lebanon (Boston Lot)	331	1997.03.31
Lebanon	City of Lebanon (Cole Park)	16	1997.03.17
Lebanon	City of Lebanon (Farnum Hill)	880	1997.03.17
Lee	Timothy and Lynn Cook	77	2000.11.29
Lee	Eleanor Earle	130	1986.08.28
Lee	Timothy and Eliza Earle	13	1986.08.28
Lyme	Katharine Beal	15	1987.04.27
Lyme	Stewart and Margaret Dall	15	1986.12.27
Lyme	George and Monique Guest	5	1986.12.27
Lyme	Lyme Hill and Valley Association	13	1986.12.16
Lyme	Lyme Hill and Valley Association	29	1986.12.16

Lyme	Lyme Hill and Valley Association	12	1987.04.28
Lyme	Donald and Keita Metz	22	1986.12.27
Lyme	Montshire Museum, Inc.	7	1989.02.15
Lyme	Everett and Verna Rich	23	1986.12.27
Lyme	Doris Schriever, Linda Fox and Karen Laudon	23	1986.12.27
Lyme	Doris Schriever	8	1986.12.11
Lyme	Bayne Stevenson	14	1986.12.31
Lyme	Patrice and Kenneth Super	18	1986.12.27
Lyme	Patrice and Kenneth Super	11	1986.12.27
Lyme	Patrice and Kenneth Super	5	1986.12.27
Lyme	Patrice and Kenneth Super	2	1986.12.27
Lyme	Patrice and Kenneth Super	3	1986.12.27
Lyme	Henry and Freda Swan	18	1986.12.27
Marlborough	Charlton and Diana MacVeagh	99	1988.12.20
Milton	Carl Siemon	1259	1990.12.27
Milton	Carl Siemon	32	1990.12.27
Milton	Carl Siemon	11	1993.12.27
Milton	Carl Siemon	246	1994.12.12
Milton	Charlotte Stewart	92	1993.05.06
Moultonboro	Richard and Elizabeth Foster	99	1986.08.27
Moultonboro	Richard and Elizabeth Foster	10	1987.11.01
Moultonboro	Richard and Elizabeth Foster	27	1991.08.24
New Boston	Louis and Gail Gallerani	89	2000.08.22
New Boston	Town of New Boston	82	1993.07.26
New Boston	Janet and David Nixon	75	1990.12.28
New Boston/ Lyndeborough/Francestown	Deland	700	1989.12.20
New Ipswich	New England Forestry Foundation, Inc.	302	1998.09.03
New Ipswich	Nathaniel Ober	44	1992.10.08
New London	James and Hilary Cleveland	21	1977.06.12
Newbury	Audubon Society of N.H.	360	1989.12.14
Newbury	William and Margaret Weiler	274	1996.12.31
North Hampton	Eugenia and David Boies	13	2000.05.23
Nottingham/ Deerfield/Raymond	Christopher Stillbach	402	1997.12.17
Orford	Katharine Hewitt and Mary Ann Lewis	8	1988.12.27
Orford	Stephen and Joyce Lamb	23	1989.03.31
Orford	Bruce and Sarah Schwaegler	196	1991.07.15
Orford/Lyme	Timothy and Lynn Cook	27	1986.12.17
Orford/Piermont	Alan Thorndike	290	1992.06.26
Ossipee	State of N.H. — Fish and Game Department	163	1984.12.27
Ossipee	Rose and Charles Smith	167	2000.12.29
Pelham	Paul and Mary Lou Fisher	34	1990.10.01
Peterborough	Perkins Bass	177	1976.12.27
Peterborough	Perkins Bass	51	1985.09.13
Peterborough	John Bross	260	1978.12.27
Peterborough	Placidia Carter	163	1976.12.14
Peterborough	Everett Clement	128	1979.12.19
Peterborough	Mary Frances Connard	52	1992.07.23
Peterborough	Richard Fernald	23	1986.12.18
Peterborough	Joanne Kane	310	1978.12.21
Peterborough	Richard Moore	65	1991.11.08
Peterborough	Anne Frantz, Mary Bowden and Abby Niss	115	1986.10.02
Peterborough	Upland Farm Corporation	60	1986.05.05

Plainfield	Achilles and Jill Rustici	19	1996.09.20
Randolph	Margaret Meiklejohn and Ellen Dempster	60	1998.02.23
Rindge	Robert Goundry	159	1993.12.21
Rindge	Daniel and Jacqueline Johnson	13	1993.12.21
Rindge/Fitzwilliam	Russell Lowe	696	1993.05.07
Roxbury	Thomas and Irene Benson	40	1993.12.13
Rumney	Loon Lake Conservation Trust	67	1991.02.22
Rumney	Loon Lake - John and Andrew Alger and Augusta Prince	11	1991.02.22
Rumney	Loon Lake - John and Judith Alger	5	1991.02.22
Rumney	Loon Lake - Andrew and Frances Alger	3	1991.02.22
Rumney	Loon Lake - Geraldine and Vickers Burdett	2	1991.02.22
Rumney	Loon Lake - Virginia Stephenson	16	1991.02.22
Salisbury	Jacob and Mary Ann Higgs	90	1990.12.28
Salisbury	John Kepper	83	2000.12.11
Sanbornton	Angelo and Romayne DiCuollo	113	2000.12.19
Sanbornton	Ralph and Olive Meader	122	1987.05.11
Sanbornton	Ralph and Olive Meader	62	1989.12.31
Sanbornton	Brian and Mary Mokler	21	1995.01.03
Sanbornton	New England Forestry Foundation, Inc.	500	1995.07.25
Sandwich	Oliver Butterworth	22	1990.09.17
Sandwich	Julianne and Richard Daniels	143	1994.12.05
Sandwich	Peter Pohl	129	1998.12.28
Sharon	Donald and Cynthia Burgess	50	2000.12.14
Sharon	Will Fenno	48	2000.12.11
Sharon	Erazim and Sheree Kohak	10	1982.12.27
Springfield	James and Hilary Cleveland	23	1977.06.12
Stark	John Kauffmann	90	1990.08.31
Stark	John Kauffmann	10	1990.08.31
Stark	John Kauffmann	130	1990.08.31
Stark	John Kauffmann	60	1990.08.31
Stark	George and Joan Lamphere	600	1990.08.31
Stark	Percy Summer Club	134	1991.09.25
Stark	Mary Sloat	100	1986.09.19
Stoddard	George Cahill	35	1989.12.22
Stoddard	George Cahill	64	1989.12.22
Stoddard	George Cahill	11	1989.12.22
Stoddard	George Cahill	800	1999.10.08
Stoddard	Lakesfalls Associates	579	1980.11.15
Stoddard	Trevor and Beatrice Price	800	1989.08.16
Stoddard	Frances Rumrill	110	1987.12.31
Stoddard	Sweet Water Trust	732	1994.10.28
Stoddard/Sullivan/Marlow/ Gilsum/Washington	Andorra Forest Limited Partnership	11000	1990.12.21
Stoddard	Andorra Forest Limited Partnership	40	1995.04.15
Strafford	George Lovejoy	200	1978.12.20
Strafford	George Lovejoy	200	1979.12.19
Strafford	George Lovejoy	507	1980.11.18
Stratford	Emmanuel Marceau	1300	1992.11.06
Success	James River Corporation	88	1989.06.12
Sugar Hill	Edna Glaessel	76	1989.06.05
Sugar Hill	Selden Hannah	645	1991.01.30
Sugar Hill	Katharine Holman	54	1996.08.30
Sugar Hill	William and Sarah Pinney	120	1989.06.05
Sullivan	Edward and Eleene McCann	35	2000.11.09

Sullivan	Craig Stockwell and Sarah Mustin	322	2000.10.31
Sullivan	Roger and Ann Sweet	82	1998.12.09
Sullivan	Erickson and Wendy Van de Poll	49	2000.11.28
Sullivan/Stoddard	John and Jean Hoffman	158	1995.09.06
Sullivan	John and Jean Hoffman	438	1998.08.24
Sullivan	John and Jean Hoffman	106	1998.12.17
Sullivan	John and Jean Hoffman	47	1999.12.29
Sutton	Roger Freeman	247	1996.03.14
Sutton	Robert Bristol	252	1992.12.28
Sutton	Edwin Keith	52	1989.12.27
Sutton	Edwin Keith	57	1993.12.16
Sutton	Edwin Keith	2	1995.06.22
Swanzey	Geraldine Hall	70	1992.12.18
Tamworth	Richard Alt	10	1983.12.15
Tamworth	Richard Alt	94	1986.12.11
Tamworth	Louis and Ruth Flaccus	38	1983.12.23
Tamworth	David Little	176	1999.12.28
Tamworth	David Little and Helen Mesick	378	1999.11.04
Tuftonboro	Jane Colburn, Kathryn Scott, Theodore Shohl	50	1991.10.31
Wakefield	Elizabeth Herberich	131	1990.10.25
Wakefield	Carl Siemon	135	1993.12.27
Walpole	Powell Cabot	461	1992.12.18
Walpole	Joan, Jan and Carol Galloway	256	1999.12.29
Walpole	Joan Galloway	352	1999.12.29
Walpole	Ann and Carl Jacobs and Francis Faulkner	49	1989.10.17
Warner	Victor and Maxine Kumin	108	1995.12.18
Weare	Greentree Land and Lumber Company	331	1999.12.22
Weare	John and Anna King	89	1991.05.13
Weare	Gordon Tiffany	112	1991.01.29
Weare	Peggy Toll	130	1997.12.30
Webster	Richard George	69	2000.12.26
Webster	Jean Talbot	56	1988.11.08
Wentworth/Dorchester	Thomas and Grace Fraser	255	1995.12.11
Westmoreland	Doris Rouner	183	1987.12.30
Westmoreland/Walpole	Philip Faulkner	302	1990.12.18
Wilmot	Robert L.V. French	467	1975.12.09
Wilmot	Lois Spearman	3	1989.06.14
Wilmot	Morton Waite	38	1989.03.23
Wilmot	Richard and Elizabeth Webb	950	1975.06.02
Wilmot	Donald Hall	7	1987.12.28
Wilmot/Andover	Donald Hall	151	1992.07.14
Wilton	Helen Rader	129	2000.12.08
Wilton	Edna Stephens	198	1988.02.10
Wilton	Stanley and Claudia Young	52	1992.04.02
Wilton	John Yurcak	11	2000.04.12
Windsor	Eric and Pauline Wilton	76	1996.12.27
Wolfeboro	Edwin and Florence Benker	65	1993.09.01
Wolfeboro	Ann Mason	112	1992.01.28
Wolfeboro	Cecily Clark, Cecily Long, Perrin Long	355	1994.05.28
Wolfeboro/Ossipee	Cecily Clark	112	1994.05.28

Society for the Protection of New Hampshire Forests
Conservation Easements (Executory Interest) as of 1/01/01

Date Acquired	Grantor	Town	Acreage	Grantee
1982.12.15	Pan Northern Company	Acworth	535	Acworth Conservation Commission
1988.04.14	Mary Burroughs	Alstead	77	Town of Alstead
1990.09.14	Sally Barbarossa	Alton	86	Alton Conservation Commission
1990.06.28	James Piper, Elizabeth Gaskell, Patricia Graves	Alton	10	Lakes Region Conservation Trust
1989.02.02	Paul and Jane Fenton	AndoverAndover	60	Conservation Commission
1982.03.22	Walworth and Mary Louise Williams	Atkinson	10	Atkinson Conservation Commission
1992.12.30	Fred Goodrich	Barnstead	116	Town of Barnstead
1993.03.01	Lynn Goodrich Guenther	Barnstead	5	Town of Barnstead
1991.08.15	James and Ann Schulz	Barrington	48	Barrington Conservation Commission
1974.09.08	Ralph and Virginia Catterall	Bristol	80	Bristol Conservation Commission
1979.12.28	Robert Burroughs	Canterbury	264	Merrimack County Conservation District
1988.12.22	Daniel and Mary Cheever	Center Harbor	2	Squam Lakes Conservation Society
1981.12.10	Edward Dane	Center Harbor	10	Lakes Region Conservation Trust
1981.12.10	Edward Dane	Center Harbor	5	Lakes Region Conservation Trust
1977.10.27	John Soper	Charlestown	40	Connecticut River Watershed Council
1990.04.11	Bois de Brodeur Trust	Concord	33	Concord Conservation Trust
1977.07.13	Warren and Elizabeth Richards	Concord	114	Richards Community Forest, Inc.
1979.12.14	Zenaide Bradley	Dalton	263	Connecticut River Watershed Council
1980.12.12	Constance Greason	Dalton	247	Coos County Conservation District
1981.11.16	Vera Smith	Dalton	14	Coos County Conservation District
1974.08.24	Dark Pond Inc.	Dublin	139	Dark Pond Inc.
1979.07.12	Alan and Judy Edelkind	Dublin	28	Dublin Conservation Commission
1983.01.31	Louisa Spencer	Dublin	5	Dublin Conservation Commission
1985.12.19	Alson and Patricia Taylor	Dunbarton	145	Dunbarton Conservation Commission
1998.03.04	Charlotte Chase	Durham	3	The Nature Conservancy
1989.09.25	Ellen Hill	Francestown	135	Francestown Conservation Commission
1989.04.28	Harold and Constance Varnum	Francestown	46	Francestown Conservation Commission
1978.07.18	Joseph and Mary Fobes	Franconia/ Sugar Hill	257	Grafton County Conservation District
1991.12.10	William Champlin	Gilford	126	Lakes Region Conservation Trust
1977.08.02	James Quigg	Grafton	400	Town of Grafton
1982.12.30	Herman and Barbara Parker	Greenland	153	Rockingham County Conservation District
1980.07.21	Walworth and Mary Louise Williams	Hampstead	58	Hampstead Conservation Commission
1983.12.15	Thelma Babbitt	Hancock	55	Harris Center for Conservation Education
1986.12.20	Mary Garland	Hancock	59	Harris Center for Conservation Education
1992.03.24	Forbes Leland and Karlene Leland	Hancock	77	Harris Center for Conservation Education
1984.12.26	Henry Grunebaum	Haverhill	39	Grafton County Conservation District
1985.12.12	Henry Grunebaum	Haverhill	126	Grafton County Conservation District
1984.03.28	Burleigh Land Ltd. Partnership - Basin Island	Holderness	1	Squam Lakes Conservation Society
1984.03.28	Burleigh Land Ltd. Partnership - Kate Island	Holderness	1	Squam Lakes Conservation Society
1991.04.15	James Crawford	Holderness	37	Town of Holderness
1992.07.30	Mary Perry	Holderness	8	Lakes Region Conservation Trust
1991.05.24	Squam Lakes Association	Holderness	30	Squam Lakes Conservation Society
1991.03.05	Pierce Beij	Holderness/ Center Harbor	175	Squam Lakes Conservation Society
1990.11.21	Pinehurst Association	Holderness/ Sandwich	173	Lakes Region Conservation Trust
1989.07.11	Harold and Elizabeth Janeway	Hopkinton	6	Hopkinton Conservation Commission
1989.07.11	Donna Murphy	Hopkinton	13	Hopkinton Conservation Commission
1977.12.30	Alex, Samuel, Robert Burgess and Abby Rockett	Jackson	120	Jackson Conservation Commission
1993.02.11	Highland Farm Trust	Jackson	73	Jackson Conservation Commission
1986.12.22	Alice and John Pepper	Jackson	35	Jackson Conservation Commission
1976.12.29	Barbara Rockwell	Jackson	224	Jackson Conservation Commission
1986.12.29	Robert and Lorraine Tilney	Jackson	49	Jackson Conservation Commission
1982.12.29	Eugene Twaronite and Josephine Kelleher	Landaff	8	Grafton County Conservation District
1999.11.17	Charles Brady	Lee	60	Lee Conservation Commission
1980.03.11	Thomas and Jean Brown	Lee	18	Town of Lee
2000.11.29	Christopher and Julie Cook	Lee	77	Town of Lee
1988.11.09	Katharine Beal	Lyme	12	Lyme Conservation Commission
1988.11.09	Katharine Beal	Lyme	62	Lyme Conservation Commission

1975.11.14	Ruth Demarest	Lyme	229	Lyme Conservation Commission
1987.12.23	Katharine Hewitt, Mary Ann Lewis, and Bayne Stevenson	Lyme	3	Lyme Conservation Commission
1987.12.23	Katharine Hewitt, Mary Ann Lewis, and and Bayne Stevenson	Lyme	18	Lyme Conservation Commission
1985.12.31	Donald and Keita Metz	Lyme	6	Lyme Conservation Commission
1985.12.31	Donald and Keita Metz	Lyme	9	Lyme Conservation Commission
1988.12.29	Jerome and Sherrill Robinson	Lyme	65	Lyme Conservation Commission
1988.12.22	Annette Schmitt	Lyme	25	Lyme Conservation Commission
1988.12.22	Annette Schmitt	Lyme	16	Lyme Conservation Commission
1990.10.30	Peter and Janice Treadwell	Lyme	27	Lyme Conservation Commission
1988.11.23	Richard Daggy	Lyndeborough/ Francestown	16	Piscataquog Watershed Association
1991.12.16	Theodore Stewart	Mason	72	Town of Mason
1999.02.22	Frederick and Virginia Hatch	Meredith	72	New England Forestry Foundation
1991.12.30	Marjorie Philippi	Mont Vernon	28	Mont Vernon Conservation Commission
1980.10.09	Kingsland and Kate Van Winkle	Moultonboro	15	Squam Lakes Conservation Society
1977.05.24	Frank Webster	Moultonboro	1	Squam Lakes Conservation Society
1989.07.26	Jonathan Brooks	New Boston	15	Piscataquog Watershed Association
1980.08.13	Samuel and Martha Brooks	New Boston	144	Piscataquog Watershed Association
1988.06.30	Elliott and Linda Hersey	New Boston	74	Piscataquog Watershed Association
1990.12.20	Louis and Kathryn Kachavos	New Boston	57	Piscataquog Watershed Association
1985.10.16	Jay Marden	New Boston	73	Piscataquog Watershed Association
1981.12.30	William and Shirley Mulligan	New Boston	32	Piscataquog Watershed Association
2000.12.20	Anonymous	Newbury	78	Ausbon Sargent Land Preservation Trust
1991.07.01	Ben and Katherine Wells	Newport	48	Newport Conservation Commission
1991.06.21	Barbara Yeomans	Newport	26	Newport Conservation Commission
1991.07.15	John and Cicely Richardson	Orford	8	Orford Conservation Commission
1989.12.27	Sarah Schwaegler	Orford	27	Orford Conservation Commission
1983.12.12	Marjorie Dunlap	Pelham	17	Pelham Conservation Commission
1987.12.17	Albert and Lois Daloz	Peterborough	40	Peterborough Conservation Commission
1986.12.30	Philip and Jennifer DuBois	Peterborough	30	Peterborough Conservation Commission
1977.06.13	Marshall Field	Peterborough	243	New England Forestry Foundation
1987.11.23	Ruth Pearson	Peterborough	8	Peterborough Conservation Commission
1976.04.12	Fairfield Raymond	Peterborough	14	Peterborough Conservation Commission
1989.11.21	Patricia Simonds	Peterborough	39	Peterborough Conservation Commission
1985.12.23	Charles and Susan Walcott	Peterborough	145	Peterborough Conservation Commission
1989.10.16	Anne Wardwell	Peterborough	53	Peterborough Conservation Commission
2000.07.14	Catherine Wheeler	Peterborough	195	Monadnock Conservancy
1977.06.10	Joanne Field Miller	Peterborough/ Greenfield	152	New England Forestry Foundation
1990.08.12	Helen Land	Peterborough/ Sharon	198	Peterborough Conservation Commission
1987.12.30	Edmond and Dorothy Goodwin	Plainfield	304	Plainfield Conservation Commission
1989.12.18	Alfred Fauver	Plymouth	105	Plymouth Conservation Commission
1984.12.28	Mrs. Marian Aikman	Rollinsford	35	Strafford County Conservation District
1988.12.16	Roger Coolidge	Sandwich	75	Town of Sandwich
1990.05.18	Dorothea Gifford	Sandwich	21	Lakes Region Conservation Trust
1989.03.08	Letitia and Rudolph Mutter	Sandwich	430	Town of Sandwich
1986.10.17	Suzita Myers	Sandwich	176	Town of Sandwich
1978.07.12	Beverly and Barbara Ridgely	Sandwich	14	Squam Lakes Conservation Society
1988.12.27	Beverly and Barbara Ridgely	Sandwich	4	Squam Lakes Conservation Society
1978.03.09	Richard Alt	Tamworth	20	Tamworth Conservation Commission
1985.10.11	Richard Alt	Tamworth	4	Tamworth Conservation Commission
1983.12.15	James, Edward and Christopher Alt	Tamworth	17	Tamworth Conservation Commission
1990.12.26	Joan Cave	Tamworth	742	Tamworth Conservation Commission
1992.11.10	County of Sullivan	Unity	230	Town of Unity
1996.12.23	Carl Siemon	Wakefield	8	Town of Wakefield
1977.01.26	Ruby Wright, Anita Aldrich, Marjorie Hudson, Maitland Hudson	Walpole	35	Walpole Conservation Commission
1978.08.08	Beatrice Graves	Walpole	65	Walpole Conservation Commission
1987.09.08	Collins Ledge	Weare	146	Weare Conservation Commission
1989.07.11	Harold and Elizabeth Janeway	Webster	7	Webster Conservation Commission
1991.10.24	Harold and Elizabeth Janeway	Webster	19	Webster Conservation Commission
1991.10.24	Harold and Elizabeth Janeway	Webster	8	Webster Conservation Commission
1991.10.22	Abby Rockefeller	Webster	268	Webster Conservation Commission
1988.08.25	John and Julie Morse	Wilmot	304	State of N.H.

Index

Author Biographies

All biographies are current as of May 2001.

David Anderson is the Society's education director. He claims he "learned everything that really matters from John Hay and the Society's Hay Reservation."

Martha Carlson has worked as a journalist and editor of *Forest Notes*. She is cofounder of the Community School in Tamworth.

Suki Casanave's work has appeared in national and regional magazines, as well as on PBS. Her book, *Natural Wonders of New Hampshire,* is available through bookstores. She writes from her home in Newmarket, New Hampshire.

Jim Collins is editor of *Yankee* magazine. His work has appeared in numerous national magazines.

Rosemary G. Conroy, co-editor, is the Society's communications director. She is editor of *Forest Notes* and co-host and writer of *Something Wild*, a biweekly natural history spot on New Hampshire Public Radio.

Carol C. Cushing is an amateur naturalist, writer, and registered nurse. She has volunteered for the Society as a docent, a leader of solar and floodplain tours, and is a contributing writer to *Forest Notes.*

Mike Dickerman is a free lance journalist from Littleton, New Hampshire. He has also authored or coauthored six books related to the White Mountains region.

Jane Difley is president/forester of the Society for the Protection of New Hampshire Forests. She is past president of the Society of American Foresters and held previous executive jobs with the American Forest Foundation and Vermont Natural Resources Council.

Peter Forbes was eastern regional director of the Trust for Public Lands. He is editor of the book *Our Land, Ourselves* and is presently a consultant and writer.

Donald Hall is an author, teacher, and poet who lives in Wilmot, New Hampshire. He is a former poet laureate of New Hampshire.

John Harrigan is an outdoor writer, sheep farmer, and publisher of the *Colebrook News and Sentinel.*

John Hay is a naturalist, author of several award-winning books, and recipient of the Burroughs Medal of Honor. He lives in Cape Cod.

Ernest Hebert is the author of several novels about New England life. He teaches creative writing at Dartmouth College.

Ralph Jimenez is a staff writer for the *Boston Globe* and lives in Concord.

Howard Mansfield is the author of several books about preserving cultural memory in New England, including *In The Memory House* (1993), and *The Same Ax, Twice: Restoration and Renewal in a Throwaway Age* (2000).

Donella Meadows was a writer, teacher, activist, and cofounder of the Upper Valley Land Trust and the Sustainability Institute. Coauthor of *The Limits to Growth* and *Beyond the Limits*, she was an inspiration to people around the world. Donella died suddenly in February 2001.

Isobel Parke is a tree farmer and senior counsel for the public relations firm Jackson, Jackson and Wagner.

Richard Ober, co-editor, was the Society's senior director of outreach programs and editor of *Forest Notes* from 1985 to July 2001. He is coauthor of *The Northern Forest* and his nonfiction work has appeared in *Yankee, Outside,* and other journals.

William T. Rotch is publisher emeritus of the *Milford Cabinet.*

Fred Taylor is a teacher and writer who lives in Putney, Vermont.

Colophon:

The page proportions and margins used in the design of this book are based upon ratios developed by Jan Tschichold with minor adjustments. The text type is Sabon 10.5 point with display type in Bellevue. The text stock is 80 lb. Productolith Recyled.

Stress Management

A Guide to a Healthier Life

Craig M. Rand

Kendall Hunt
publishing company

Cover image © Shutterstock

Kendall Hunt
publishing company

www.kendallhunt.com
Send all inquiries to:
4050 Westmark Drive
Dubuque, IA 52004-1840

ISBN 978-1-4652-0189-8

Printed in the United States of America
10 9 8 7 6 5 4 3 2

Contents

Chapter 3 The Power of Our Healing Breath

Chapter 4 To Journal or Not to Journal

Chapter 5 Time Management: What Are We Doing to Ourselves?

Chapter 6 Meditating and You: Taking the First Steps

Chapter 7 The Value of Exercise and Play as Great Stress Management Techniques

Chapter 8 Discussion of Our Social Health

Chapter 9 Emotional Wellness

Chapter 10 Intellectual Wellness

Chapter 15 Walking Meditations: Experience the Labyrinth

Chapter 16 Next Steps to Wellness: Lowering the Impact of Stress on Your Body

Acknowledgements

There are many people who have influenced my thought process within the perspective of stress management and wellness. First and foremost is my wife Marianne, who has always supported the decisions I have made and has always been my best friend. My children Shawn/Sandra, Justin/Claire, Kyle, and Connor, who have added joy, love, laughter, and even some stress occasionally into our lives. They make me proud of whom they are today and will continue to be in the future.

Additionally, the faculty whom I work with at Monroe Community College, listening to all of the stress management teachers and their new and innovative ideas of teaching pedagogy for this amazing class. The students with whom I have had the pleasure to teach this course for the last fourteen years and who I hope I will enjoy teaching for the next decade or more. I write this book for you and my hope is that it will make a difference in your lives after the class experience.

My classmates, Jill, Trish, Beth, Jane, Mary Sue, and faculty, Janet, Troy, Nancy, et al, the wonderful staff at Rocky Mountain University of Health Professions, Provo Utah, (HPW 1) you have helped frame my perspective on wellness and we all supported each other throughout the amazing learning process. I am so proud of each of you for completing the doctorate that I was unable to complete. My hope is that you will each enjoy this book and see yourselves within the pages I have written.

Lastly, I would like to thank Brian Luke Seaward, the foremost expert on stress in this country (my opinion, I know) for being my friend. You have impacted my journey more so than you can imagine and I say thank you.

Foreword

The overall goal of this textbook is to help you grow the stress management tool kit you currently have. You may ask, what is my personal stress management tool kit? I have used that metaphor for as many years as I have been teaching this course on Stress Management.

What are some examples that you currently have in your toolkit? Perhaps driving in anger (road rage), screaming at someone, swearing, physical aggression, drinking, taking pills for your headache (caused from stress)? These are what I would consider to be more negative ways to deal with stress. They may offer some short-term relief, but if these techniques are first and foremost in your tool kit, then you already know there are often negative consequences to handling stress this way.

Some techniques I will present within this text that I believe to be more positive methods for dealing with stress include: exercising (I actually prefer playing), taking deep breathes (one or several), meditation, journal writing, walking a labyrinth, using Complementary and Alternative Medicine, massage, connecting with the beauty of nature that surrounds us, and many more. We will practice each of these and introduce others throughout the book. To practice changing your response to stress is the goal I have for each of you. Then you can change the impact of stress on your life. When you have stress, you can continue the traditional responses you have always used, or you can add these new techniques (not actually new as some of them are thousands of years old), but they will be new to you and your response to stress.

The focus will not be on the physiological aspect of stress. Yes, it will be discussed, but my focus will be to help you identify the stressors in your life and to help you develop coping mechanisms, skills sets that you can use daily to lower and hopefully eliminate stress in your life. In this

day and age, that may be asking a lot from a textbook, but my desire is to help you make changes in your reactions to stress that will help you increase your wellness and hopefully the joy you will find around you.

The approach we will be taking on this journey is to examine the components of wellness. We will discuss each component and take some time within the reading, the homework assignments, and reflective comments and questions to ask this primary question: *Am I well today?* This is a complicated question, and the answer is that each day our wellness is impacted in some way. Not knowing what wellness is makes it harder to right the ship and get back on the right track.

An example of what I mean: I once had a student show up to my stress management class at 9:00 a.m., and she was obviously distraught. When I asked her what was going on, her answer surprised me. She stated, "I just found out my father was killed in Iraq." I asked what I could do for her, even offering her the opportunity to miss class. Her reply was, "I need to be with people that I trust, and I need the quiet and meditation time that we do in class each day." She stayed, and being with people she trusted in the classroom community, started the healing process. Yes, she did miss several classes over the next several weeks as she dealt with burying her father in Arlington Cemetery, but her experiences and the tools she had added to her tool kit, helped her to deal with her tragic loss.

I hope you appreciate my viewpoint and I hope that we can indeed add new tools to your personal stress management toolkit.

Namaste

Chapter 1 Introduction to Wellness and Its Importance in Dealing with Stress

Goals for This Chapter

- To be able to define stress.
- To be able to identify the categories of stressors in our lives.
- To be able to identify the current stress management activities you use to lower your stress.
- To be able to name and understand the dimensions of wellness.

KEY TERMS

stress
eustress
distress
burnout
environmental stressors
physiological stressors
psycho-social stressors
wellness

DEFINING STRESS

The primary question as we start this journey is: Why are you taking this class? Is it because you are currently dealing with a lot of stress in your life, or are you currently stressed out and are hoping to learn how to minimize its total impact on your life? Perhaps is it because this section just fits into your schedule, or a faculty advisor/friend suggested taking the course.

Stress

an absence of inner peace; emotional and physical wear and tear on the body; emotional and/or physical turmoil.

Whatever the reason that has brought you to this class, the focus of the course and your outcomes will still be the same. We will introduce you to **stress** and help you develop a better understanding of how stress impacts your daily life and those with whom you interact on a daily basis, as well as what and how stress impacts your health (often negatively). We will also introduce you to a wide variety of stress management techniques to enable you to lessen the impact of stress on your life. There is no one reading this book, sitting in the classroom next to you, engaged in classroom discussion, or in the online work, who can honestly state that stress is not relevant to his or her life. Each of us has a variety of stressors bombarding us each day. How we let them impact our emotions, our health, and our energy levels is critical. It is my hope this course will help you lessen the impact of stress in your daily life.

We will also be examining wellness and assessing your current wellness. It is my belief that no stress management strategy can move forward without a certain amount of knowledge and more importantly, a certain commitment to taking care of ourselves each and every day.

Lastly, we will introduce you to a wide variety of stress management activities that will enable you to win the battle against stress. We will help you assess the current tools in your stress management tool kit, learn what we can add, and why we would add these techniques into a stress management tool kit.

Let us then first discuss stress, develop some basic understandings of what stress is, how stress impacts our health and wellness, and how we can lessen the impact of stress within our lives. This much I am sure of, stress surrounds us each and every day; some of us are able to address stress and it has minimal impact on our day-to-day lives. Others of us wake up and the stress has already impacted our day; perhaps our sleep was restless or absent completely, we feel unhealthy, our emotional responses are angry, full of negative emotions, and we are unhappy. Often we don't even understand that the stress in our lives is contributing to our start of the day. Without the ability to see the impact stress is having on our lives, how can we change our attitude, our focus, and our health?

If you have even awoken and didn't feel right, you can utilize positive thoughts and start to change your focus and the intention of the day. You can change the impact of stress on your life, as long as you agree that we are all surrounded by stressors and many may have to be addressed today.

Some definitions that I have read over the years that make the concept of stress come to life for me are: an absence of inner peace; emotional and physical wear and tear on the body; emotional turmoil; and even a crappy day (week, month, or year). Do they make sense to you? Can you relate to any or all of these definitions? Each definition may be simplistic in length but important in helping understand the premise of stress. By beginning our conversation with these definitions of stress, I hope they provide you with something that you can relate to, something that makes stress real, and yet easier to start to understand.

Eustress

good stress; a stress that brings joy and happiness such as the birth of a baby.

If you had to develop your own personal definition of stress, how would you frame your answer?

____

As we explore stress, we need to understand that there are several types of stress that we face each and every day. **Eustress** is commonly considered to be good stress, a stress that brings joy and happiness into our lives. Often when I ask this question of my students, the common response I receive to this question is having a baby. Having been in the delivery room with each of my four sons, I doubt that my wife thought the act of having a baby (the actual delivery) was an example of eustress, although I also know that when each son was delivered and handed to my wife and me, the fact that we had a beautiful new son would become a great example of eustress. Can you give an example of an eustress in your own life?

The opposite of eustress is **distress**, which is considered to be a negative stress that has negative consequences on our body both mentally and physically. An example of distress that perhaps you have experienced is being pulled over by a police officer for speeding. Think about the physiological changes that occur as you first see the red lights flash behind you. Your heart starts to race, your palms become sweaty, and you may feel muscle tension in the back of your neck or head. Each feeling gets stronger as you pull over, thinking what did I do wrong? Then think of the emotional release as the cop speeds up around you and continues on; it is as if a weight is lifted off your shoulders. A smile and a deep breath help you relax. Of course, the distress response continues to occur if the police car pulls over, puts the spotlight on your car, and the officer comes over to your car.

Distress

bad stress; negative stress that has harmful consequences on our body both mentally and physically.

Another concept related to stress is known as **burnout**, a complete overwhelming of stress, which causes one to shut down both personally and professionally. This term started to become mainstream in the late 60s and early 70s and was often found within professionals whose jobs included being first responders (firefighters, paramedics, police officers). During the course of their daily work lives, these people saw horrors at accident scenes, murders, fires, and violence, and when they were done with that incident, they went to the next call. By the end of their shift, the end of the week, month, year, career, they had seen so many horrible or violent things that negatively impacted their spirit, their emotions, their joy within their jobs, they were massively stressed. If you ever thought about entering one of those noble careers, when asked why, you would probably answer that you want to make a difference, you want to help individuals. I doubt you would respond that you want to see people's pain and suffering. You would not be ready emotionally, physically, or mentally to experience this and handle the physiological responses the first couple of times (hundreds of times) that you experienced such trauma while at work. Because these professionals were severely impacted, many left the profession due to all that they had seen and experienced. Today, we know that when people see a horrific accident or crime scene, they may need to be referred to counseling to help them work through what they saw and how it impacted them. They will talk and share the experience with a trained professional who will help them. For example, if police officers discharge their guns during work, they are often put on desk duty to ensure they are okay and will return to the field only when they are ready.

Burnout

completely overwhelming stress that causes a person to shut down both personally and professionally.

You see the same scenario played out in every community when there is a death of a student, a beloved teacher, or administrator. The school district announces that the school will have counselors available to talk to students, faculty, staff, and parents; anyone who is hurting emotionally. We are now acutely aware that people often need help when dealing with life situations. We know that counseling services, an ear to listen to the pain, share the anger, and process the emotions that come with any sudden death are beneficial and have become the SOP (Standard Operating Procedure).

To help you further understand the concept, think back to September 11, 2001. What impact did that have on the first responders, firefighters, and police officers who were at

Ground Zero for that day and for the weeks after? How did they overcome the tremendous sorrow, the sights they saw, and the friends they lost? They likely needed support, support from their colleagues, and love from their friends and family to move forward after all was said and done. Whole towns were impacted, and I can remember travelling to the Long Island area and seeing support for the individuals who died and for those who tried valiantly to rescue them.

Perhaps you have heard in the news, on television, or the internet about post-traumatic stress disorder (PTSD), a similar response to burnout that occurs with soldiers returning from the battlefields of war. There they see so much death, loss of friends, unimagined destruction, and edginess from being on the frontlines, that it damages their emotional and physical spirit. They have suffered tremendous emotional, spiritual, physical wear and tear on their bodies. They come back with battle scars (that we cannot always see, and sometimes, even they are not aware of the impact the war made on them) both physically and emotionally. What they have seen and or experienced makes it hard to transition back to a normal life. Some soldiers are unable to return to the main street life they left. Military branches are developing policies and procedures to provide support, someone to talk to, someone to share the horrors, and through this support and help, encouraged the soldiers in the transition process. They also include the soldiers' families to ensure that all are aware of the issues and concerns for the soldiers and share the goal of helping them to successfully transition to a normal life.

With understanding and support, we each can help ourselves manage the stress in our lives and begin to take a step in the right direction. Each step we take will hopefully include lessening the impact of stress on our lives, our relationships, and our spirit, as well as have a positive impact on our health and wellness.

Environmental stressors

any external factors such as weather conditions, noise, and crowds that create stress.

CLASSIFYING STRESSORS IN OUR LIVES

The next step is to label and or identify the gamut of stressors we face in our lives. The stress of being a teenager and trying to fit in are no different for a new college student looking to start the next life chapter, or an adult learner who has come back to school to begin a new career, or the husband and wife whose children have left the nest and now realize it's time to focus on themselves. Each stage of our life story will have the same classification of stressors. They may vary, depending on where you are in your life story.

© kohy, 2012. Under license from Shutterstock, Inc.

Environmental Stressors

The easiest way to make **environmental stressors** understandable is to ask: Do you dislike weather in Rochester? If you answered yes, then you have acknowledged an environmental stressor and then, the recommendation I would make to you is quite simple: move. Now if life were only that easy! Moving is not always a realistic possibility, but if it were, then you would have be able to change an environmental stressor since Rochester weather has been this way forever and is not likely to change in the near future. (Well, maybe not. I remember an article I read several years ago which discussed global warming. It suggested that by the year 2050, the weather in Florida will resemble living at the equator; weather in North Carolina will be like Florida, and the weather in upstate New York will be like today's North Carolina. So if you are still living in Rochester in the year 2050, perhaps weather will not be an environmental stressor.)

There are other examples of environmental stressors that surround us both in our college environment and in our homes. They run the gamut, but here are several that fit into the environmental category. Parking at the beginning of any semester at most colleges would be an excellent example. We can control or lessen the impact by better planning or by scheduling college courses at the 8:00 to 9:00 a.m. times when parking is abundant. Another example of parking being an environmental stressor is going to any mall during the holidays; parking spots are at a premium and people actually follow you to your car to grab your spot. Add the stress of the holidays and we see a variety of examples of stressed-out people, who behave uncharacteristically badly. The last example of an environmental stressor would be noise, whether it is in college classroom, in the residence halls, or your home or apartment. I have often been assigned to teach stress management in the college's dance studio, which is a beautiful space with great acoustics and lots of space to practice different techniques. The only problem is when I am teaching meditating next door, there is the smashing of racquetballs, laughter, and lots of energy. I am all for exercise; I think it is one of the best stress management tools we can add to our toolbox (more on that later), but while we are practicing meditation, it is hard for the students to focus on the guided imagery as it is being presented.

Other examples of environmental stressors could be the heat during the summer (Why does violence increase in the summer? Could it be related to the environmental stressor?) Think about traffic congestion. Have you ever sat in a traffic jam for two hours plus? I guarantee many drivers become agitated, frustrated, and lash out at anyone they see. Other stressors include overcrowding at places you enjoy, waiting in line at a restaurant on any Friday or Saturday evening, waiting in line at the DMV, waiting to pay your phone bill, having the folks in the apartment or residence hall next to you playing a huge sound system 24/7 without any concern for your well being or your friendly complaints. Each of these is examples of environmental stressors.

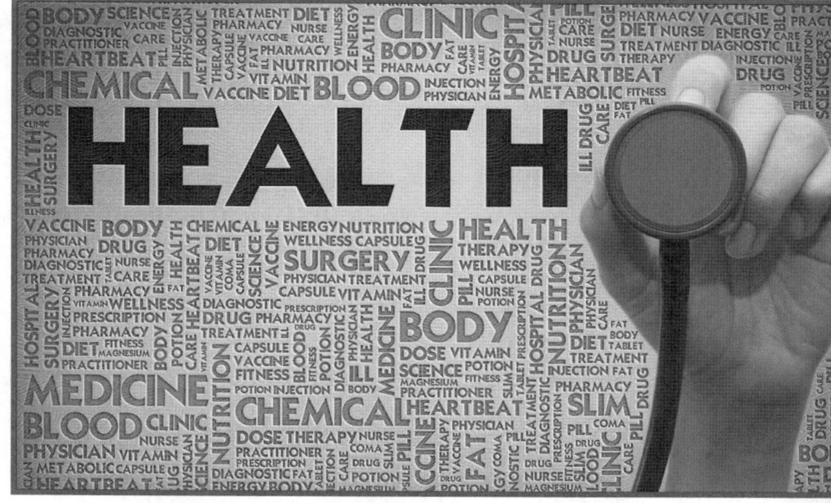

© basketman23, 2012. Under license from Shutterstock, Inc.

What are your current environmental stressors in your life?

____

____

Health or Physiological Stressors

Physiologoical stressors

factors that are damaging to emotional or psychological health such as injury, serious disease, depression, or serious drug and alcohol use. These generally are long-term stressors.

The next category of stressors is health or **physiological stressors**. These stressors tend to be more damaging to our emotional and psychological psyche, whereas most of the examples of environmental stressors tend to be of shorter duration (except for the Rochester weather.) When we discuss health and physiological stressors, they tend to last longer, often times the outcomes are not as we hoped, and the pain, the loss, the sickness lingers for months or years.

Think back over your life. Have you suffered a serious illness or injury or has someone in your family or close friends received an unwanted health diagnosis that sent that person and their family reeling? The diagnosis of heart disease, cancer, diabetes, or serious drug and alcohol use can be devastating to the person, and the stress can increase the impact of the disease on the person. In my opinion, these stressors are often extremely damaging as they impact more than the person with illness or disease. They affect all those who love the person, who are afraid of the disease, who are afraid of losing the person to the disease. The impact of this category of stressors will have a long-term effect on our overall health and wellness.

I recently read an obituary in a paper, and the person who died was young (at least by my standards), and the lead comment was that the person lost her life due to losing the battle with her drug and alcohol addictions. I am sure that her family stated this as a lesson to others, but also to acknowledge the battle that this person struggled with for many years.

One of the life experiences as we age is that we, unfortunately, see more and more health or physiological stressors. In my life, I have lost my father to lung cancer, where the diagnosis indicated that he had less than five years to live (a 5 percent chance of surviving five years), but he died within three months of the diagnosis. Several other family or extended family members have suffered with serious illnesses or died younger than any ever expected. But it isn't always those who are older. I sat with my son when his girlfriend in third grade was diagnosed with cancer and who died much quicker than anyone thought. My hope for you is that you don't have to deal with this category often in your lifetime.

In the last year have you experienced any stressors that fell into this category? If so list them and describe how you dealt with these stressors?

Psycho-social stressors

the ordinary stresses of daily life such as losing your job, moving, ending a friendship, divorce, getting a speeding ticket, car accident, starting or stopping school, illness, etc. These tend to be of shorter duration and/or are self-limiting.

Psycho-Social Stressors

The last categories of stressors we will encounter during our lifetime are known as **psycho-social stressors**. These are the wide variety of stressors that we encounter often in our day-to-day life. As an example: You go home after your classes today and you are met by your parents who inform you that you are moving in a week to Nome, Alaska. Now, there is nothing wrong with Nome, Alaska, but you're already enrolled in college, you have friends, family, perhaps a significant other in your life, and your parents have made the decision to move and you have to make the move with the family. Think of the turmoil this decision will make in your life. What is the range of your feelings, emotions, the tears, the laughter, the anxiety of starting a new life? You are leaving your comfort zone and, moreover, this huge change will be happening shortly.

© Stuart Miles, 2012. Under license from Shutterstock, Inc.

How many of you could feel the impact as you read this scenario?

Some might look at this as a wonderful, new opportunity to grow, to experience new things and new people, to see another part of the country. The student who has that outlook is well grounded and this event may not cause them any significant change in their stress levels. However, they are usually the exception, not the rule in their response.

Others of us may view this as our world has just been destroyed. We don't think there is enough time in a week to say good-bye to friends and family, give our job appropriate notice, decide what and how the relationship with our significant other will be (stay committed or break up knowing that the distance is likely to cause it to end eventually anyways). There is just so much to do, so little time to process it or even work through the range of emotions. If you felt your stomach knotting up, if you could feel a tension headache developing, muscle tension in your upper neck and shoulders, then you are beginning to relate to psycho-social stressors and their impact on our lives.

Other examples stem from daily life occurrences: losing your job, breaking up with someone you loved, ending a friendship, parents or you going through a divorce, being bullied, an unplanned pregnancy, a speeding ticket, car accident, failing an exam, sleeping though a presentation, missing a class due to no parking, an injury, feeling overwhelmed with homework, tests, roommate issues, trying out for a competitive college team and being cut, starting over in college making new friends, joining a club, changing careers, changing or stopping your religious beliefs, a family member or close friend being seriously hurt or dying. These things and others like them will happen to us throughout our lives. The significance each of these stressors has on our lives may be lessened by the tools we develop to handle stress.

What are some current psycho-stressors ongoing in your life today?

____

____

DEVELOPING AN UNDERSTANDING OF WELLNESS

Wellness

the state of being in good mental, emotional, physical, and spiritual health.

Wellness is a relatively new concept that first came to the forefront in the 1950s, but as we come to better understand our human condition, we are developing a more thorough concept of wellness. The World Health Organization in 1959 described health as "a state of complete physical, mental, and social well-being and not merely the absence of disease or infirmity." H.L. Dunn describes wellness as "an integrated method of functioning which is oriented toward maximizing the potential of which the individual is capable." To better understand wellness, we need to discuss the categories to look at our individual health and wellness. You have likely heard of mind, body, and spirit which are often used to discuss wellness. A more inclusive wellness model includes the following dimensions: physical, social, intellectual, emotional, spiritual, and occupational. Additionally, other models are expanding to include an environmental dimension, and I believe no conversation about wellness can be complete until we add the dimensions of nutrition and diet.

Let's develop a broader understanding of each dimension and as you read each section, I would ask that you reflect on your current status within the dimension being discussed.

Physical. Within the physical dimension we will be discussing such things as regular exercise, both cardiovascular and weight training; making appropriate medical visits; doing regular self checks to monitor changes within your body and calling your physician when you notice changes; knowing your numbers including resting pulse, blood pressure, cholesterol scores (high density lipids and low density lipids), healthy weight range, muscular strength, muscular endurance; maintaining your flexibility; managing your stress level, avoiding tobacco and illicit drugs, and practicing safer sex. Later we will discuss a wide variety of types of activities that will enable you to improve, maintain, or change your physical wellness.

How would you rate your current physical component of wellness?________________

____

____

and is this an area you could improve? YES NO

If the answer is yes, how?____

____

____

Social. The focus of this dimension will be on interactions you have with family, friends, colleagues, knowing yourself and being happy with who you are, giving back to your community, active and involved with clubs and organizations, playing on a team whether it is a college team or being on kickball team, hanging with your friends, being able to go into a new environment and be comfortable, being able to share your thoughts and feelings, making new friends, maintaining friends and family as an integral part of your support network, and enjoying being with people you care about.

How would you rate your current social dimension? ______________________

____

____

and is this an area you could improve? YES NO

If the answer is yes, how? ______________________________

____

____

Intellectual. For this dimension the focus is related to your healthy or unhealthy mind, imagination, observing the world around you, listening, questioning to learn more, staying current on world events (which means more than YouTube), reading, communicating, exercising creativity (right brain versus left brain), desiring to be a life-long learner, and enjoying the process of learning. Do you know what kind of learner you are? Are you an auditory learner, an experiential or kinesthetic learner, logical, verbal, or visual learner? Each style will influence your intellectual experience.

How would you rate your current intellectual dimension? ______________________________

____

____

and is this an area you could improve? YES NO

If the answer is yes, how? ______________________________

____

____

Spiritual. In this area people often confuse spirituality with religion. I would state to you that I am both religious and spiritual, and yes there may be some overlap within my life. I can distinguish the difference in my religious experiences and my spiritual connections that I have developed during my life. We will explore this further, but for now, we will define spirituality. This discussion includes our sense of meaning and our purpose of our life, our values, intuition, being aware of others diversity within cultures and their religions, developing a practice of quiet time in reflection, engagement with spiritual activities, developing our thoughts and actions to be more congruent with our values, kindness, faith, compassion, service to others, respect for nature, and a possible belief in a higher power. It also includes a spiritual connection to Mother Earth and taking care of her as many indigenous tribes do. Each of these concepts will help us develop a better understanding of our personal spirituality.

How would you rate your current spiritual dimension? ______________________________

____

____

and is this an area you could improve? YES NO

If the answer is yes, how? ______________________________

____

____

Emotional. This dimension includes the range of feelings that we as humans experience: joy, love, anger, angst, happiness, sense of our own worth, positive self and positive attitude, pain, depression, sadness, ability to deal with stress, crying, frustration, and more. Sometime emotions are like riding a roller coaster with dramatic changes in our ups and downs. I would state that the emotional dimension is perhaps the hardest dimension to share or discuss from the male perspective. Many men have been raised to not show your emotions, as they may be seen as a sign of weakness. A good example of this is to ask the male readers if they would cry in public. Most often when I ask this question in class, most males say that crying in public is not something they can or would do. I hope we can slowly change the answer to this question, but it is both a cultural response and a learned behavior, so the change will likely be glacial.

How would you rate your current emotional dimension?________________________

____

____

and is this an area you could improve? YES NO

If the answer is yes, how? ____

____

____

Occupational. It is likely the dimension we understand the most and often is at the root cause for much of the issues within our lives. Here we are talking about our careers, our job, our college choices, if we find job satisfaction or just view the job as a paycheck, quality of life as it is tied to our occupation, how our job relates to career goals, our dreams, as well as respect at our workplace. In boom economies, it is easier to leave a job, but in current times many are forced to keep a job that is not satisfying as there may not be other jobs available.

How would you rate your current occupation?_______________________________

____

____

and is this an area you could improve? YES NO

If the answer is yes, how? ____

____

____

Lastly, I would like to include two additional dimensions to the wellness continuum. They are environmental and diet and nutrition. Both are significant and I believe should be added into the overall discussion within wellness.

Environmental. This dimension includes the areas where we reside, work, and play. Factors that influence this dimension are air quality, water quality, noise pollution, traffic, overcrowding, pollution, and even at the start of the college year or during the holiday shopping season. Parking would be considered an environmental problem. As you think about this dimension, are there examples you can think of that impact your wellness? Consider how you would feel if you found out out there is lead paint in your home or you show up to work and there are signs for asbestos removal in your place of employment? These would be relevant examples of environmental factors.

How would you rate your current environmental dimension of wellness? ____________

____

____

and is this an area you could improve? YES NO

If the answer is yes, how?____

____

____

Nutrition. The last dimension I would add to the dimensions of wellness would be nutrition. If there is any area of knowledge that needs more understanding, it is the foods that we consume and how they impacts our wellness. Some models add nutrition under the physical dimension, but after working in the fitness and education arenas for all of my professional life, the one constant has been the wealth of misunderstanding about the impact of nutrition.

The role of wellness models is to incorporate better, more simplistic approachs to nutrition and create and understand how the foods we consume significantly impact our wellness. There is so much misinformation as to what it means to eat healthy. The actual food pyramid which we were all introduced to as children has changed several times over the last twenty years; not to mention MyPlate, which makes sense but I believe has caused more confusion instead of the desired effect to make our meals easier to create and seek balance. In later chapters, we will spend more time breaking this down.

How would you rate your current nutritional dimension of wellness? ____________

____

____

and is this an area you could improve? YES NO

If the answer is yes, how? ____

____

____

WELLNESS AND STRESS

As we travel together in this journey to look at your personal wellness, your stress management, and to grow your tools to help you develop stress strategies, we will always look at the symbiotic relationship that we have between our health and wellness and the impact stress does within each dimension.

REFERENCES

World Health Organization. "Constitution of the World Health Organization." *Chronicle of the World Health Organization* (1947): 1, 29–43.

Dunn, H. (1959). "High-level wellness for man and society." *American Journal of Public Health* 49(6) (1959): 786–792.

National Wellness Institute. Accessed February 2012. www.nationalwellness.org.

Name____ Class Days and Time ________________________

1.1

REALAGE QUIZ

Go to www.realage.com and do the quiz that will come up on the first page. Be honest with your answers and watch your age as it changes with each answer. The focus of this assignment is easy. Each question is related to health and wellness components and your answers will show up in your real age in the corner. So let's use the example question: do you smoke tobacco products? If your answer is no, then your age will not change; if you answer yes, and then state that you smoke a pack a day, it will add years to your chronological age. At the end of the realage quiz, you must print the final page, which will state your chronological age and your realage based on the answers to the questions within the quiz.

After you have printed the last page, write a one-page paper discussing the differences in your ages, discuss your responses to your realage, and whether you were surprised to see the age the program projected. What are the items you answered that impacted your age the most either positive or negatively?

Name____ Class Days and Time ________________________

1.2

BASELINE INFORMATION

The second assignment is to start to determine and record the following vital health and wellness information. All this information should be completed by the end of semester. Then you will have a baseline and if changes occur, you will be able to work with your physician to correct or minimize the outcome.

Height ____________ Weight ______________ Age______________

Date of last physical ____________________ By whom ________________

Resting pulse _________________ Resting blood pressure _______________

All vaccines current: yes no Total blood cholesterol levels _______________

Triglycerides __________ HDL "good" __________ LDL "bad" __________

BMI ___________ Hip/waist ratio ___________

Frame size ___________

Recommended normal body weight for your age ___________

1 -mile walk test __________, which indicates your fitness level to be __________

Cooper's 1.5 mile run (walk, crawl) test ___________ , which indicates your fitness level to be ___________

Are you happy with your current fitness? If yes, why. ______________________

____

____.

If no, why and what are you willing to do to make a change in your overall fitness?

____

____

Are you happy with your wellness today? If yes, why. ______________________

____

____

If no, why and how could you improve your wellness dimensions?

____

____

Health issues that you currently have or a history of disease in your family. Go back at least three generations, if possible.

Name____ Class Days and Time ________________________

1.3

TECHNIQUES TO MANAGE STRESS

Develop a list of current techniques that you utilize to manage your stress level. After making the list, decide if you view that technique as a positive or negative method for managing stress in your life and why you view it as either positive or negative.

____

____

____

____

____

____

____

____

____

____

____

Name____ Class Days and Time ________________________

1.4

DIMENSIONS OF WELLNESS WHEEL

Using the wheel below, place each of the eight dimensions of wellness as introduced earlier in this chapter in a segment of the circle. Then place a + or a – to indicate your current status within the dimension. Within the circle, add descriptive words which support your wellness status. This will be a personal reflection of your current wellness viewpoint. Good luck and be thorough. At the end of the semester, you should revisit your wellness wheel as our dimensions of wellness can change often, depending on many of life's changes.

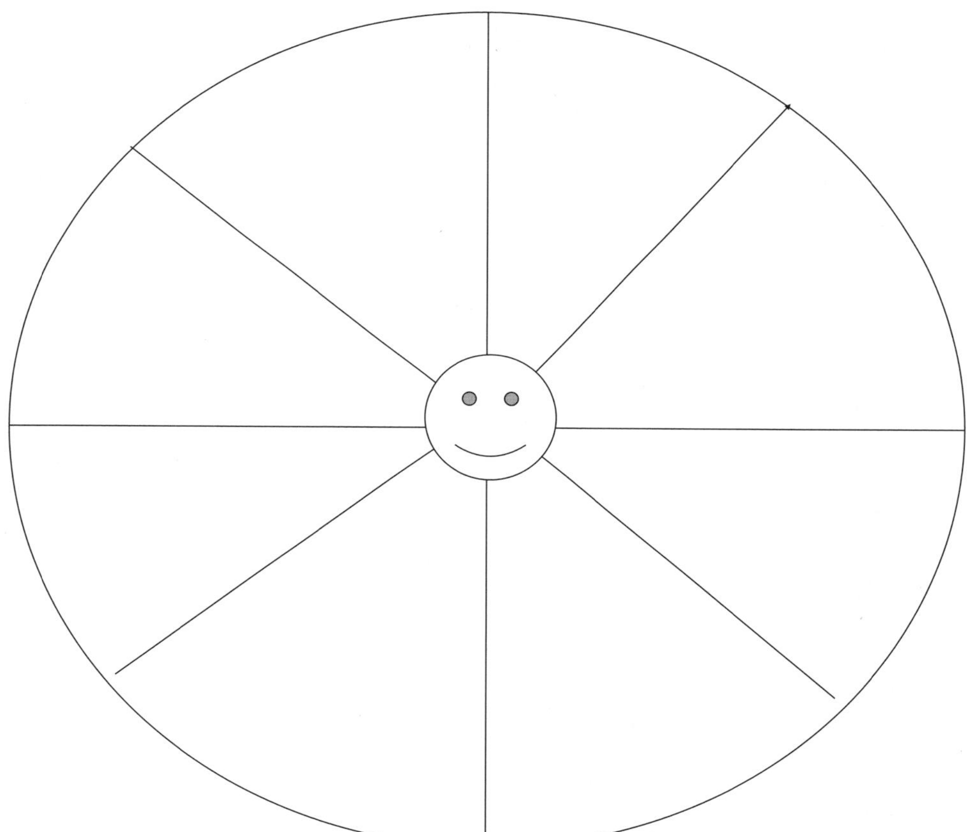

My Current Wellness Dimension Status

Chapter 2
Stress and Its Impact on Our Bodies and Our Lives

Goals for This Chapter

- To understand the General Adaptation Syndrome.
- To be able to explain the top ten health anti-oxidants as described in the chapter.
- To understand the fight or flight response to stress.
- To be able to show comprehension of a variety of strategies to utilize while stressed.

KEY TERMS

General Adaptation Syndrome (GAS)

fight or flight response

FURTHER REVIEW REGARDING STRESS

In Chapter 1, we introduced the concepts of both wellness and stress and began the process of linking them together. If we can develop an appreciation of maintaining our health and wellness, then in the process of taking care of ourselves, we will also be developing and maintaining stress management strategies. These strategies can make a huge difference in the impact that stress has on our lives, but no strategies that we will present in the class or this text are inclusive. In other words, they work, but it is best to have a variety of techniques to utilize since we never know the depth of the stressor nor how we will react to each stressor.

Stress is created when a real or imagined threat is perceived and causes a physiological response within our bodies. This physiological response includes muscular tension, increased perspiration, a change in our emotions, a release of adrenaline and cortisol into the bloodstream, increased blood pressure, increased heart rate, increased breathing rate, and a heightened alertness. Other definitions include any physical, mental, or emotional event that causes a bodily or mental response that impacts our mind, body, and/or spirit.

Fight or flight response

the first stage of GAS in which the sympathetic nervous system automatically prepares a person to either confront (fight) or escape (flee) from a threat.

The classic, automatic response to stress is known as the **fight or flight response**. In reality, the fight or flight response started back with our prehistoric ancestors who, when confronted by a woolly mammoth or saber-toothed cat, had to either fight the animal as a food source or become its food source, or decide that this battle was not in their favor and flee (the flight response). Over the countless generations since the first hunters and gatherers, this response became automatic and designed to protect each of us.

In today's version, we still have a fight or flight response, but the stakes are different, although the physiological outcomes are still similar. Perhaps you are having a truly lousy day; after school you go home to study for a big test tomorrow, but you are emotionally spent, so you take a nap. At first, you may think it is a good idea to take time to care for yourself and study later. Well, the nap is not a power nap and lasts the rest of the evening or even into the next morning. When you wake up, the flight response (the nap) has now increased your stress level as you are not prepared for the exam. Now one stressor has created a second, and the negative energy overtakes you. If you had chosen to fight no matter how bad the day had been, using some of your stress management tools in your tool kit, you could have worked out, worked on a hobby, or called a friend. Each of these could be seen as the fight response. You would be taking on the stressor and by using your techniques, your fight response would be appropriate. You would be able to study, get a good night's sleep, and hopefully nail the exam the next day.

When you have a stressor come at you, what are your personal physiological responses to the stressor?

____

____

What might be your current fight responses?______________________________

What are your current flight responses?_________________________________

The scientific community is in agreement that being exposed to some stress is beneficial to us and helps the body adapt to the times when we face stress. The question is how much we can be exposed to before it has a negative impact on mind, body and spirit, or our wellness. The answer is convoluted as each of us responds differently to the stressors in our lives. We can take a similar event in the lives of everyone in this class, and many responses would occur from that one stressor based on our current life experiences or expectations.

Remember there is both eustress (positive or joyful stress) and distress (negative stress) within our lives. Words associated with distress are anger, impatience, frustration, hostility, anxious, irritable, and worry, among others. With distress, it is further broken down to acute stress (short and of intense duration, fifteen to twenty minutes). An example of this might be losing a paper on your computer because you didn't back it up. The other kind of distress is called chronic stress; the intensity is lower, but it lasts for days, weeks, or even months. An example would be working at a job you find no joy in or staying in a relationship that is over, but you are afraid to move on. This stress is not immediate, but over time does the same damage to our wellness. We need to be aware of the impact of stress has on each of us, and develop strategies to lessen its overall impact on us.

When discussing the fight of flight response to stress, we need to look further at the physiological response the body has to the stressor. The **General Adaptation Syndrome (GAS)**, was originally developed by Hans Selye (considered to be the father of stress research) to describe a three-stage response to stress he was investigating. This response involves both the nervous system and hormonal systems of the human body. Following is a brief overview of the GAS.

General Adaptation Syndrome (GAS)

a term used to describe the body's short-term and long-term reactions to stress. It consists of three stages: alarm, resistance, and exhaustion.

Stage 1. The alarm stage is the immediate response to the stressor. This stage is the preparation for the fight or flight response we earlier discussed. The body releases cortisol and adrenaline, which provide the energy to deal with the stressor.

Stage 2. In the resistance stage, also known as the adaptation stage, the body reacts to the stressor. Especially if the stressor continues, the body begins to make changes to lessen the impact of the stressor. If the stressor lessens, the body struggles to return to homeostasis (a physiological balance) and recovers from the stressor. If the stressor remains for a longer period of time, then the body moves into the last stage.

Stage 3. The exhaustion stage occurs when the body's response to the stressor is weakening. The longer the duration of the stressor, the more likely this response will be impacted. As indicated by the name, the stressor has lasted a length of time and the body is at an overload or truly fatigued. The indication is that the body's immune system is weakened and making the individual more likely to become ill. When the individual reaches the exhaustion stage, this is where the serious health consequences from stress impact us.

"It's your choice, medicate or meditate?"

www.CartoonStock.com

STRESS AND OUR HEALTH

It is stated within much of the health and wellness literature, that approximately 75 to 85 percent of all illness is related to stress. That is a huge number when you consider the current cost of healthcare in this country and the number of individuals who are unable to afford or get coverage. If we can lower our stress level, then it makes sense that we will not be sick as often and perhaps healthcare coverage can be available to more citizens. We need to emphasize a movement from our current healthcare program, which in reality is more of a sick care program, and move into a well care program. Our focus has to change to emphasize taking care of ourselves, maintaining our health and wellness, and our stress levels, thereby lowering our healthcare costs. This is a better way to make healthcare affordable than to continue to have people running to the ERs whenever they don't feel well.

What are some of the major healthcare issues of this country? Currently, the leading diseases in this country are heart disease, cancer, metabolic syndrome, depression, and obesity. Each of these classifications of disease is very expensive to treat, to manage, to care for, and a tremendous drain on our healthcare resources. If we could lessen the total number of individuals with these diseases, then we could change the face of healthcare in this country. Perhaps we could move from our current model to a newer and improved model.

Dr. Karen Wolfe stated in 2009, that the top 10 Lifestyle Oxidants (harmful attributes that impact our life) are as follows:

1. Cigarette smoke
2. Excessive stress
3. Diet high in saturated and transfats
4. Exposure to ionizing radiation
5. Exposure to air, food, water pollution
6. Lack of exercise
7. Exposure to petrochemicals and heavy metals
8. Excessive alcohol consumption
9. Cooking on gas/charcoal grills
10. Lack of sleep

We often face each of these ten attributes on a daily basis. The impact of each of these harmful attributes impacts our overall wellness. We must begin to take ownership for what we do to our bodies and understand the damage and wear and tear we face. We can change our wellness and lessen the damage or long-term impact of stress.

The choice is truly ours. What will it take to move forward to develop a thorough tool kit for us to manage our stress and to increase our wellness? Following are some beginning suggestions to contemplate stress management techniques. As we move through the book, we will expand on some new concepts and discuss ways to examine our wellness and make changes in our life.

We can consider these ideas to be the building blocks from which our foundation will be built. As we practice them and utilize the ones that work for us, we will begin to lessen the negative responses that stress creates for each of us.

1. **Don't keep it to yourself.** If something is bothering you, find someone with whom you can communicate with. Hopefully, it will be someone you trust and whose opinions you value. You have to be able to be open, honest, and have the ability to listen to what the person whom you trust gives you back.
2. **Exercise.** Play a physically active game; do something to expend the negative energy that stress often brings. Imagine working out after having an argument with a co-worker and taking the energy from your anger into your workout into the physical activity. You will work out harder, and when you are done, you will feel better, expended the negative energy, and the anger should be gone or lessened.

3. **Breathe.** Take several deep breaths, whether it is while stuck in traffic, taking a test, or fighting with a friend, a work colleague, or a family member. Often by remembering to take several deep breaths, you lessen your stress level and are able to work through the issue.
4. **Count to ten.** I know it is a simple solution, but it is an effective one. How often in your life have you reacted immediately and said something hurtful or in anger that caused more pain? If we all could just count to ten and think before we react, the world would be a much better place.
5. **Take some ME time.** Find your quiet and comfortable place to escape from the world around you. Remember that each and every day you must find and utilize your ME time. I have several small ponds in my yard where I can go to meditate or just watch my fish swim. They make me feel better; it truly does work if you create such a place. My office is the same kind of place, decorated to help me and students who visit to relax and calm down. I always have quiet or meditative music playing. I have stress toys, such as a sand garden that students can rake, create designs, and just take a moment to just be. Create or identify such a place for you.
6. **Volunteer.** Give back to someone else or pay it forward. Make a difference in someone else's life. No matter how bad we feel our life is today, all around us are people who have more stress and turmoil in their lives than we can imagine. Make a difference by volunteering at a soup kitchen, a homeless shelter, an animal shelter, or volunteer at a hospice house where people know they are going to die and do so with grace and dignity.
7. **Be less critical.** Unless you are perfect, do not be so critical of those around you. The sting of words can last for days, months, and unfortunately sometime years. Think before you speak and try never to say a disparaging word. Look at the growing number of cases of violence and getting even with those who have hurt us. Our words do make a difference and so do our actions. Make sure your words and actions send the right message.
8. **Be honest with your feelings.** Tell someone you care. Don't wait until it is too late. It is okay to say, "Thank you," "I love you," "You make a difference in my life," "I am thankful you are my friend." Each of these statements has beauty and honesty within it. Use them.
9. **Laugh at yourself.** We all will end up doing stupid things in our lifetime, and it is better to laugh at yourself when others are laughing at you. Then the laughter is infectious and it doesn't hurt nearly as much. Remember the poor kid in the lunchroom who dropped his tray? Well, some of you may have laughed at that kid, causing him pain and embarrassment. If the response was to laugh with him, then the laughter would not be as hurtful. Life will be full of moments when laughter is a great way to relieve the stress of the moment. Use laughter whenever you can.
10. **Smile!** It amazes me as I walk around a college campus how many people are engrossed in texting, listening to music, and not engaging in the college experience. Whenever I walk around the campus, I make eye contact with those coming at me. I try to smile, say hello and, if at all possible, ask how they are doing. Often, I am ignored, but I will continue to smile as I walk to and from my classes. There is an old adage: Smile. It makes them wonder what you are up to. I just smile because it makes a difference. So smile, especially when you see me coming down the hallways.

What other suggestions or strategies can you add to this list? List some methods you are using or have heard of that may help lessen your negative stress response.

____

____

____

____

The homework assignments will help you examine some of your personal and physical responses to stress and to look at a list of common stressors that each of us may have experienced in the last six months. They will help you begin to examine the physiological response you experience when you are subjected to stress.

See you in Chapter 3.

REFERENCES

Selye, H. "Stress and Disease." *Science* Vol. 122, Number 3171 (1955): 625–631.

Wolfe, K. Keynote Presentation. *Inflamming-aging: Keys to Longevity and successful aging.* Wellness Conference, Stevens Point, Wisconsin. July, 2009.

NAS Database. Stress Management for the Health of It. Accessed March 30, 2012. www.nim.nih.gov/stress:medline

College Readjustment Rating Scale, Accessed March 30, 2012. www.uic.edu/depts/stress

Name________________________________ Class Days and Time ________________________

2.1

HOW DO YOU RESPOND TO STRESS?

Stress affects us on many levels. The following is a list of stress symptoms that are the most typical reactions. Go through and check all that apply. Next, go through and circle the ones that occur the most frequently.

Physical

_______ headaches

_______ fatigue

_______ insomnia

_______ weight change

_______ colds

_______ digestive upsets

_______ pounding heart

_______ accident prone

_______ teeth grinding

_______ restlessness

_______ increased alcohol, drug, tobacco use

_______ neck and shoulders tighten up/ache

Mental

_______ forgetfulness

_______ dull senses

_______ poor concentration

_______ low productivity

_______ negative attitude

_______ confusion

_______ lethargy

_______ no new ideas

_______ boredom

Emotional

_______ anxiety

_______ the "blues"

_______ mood swings

_______ bad temper

_______ crying spells

_______ irritability

_______ depression

_______ nervous laugh

_______ worrying

_______ easily discouraged

Social

_______ isolation

_______ resentment

_______ loneliness

_______ lashing out

_______ clamming up

_______ lowered sex drive

_______ nagging

_______ fewer contacts with friends

_______ using people

Study your list.

1. Which of your reactions cause you the most concern? _______________
____

2. Did any patterns surface? _______________________________
____

3. Can you name one effective way of coping with each of your stress reactions?
____
____

After you recognize the stress reactions and patterns and your best coping mechanisms, you can then create a stress management program to address the stressors in your life.

Source: NASD National Ag Safety Database, Clemson University Cooperative Extension Service. http://www.clemson.edu/extension/

Name________________________________ Class Days and Time ____________________

2.2

COMMON STRESSORS AMONG COLLEGE STUDENTS

Life Event		Value	Check if this applies
1	Death of spouse	100	
2	Divorce	73	
3	Marital separation	65	
4	Jail term	63	
5	Death of close family member	63	
6	Personal injury or illness	53	
7	Marriage	50	
8	Fired at work	47	
9	Marital reconciliation	45	
10	Retirement	45	
11	Change in health of family member	44	
12	Pregnancy	40	
13	Sex difficulties	39	
14	Gain of new family member	39	
15	Business readjustment	39	
16	Change in financial state	38	
17	Death of close friend	37	
18	Change to a different line of work	36	
19	Change in number of arguments with spouse	35	
20	A large mortgage or loan	31	
21	Foreclosure of mortgage or loan	30	
22	Change in responsibilities at work	29	
23	Son or daughter leaving home	29	
24	Trouble with in-laws	29	
25	Outstanding personal achievement	28	
26	Spouse begins or stops work	26	
27	Begin or end school/college	26	

continued

Life Event		Value	Check if this applies
28	Change in living conditions	25	
29	Revision of personal habits	24	
30	Trouble with boss	23	
31	Change in work hours or conditions	20	
32	Change in residence	20	
33	Change in school/college	20	
34	Change in recreation	19	
35	Change in church activities	19	
36	Change in social activities	18	
37	A moderate loan or mortgage	17	
38	Change in sleeping habits	16	
39	Change in number of family get-togethers	15	
40	Change in eating habits	15	
41	Vacation	13	
42	Christmas	12	
43	Minor violations of the law	11	
	Your Total		

Note: If you experienced the same event more than once, then to gain a more accurate total, add the score again for each extra occurrence of the event.

Score Interpretation

Score	Comment
300+	You have a high or very high risk of becoming ill in the near future.
150–299	You have a moderate to high chance of becoming ill in the near future.
<150	You have only a low to moderate chance of becoming ill in the near future.

Reprinted from Journal of Psychosomatic Research, Vol. 11, Issue 2, August 1967 by Thomas H. Holmes and Richard H. Rahe. "The Social Readjustment Rating Scale", pp. 213-218, Copyright © 1967, with permission from Elsevier.

Chapter 3
The Power of Our Healing Breath

Goals for This Chapter

- To understand the importance of breathe in healing the body and maintaining our health.
- To understand the concept of diaphragmatic breath.
- To understand the concept of resilience and how it can be a great tool in our stress tool kit.

KEY TERMS

breath
second-hand smoke
third-hand smoke
diaphragmatic breath (cleansing breath)
lotus position
resilience

Have you ever thought about the importance of your **breath**? Often we just take for granted this wonderful aspect of being alive. Many people have never taken the time to reflect upon their breathing, the pace of their breath, and the depth of each breath. After all, you automatically breathe about every three to five seconds, or twelve to twenty breaths per minute on average. When using fifteen breaths per minute, you take 900 breaths in an hour, 21,600 in a day, and over

Breath

exhalation and inhalation of air from the lungs.

7.8 million breaths in a year. Yet, we don't think about it; it just happens. The body automatically inhales, and then exhales every three to five seconds supplying oxygen to each cell of the body with each inhalation and with each exhalation removing carbon dioxide, the by-product of cellular respiration.

This is an understanding we must come to if we want to continue on this journey of wellness and stress reduction. We must not take our breath for granted; we must further explore and reflect on how our breath can help us manage our stress and how our breath can improve our health. We must monitor and take time to better understand the value of our breath. The focus of this chapter will be to help you better understand your breath as well as the connection between the breath and the heartbeat.

A QUICK REVIEW OF THE BREATHING PROCESS

How do you breathe and what happens when you do breathe? Answer this by demonstrating your understanding of the breathing process. ______________________________

____

____

____

____

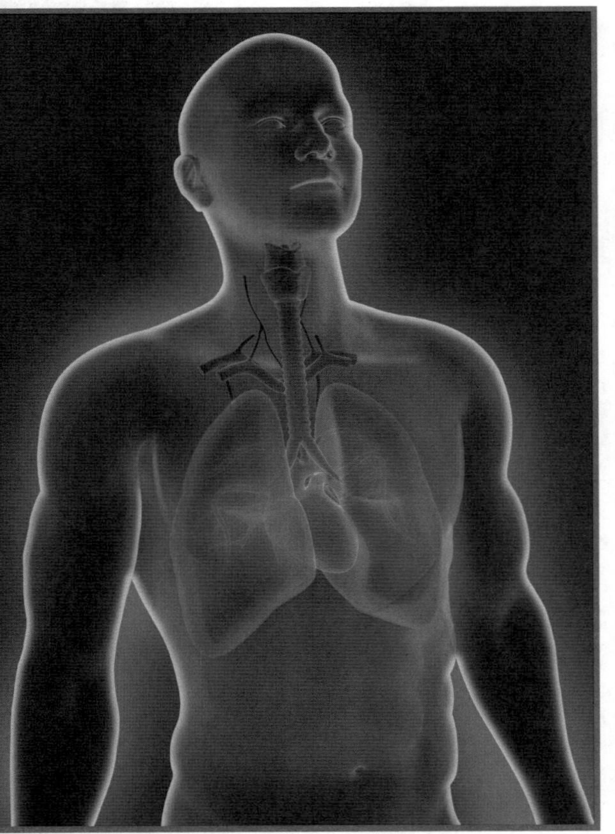

How was your explanation and overall understanding of the breathing process? The automatic nervous system (ANS) automatically handles all of the involuntarily bodily functions. It is an amazing concept that our body is able to have so many automatic bodily responses such as our heart rate, our breathing, our digestive processes. Could you imagine how complicated our lives would be if we had to concentrate on breathing or telling our heart to beat? Our minds would be so overwhelmed, we would be able to do little else.

The breathing process involves the nose, mouth, lungs, diaphragm, alveoli, and the heart to provide oxygen to each cell of the human body. When we take a breath, called either inspiration or inhalation, the air flows through the nose, into the pharynx, down the larynx into the trachea, into the lungs (the right lung has three lobes and the left lung has two lobes) through the bronchi and then into the bronchioles. Then the air travels into the alveoli (think a bunch of grapes) where the alveoli are surrounded by capillaries, which take the oxygen from the breath into the blood stream. The blood circulates back to the heart, where it is pumped throughout the body. Each cell within the body requires oxygen, and with this cellular respiration, there is a byproduct of carbon dioxide. As the blood circulates back to the lungs, the carbon dioxide is released back into the alveoli sacs and on expiration or exhalation, is removed from the body. The diaphragm muscle and the intercostals are the primary muscles involved with taking a breath. Additionally, the heart muscle is involved in the circulation of the new oxygen to the cells and the removal of the waste of carbon dioxide.

What simple and effective process breathing is and one that works as long as we are alive!

BREATHING AND OUR HEALTH

As efficient as the respiratory system of the body is, it can be negatively impacted by a wide variety of determinants to our health. Some of these are self-inflicted, such as smoking or second-hand smoke. Others include pollution (consider Los Angeles when there are smog alerts where the citizens of California are asked to stay inside or be less active because of the harmful particles in the atmosphere) or the spring when the flowers and trees start to bloom and pollen fills the air, making it harder to breathe.

I am positive that each of you are acutely aware of the negative impact smoking has on our health, and unfortunately, I also know that many people smoke and are not worried about the impact of the tar and nicotine will have on their breathing and overall health. This is an area that I have a hard time understanding: the allure of starting or continuing to smoke. It is not cool; it is a BAD habit that not only affects your health, but seriously impacts the health of your friends and loved ones if you smoke around them. We know that smoking is the number one determining factor for lung cancer! We know that smoking contributes to 80 to 85 percent of lung cancers developed each year. Why do we continue to smoke?

© Stocksnapper, 2012. Under license from Shutterstock, Inc.

I have personal experience with lung cancer and smoking. My father died in the year 2000, after being diagnosed with lung cancer in early January of that year. He passed away in March after going through chemotherapy and radiation for eight weeks. My father was a moderate to heavy smoker from the age of 18 until his 40s, when he began to try to lessen the negative impact of smoking on his health, and switched to smoking a pipe. He smoked his pipe until he was diagnosed. When his diagnosis was made, he didn't want to take ownership of the cancer as it related to his smoking. He chose to try to blame it on growing up on a truck farm outside of Cleveland, where as a teenager, he would mix the chemicals by hand with no breathing protection. Now, I know that was probably not a healthy choice either, but my grandfather did the same mixing for many years and lived until his mid-80s and he did not die from cancer. I had to call my dad on that, because all of the research continues to show a connection between smoking and lung cancer. Unfortunately, his smoking contributed to his early death. (He was 65 at the time and still working as a college faculty member). The effects of smoking are traumatic to our health and have long lasting impacts to our overall wellness.

The research is beginning to show that when you stop smoking, your body begins to heal itself within a matter of days. The lungs start to become pinker and the oxygen flow becomes stronger. The exchange of the oxygen at the alveoli level is more efficient, the amount of oxygen brought in with each breath is larger, and you begin to feel better. Do you remember the television commercials that discussed each cigarette taking six minutes of your life? I want to enjoy every minute of life that I have been given and losing six minutes for each and every cigarette seems like such a waste within my time on this earth.

As the cost of health insurance continues to rise and it becomes harder to obtain healthcare coverage, I believe we will see people denied health insurance due to smoking. It is on the radar and the choice is yours. So if you smoke, stop! That is as simple of a health promotion statement that can be made in relationship to smoking. Yes, I am acutely aware of the nicotine addiction and how hard it is to stop smoking. We are lucky that science has continued to help with many options to assist with nicotine addiction such as patches, gum, and other tools. Two websites that you may want to visit if you smoke and want to quit are: You Can quit smoking/cdc.gov at www.cdc.gov/quittingtips and New York State Smokers Quit line (1-866-NY-QUITS) at www.healthny.gov/prevention/tobacco.

Here is what I know from first-hand experience: quitting is very difficult, but it is not as difficult as your family watching you suffer, or having to adjust to life without you because of your dying from lung cancer and leaving your family way too early.

SECOND-HAND AND THIRD-HAND SMOKE

Second-hand smoke

inhalation of smoke in the environment from tobacco products used by others.

Third-hand smoke

inhalation of lingering chemicals within upholstery, bedding, curtains, and other material resulting from the use of tobacco products.

The negative impact of **second-hand smoke** is becoming more and more a focus of health research and the evidence is strong that second-hand smoke is extremely bad for all of us. It may not have the same impact on our health as directly smoking, but the research is united in the message that second-hand smoke is dangerous and a cause of a variety of health issues in this country. A big concern is how much exposure we each have to second-hand smoke. Additionally, they have now added another layer called **third-hand smoke**, which is the lingering amount of noxious chemicals that stay within the car seats, upholstery, bedding, curtains, and other materials in our environments. With second-hand smoke, the thought was once you stopped seeing the smoke the chemicals were assumed to be gone. Now we are concerned with the absorption of the chemicals from tobacco being absorbed into the environment and keeping the exposure high. This exposure is putting us at risk, even when there is no smoke visible. An example of this might be checking into a hotel and asking for a non-smoking room. When you enter the room, you can smell the smoke, because someone smoked in the room and no amount of cleaning or air-fresheners really remove the chemicals that were absorbed by the bedding, carpet, and curtains. This exposure is from third-hand smoke and we must understand its health complications and lessen our exposure to both second- and third-hand smoke.

MAKING OUR BREATH AN ALLY IN OUR WELLNESS

If you have ever been part of the child birthing process (either the women delivering or the birthing coach), then you have an awesome example of the power of breathing to achieve or overcome a painful process. If you have run up five flights of stairs until the top, and at the top are winded and light headed, then you know that focusing on your breathing will help you recover. If you have ever run a race and were breathing heavily, then you know with your breath you can regain how your body feels. Even if you have participated in a haunted hayride and you were scared to death, you can calm yourself down by focusing on your breathing. This is what we are talking about in this section. Using our breath to help us maintain our health, to take care of ourselves, and use the centering process of breathing to calm ourselves down.

There are many cultures throughout the world that discuss, practice, and believe in the power of breath and or life energy. These cultures teach that breathing is the life force within each of us, which is indeed true. Within Indian Sanskrit the word for breath is *prana*, the life force or energy within, similar to the Chinese word *qi*, which is thought of as life energy, or *qigone*, a practice of using breath for cultivation of life energy. In Japan, *reiki* is your life energy, your spirt. Each of these concepts is thousands of years old and still in practice around the world today. So the power of our breath is a reality; the only roadblock is our own viewpoint as to the power of our breath and our commitment to try to make use of our *prana*.

HOW TO BREATHE!

Let us review how to breathe. I am sure that you never expected to hear this assignment when you signed up for a class on stress management. You have been breathing since your first breath as you left the womb. It is automatic and you have never spent much time thinking about your breathing. That is until now.

I want you to learn how to breathe and begin to practice your breathing techniques as needed. So just sit there for a minute or so, with your eyes closed (no sleeping) and just breathe. Listen to your breath. Do you feel the synergy between your breath and your heartbeat? How deep is your breath? Do you fill your lungs completely? Do you breathe through your mouth or nose? Are you expanding the lungs completely and with exhalation are you emptying your lungs as well as possible? Each of these answers is an indication of how well you breathe. The overall question is how well do you breathe and then how can you improve or change your breathing to be better for you and your body.

First, the focus on breathing has to go deeper and beyond the automatic pilot you are currently on. So as you practice your breathing, I want you to take deep breaths in a variety of poses, from sitting in a chair, to lying down on your back, to standing up. Within each breath in each position you should notice a difference. Gravity does impact the depth of your breath; we need to appreciate this and focus on changing our breathing pattern for different events throughout our day.

So read this section and then, after you understand how I would like you to try to breathe, go ahead and follow these guidelines. Lie on your back on the floor (on a mat) or your bed, place one hand on your belly and place the other hand on your chest. Now take a deep **diaphragmatic breath** (often called a **cleansing breath**), through your nose, filling your lungs completely. Feel your chest rise up from the surface you are lying on as it fills with "new air." When you have taken a deep breath, deeper than you would normally take, then slowly exhale and remove the "old air" from your lungs. The inhalation and the exhalation should take the same amount of time. Repeat this process between five to nine times, with each breath filling the lungs completely and with each exhalation removing as much of the air in the lungs as possible.

Diaphragmatic breath (cleansing breath)

a deep breathing technique that draws air deep in the lungs by using the diaphragm rather than by flexing the rib cage.

While practicing your new breathing technique, you can add the aspect of turning your mind down, emptying your body, and becoming focused on your body. Listen to your body and hear the connection of your breath and your heartbeat. Diaphragmatic breath will become the beginning stages of each our meditations as we add meditation into our stress management tool kit. (More on that in the next chapter.)

**You may have noticed that I have added the descriptors of breathing in new or good air and exhaling old or bad air. By taking these deep breaths, you are getting rid of the stagnant air in the lower lobes of the lungs, thereby increasing the overall impact of these deep, cleansing breathes. As you take these deep cleansing or deep diaphragmatic breaths, you are increasing the life energy within your body.*

FINAL THOUGHTS ON DEVELOPING YOUR BREATHING

As with any skill from typing on a keyboard, hitting a softball, being a skilled artist, a poet, or a great student, we need to practice and maintain the skills that will enable us to be good. The same philosophy applies to learning how to breathe. We must create an awareness of working with our breath and then introducing it as a stress management tool as well as an adjunct to be used as part of our wellness plan.

Some possible strategies would be to take time over the next week to find a quiet moment, and a place to lie in a recumbent position (lying on your back, not on your stomach) to practice the deep diaphragmatic breath we have been discussing. Take somewhere between five to ten deep cleansing breaths, focusing on making your chest rise and fill completely. Make each inhalation and exhalation be the same length in seconds, and with each breath, turn your mind down. The focus of deep breathing is internally within you, letting go of the outside distractions and taking this time to become at peace, calming your body down and removing the old air that is deep within your lungs. After you have completed the five to ten deep breaths, just lie still and breathe, not as deeply, but keep still and focused internally.

How do you feel? What are your thoughts? Are your thoughts clearer? What is your overall reaction to focusing on your breath?

____

____

The next step is to try to focus on your diaphragmatic breath while sitting in the **lotus position**. The lotus position is a favorite pose for breathing and meditation. Sit cross-legged on a large pillow with your opposite foot on the other leg and vice versa. If you are a beginner or lacking some flexibility, then sit with your legs crossed in front of you, touching your each foot to the opposite calf. As you practice this technique, your flexibility may increase and you may go from a partial or modified lotus position to the full lotus position. You want your back and shoulders directly over your hips, head straight, elbows at 90 degrees, with your forearms resting on the upper leg. Palms should be opened and facing up towards the heavens. At first this position may seem awkward but with practice it will become more comfortable. One of the primary reasons that I prefer this position to lying prone on your back is that when students lie on their backs, occasionally they will fall asleep and then they are no longer practicing deep diaphragmatic breath or meditating. They are just sleeping, which may be a good strategy for managing your stress but is not the outcome we are trying to learn.

Lotus position

a cross-legged meditation position for meditation, with the left foot resting on the right thigh, and the right foot resting on the left thigh.

After you are comfortable in either the modified or lotus position, you will follow the same strategies from above. Take between five to ten deep cleansing breaths, focusing on making your chest fill completely. Leave a hand on your stomach to feel the work of the diaphragm. Focus on each inhalation and exhalation of being the same length, and with each breath, turn your mind down. The focus of deep breathing is internally in you, letting go of the outside distractions and taking this time to become at peace, calming your body down and removing the old air that is deep within your lungs. After you have completed the five to ten deep breaths, just sit still and breathe, not as deeply, but keep still and focused internally.

How do you feel? What are your thoughts? Are your thoughts clearer? What is your overall reaction to focusing on your breath?

____

____

These are two primary techniques for practicing your breath and both will be the positions we will utilize when we learn how to meditate in the next chapter. To take this practice and make it practical in our day-to-day lives, we have to utilize the breathing techniques in real life situations. Have you ever taken an exam and felt the stress overtaking your mind and body (especially in the shoulders and neck area)? This would be a wonderful opportunity to practice your breathing techniques to calm yourself. By taking a few moments to take five to ten deep cleansing breaths, you will clear your mind, calm your energy, and perhaps some answers will become more apparent. You know that if you studied, the material is somewhere in the brain. Use the breathing techniques to open your mind, to center yourself, and hopefully to be more successful with the test.

Have you ever been stuck in traffic? If you have, you are acutely aware of the stress level increasing as you worry about arriving at your final destination. As you sit, you feel a sense of muscle tension and headache developing. You begin to honk the horn, and perhaps you even gave the one-finger salute, all to no avail. Traffic will not part for you as everyone is stuck. The difference is how you respond to this stressor. If you are stuck and the traffic is not moving, perhaps place the car in park and take some deep cleansing breaths to help you remain calm. As the traffic jam starts to move, then you can be ready to continue on this journey with a better viewpoint.

Another example of breathing in during a life experience would be during your work environment, whether it is dealing with a rude colleague or a customer who just continues to push your buttons. You just want to say what is on your mind. If you do, you will likely lose your job, and if you don't you, will be aggravated for some time. Here is a great time to focus on your cleansing breath. Just breathe and get past the situation without ruining the rest of your day or impacting your health by developing a headache, stomachache, or even heart palpitations. Just breathe through this and don't let the other person win. Take care of yourself both in the short term and in the long term.

Resilience

the ability to adapt quickly to the situation and move forward positively.

A word that needs to be added to our stress reduction vocabulary is **resilience**. Resilience is the ability to go with the flow, adapt to the situations life is presenting us, and move forward, bouncing back from challenges within our lives, recovering from an illness, quickly adapting to what life hands us. Incorporate this word into your responses to stress and life will enable you to be that much the better.

My favorite example that confirms a group demonstration of resilience is the news article I remember seeing in January 2011. On New Year's Eve in Atlanta, Georgia, everyone was getting ready to travel to the New Year's Eve parties throughout the city. At the same time, a strong ice storm hit and basically closed the roads down. Well, many people were stuck in traffic, getting angry, honking the horns (like that will melt the roads), and increasing their stress levels. Another group of folks who were also stuck on the main arteries within the city, decided to get out of their cars, turn their car stereos on to the same station, get out the food and alcohol they were bringing to parties, and celebrate New Year's Eve with a party on the interstate. They were shown having a great time, making the best of a bad situation. To me that is a terrific example of resilience. Making lemonade out of lemons is not a bad life lesson; it's one we can all learn from.

Name____ Class Days and Time _________________________

3.1

BREATHING

1. After you have practiced the breathing techniques as described in the chapter, discuss the process and how your body felt. Did you prefer lying prone or in the lotus position as you practiced and why?

2. Give an example within your life that you have or could see using the breathing techniques as discussed in the book.

3. How do you handle second-hand or third-hand smoke as a serious health risk for you and your families?

4. Give an example within your life that you have demonstrated resilience and how it helped you with the situation.

Chapter 4
To Journal or Not to Journal

Goals for This Chapter

- To develop journaling skills.
- To be able to understand the usefulness of journaling as an effective stress management technique.
- To develop a journal and begin to write in it each week.

KEY TERMS

journaling

BRIEF REVIEW OF JOURNALING

As you read the title of this chapter, it is likely that several of you raised your eyebrows and said "No way." Others have used writing in a journal often during your lifetime. I want you to understand **journaling** and begin to develop an action plan. During the class, journaling is an assignment that will be expected for all of you.

Journaling

private writing for either record-keeping or thought-processing, often used as a stress reduction technique.

You have likely read or at least know some of the greatest journals of the last 150 years. You may have read *Little Women* written by Louisa May Alcott or *The Diary of a Young Girl* by Anne Frank. Both are personal reflections from their life experiences. *Little Women* is a story of a family in Concord, Massachusetts in the post-Civil War era of this country. It tells the story of four sisters through their life experiences of good, bad, and life changes. *The Diary of a Young Girl* was Anne Frank's account of being a young Jewish girl in hiding during the Nazi occupation of the Netherlands. Both are examples of using a journal to describe life experiences and share them with others.

A journal can be simply a place to write down your day's activities, your frustrations, your joys, and anger. Another method of using the journal is to keep track of your life story as the two authors previously mentioned. If you kept a journal for the rest of your life, imagine the experiences you will have and could share with your family members. Just in my lifetime, I have seen some amazing changes, which I will likely forget about or not share. A journal kept in this format will actually be your life story. Can you think of a better way to share your life with the generations after you?

If I had kept a journal, I would have written where I was when President John F. Kennedy was shot, or when I watched the first man on the moon, stating "one small step for man, one giant step for mankind." I can tell you what I was actually doing the morning of September 11, 2001 and share my fear as I watched the second plane hit the second tower; as I worried about friends who worked in the next building and hoped they were okay. In my journals, I would be able to describe growing up with a phone party line. For those of you who are asking what that is: we had multiple phones from different families on the same line. We each had a different ring, but if I wanted to listen to a neighbor's conversation I could lift the phone and either join in or listen. I would be able to tell my children and their children we had three channels, ABC, NBC, and CBS, and every day at midnight the *Star Spangled Banner* was played and then a test screen appeared until 7:00 or 8:00 a.m. the next morning. Today we have access to hundreds of channels, and Bruce Springsteen summed it up best with his song "57 Channels (and Nothing On)."

Another aspect of my life journal would include the aspect of my first computer I used in college to complete the statistical analysis of my master's research. The computer was the size of an average classroom. We had to key punch the data onto cards, then run the data, and finally get scrolls of computer paper from a huge printer. Today's phones have more capabilities than the computer I was using. These are just a few examples of what could be included in my journal if I had started early in my lifetime. Now all I can do is to try to recreate my life. Keeping a life journal would be so much easier.

MEN VERSUS WOMEN WITH A JOURNAL

Women are generally more likely comfortable with using a journal than men. My bet is that almost every woman reading this chapter was given a diary sometime in her lifetime and used it for a while. They always displayed the favorite cute character of the time on the cover and were equipped with a small lock designed to keep wandering eyes away from private thoughts, dreams, and hopes. You may have discussed your friends, your loves, as well as your enemies. If you still have yours someplace, go back, unlock it, and take a moment to go back in your past. What was your focus of your diary?

Men not so much. We didn't have time to write down our thoughts. We were too busy playing. The difference today is that both sexes are keeping journals and finding them to be wonderful ways to help manage stress. For this course, I believe each faculty member will expect that you will keep a journal. Not to worry; we won't actually read them. Our focus will be on this fact that you have a journal with at least three entries a week for the semester. I have been amazed when I read the final papers at the end of every semester. One of the common statements from students is how many of them (both sexes) enjoyed keeping a journal. They found it helped them review the issues of the day, as well as the emotions of the day. They often say they plan to continue to use a journal as they leave the class. They were skeptics who have added keeping a journal as tool in their tool kit.

STARTING A JOURNAL

The first step to writing in a journal is to have a journal. We know if you have ever spent a few moments in a Barnes and Noble or your local bookstore, that you can spend a small fortune for a journal. If you are planning on keeping a life journal, then perhaps the investment of a quality journal built to last a lifetime or longer may be worthwhile investment. For the average person, I would not start with that financial commitment. One of the most reasonable starting journals is the marbled-cover composition book that you have used throughout your school years. They are usually available for about a dollar. They have enough paper to last you for most of the semester. What you decide to use is up to you, but you will want to have something that is sturdy and not fall apart immediately.

The next step is to develop some guidelines for your journal. Some journals I have experienced are words only; others are a combination of sketches, doodles, art works, and cut outs of pictures and/or emotions. One of the methods I like is when people actually use different colored ink to represent their moods. There is no limit to the creativity that people use to reflect their personalities and their emotions. I have seen people write in huge letters, or big swear words, or in their own version of some secret code. I have seen people write on computers and print out their words and add them to the journal. Be yourself, and if you are creative, then let it out. The most important rule is to use your journal and write in it. When you write in the journal, try to develop more than a paragraph, but if you have little to say, then you have little to say.

The second guideline is to determine how often you will write in your journal. Some folks write every day; others write when they need to express their emotions of the day. How do you imagine using your journal? This will help you determine the question of when and how often to write. ____

____

Lastly, I would recommend you keep your journal in your room and write in it at the end of the day. If you feel the need to have the ability or access to write in the journal throughout the day, I would highly recommend making use of the technology available, verbal to your phone, an app on your smart phone or tablet device (remember to keep locked so no one can access your thoughts and emotions), and then add to your home-based journal at the end of the day.

Suggested Possible Journal Entries

Often people ask: where do we begin if we have never before kept a journal? The answer is simple: be open to any of the suggestions below. These are some possible concepts or starting points to enable you to start to journal. Here is a poem which I believe will also help you decide how to write in your journal. It is called "Most Important Words", author unknown, but I have used this poem for many years. See if you know the answer to each line?

> Six most important words: I am sorry, please forgive me.
> Five most important words: We can work this out.
> Four most important words: I will help you.
> Three most important words: I love you. (I bet you answered this one.)
> Two most important words: Thank you
> The most important word: Us
> The least important word: Me

Although I would have changed this last word to "I" because throughout this textbook, the focus is that we have to take care of ourselves, so the most important person to start with is me (yourself). Once you have taken care of yourself, you can then take care of your family, your friends, and your loved ones.

Using this variety of simple statements and these simple concepts may indeed help you start to develop thoughts for your journal. Below are some other common topics to help you get your thoughts onto paper.

- Gratitude—list five things you are grateful for. I think is a great one to start with. We often forget to show our gratitude to our family and loved ones. If you start with writing what you are grateful for, you may continue and show your gratitude to friends, family, and loved ones.
- Express any emotions you are feeling that particular day. If you are having a highly emotional day, your responses throughout the day may have been wrong, inappropriate, or hurtful. By discussing your emotions, the cause of the emotional response, and how it made you feel will enable you to look back with a reflective eye. A common comment when you write about your emotional responses for the day is this: how stupid, crazy, or silly that response was. We are emotional creatures who at times let our emotions take over or get the best of us. By reviewing the day, you may see how inappropriate your response was to something minor. At the same time, you may understand how much the event hurt you and by writing it down, you are removing the negative energy that came up.
- Your journal may include letters, paintings, collages, quotes, readings, drawings, photos, dreams, or poems. Nothing is really taboo within your journal, but remember your words within the journal can be hurtful and damaging if someone ever reads them.

- When writing in your journal, there are no grammatical consequences. You do not have to follow proper English. No one cares about your spelling, and no one will be upset if you did not follow the APA (American Psychological Association) format. If you choose to write your paragraph or pages in text language, that is your choice. Your grade will not be impacted by your writing style. A journal is yours to develop and create as you see fit.
- Your journal is a place for self-inquiry, focusing, creativity, mindfulness, and compassion. Don't be afraid to let your emotions out; joy, happiness, anger, or frustration can all be expressed in your writing. Lastly, *no one will read your journal, only you.* (Unless you keep your life history, so in a hundred years, when you have passed away, perhaps some family member will find it and read it. Then they will have an amazing history of an amazing person who will have had a great life.)

© casejustin, 2012. Under license from Shutterstock, Inc.

This is a quick overview and a suggested method to start journaling. I know that some of you will reconnect with this technique and be elated. Others will think this is not for you, but at least for this timeframe of the semester, give it a try. Remember we are developing a multitude of tools to add to your stress management tool kit and you may find this one to be a more useful approach than you first expected. You may be surprised at how a journal will keep you healthy, maintain your sanity, allow you to reflect on the variety of emotions you have shown throughout the day, and it may make the day end on a good night. Perhaps by letting go of the life experiences that challenged you today, you will sleep soundly tonight.

Name____ Class Days and Time ________________________

4.1

START TO JOURNAL

Your assignment for this chapter is to start to journal. Below are several statements that could be used in a journal. You are asked to give an answer and do so as this was a journal entry. Answer each of these questions in one or two paragraphs. They are designed to make you think.

1. The qualities that make a best friend are…

2. Describe a life event which has caused a change in you…

3. The best lesson any relative ever taught me was…

4. What kind of animal would you like to be and why…

Chapter 5

Time Management: What Are We Doing to Ourselves?

Goals for This Chapter

- To develop an understanding of the intrusive nature of technology into our lives.
- To understand how to improve our time management.
- To develop plans to better utilize our time usage.
- To comprehend and implement time management strategies to be a committed student.

KEY TERMS

time management
time management strategies
plan of action
to do list

INTRODUCTION TO THE TIME MANAGEMENT ISSUE

If ever there was a topic that the population of the United States needs to re-examine it is the obsession we have with having access 24/7 every day of our lives to our friends, work, and school. Where did this come from and why do we continue to allow it in our lives? I remember as a child visiting Disneyworld in Orlando, Florida and specifically the exhibit called Future World. Within the exhibit, along with many examples of dreams that actually became reality for each of us, the biggest idea was how computers were going to make our lives so much easier. They would do the work quicker, faster, and more accurately. They actually predicted computers would give us more leisure time; all Americans would have more time for recreation and their families. I think (well, I hope) we agree that computers have significantly changed our lives; unfortunately they have not given us more time for recreation. Our ME time was not increased. Instead, it has been attacked.

Here are some examples of technology impacting us. I was on a vacation where a businessman stood in the water of the Gulf of Mexico for forty-five minutes arguing with someone at his work. My suggestion was, if you are on vacation, let it go. Recently my niece had emergency surgery to remove her appendix. In the middle of the night as the drugs were wearing off, she went online to update her Facebook page! I was recently at a family get together, and as I looked downstairs where a dozen or so cousins were watching a movie, the majority of them were texting others instead of catching up with their cousins whom they hadn't seen in six months or longer.

Technology is and can be very intrusive in our lives. We need to take our valuable time back and use it wisely.

TIME MANAGEMENT STRATEGIES

Time management

the act of organizing the way you spend your time so that the most important and/or the most necessary activities are prioritized and accomplished first.

The first mistake we commonly make as related to **time management** is not creating or understanding the commitments we have in our lives. We all have a lot on our plate; the question is do we understand how much we have and tackle the most important aspects or the ones that are fun? I hope that the number one priority in your life is the reason you are sitting in a class in college. You want to develop a professional career that will hopefully lead you to a good life. So the goal is to complete your degree and obtain a job in your profession. Do you agree with this statement? If so, then for the time you are in college classes, the number one priority is to attend class, study, and do the work, projects, papers, and tests that are assigned throughout the semester. Yet, we all know countless students who do not follow through; they do not hold that priority to number one. If they did, then they would focus on being successful in each and every class.

Time management strategies

the skills, tools, and techniques used to manage time when approaching specific tasks, projects, and goals.

To help you develop this success within your college program, there are a wide variety of **time management strategies** that will enable you to work towards this goal. The first day of class you are given a course information sheet or a syllabus, which explains the course, the expectations of the professor, and the guideline for reading, homework, labs, and exams. At the end of each first day, do you go home and map out all of the assignments, the tests, and all related work for the semester? If you do, you will see a visual aid as to what the semester looks like as related to school work. You can even see some weeks that look like hell weeks, but if you know they are coming, you can prepare, do some work early, and still be up to the challenge. This is the start of a good time management program: taking an action step and planning out the week, month, or semester.

Students who struggle with time management do not often take this first step. They take the day as it comes, not looking too far into the future. They often live for the moment. They add more stress to their lives by waiting until the last minute and then wonder why they often fail or are not very successful. I have students I advise who find certain courses like anatomy very difficult. I walk them over to the science lab where there are advisors and faculty available to help them. I ask have they ever been and they say no. Then I ask if they are in a study group, and they say they thought they could do it themselves. When they finally determine they are in over their head, they often quit. My advice is to fight through it. We all will face failure in our lifetimes; the question is do we learn from our failures and change the strategy, or do we repeat the same process the next time?

Before we continue with other time management strategies, I would like to talk about habits of successful students. These are related to strategies, but are helpful to all.

Habits of Successful Students

1. Attend class, be on time, be prepared to be engaged in the lecture, and ready to learn. This may seem simple, but you would be amazed how many students fail a class or even drop out of college because they didn't attend classes.
2. Read the assignments before the class. Then if the reading and the lecture still don't make sense, you know you will have to work harder on the chapter. It amazes me when a student doesn't read before the lecture, and then reads before the quiz and gets lost. If you are prepared and the material is not making sense, ask questions of the faculty member to help you better understand the concept. If you haven't read the material, you will never be able to ask the questions or be involved within the class discussion.
3. Treat coming to a college class like a job. If you don't show up for work what happens to you? Well, if you are lucky, you may get a warning the first time, but likely the second time you will be fired. Within the work environment, we understand that. Use that same strategy with each of your classes. If you are not there, you will not be successful.
4. Build relationships with your faculty members. Most of us are good people who want you to be successful. If you need help, visit us during office hours. If you are scheduled to be in a lab for review, attend, and reach out early and often as needed. Don't wait until the last couple of weeks and then ask for extra credit. If you haven't felt the class was worth your time, why would we go the extra mile for you?
5. Know when all of your assignments, tests, papers are due and have them completed and ready to turn in. If you are a weak writer, finish the first draft of the paper early and take it to the writing center for feedback. Take their comments and integrate them into the paper to have a much better finished product.
6. Sit in the front half of the classroom. Here you can be engaged with the faculty member and answer or ask questions. Be an active participant in the learning process; become a sponge. I always wonder about the students who always sit in the back row.
7. Come prepared to class with a notebook, writing instrument, book, and appropriate lab supplies. It always amazes me when a student comes to class without a notebook or pen. If you are taking notes on a laptop, make sure you are taking notes and not playing games or talking to your friends.
8. Turn your phone off during the class time. If there is a crisis in the world, I believe we will all find out at the same time. How many times do we have to hear from our

significant loved ones to know that they love us? Honor their love by focusing on being the best student you can possibly be to make a better life for both of you.

9. Set academic goals for yourself for each course, each semester, for your undergraduate degree. This will make you focus and be accountable for your actions. If you want an "A" in a hard course and only study an hour a week, then you are not trying to achieve academic success.
10. Take risks. It is okay to take risks as a student; we all learn from our successes as well as our failures. No excuses! You are accountable for every action you make from this day forward. When you fail, move forward, examine why and make changes so that it doesn't happen again.
11. No sleeping in class. A simple rule that is often broken by students who are burning the candle at both ends.
12. If you miss a class, send an email to the faculty member before class. At least they know you care about missing their class. Ask if they have the notes available online; contact a classmate to obtain a copy of their notes. If you miss a class, you must keep up with the work.
13. Take advantage of the wonderful diversity of your college, the community; meet new people, learn about their cultures, reach out and make a friend. In a global society, being able to understand individuals from different cultures, different religions, and different viewpoints will pay off during your lifetime. At college this may be the best opportunity to explore diversity.
14. Work with your classmates on class projects and become a vital member of the group. Don't become a slacker, as this will affect not only your grades but others' grades as well. If you develop a reputation of being a slacker within your academic program, eventually no one will want to work on group projects with you. What message is that sending from your peers to the faculty member?
15. Enjoy this time of your life. Yes, it will be hard and at times stressful. But this is an exciting time, so make the most of it. Enjoy your educational experiences. Become involved on the campus; join a club or an organization. If there is a faculty advisor, get to know him or her. Someday you will need a letter of reference and having a faculty member who knows you both as a student and from other perspectives will enable him or her to write a strong letter.
16. Lastly, remember to SMILE; it will brighten the attitudes of those whom you meet and you will make a difference. Smiles are free and the return of your investment may be hard to measure, but it does make the world around us a better place to live in. May your smile be contagious now and forever.

As we discuss your commitments, take a minute and list the top five commitments you currently have in your life. Then next to each commitment that you currently have, identify how much time you believe you give to each. ______________________________

____

____

We will review your commitments at the end of the chapter. This is the first step as we try to develop a strategy for time management. Understand your commitments and how far you are extended.

The next step is to develop a **plan of action** by the day or week. Here is where your technology can help you stay of task. Likely, you have a calendar on your phone or computer. Use it. Develop a plan for all that you have to accomplish this week. Plan your study times, plan your time at work, and don't take extra shifts at work unless you have accomplished everything on your day. Remember, you are in college and that is your number one priority. No smart phone? Then I guess you will have to go old school with a day planner or a desk calendar. Map out your semester and make a commitment to follow the map you have prepared. What happens when you travel to a new area without a map? You likely will become lost. The same principle applies here. Stay focused and committed to your success.

Plan of action

the means by which you focus your thoughts and decide what steps are needed to take to achieve your goals.

When discussing planning study time, do you know what is recommended for course work? An approximate guideline is that if you want to receive a "C" in a course, for every hour you are in class, you should plan on two hours of studying and homework outside of class. So for a three-credit course, you should build in six hours of studying. If you want a "B," then they suggest you should plan three hours outside of class for every hour in class. If you want to earn an "A", then you should plan four hours of outside studying. So if you have a hard anatomy or chemistry class and want to earn an "A," the class meets five hours a week and four hours per class, you will need to study around twenty hours a week to earn the "A." This is only a suggested guideline, but if you are struggling in a class, the first question the faculty member will likely ask you is how much time you are putting into the class.

The next step in your studying plan is to never study a course material for more than one hour at a time. I recommend studying for fifty minutes and then taking ten minutes off. During the rest period, you may check your texts, go to the facilities, grab a bite to eat, and when the ten minutes are up, go back to studying. Except now, move on to another subject for the next fifty minutes. After the next break, if you need to study or do more work for the first course, go back to it. This will keep it fresh and enhance your overall retention of the subject matter.

To do list

a list of things you want to accomplish within a given time period.

The next recommendation which I have found useful is to develop a **"to do" list** for the day. How many of you would consider yourself good at multi-tasking? Unfortunately, many of us believe we are, and then we continue to fail or not finish something, which increases our stress level. A simple suggestion is to create your to do list the night before, so that as you prepare it you will start to see what lies ahead of you. Create the list from the most important to the least important. When you complete the first task on the list, cross it off, then move on. Each time you cross something off, you will feel a sense

© Melinda Fawver, 2012. Under license from Shutterstock, Inc.

of accomplishment. Of course, during the day you may have to modify your list. Keep working on your list, and at the end of the day, you can feel good for what you completed. Whatever is left on the list can be moved to the next day, but you will have to reassess where it fits on the next list.

I have found lists are very helpful, especially when people want to add to your list, or your friends want you to come out and hang. If the list is complete, you can go without any guilt, but if there are still important activities to be completed, then you have to say no to your friends.

This leads us to the next concept for managing your time well. The best word you must add to your vocabulary is the word "no." Too often we become "yes" people to our bosses, to our family, to our friends, and we lose track of what we need to do. I am not saying your boss, family, and friends or significant other are not important, but they have to respect you for what you are trying to accomplish. Try not to take extra shifts at work very often, because as you will see, you are likely overextended and by taking those extra shifts, you will impact your weekly plan. This may cause the plan to fail, which means the next week you will have to catch up. For every decision that is not supported by your plan there is often a negative reaction or outcome to your plan. You are the only one who has ownership of the plan.

The same concept works with friends and family. You are now a college student and it may not be reasonable to be able to make every family outing or hang with your friends all day Saturday. If possible, you will add it in, but on the list of priorities, sometimes you will have to make hard choices. Make the choices that will make you better. Yes, sometimes your friends will give you grief, but if they are your friends, I hope they support and understand your long-term commitment to becoming a professional.

Learn to say no whenever you feel that saying yes will add stress to your life. It takes practice, but once you start to use the word, people are not so surprised when you do. It may take practice, but saying no will make a huge impact of being successful within your plan and college.

The last strategy for improving your time management is to work on developing goals, both short-term and long-term. Sometimes we need extra motivation, an extra incentive to help us stay focused on the long-term outcomes. So as you develop your weekly plan, if you complete everything, give yourself something more than a gold star. Heck, maybe the gold star would work, but not for long. So if you complete your plan for the week early, go hang out with your friends, go to dinner with a loved one, go for a walk on your favorite hiking trail. Thus the reward acts as congratulations for doing a good job and you can enjoy the fruits of your labor. If your goal is to achieve a 3.0 this semester and you do, celebrate the accomplishment, buy a new outfit, or a new toy, or the latest CD of your favorite artist. The goals do not have to be costly; sometimes we are motivated by the simple pleasures that occur around us all the time. (An example is as I type this, out my window I am able to see a new moon with both Venus and Mars in view nearby. It is a beautiful example of simple pleasures of our life.)

Keep a list of your goals on your desk, your smart phone, and share with those who are supporting you and make them a part of your success.

FINAL THOUGHTS

Time management will enable you to stay focused, will help you be successful in your life, and will tremendously help lower your stress level. Likely, you know people who always wait to the last minute to accomplish their work or study for a test. More frustrating is that some of these procrastinators are successful in their lives, but many end up crashing and burning at some point. Don't stay a procrastinator or even worse, emulate their behavior that is likely a sure path to failure!

Each of the strategies for time management is based on you making a change or improving strategies you are currently using. If your strategies are working, keep using them, but perhaps take some of the suggestions to improve your overall plan.

We have become a twenty-four hours a day, seven days a week world. We must take control of our time and make the most of it. Those twenty-four hours a day equal 168 hours in a week, and 8,736 hours in a year. Make the most of every hour and always find time for you every day.

Name________________________________ Class Days and Time ____________________

5.1

COLOR-CODED SCHEDULE

The assignment for the week is to keep a color-coded record of how you spend your time. Record when your classes are, your studying schedule, your work schedule, time on Facebook, time playing games on technology, time outside, exercise, hanging out with friends/family. I want you to capture how you spend your week and then answer the questions at the end.

Time of Day	Sun	Mon	Tues	Wed	Thur	Fri	Sat
6:00 a.m.							
7:00							
8:00							
9:00							
10:00							
11:00							
Noon							
1:00 p.m.							
2:00							
3:00							
4:00							
5:00							
6:00							
7:00							
8:00							
9:00							
10:00							
11:00							
Midnight							
1:00 am							
2:00							
3:00							
4:00							
5:00 a.m.							

Add your color codes here (add others as needed):

Classes

Significant other

Commuting

Showering/getting ready

Work

Studying

Watching TV

Clubs/organizations/ volunteering

Eating

Exercise/play

Hanging with friends

Texting/Facebook

Family time

Computer time

Sleeping

Answer the following questions after you have completed recording your time usage for the week.

1. Were you surprised at how busy you are? Explain?

2. How much non-productive time did you record for the week? What were the biggest non-productive users of your time? Can you change them?

3. Do you preplan your week to manage your time?

4. Do you schedule your time to study each week or on an as needed basis?

5. Did you meet the goal of at least 150 minutes of moderate physical activity or exercise this week? If yes, good job. If not, why not?

6. While reviewing your week, what changes do you believe you need to make to better manage your time?

7. Did you find time each day to do something for yourself? If no, why?

8. Did you average seven to eight hours a sleep each of the nights you recorded? On the days you didn't get seven to eight hours, what was your next day like?

9. List your biggest time consumers of the week. How much of an impact do they contribute to the stress in your life?

10. After reviewing this week, what suggestions do you have for yourself to make better use of your time?

Name________________________________ Class Days and Time ____________________

5.2

LIFE BUCKET LIST

One of my favorite assignments for this class is this one: the Life Bucket List. First, it surprises me how many people are limited in their life goals. They have limitations, they lack vision. So for this assignment I want you to create a Life Bucket List. The guidelines are fairly simple; look forward in your life, develop the goals and aspirations you hope to accomplish, and write them down. Then every year on New Year's Day or your birthday, take out the list and check off items you have completed, and perhaps add new items that you have decided to do. I don't really want to see how many cars, homes, and toys you hope to own. I actually keep in touch with many students and one I know for sure still uses his bucket list. Good luck, have fun, and when this is returned, place it in a safe place and start living and checking off items after you have done them.

1. ____________________
2. ____________________
3. ____________________
4. ____________________
5. ____________________
6. ____________________
7. ____________________
8. ____________________
9. ____________________
10. ____________________
11. ____________________
12. ____________________
13. ____________________
14. ____________________
15. ____________________
16. ____________________
17. ____________________
18. ____________________
19. ____________________
20. ____________________
21. ____________________
22. ____________________
23. ____________________
24. ____________________
25. ____________________
26. ____________________
27. ____________________
28. ____________________
29. ____________________
30. ____________________
31. ____________________
32. ____________________
33. ____________________
34. ____________________
35. ____________________
36. ____________________
37. ____________________
38. ____________________
39. ____________________
40. ____________________
41. ____________________
42. ____________________
43. ____________________
44. ____________________
45. ____________________
46. ____________________
47. ____________________
48. ____________________
49. ____________________
50. ____________________
51. ____________________
52. ____________________
53. ____________________
54. ____________________
55. ____________________
56. ____________________
57. ____________________
58. ____________________
59. ____________________
60. ____________________

Chapter 6

Meditating and You: Taking the First Steps

Goals for This Chapter

- To understand what meditation is and how it can be used to manage our stress and our wellness.
- To be able to explain the differences between mindfulness, exclusive and guided imagery meditation styles.
- To practice and experience at least five meditations as developed in the appendix.
- To create your own meditation that you find beneficial.

KEY TERMS

meditation
mindfulness meditation
exclusive meditation
inclusive meditation
guided imagery meditation

ADDING MEDITATION TO OUR TOOL KIT FOR STRESS MANAGEMENT

In the previous chapters, we have introduced the concept of wellness. We have provided a brief overview of stress, its definition, and the types of stress we are exposed to, as well as the common categories of stressors we are faced with. We have started to use our breath as a tool within our tool kit and have started to consider time management and journaling as strategies to lessen the impact of stress in our lives. The next technique to be added is meditation. Now, don't start with any number of previous misconceptions such as: "I can never see myself meditating," or "That is so weird, it takes too long, and people will think I am funny." The focus of this book is to introduce you to a variety of techniques that will make a positive improvement within your wellness and to grow your stress management tool kit and meditation is one of those techniques.

One of the constants since I began to teach this class is the amazing growth and willingness of my former students to try meditation. (Many students were worried if they could meditate and were afraid it wouldn't work. They felt it was outside of their comfort zone or just couldn't focus on keeping the practice alive. The great aspect is that a common theme in the final lifestyle papers has always been that although the students were intimidated by meditation at first, many have become fond of the practice and hope to continue using meditation in their lives. Another example of students' responses to practicing meditation in class is that occasionally during the semester, I will lecture too long and not leave time at the end of the class to lead them in a guided imagery meditation. Often they complain that they wanted or needed the meditation or even that the meditation was the primary reason they came to class that day. So my experiences have been, if you give it a chance, many of you will begin to see the value of meditation and will likely continue to use this technique long after you have received your final grade.

Meditation

contemplation; a quiet, alert, yet focused state of mind often used as a relaxation technique.

My request is quite simple: open your mind to the possibility. We will practice often throughout the semester and if you find it works, terrific, and if you find it doesn't work for you at this time, at least you have made a decision based on the experience of meditation, not the assumption of what you think meditation is.

© Malyugin, 2012. Under license from Shutterstock, Inc.

WHAT IS MEDITATION?

My first actual experience with any meditation was in 1975 when I moved into a fraternity house as a freshman at Ithaca College and my senior roommate was practicing Transcendental Meditation almost every day. I was unsure of what he was doing, but I remember that when he practiced, he would sit in the middle of our dorm room for sixty to ninety minutes totally unaware of what was going on around him in the room. I could have music on, fraternity brothers would stop by, and he never knew it. When we discussed his actual meditations, he always described it as going down deep within himself to find his center and calmness. I have lost track of him, but my guess is that he still is practicing almost forty years later.

To define **meditation**, I would frame it around these concepts. Meditation is indeed a relaxation technique, which is based on practices thousands of years old. It tends to be a solitary practice (although Buddhist monks, among others, practice meditation in larger groups;

even prayer within church has been considered as a form of meditation). It is used to clear the mind of thoughts and the outside stimulus of the world. The focus of meditation is to create an inner peace within your spirit. The focus is also to create a self-awareness and in many cultures, the focus of meditation is to heal your body, your spirit, or your mind. You may ask if this is really possible, and I can only answer in the affirmative for myself and for the many students who have learned how to meditate within this class.

The National Institute of Health considers meditation to be a category under Complementary and Alternative Medicine (CAM), and meditation is further classified as a mind-body medicine. A mind-body medicine focuses on the integration of the mind and other parts of the human body. A mind-body medicine influences many of the components of wellness, specifically emotional, mental, social, and spiritual by changing or impacting our health. Imagine a medicine that we do not need a prescription, that has no real cost, and makes a difference in our health and our stress levels.

**A warning thought: just because meditation is classified as a mind-body medicine, I am not suggesting that we should start managing our medical care without talking and including our primary physician. I truly believe for my own personal health care, a combination of Western, scientific medical practices, as well as the use of and integration of Eastern Philosophy and the use of complementary and alternative medicine are a part of a thorough and comprehensive approach to my healthcare. University and medical schools have begun to teach CAM classes in medical school, and slowly Western doctors are becoming more aware and asking more questions of their patients. If you are using any CAM techniques, you must share and discuss them with your doctor. Then we can work with our doctors to develop a comprehensive plan to improve or maintain our health! More on this in Chapter 14.*

In a Welcoa 2010 online bulletin, five types of meditations were discussed. They are mindfulness, insightfulness, loving-kindness, exclusive, and inclusive. Brian Luke Seaward, a foremost expert on stress in this country discusses three primary types of meditation as inclusive, exclusive, and mindfulness. So you will likely hear differences in techniques, but the focus and framework for all meditations remains centered around the premise of taking time to enter yourself, to relax and listen to your body, your mind, and your spirit.

The most common and likely the most researched form of meditation is called **mindfulness meditation**; Jon Kabat-Zinn is one of the world's experts on mindfulness meditation. The

Mindfulness meditation

a type of meditation in which you are engaged with and focused on a single activity, without letting your thoughts wander.

focus of mindfulness is to be fully present with whatever activity you are doing. Whether that is driving home or walking in the neighborhood, the concept is to be fully aware of everything related to the activity. You should not let your mind wander. By being mindful, you are more aware of your surroundings, which allows you to have a better understanding of your thoughts, your emotions, and how they affect your health. The only requirement is to be fully engaged with your activity and take in everything, without letting your mind wander to some other pressing thought. In principle, it is an easy concept, but it takes practice to be able to stay fully present in the moment, especially in our society which is based on 24/7 access. Give it a try and see if you can develop a practice or experience based on mindfulness meditation.

Exclusive meditation

a type of meditation in which you focus on one thought, slowing the mind, concentrating on the breath and often using a mantra such as the word "OM."

An example of a mindfulness meditation would be to eat an orange. Not just eat the orange, but to be fully present while eating the orange. Feel the texture of the skin as you peel it, smell the citrus oils in the air, and feel them on your hand. Taste the sweetness of the juice and flesh as you bite into the fruit. Actually be a part of each step as you prepare and then eat the orange. It is truly a difference between eating an orange and appreciating the opportunity to eat the orange.

Inclusive meditation

a type of meditation in which you focus on the range of emotions you have experienced throughout the day without passing judgment on your thoughts or feelings.

Guided imagery meditation

a type of meditation in which you use hypnosis-like suggestions to create images in the mind, which elicit positive emotions such as joy, love, happiness, and calmness.

Another common type of meditation is known as **exclusive meditation**, where the focus is on one thought. You are trying to slow your mind down. Often someone who is practicing exclusive meditation will use a mantra such as the word "*Om*", which is repeated over and over to help calm and center the mind. At the same time you are speaking your mantra, you will still focus on your breath. The repeating of your mantra and the focus on your breath helps you quiet your mind. Once the mind is quieted, you will be able to focus your energy on a thought, perhaps creating depth within the thought or taking that thought to a reality with clarity and purpose.

Inclusive meditation is another type of meditation that allows you to focus on the range of emotions you have experienced throughout the day. Inclusive meditation is suggested as an emotional detachment to the range of human emotions you have experienced that day. During this process, you do not pass judgment on your thoughts or feelings. Zen meditation would be a good example of an inclusive meditation.

The last category of meditation is **guided imagery meditation**, which is the type we often use within class. The focus is to develop imageries in your mind that create joy, love, happiness, relaxation, calmness that help contribute to changing your emotional and mental response to the day. I use guided imagery most of the time. Over the years, I have found it is easier for students to listen as I create a place, doing an activity that I hope they can relate to. The focus is for the mind to create the images that are being presented. Within guided imagery, it is important to try to use as many of the five senses as possible. When I present a meditation on the beach, I add the element of the breeze blowing across your body, the warmth of the sun on your face, the taste of the salt water as you dive into the ocean. Each of the senses adds depth to the created image in your mind. The images that I utilize within this category are related to things that I have experienced within my life. I try to take the lasting image and recreate for you, the student. So when we use a beach image it is because I believe most of us have experienced a beach and it is easier to recreate in your mind. The image is imprinted in your mind and we are embellishing it and or giving more suggestions to make the image come alive in your mind.

You now have an introduction to the types of meditations that are commonly practiced in the world. Before we continue with learning how to meditate and to begin the practice of meditation, it is appropriate to discuss the health benefits of meditation. The health benefits are not only limited to the calming of the mind, which is a stress management tool in our tool kits, but the overall benefits of meditating, which will have a long-term impact on our wellness.

© Markus Mainka, 2012. Under license from Shutterstock, Inc.

HEALTH BENEFITS OF MEDITATING

If you were to Google "health benefits of meditating" the search would likely come back instantaneously with thousands of hits and possibilities to read and review. The search would show how much interest meditation has received from scientific evidence based on research communities around the globe and how it is becoming better understood and more mainstream in the scientific community. Although the benefits have been reported for thousands of years, sometimes we need scientific proof to support our choices. I am summarizing the concept that the literature does support meditation as both a stress management tool and as an adjunct to help us improve our wellness. Take the time to do a search and read some articles on the value of meditation for yourself.

This list is by no means all inclusive, but is a good sampling of the reported and researched health benefits of meditation include: helps us regain a calmness, increases our relaxation response, reduces our stress and anxiety, helps strengthen our immune system, increases our creativity, improves the quality of sleep, lowers our resting heart rate, lowers our resting blood pressure, improves our mental acuity or sharpness, lowers our fatigue level, recharges our "battery," improves memory function, improves our physical and emotional resilience, increases our happiness and joy, increases our reception to love, forms a connection to our spiritual self, as well as lowers our levels of aggravation and impatience.

As you review the list, is there anything listed that has a negative impact on your overall stress levels or your health and wellness? None of these reported benefits of meditating that I can see or imagine appears to be harmful. The positive outcomes of meditating are making inroads in this country. In our culture, in the American mindset, instead of meditating to achieve these results, we go to our physician and take pills to create some of these same outcomes. As the cartoon shown earlier says, we have a choice medicate or meditate. I hope you will give meditation a serious try and awaken your mind, body, and spirit to a new level of consciousness and happiness. Namaste!

© StockLite, 2012. Under license from Shutterstock, Inc.

STARTING YOUR MEDITATION PRACTICE

To start, you need to designate an area that you will feel relaxed in, absent from normal distractions of everyday life. In my home, I have several small ponds with small waterfalls, which make a great place to meditate. The calming sound of the waterfall actually blocks the other sounds in my yard. So if the weather is nice, go outside and sit under a tree on the grass. If you have to meditate inside, turn your cell phone off, turn your computer to sleep mode, leave the house phone in another room. If you have a pillow to sit on, good; if not, then a clean space on the floor will do. If you like music that is instrumental (suggestions in Appendix B) and you find it relaxing, then having your iPod, iPad, or disc player is a good addition to the meditation. I would not wear headsets as that may be distracting while you are meditating.

The next step is to make yourself comfortable and to assume one of two recommended meditation poses: lie on your back or to sit in the lotus position. A worthwhile suggestion is to start your meditation practice at no more than five minutes. Then slowly build time on as you become more comfortable until you are meditating for fifteen to twenty minutes.

Hint for a successful meditation: Read the following guided imagery once before you attempt it. It is hard to meditate and read the cues. If you have access to a voice recorder, you could even read the following and play it as a guide.

If you choose to lie on your back, make sure your body is in a straight line from head to shoulders, hips, and legs. Let your legs relax and drop open a little to the side. Have your hands lying next to you on the ground, palms facing up. If you choose to meditate in either a modified or the lotus position, make sure to keep your hips, shoulders, and head in good alignment, with arms bent at 90 degrees at the elbow, resting on the top of your legs. The last step is to form a circle with your thumb and longest finger letting the rest of the hand remain palm open and facing up. (The intent with both positions and the position of the hands is to be open to receive gifts from above.)

Once you are comfortable, you are ready to begin. Keep your eyes closed and begin with your deep diaphragmatic breath (often called a cleansing breath). Breathe through your nose, filling your lungs completely. Feel your chest rise as it fills with new air. When you have taken a deep breath, deeper than you would normally take, then slowly exhale. The inhalation and the exhalation should take the same amount of time. Then repeat this process between five to seven times, with each inhalation filling the lungs completely and with each exhalation removing as much of the air in the lungs as possible. While focusing on your breathing technique, start the process of turning your mind down; empty your thoughts and become focused internally on your body. Listen to your body; hear the connection of your breath and your heartbeat. When you feel the connection of your breath and your heartbeat, you are in contact with what we would consider being our life force within us. Embrace your heartbeat and slow it down by telling your mind to slow the heart rate down.

In the next step for this beginning meditation, I want you to see your favorite color in your mind's eye. Make this color come to life in your mind. Can you see the color, focus on the color, make the color more intense, and add depth, to the color? Good, the next step will be to imagine in your mind something that is made of that color. So if you chose blue, you might see the sky or some beautiful ocean. If you focused on red, perhaps you see a fire truck. Whatever the object is, bring all of its details into the vision you have created in your mind. Once you have focused on the details, then fade the object back into the color you selected. Remain focused on this color for a minute or so, then close the image of the color and as you end the image, come back to blackness within your mind. Keep your mind turned down; don't let the outside world in yet. As you make the transition back to the present moment, come back to this space with your deep cleansing breath (five to seven deep cleansing breaths). Then when you are ready, you roll onto your right side (if you are meditating in the prone position) and take another deep breath. Slowly open your eyes, become aware of your surroundings, and slowly sit up.

That is a beginning meditation in the form of a guided imagery. I have chosen to keep the image simple the first time for many reasons. The first reason is that color is something we are often able to create within our mind. Were you successful? Not to worry if you were unable the first time to close your mind down or were unable to develop the color. It will take practice. The hardest aspect for most students who are new to meditating is to be able to actually shut their minds down. They think about their next class, lunchtime, and their significant other. We all have so many distractions and sometimes the distractions win in our mind. Sometimes we cannot shut them down, but don't give up. It will happen with practice and commitment. You just have to continue to try and not become so frustrated to give it up without giving meditation a fair chance.

One suggestion is to make a commitment to take the time to meditate and to quiet your mind for the period, while at the same time acknowledging the items that are pressing on your mind that you will focus on after the meditation is complete. Remember, your first meditations can be as short as five minutes and you will find even in that short time to experience some of the benefits discussed.

You may have found that guided imagery very uneventful, but I have found over the years to introduce meditation in its simplest form. If you go to Appendix A, you will find several of my favorite meditations that I have created over the years. I hope you enjoy them. As already mentioned, if you can reread them so you know what the image we are creating is, or have a friend or family member read them to you, or record them and then play them with the instrumental music. I believe you will experience some wonderful images within your mind that will leave you refreshed and ready to take on the rest of your day. I wish you many successful meditations, which I know will be helpful both within your stress management tool kit. I also believe that by adding meditations into your life you will make a positive impact on your wellness from here forward.

REFERENCES

"5 Types of Meditation." *Welcoa Online Bulletin* (Spring 2010).

Seaward, Brian Luke. *Essentials of Managing Stress*. Burlington, MA: Jones and Bartlett Publisher, 2011.

National Center for Complementary and Alternative Medicine. Accessed March 2012. http://nccam.nih.gov/health/meditation/overview.htm.

Name____ Class Days and Time ________________________

6.1

MEDITATIONS

In Appendix A, there are examples of ten different guided imagery meditations that I have developed over the years. Your assignment is to look at them and decide to try at least five meditations this week. Then, write about the experience. Were you able to create the image in your mind? Would you use it again? Describe the time and environment you were practicing each meditation. Did you enjoy the concept? How did you feel at the end of the meditation? Write a paragraph or two for each of the meditations. Try to do only one meditation a day if at all possible.

Answer the following questions after you have completed recording your time usage for the week.

1. Meditation title ______________________________
2. Meditation title ______________________________
3. Meditation title ______________________________
4. Meditation title ______________________________
5. Meditation title ______________________________

Name____ Class Days and Time ____________________________

6.2

CREATING YOUR OWN GUIDED IMAGERY

Now that you have experienced some meditations within the class and practiced several of the ones in the Appendix, the next step is to create your own meditation. As you have practiced within the class, you likely know that my meditations are based on a connection to a place, an activity, and a time with family and or friends. So the assignment is to create your own guided imagery meditation and share with us. I look forward to reading these and see what thoughts you have as you create your personal meditation.

> Develop and write out your personal meditation. Start with the breathing process and make your meditation as inclusive as possible, using as many of your senses as is reasonable for your meditation.

Chapter 7
The Value of Exercise and Play as Great Stress Management Techniques

Goals for This Chapter

- To understand, define, and discuss the concept of physical fitness.
- To understand the FITT Formula for exercise program development.
- To be able to calculate your personal Target Heart Rate and understand its value with aerobic activity.
- To be able to complete the PAR-Q questionnaire and understand its use for starting a safe exercise program.
- To be able to demonstrate the strategies needed to maintain a fitness plan for both stress management and wellness.

KEY TERMS

physical fitness
cardiovascular
presentism
Physical Activity Readiness Questionnaire (PAR-Q)
FITT Formula
target heart rate (THR)
weitgh taining
aerobic activities
basal metabolic rate
exercise metabolic rate
talk test
rate of perceived exertion (RPE)

EXERCISE/PLAY FOR STRESS MANAGEMENT

In Chapter 1, we asked you to develop some stress management tools. I hope many of you listed exercise as one of your top strategies. Unfortunately, we know that many Americans are not using exercise as a technique very often. You will notice that I interject the word play with exercise. I do so with a purpose. As a child, play was an essential part of our lives. With each generation, play has taken on different forms, i.e. watching too many hours of television, playing video games on the television, game systems, or computers during the day. How many of us spend time on the computer changing our status or checking our friends' Facebook pages? Heck, now we have to include playing games on our phones, such as Angry Birds, Words with Friends, and Hangman. How many hours a day do you waste with each of these activities? Additionally, we also tend to play these non-movement games while eating a variety of unhealthy foods, washed down with some kind of sugary drink. This has created a double whammy, and in my opinion, created a perfect storm as to the reasons we are no longer as active in the United States as in previous generations. Then we wonder why the youth of the country are gaining weight at a pace never before seen.

The primary reason why I interject play instead of talking about exercise is simple. Many of us have had bad experiences; maybe it was a physical education teacher who catered to the athletes, a youth coach who used exercise as either punishment or motivation, or a high school coach who had the philosophy, "We will never lose due to our fitness level." Or perhaps you joined a fitness center, and the first week you worked so hard you could hardly walk, let alone continue the program. The good news is that the concept of "no pain, no gain" is slowly slipping into obscurity. When I discuss the value of exercise as one of the best stress management techniques we have, the challenge before you is to bring play and all of its positive benefits back into your life. You must decide the importance of play and becoming more physically active within your life. Exercise and play have many benefits that will enable you to not only manage your stress better, but will help you maintain and/or improve your overall wellness, not to mention, help you live a longer and healthier life. It is truly a win-win for all of us.

Physical fitness

having enough physical energy to go through a normal work and leisure day as well as maintaining sufficient reserves to handle emergencies.

PHYSICAL FITNESS

What is **physical fitness** and why is it so critical to our life? Here is a simple definition that I use: Physical fitness is having enough energy to go through a normal day (as a college student going to class and perhaps working a part-time job), having enough energy for leisure pursuits (play, exercise, or recreational activities), and then having enough energy to handle any emergency that happens. To help you imagine this, picture if during class we decide to go out and run a mile and a half, which is the standard test to measure your **cardiovascular** endurance. Well, coming to school was part of your normal day, then running the 1.5 miles would be your exercise session for the day. The last aspect of the definition is all that is left. How do we create an emergency to see the status of your physical fitness? My experience is that after running the 1.5 miles some of you will breeze through it under the time required. Others will finish, not in the correct time and will crash on the infield, trying to catch their breath. Now, I release two pit bulls, which have not been fed today. Everyone will likely sprint back to the building; those who make it into the building have survived the emergency and would meet the definition of being physically fit. Those who don't have the

Cardiovascular

pertaining to the heart and blood vessels; often referred to as a type of exercise that strengthens the heart and lungs.

energy or stamina to run back into the building, well they may be part of the dogs' lunch, and would not meet the definition of being physically fit. Which one would you have been?

Before we discuss the value of play/exercise as a quality stress management technique, we must examine some of the physical and mental benefits exercise has on our bodies. Research has shown that physical activity improves the physical functioning of the human body. Physical tasks can be performed more readily and with less fatigue. Some of the physical benefits of exercise include: increased muscle tone, strength, flexibility, and endurance; an increased ability to take in oxygen and circulate the oxygen to all cells in the body; greater work efficiency (employees who are physically fit miss less work due to sickness, and have fewer issues with presentism); lower blood pressure; lower heart rate; lower body weight; higher self-worth; not to mention, individuals who exercise usually live longer.

You may ask what **presentism** is. It is a relatively new word utilized within the wellness world. An employee who is demonstrating presentism is one who is at work, but is not really working, instead doing other things that are not relevant to work such as checking Facebook, shopping on Cyber Monday, watching the NCAA basketball tournament. In industry, it has become a large problem in which companies are struggling to address.

Presentism

the act of being physically present in a workplace, but either not working or being inefficient at work by doing non-work related activities such as checking personal email, going on Facebook, or playing games.

Many other benefits to exercise should be mentioned here. Each of these benefits has a positive outcome related to our wellness: a decreased risk of developing or dying from a chronic disease; less likely to develop or die from heart disease; more likely to survive a heart attack; less likely to lose balance and suffer hip fractures; and more enjoyment out of life. Often when we are active, we develop new friends and new acquaintances, thereby having a positive impact on our social well being. Many people start an exercise program for health reasons and benefits. After a few months of regular exercise, they will tell you they are exercising because it makes them feel good and that they don't feel as well on days they miss a workout. This is an example of a runner's high that many runners report while running. It is the release of catecholamines and endorphins from the exercise that provides this almost euphoric state to the body and brain.

The last benefits are also important to this discussion as they are to add the psychological benefits attributed to exercise as a management of stress: the increased ability to cope with stress; increased ability to resist or lessen depression; better responses to relaxation techniques; and better sleep patterns. Physical activity provides greater relief from mental stress than any other techniques you may have listed in Chapter 1, especially drugs, alcohol, and food. It provides better outcome without any negative consequences. That is why I will always list exercise as my favorite stress management tool. By using exercise to manage our stress, not only do we get to lessen its impact on our lives, we also receive all of its health and wellness benefits.

FITNESS PLAN

As we further explore the concept of exercise and play as an effective stress management tool, we should spend time discussing basic principles of starting a fitness plan, which will enable us to continue with the activity and manage our stress and improve our health and wellness. Starting an exercise/play program is not as easy as just beginning. Well, I guess you could just start, but the likelihood of finishing is not very strong. One summer in college I started a running plan, and my friend who was already running, decided the first day

© Monkey Business Images, 2012. Under license from Shutterstock, Inc.

we should run one mile, the second day we ran two miles, the third day three miles, the fourth day we ran four miles. On the fifth day, I quit. Not really, but the experience impressed on me that we must have a plan in place.

There are several steps we must complete before beginning our exercise plan. You may go out of order, but each should be checked off. I always recommend any time I work with someone starting a program to develop goals. A goal cannot be so absurd as to not be reasonable to achieve. So if we state we are going to lose fifty pounds (a reasonable goal) and then we state we want to lose the weight in one month, that is not reasonable. The goal to lose fifty pounds will need to be spread over the right amount of time. A recommended plan is to lose one to two pounds a week. So losing fifty pounds we will between twenty-five and fifty weeks. Now you may be saying that will take forever, and my response would be to ask how long did it take for the person to gain the weight? There are no quick fixes for returning to a better fitness level. It will take work, commitment, and a desire to achieve the goal the person sets. Develop several goals, write them down, develop a timeline, perhaps develop incentives (if I lose ten pounds, I will buy a new outfit), and keep a journal.

Another pre-step is to find a training partner with similar abilities and similar goals. This is someone who can motivate you and you can motivate them. Additionally, your training partner has to have the same time frame to work out with you or you will stop before you even start. Your training partner will help you focus, give you encouragement during the workout time, and a smiling face on those cold and dreary days when you just want to roll over and hit the snooze button. They will help you stay motivated and you will do the same for them.

What equipment is needed to begin your exercise/play program? If you start a walking program, which is the easiest program to start, then you need comfortable clothes, good walking shoes, a reusable water bottle, a pedometer (to achieve the 10,000 steps everyday), and several walking routes which have been premeasured and which are safe. If you are biking, then you need to have a working bike with new tires, a helmet, water bottle, and a variety of routes and distances. You may have noticed I did not mention music. It is not that I don't believe in having tunes to work out with, but if you are working out with a partner, as soon as you start to crank the music, you lose the social content of having a workout buddy. Additionally there is a safety concern. If you work out to music in the "world," never, never, ever have both ear buds in. You will miss warning signs from cars, dogs, and other people.

Physical Activity Readiness Questionnaire (PAR-Q)

a questionnaire to help you determine if it is safe to begin an exercise program in your current physical condition.

Develop a workout calendar for the week, then the next week, and on and on. One suggestion I always make is to schedule your workout time into your calendar, your day planner, even your phone and make it a firm commitment. Other options should not take precedent over your workout. With the technology available, you can find apps that offer workout programs, yoga workouts, different routes in your town; some even offer the ability to record your workout data and keep track of how many steps you take in the day.

Now the preparation process is almost completed. The last step before starting is to either contact your primary care physician to schedule an appointment for a physical or at least discuss any issues with you start an exercise program. If you are under thirty-five years of age and in good health, with a good family history for cardiovascular disease, you should be able to start a program without a complete medical exam. In this case the **Physical Activity Readiness Questionnaire (PAR-Q)** is the industry standard. See **Figure 7.1** and take a moment to review and honestly answer the questions as the last step before you begin your exercise program.

FIGURE 7.1 Physical Activity Readiness Questionnaire (PAR-Q)

Physical Activity Readiness Questionnaire - PAR-Q (revised 2002)

PAR-Q & YOU

(A Questionnaire for People Aged 15 to 69)

Regular physical activity is fun and healthy, and increasingly more people are starting to become more active every day. Being more active is very safe for most people. However, some people should check with their doctor before they start becoming much more physically active.

If you are planning to become much more physically active than you are now, start by answering the seven questions in the box below. If you are between the ages of 15 and 69, the PAR-Q will tell you if you should check with your doctor before you start. If you are over 69 years of age, and you are not used to being very active, check with your doctor.

Common sense is your best guide when you answer these questions. Please read the questions carefully and answer each one honestly: check YES or NO.

YES	NO	
☐	☐	**1. Has your doctor ever said that you have a heart condition and that you should only do physical activity recommended by a doctor?**
☐	☐	**2. Do you feel pain in your chest when you do physical activity?**
☐	☐	**3. In the past month, have you had chest pain when you were not doing physical activity?**
☐	☐	**4. Do you lose your balance because of dizziness or do you ever lose consciousness?**
☐	☐	**5. Do you have a bone or joint problem (for example, back, knee or hip) that could be made worse by a change in your physical activity?**
☐	☐	**6. Is your doctor currently prescribing drugs (for example, water pills) for your blood pressure or heart condition?**
☐	☐	**7. Do you know of any other reason why you should not do physical activity?**

If you answered

YES to one or more questions

Talk with your doctor by phone or in person BEFORE you start becoming much more physically active or BEFORE you have a fitness appraisal. Tell your doctor about the PAR-Q and which questions you answered YES.

- You may be able to do any activity you want — as long as you start slowly and build up gradually. Or, you may need to restrict your activities to those which are safe for you. Talk with your doctor about the kinds of activities you wish to participate in and follow his/her advice.
- Find out which community programs are safe and helpful for you.

NO to all questions

If you answered NO honestly to all PAR-Q questions, you can be reasonably sure that you can:

- start becoming much more physically active – begin slowly and build up gradually. This is the safest and easiest way to go.
- take part in a fitness appraisal – this is an excellent way to determine your basic fitness so that you can plan the best way for you to live actively. It is also highly recommended that you have your blood pressure evaluated. If your reading is over 144/94, talk with your doctor before you start becoming much more physically active.

DELAY BECOMING MUCH MORE ACTIVE:

- if you are not feeling well because of a temporary illness such as a cold or a fever – wait until you feel better; or
- if you are or may be pregnant – talk to your doctor before you start becoming more active.

PLEASE NOTE: If your health changes so that you then answer YES to any of the above questions, tell your fitness or health professional. Ask whether you should change your physical activity plan.

Informed Use of the PAR-Q: The Canadian Society for Exercise Physiology, Health Canada, and their agents assume no liability for persons who undertake physical activity, and if in doubt after completing this questionnaire, consult your doctor prior to physical activity.

No changes permitted. You are encouraged to photocopy the PAR-Q but only if you use the entire form.

NOTE: If the PAR-Q is being given to a person before he or she participates in a physical activity program or a fitness appraisal, this section may be used for legal or administrative purposes.

"I have read, understood and completed this questionnaire. Any questions I had were answered to my full satisfaction."

NAME ______________________

SIGNATURE ______________________ DATE ______________________

SIGNATURE OF PARENT ______________________ WITNESS ______________________
or GUARDIAN (for participants under the age of majority)

Note: This physical activity clearance is valid for a maximum of 12 months from the date it is completed and becomes invalid if your condition changes so that you would answer YES to any of the seven questions.

CSEP | SCPE

This questionnaire will indicate if you have any health concerns that should be discussed with your physician before starting. If you are over the age of thirty-five or have any pre-existing illnesses or diseases, then it is strongly recommended you schedule a physical and discuss your concerns with your physician before starting your exercise program. After this, it is time to get moving and improve your stress management tools and to begin to improve your health and wellness.

FITT Formula

a way to design an exercise program based on Frequency, Intensity, Time, and Type of exercise.

We are ready to start, but I want to explain a basic premise of exercise design before we actually begin the workout. I want you to understand the **FITT Formula** as you begin the design of your actual program. (See **Figure 7.2**.)

Frequency indicates how often a workout program should be implemented. When I sat where you are sitting, the American College of Sports (ACSM) recommended all exercise programs should be three times a week for twenty minutes. Obviously, that plan has not worked out so well for our country. Today, the ACSM recommends that we should work out five or six days a week for a total of 150 minutes or more during the week. The American Heart Association suggest at least 150 minutes per week of moderate exercise or seventy-five minutes per week of vigorous exercise (or a combination of moderate and vigorous activity). I agree. I never recommend anyone work out seven days a week. Our bodies need some recovery time and taking a day off each week will make a great difference in your mental and physical attitude.

Target heart rate (THR)

a guideline for safe cardiovascular exercise based on age and workload on the heart.

Intensity when discussing aerobic activities is measured through the use of your **target heart rate (THR)**. (See **Figure 7.3**.) The THR is a guideline for cardiovascular exercise that is based on age and workload on the heart. It is a safe and easy method to calculate a range for your heart rate during exercise

FIGURE 7.2 FITT Formula

F = Frequency—the number of exercise session each week.

Example: Moderately fit individual—
3 to 5 days per week.

I = Intensity—How hard a person has to exercise to improve fitness, indicate by calorie cost.

T = Time—The number of minutes spent in each exercise session.

T = Type—The mode of exercise chosen.

Aerobic—Exercise that requires oxygen to produce the necessary energy to carry out the activity, low to moderate intensity lasting 20 minutes minimum. Examples: Jogging, walking, or swimming.

Anaerobic—Exercise that does not require oxygen to produce the necessary energy to carry out the activity, high intensity for short periods of time. Examples: weight training, sprinting, racquetball.

Source: Hoeger and Hoeger, 2009. Fitness and Wellness, 8th ed. Wadsworth Cengage Learning.

for an effective and safe range. The formula is to take 220 minus age = your maximal heart rate. Then take that number and multiply it by 60 to obtain the lower range of heart rate to earn cardiovascular benefits. Take the maximal heart rate and multiply it by 85 to calculate the upper range of your heart rate to not over tax your heart. So if I am 20 years young, the calculation would look like this: 220-20 = 200 (maximal heart rate). Then take 200 and multiply 200 by .6, which gives you 120 beats per minute, the lowest number to obtain successful cardiovascular benefit. Take 200 and multiply it by .85 which gives you the upper limit, which in this example would be 170. So a 20-year-old student who was participating in cardiovascular exercise for either wellness or stress management would want to exercise hard enough to have his or her heart rate between 120 to 170 for 30 minutes or more. The exercise literature recommends 150 minutes a week of cardiovascular exercise and additional time working with weights of at least two to three days a week also.

Intensity measures within a weight training programs are based on sets and reps in defining workload on the muscles involved. A repetition is considered doing the activity one time, and each additional time is considered another repetition. A set is a grouping of reps, which is then repeated for a second set. If you were asked to twenty-five repetitions of abdominal crunches and perform four sets, how many total crunches would you actually do?

Answer (25 X 4 = 100 crunches)

The last components of an exercise program design are time and type. As already discussed, it is expected our workout time will be between thirty to sixty minutes based on the day and the activity we are doing. On aerobic days, we may want to exercise for sixty minutes (at an moderate intensity), and on days when we are combining both aerobic and weight training, we may want to spend thirty minutes or more in the weight training area and then spend thirty minutes on cardiovascular at an intense level.

FIGURE 7.3 Calculating Your Target Heart Rate

Step 1: 220 - age = ______ estimated maximal heart rate (Max HR).

Step 2: Take your pulse for 1 minute as soon as you wake up in the morning but remain laying flat = ______ Resting Heart Rate (RHR).

Step 3: Take your estimated Max HR - RHR = ______ Heart Rate Reserve (HRR)

Step 4: Set your target heart rate (THR) ranges using 60 to 80% of your HRR:

a. ______ (HRR) × .60 + ______ (RHR) = ______ bpm THR @ 60% HRR / 4 = ______ beats per 15 sec

b. ______ (HRR) × .70 + ______ (RHR) = ______ bpm THR @ 70% HRR / 4 = ______ beats per 15 sec

c. ______ (HRR) × .80 + ______ (RHR) = ______ bpm THR @ 80% HRR / 4 = ______ beats per 15 sec

*40–50% HRR is reserved for people who are currently sedentary and/or have not exercised due to injury or illness

d. ______ (HRR) × .50 + ______ (RHR) = ______ bpm THR @ 50% HRR / 4 = ______ beats per 15 sec

e. ______ (HRR) × .40 + ______ (RHR) = ______ bpm THR @ 40% HRR / 4 = ______ beats per 15 sec

From Wellness: The Total Package *by Mindy Mayol. Copyright © by Kendall Hunt Publishing Company. Reprinted by permission.*

The one significant change that has occurred over the last decade is the fact that all of the exercise does not have to be done at the same time. If your time is limited, then you can do ten minutes in the morning when you wake up, take a twenty minute walk at lunch time, and walk or jog for thirty minutes before dinner. You have met your goal. Good job. If you want a quick and easy addition to your workout program while watching TV, get down on the ground and do a variety of crunches during every commercial. The average thirty minute show lasts only twenty-two minutes, so you will spend eight minutes working on your abdominals. An additional advantage of this approach is you will avoid what many Americans do all too often during commercials, which is eat junk food.

Take the time to buy a pedometer (average cost is $5.00 to $25.00) and wear it for a week. Measure how many steps you take each day. How close are you to the recommended 10,000 steps we need to take every day? If you are low, figure other ways to increase your step total each day (park farther away in the parking lot, walk around the campus), to accomplish 10,000 steps.

You now should have a basic knowledge of the value of exercise and play in your life. You likely understand how this helps either improve or maintain physical fitness and contributes to your overall wellness. The only question that remains is if exercise really contributes as an important stress management tool. I want you to think about that question and write down your answers in the space provided.

What are your thoughts? Can you make the leap as to how valuable exercise and play is in the management of your stress level?

____

____

The answer is quite simple; you take the negative energy from the stressor and use it to complete your workout. A harder workout likely will be the outcome. Let's use an example: you are having a bad day. Everything you do is wrong; a faculty member or your boss are riding you, trying to get a response. Perhaps you can laugh it off and not let it bother you, but many of us have a cracking point (or boiling point) and you have reached yours. It's not recommended to tell the faculty member or your boss to shove it. If you do, you may lose your job, receive a failing grade, or be suspended from your college. So how can you take this negative energy and lessen your stress level?

Exercise is a great solution. Take the energy that is pulsating through your body and use it in your workout. If you are running on the treadmill, imagine the face of the person who is frustrating you on the treadmill. Every time your foot touches the treadmill, you are running over them. Your workout will be intense, and when you are done, you will be tired but the negative energy will have left your body. A win-win situation, since you utilized the negative energy and focused it into your workout and refrained from speaking your mind and compounding the stressor.

Need another example? What if you were having an issue with your significant other? You can yell at them, swear, or even threaten them, and unfortunately sometimes violence occurs as our anger or rage explodes out of us. This approach will just compound whatever the issue was. Sometimes when we are done with our anger and rage response, we will not remember what lit the fuse, and we will be backpedaling, asking our partner for forgiveness, trying to make it up to them, but we have hurt them and caused damage to the relationship. Sometimes we may not recover from this stress response. Imagine if, instead of blowing up, you decide to go out and play some racquet sport, and each time you hit the ball, you visualize hitting a body part of your significant other. You will likely play really well, perhaps even win the match, which will improve your mood and the negative energy will leave your body. With the negative energy removed from our body, you can likely go back and have an open, honest discussion regarding what occurred. Good communication with a colleague, a significant other, a family member is more likely to be successful to manage the stress than screaming and yelling at the person. Give it a try and see the results.

Some of the issues that develop after we start an exercise program need to be mentioned. The two biggest issues I have heard over the last thirty years of working in the physical fitness arena are that the person becomes bored with the program or that they don't have time to work out. Here are some suggestions to help you raise your awareness, so that your program will become successful.

First, to deal with boredom, I highly recommend that you have a wide array of activities to chose from that can be done inside or out. When exercise is being used as a valuable stress management technique, you need to have a variety of activities, as sometimes you may not have enough time for your normal exercise response. When stress is developing while taking a test or driving in rush hour, I don't believe we can do a full exercise program, but we can do light stretching. Moreover, the body responds better when given a variety of exercise options and by changing the intensity of our workout as well. By changing our workout intensity, we can overcome boredom, keep our bodies challenged, and keep ourselves fresh. A basic premise is to do cardiovascular work four or five days a week and then mix in some strength training activities. In the summer, you can train like a triathlete: swim two days, run two days, and bike two days. If you keep the workouts fresh and changing, it will be easier to overcome the boredom that will set in.

The second issue of lack of time is a little more complicated, but I believe if you follow the beginning guidelines you can overcome it as well. It is imperative you schedule a normal workout time, which can change occasionally if needed. The focus has to be not breaking the appointment. This is your time. Think of its importance as not forgetting your wedding date, a friend's birthday, or any other important date. There are better times of the day to workout, but the cardinal rule is to work out with what works in your schedule. If that is first thing in the morning, then work out then; if you can only workout in the evening, then work out then. Just make the time to take care of you and help lower your stress level.

If you work out at home, utilize your DVR to record your favorite show and work out while watching it. With the technology currently available to you, you can watch your favorite shows on your phone or your tablet, while multitasking and taking care of yourself at the same time. During the summer months, you likely will find others at work or in your neighborhood who go for walks every lunch hour. Don't be shy; join them. If you travel, find a place to walk whenever possible. Whenever I travel, I always walk around the city; while doing this, I actually experience the vibrancy of the city.

INTRODUCTION TO A WIDE VARIETY OF GOOD EXERCISE AND PLAY OPTIONS

There are so many choices for working out and playing, I hope you can try some that will work for you and help you stay active. If you asked what my goals would be for you, the reader of this book, they are twofold. The first is to help you identify stress in its many varieties and to develop a large tool kit to help lessen the impact of stress in your life. The second goal would be to have you be observant of your wellness and to continue playing and working out for the rest of your life. To emphasize the point, I plan on working out on my last day on earth (which hopefully is many years off in the future).

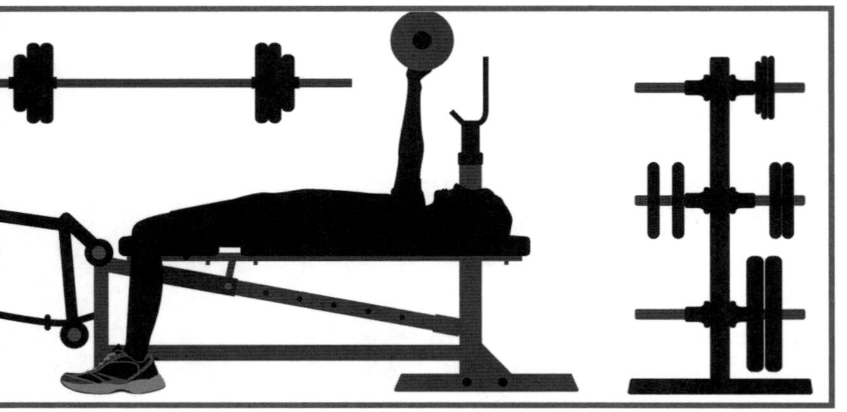

Weight training. Your choice of what type of weight training system to use will be decided by not only your goals, but more importantly your time. There are actually three choices to consider with weight training: your own body weight as the resistance, using a form of stack weight equipment, and free weights. Each brings value to your workout. You will have to see which program works for you.

> ***Weight training***
>
> exercise using your own body weight as resistance, a form of stack weight equipment, or free weights.

Using your own body weight as the resistance, think P90X, Insanity, The Firm. These are all examples of programs that utilize your own weight in many of the activities before adding dumbbells to further challenge the body. You will be amazed at what you can do to your body with just push-ups, crunches, chair-dips, pull-ups, and dips. Often folks are intimidated by all forms of weight training, so using your own body weight is a great starting program to develop your confidence and commitment.

Another choice would be to start with some form of weight stack equipment found in most gyms, fitness centers, hotels, and college campuses. Using stack weight equipment is easy to learn, of short duration, and the directions for muscles to be trained are posted on each machine. The beauty of stack equipment is the time to complete a circuit is usually less than thirty minutes. The concept of stack weight equipment is slower muscle growth, with emphasis on increasing strength and tone, but you will not see the same growth of muscle as compared to free weights. A normal program here would encompass working out three times a week, completing the circuit each time.

After you have experienced the other forms of weight training choices, then free weights (throwing iron) is the next option. The fear many individuals have is that they will become large, muscular individuals. Maybe that was true in the past, but today we see folks of all ages and sizes who want to experience the mindset and intensity from free weights. It is a different experience from stack weight equipment and one I suggest everyone should experience. A recommendation I would make as you add free weights into your program, is to not get concerned about how much you lift, but keep your focus on good form and technique. The results will come with time. We need to remember that the large, muscular individuals have developed their muscle mass from hours and years of lifting iron. At one time, they were likely your size and had the same trepidation of trying to lift in the free weight area. They too may have been scared of trying this area of the fitness center. When you are ready to enter the free weight area, try a beginning exercise with light weights. Start with lunges, or the bench press, biceps curls, or triceps kickbacks. Focus on developing good form and technique. As your comfort level grows, add other lifts to develop your overall strength program. Utilizing free weights is a great method to develop muscle mass, but the time commitment is different. You can expect to double or triple your workout time while in the free weight area.

A reminder, as you consider weight training options, review the personal goals you are trying to accomplish. This will help you determine how weight training will become part of your wellness plan. I would also strongly suggest taking a class or joining a fitness center that has trained fitness instructors to help you get started. The variety of differing views of what a good workout consists of is overwhelming. If you Google fitness weight training programs, you will be amazed at the thousands of hits, and I doubt you will read all of them. So spend the money, be trained by someone who is knowledgeable, and begin to workout.

Aerobic activities. There are so many choices within this area of a fitness and wellness plan. There is so much to experience, it is easy to find activities that are fun and good for your heart and body. We can run, bike, walk, play golf, canoe, kayak, Zumba, aerobic dance, box, ice skate, cardio boot camp, yoga, Tai Chi, Taekwondo, disc golf, rugby, kickball, dodge ball, swim, hike, tennis, racquetball, pickle ball, platform or paddle tennis, ski, snowboard, mountain climb, indoor rock climb, paddle board, cross country ski, water ski, gouache, basketball, ultimate Frisbee, soccer, ballroom dance, line dance. The choices are almost limitless. We should be able to find activities that we enjoy that are good for our hearts and good for lowering our stress levels. Not only that, many of these have a strong social component. It is easy to understand why participating in most aerobic activities provides a significant value to our psycho-social health.

Aerobic activities

physical activity that uses oxygen, increasing the heart rate and breathing.

When we are discussing aerobic activities, there are basic rules to apply. The benefit of aerobic activity is to strengthen and condition the most important muscle within the human body.

Basal metabolic rate

the rate at which your body uses energy while at rest to maintain vital functions such as breathing and body temperature.

What muscle is that? ______________________________

Your heart is the most important muscle in the human body. We can actually survive with damage to any other muscle, but when the heart stops pumping, we die. So I truly believe if you don't have time for both types of exercise, then condition the heart (cardiac) muscle. It will pay off with great dividends over your life. Cardiovascular exercise helps provide more energy, maintain or lose body weight, stimulate our **basal metabolic** and **exercise metabolic rate** (how many calories we consume at rest or during and after exercise), and is fun.

Exercise metabolic rate

the rate at which your body uses energy while exercising.

As you start to participate and experience the wealth of aerobic activities, remember to utilize basic safety guidelines for aerobic activity. Earlier in the chapter we discussed target heart rate. Now we will actually use it to ensure our workouts are performed at the right intensity. If you haven't already calculated your target heart rate, do so now. The formula is 220 minus current age, to give you X, then take X and multiply it by .60 for the bottom number. Then take X and multiply by .85 for the upper number. During your aerobic activity, you want your heart to be beating in between the ranges you just calculated. If you are exercising within this range, you are effectively conditioning your heart.

Talk test

a method of determining exercise intensity based on your ability to carry on a conversation during the exercise.

Other guidelines for safe cardiovascular activity are to utilize the **talk test**, and/or the RPE model to monitor the intensity of your workout. The talk test is simple: Are you able to carry on a conversation with whomever you are working out with? If yes, then you are not working out too intensely. If you are unable to talk to the person running next to you on the treadmill, you are working too hard and need to slow down the intensity. This is a simple and very effective guideline.

Rate of perceived exertion (RPE)

a method of determining exercise intensity by using a scale of 1 to 10 to estimate how much energy you feel you are exerting during a workout.

The last guideline to help us safely do cardiovascular activity is to use the **rate of perceived exertion (RPE)** model. (See **Figure 7.4.**) The RPE is another useful method to approximate the exercise intensity for any age group. The RPE asks the individual working out how much energy is being exerting during the exercise program. RPE is a good measure of intensity of your workout because it is your perspective of your workout. It can be adjusted by how you feel, your overall fitness level, and your effort while exercising. The scale ranges from 1 to 10, allowing you to rate how you feel physically while participating in an aerobic pursuit.

During your cardiovascular workouts, the goal for the RPE is between 5 and 7 on the chart. This is the recommended target to aim for to ensure the intensity is significant of enough to cause a healthy benefit. So when you are working out, you would want to feel you are working somewhere between "somewhat hard" to "hard."

When we talk about the boredom aspect of working out, the variety of activities that are aerobic (requires oxygen at the cellular level) enables us to try many and each of them are good for the heart, good for body, and good for our spirit. If you haven't tried any of these, then sign up for a class at the fitness center, at the college, at the YMCA, or your town's recreational program and give it a chance. You will be surprised how much fun these activities are and how much they challenge our bodies. Go ahead and try several new aerobic activities over the next couple of weeks. Keep track of how your body feels. Then ask if your energy level has improved, if you have made new friends, and if you are having fun.

FIGURE 7.4 Rate of Perceived Exertion (RPE) Model

10	Maximal exertion
8	Extremely hard
7	Hard (heavy)
6	
5	Somewhat hard
4	Fairly light
3	Light
2	Very light
1	Rest

REFERENCES

American College of Sports Medicine, Health and Fitness Journal vol. 16, Number 1 (Jan./Feb/ 2012): 5–7.

American Heart Association. Accessed February 2012. www.Heart.org.

Fitness Things. Accessed February 2012. www.fitnessthings.com

Name________________________________ Class Days and Time ____________________

7.1

YOUR PERSONAL TARGET HEART RATE

1. Calculate your personal target heart rate using the formula shown in the chapter. Show all work. After you have completed your target heart rate, choose an aerobic activity and attempt to work hard enough to raise your heart rate above the threshold level. If possible, try to maintain this level for twenty minutes. Give your responses of what the activity was and how easy or hard it was to raise your heart rate into the safe range the THR provides. How did you feel when you completed the workout? How did you feel the next day? Good luck and have fun.

2. Describe your areas of weakness as related to weight training and cardiovascular work. Then develop a two-month long workout plan in this space. After you completed the design using the FITT principles, do you believe your program is reasonable and you could complete it?

3. Describe at least five aerobic or cardiovascular activities that you have tried or are utilizing now. Within each, describe equipment needed, overall cost, how hard the activity is, and the fun factor you have from trying or playing.

a.

b.

c.

d.

e.

Chapter 8
Discussion of Our Social Health

Goals for This Chapter

- To understand what social health is.
- To be able to explain self-efficacy and resiliency and apply to yourself.
- To understand what depression is and recognize some of the signs of depression.
- To understand the part self-esteem plays in making our social health stronger.

© Rafael Ramirez Lee, 2012. Under license from Shutterstock, Inc.

KEY TERMS

social health
self-esteem
resiliency
self-efficacy
helplessness
depression
happiness

INTRODUCTION TO SOCIAL HEALTH

When we begin to look at our **social health**, we have to reflect on where we are today in relationship to our family, our friends, our community involvement, our world involvement, and ourselves. As you begin this reflection, where you currently are is not a limit, as many of us could use more social interaction and social support in our lives. You may even question why I added

Social health

the economic and social conditions under which a person lives or a society functions.

© Ginko, 2012. Under license from Shutterstock, Inc.

world involvement as part of our social health, but all you hear in the media and in your college classes is how the world is shrinking quickly and how we are entering a global economy. Heck, many of you already may already have a world connection through Facebook and other social media forums. Each of these components will impact our social health either positively or negatively. We have to consider what are personal needs are and what we are able to provide our friends and families as we grow and nurture our social health. So the beginning discussion of social health will examine where you are with each of these.

PERSONAL REFLECTION ON SOCIAL HEALTH

As you begin to read this chapter, consider these questions: Do you see your life as half empty or half full? Why or how did you arrive at this perspective? You have likely heard this question before. Perhaps you have even answered it before. I want you to understand that we all have an answer as to how we view our current life. Perhaps we dream we are better off financially, have more friends, do better in school, and have families who love us, have more friends than we can count. If we dream of these things, then the secondary question is how we can make the dreams become closer to reality.

I remember when one of my sons came home from his girlfriend's home, walked in and stated as a matter of fact, that our home sucked and we needed to move to a better house. The comment was funny but still stung a little, as I live in a home I never imagined I would own—much different from where I was raised. I love my house and the home we have made it into. But he came from his girlfriend's home, which was on top of a hill, was a gorgeous home, one that I could likely never afford, but my son thought we should have a better home. Perspective is very important and I reminded him where I grew up and what my parent's home was like. I stated that I was more than happy with my home and I was sorry it didn't measure up to his expectations. I still haven't moved.

In a discussion of our social health, we must introduce the following words into your vocabulary: self-esteem, resiliency, self-efficacy, helplessness, depression, and happiness. Each of these words will help us to better understand our perspective of our social health and can help us grow to the next version of ourselves.

Self-esteem

a feeling of self-worth; the ability to meet life's challenges with confidence.

Self-esteem is a feeling of self-worth, how you view yourself, happiness within your spirit, and the ability to meet life's challenges each day. What number would you assign your self-esteem on a scale of 1 (being the lowest) to 10 (being the highest) today? __________ Explain the number you chose to help you reflect on your self-esteem.

____

____

Resiliency is having the ability to bounce back from obstacles and adversity within our daily lives by having the ability to cope with the life stressors we face. I love this word as it describes people who have this amazing ability and do it with such a strong resolve that is actually inspiring.

Give an example of a time you demonstrated resiliency:

____

____

____

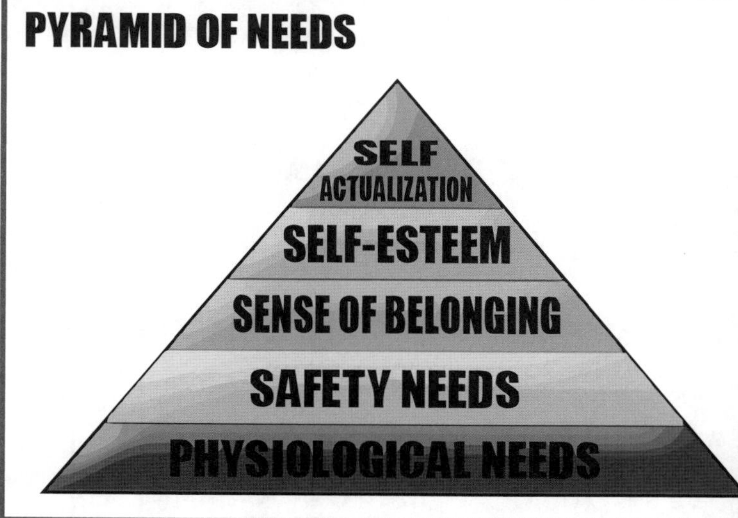

Self-efficacy is having the confidence in yourself to make things happen and believing in your ability to succeed in all or most of the situations that you face in your life. When we have self-efficacy, we have an innate ability to bounce back from failures, set-backs, and disappointments that arise within our life. We face the challenges given to us and believe we will overcome and be stronger for the experience. You will often see self-efficacy discussed within positive psychology and health and wellness concepts. If self-efficacy becomes a part of the management of our stress levels, then we will be healthy persons. Name a challenge you thought was going to be impossible, but you stuck with it, worked hard, and overcame it. How did your persistence and confidence help you be successful?

____

____

After you have completed the thought, remember the sense of accomplishment you felt immediately afterwards and how that positive viewpoint helped you the next time you faced a challenge. Failure is only a failure if we take nothing away that can help us the next time we face the same or a similar situation.

Of course, there are some opposite or negative words we need to at least discuss within the sense of self and they are learned helplessness and depression. Obviously, these words have a negative connotation and likely we would not like these words to be used to describe our current sense of self. Unfortunately, many individuals experience these feelings. They struggle with their lives and wonder if they will ever turn the corner; will their lives get better? There are very hard questions to answer within any certainty, but if you are in those situations, we want to help you understand the changes required to reach out and get support and help as needed.

Learned **helplessness** is the anticipation or action that the individual has no control over a situation and can see no positive outcome, so they flounder with whatever occurs. An example of learned helplessness is shy persons who are very introverted. They feel they have no control or ability to change their shyness, so they begin to stay away from social situations at work, home, or in the community. This, unfortunately, only exacerbates their shyness and they withdraw even more, which makes their shyness even harder to overcome.

Resiliency

the ability to bounce back from obstacles and/or adversity in daily life; the ability to cope with life stressors in a positive way.

Self-efficacy

the confidence in yourself to make positive things happen; a belief in your ability to succeed in all or most life situations.

Helplessness

the feeling that you have no control over a situation or action and can see no possible positive outcome.

Depression

a sense of despondency and dejection, often accompanied by feelings of hopelessness and inadequacy.

Depression is a growing health concern in our country, and it affects people across every age category. If I had asked back in the 1970s when I was in college, how many of the students who know someone who has been diagnosed as being clinically depressed, it was likely that no one would have stated yes. When I ask the same question today, usually one-third to one-half of the class will raise their hands as they know someone who has been diagnosed as being depressed. Why such an increase? There is no definitive answer, just as there is no known exact cause of depression. Sometimes it runs in families, but people develop depression with no family history. Some of the other causes being investigated range from our stressful lives to alcohol and drug abuse, among others. When we discuss depression you will often hear these descriptive words: feeling of deep sadness, unhappy, anger, lethargic, thoughts of suicide, troubled sleep, joyless, isolation from family and friends. Each of us has experienced some or all of these feelings and thoughts at some point in our lives, but with depression the mood changes are deeper and longer. They interfere with our day-to-day activities for long periods of time. Counseling and drug treatments are the most often medical approaches chosen.

© Rafal Olechowski, 2012. Under license from Shutterstock, Inc.

If you know someone who is exhibiting signs of being depressed, reach out, try to help them by talking to them, and suggest that they may need somebody to talk to such as a professional counselor. Try to make a difference in their overall outlook. We all need to understand that depression is an illness that needs medical attention, which is why it is important for each of us to reach out and make a connection to a depressed friend or family member and try to get that person help.

So quick checks: Where do you see yourself at this moment? Are you joyfully enjoying life and making the most of your moments? Or are you sad, struggling at times throughout the day/week/or months? Whichever answer you chose, the following sections will discuss ways to strengthen either answer.

© iQoncept, 2012. Under license from Shutterstock, Inc.

CONNECTIONS AND SUPPORT FROM FAMILY AND FRIENDS

A discussion of our social health has to include all of the connections we have made during our lifetimes. The text in the heart-shaped graphic art encompasses the words we use when we discuss our family and friends. Perhaps the most important social connections we can consistently count on are the emotional support, friendship, patience, love, understanding of our families, and being there to pick us up when we are down. Family and friends have grown up with us; they know us, can read our emotional responses, understand our mood swings, and love us unconditionally when we screw up. Yes, we all screw up during our lifetimes, and those screw-ups are actually life lessons that help us develop into who we become. As you reflect on your past life lessons, who were the people there supporting you, helping you pick up the pieces, and move forward to the next chapter in your life story?

Something I would like you to consider is an act of thankfulness to your friends and family members who have been there sharing the good times, and more importantly, who were with you during the bad times helping you come back from your sadness. They are gifts in your life, and I hope you show them how much they mean to you. I hope you help them when they need you to be there for them.

© Leremy, 2012. Under license from Shutterstock, Inc.

COMMITMENT TO OUR COMMUNITY, TO THE WORLD

The question as we begin this section is, how would you rank your involvement and commitment to making your community better? As you look around any college in this country, you will obviously see a wide spectrum of students who have different levels of social engagement. We have courses that provide service learning where you take materials related to your college courses and engage in experiential activities to immerse yourself in the learning. Most college campuses have a plethora of clubs and organizations; many are geared to provide leadership opportunities; others are created to have like-interested people who share the same passions, and others are geared as service clubs whose goals are to make a difference within the college or local community. These types of activities are the foundation for making the world around you a better place. Whether it is within the classroom experiences or from actually volunteering somewhere in your community, giving back can make a wonderful change in your attitude and increase your self worth.

© mangostock, 2012. Under license from Shutterstock, Inc.

Have you ever volunteered or made a difference in someone's life? If you have, then you understand my thoughts and know how valuable it is to our self worth. If you haven't, then I would highly recommend that you try volunteering to see what a difference it can make in your life.

I often challenge students who are feeling sorry for themselves because they don't have the most current phone, hottest car, newest shoes, or whatever they think they are missing in their lives to go volunteer. It could be at a homeless shelter to see how well they have it compared to those who are relying on the food, clothes, and shelter provided by the volunteers. Or spend time with a dying person staying in a hospice house as they face the prospect of their death. I truly believe we need to develop an understanding of how well most of us have it; it may not be as good as you had hoped at this stage of your life, but as you look around, you will see that we are truly blessed. One comment I heard several

© joana3d, 2012. Under license from Shutterstock, Inc.

years ago, was that the average American is in the 95 percent of wealth in the world. That amazes me, especially when you consider that an average American's cell phone bill is approximately the annual income for many third world families. It provides something for each of us to reflect on and remember when we are feeling that life isn't fair. Make the most of your life. We all experience highs and lows within our life story sincere. My wish for each of you is to have more highs than lows in your life. When you have the lows, remember to reach out to friends and family and work past them.

HAPPINESS AND JOY

Have you ever tried to describe what happiness means to you, or how to explain joy? Take a second and define happiness in your own words. ____

____

____

Now describe what joy means to you. ____

____

How do you know when you are happy? Is there a feeling you have inside, or is it a feeling that exudes from your soul, your personality? Can we tell you're happy by your smile, your body language, how you treat others around you? What are your indicators that you are happy? Would your friends and family describe you as a happy person? I hope happiness is a part of your overall make-up and a strong aspect of whom you are.

Happiness

state of positive emotions.

Happiness and joy are often interchanged to mean the same idea. I think that happiness and joy are similar, but I view joy as a more intense experience that is of a shorter duration, and happiness is a sense of positive well being, excitement, and contentment with your life at that moment. My experience is that happy people tend to stay happy most of the time; additionally happiness can be contagious.

Some further discussion to help frame these ideas would be the following examples. I love my family and they bring happiness to my life every day. Not to say that they have not brought a wide range of emotions over the twenty-eight years I have been a parent, but if I were to chose one word to describe my family, happy would be it. Another example of happiness is what I feel every day I come to teach at this college. I truly find passion, excitement, and happiness thorough my teaching. I have always stated to my colleagues that the day I no longer enjoy coming to teach is the day I will retire. Luckily, that day has not arrived as of yet.

An example of joy (remember I believe this is of shorter duration and more intense) would be the birth of each of my children. It is an incredible joyful time, but eventually reality comes back to remind you of diapers and sleepless nights. Another example of joy would be at each son's wedding, when my sons do the mother-son dance, I sit watching with tears of joy and pride at the moment to see what fine men they have become.

Find ways to add joy and happiness into your life. Whether it is with your family, friends, or your career, joy and happiness are strong words that make life more enjoyable. When you have joy and happiness within your life, it will be easier to adjust to the life's speed bumps which we all face.

THE WORLD CONNECTION YOUR GENERATION IS EXPERIENCING

A huge difference between my generation and your generation is global shrinking. As the picture above suggests, the world is shrinking and those landmarks are more relevant as an indication of the society and institutions that reflect the city or culture. The Internet and computers have shrunk the world more than the original designers could have ever imagined. It wasn't that long ago (in the early 80s) there were less than a thousand websites on the World Wide Web. Today there are over 185 million websites and almost double that for inactive websites. The web, Skype, and Facebook have made it easy to find out information and contact people from other countries. Instead of writing pen pal letters (my generation) and waiting months for a reply, you go on and talk instateously in real time to anyone, anywhere in the world.

We can talk to the base camp of Mt. Everest with ease and see live video from the climbers and the base camp operators. To me, that is amazing. You probably think no big deal.

I remember the first computer I worked on in college; it was the size of the average classroom, and we had to keypunch individual cards for it to be able to do the statistical analysis. It was superfast compared to doing it by hand, but each of your smart phones has more capability than the original computer I used.

Due to technology, the world is starting to shrink, the economy is global, and the contacts in our lives are worldwide. An example, my son is studying abroad at University of Auckland in New Zealand. During his time there, he has traveled to Australia to meet up with friends from school. When the semester was over, he traveled around the country. Then he

© zeber, 2012. Under license from Shutterstock, Inc.

was off to the Fiji Islands where he has friends he was able to stay with. He was able to Skype us with live video from over 8,000 miles away.

Some drawbacks we encounter are that we have started to forget how to communicate in face-to-face conversations. We use abbreviated words in our text messages. I even have had students use text language in papers. They become upset when they have to redo the papers. They argue that text language is acceptable, and my response is always the same, "Perhaps it acceptable on the phone or computer emails, but it will never be accepted in college level courses."

Technology has both a positive side and negative possibility when discussing our social health. Remember that human contact? Human touch cannot be replicated or nothing can soothe a broken heart the way we do with each other.

Name____ Class Days and Time ______________________

8.1

SOCIAL HEALTH

1. List the characteristics you expect from a close friend.

2. Do you have one person whom you can talk to, share your emotions with, and find support and comfort? Do you use them when you face your life issues?

3. Have you ever had a friend who broke your trust? If your answer is yes, did you ever give them a second chance after communicating with them what they did? Did it work?

4. Have you taken the time to let a good friend or family member know how important they have been to your life at this time? If not, consider taking a moment to write them a note, post a Facebook comment, or e-mail them and let them know how they influenced your life.

5. Discuss what makes you happy in your life.

6. What is the worst thing that has ever happened to you and how did you survive it?

7. Give an overview of your current social health in your viewpoint. How can you make your social health stronger and healthier?

8. Have you ever done any volunteer work? If your answer is yes, explain how it impacted your life. If your answer is no, discuss what kind of volunteer work you would consider and why you haven't gone forward to make a difference in your community.

9. Do you communicate with anyone in another state or another country? If your answer is yes, how did you make this connection?

Chapter 9
Emotional Wellness

Goals for This Chapter

- To understand the nature and value of emotional strengths as expressed in the concept of emotional intelligence.
- To be able to identify four abilities associated with emotional intelligence.
- To begin identifying emotional strengths in your life.

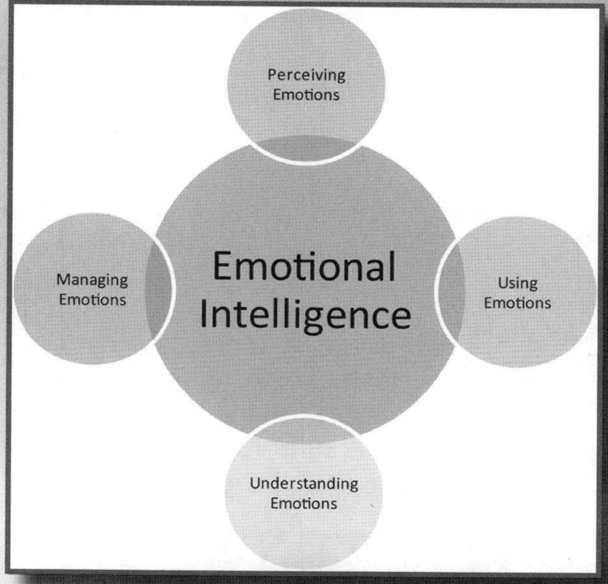

KEY TERMS

emotion   environment   feeling

CONCEPTS

What are the most important and significant experiences you will have during this school year? If you start to list them in your mind, you will find that they will likely be full of emotion. You may go to your first class and feel both excitement and apprehension. You may get your first "A" in college and feel pride and satisfaction. You may make a new friend and gain a real sense of belonging. You may give your first speech or class presentation and feel nervous. You may try out for the varsity basketball team, and if you don't make the cut, you may feel depressed or angry at what you see as rejection. Whether they are positive, negative, or neutral, **emotions** play an important role in our lives because they alert us to something important in ourselves or our **environment**.

Emotions

that part of the consciousness that involves feeling and the capacity to detect and respond to sensory stimuli.

Environment

the totality of surrounding things, conditions, or influences.

Feelings

nonrational, internal sensation not connected with sight, hearing, taste, smell, or what is classically correlated to touch.

Successfully navigating your college experience will likely call into play your ability to effectively work with your emotions, and this takes us to the concept of *emotional strengths*. We defined the emotional strengths domain as the capacity in our lives that enables us to experience **feelings**. What do we mean by these terms? When we talk about our feelings, we are describing an experiential state that builds within us in response to sensations, sentiments, or desires we encounter. Sensibility refers to our responsiveness toward other things or persons, such as the feelings of another person or changes in the environment.

If we were to collect all the words in the English language that express our emotions, they would probably number in the hundreds. The paradox, however, is that with all those words, we still have great difficulty describing our emotional experiences to others. Why is that? Perhaps it stems from the view of emotions throughout the history of Western civilization. Emotions have, for the most part, been seen as a disruption to rational thinking and a hindrance to making good decisions. But now that view is changing.

John Mayer, a psychologist at the University of New Hampshire, and Peter Salovey, a psychologist at Yale University (currently Dean of Yale College), proposed the concept of emotional intelligence, defining it as "the ability to monitor one's own and others' feelings and emotions, to discriminate among them, and to use this information to guide one's thinking and action" (Mayer & Salovey, 1993; Salovey & Mayer, 1990). Mayer and Salovey have been joined by another psychologist, David Caruso, in systematizing the study of emotional intelligence and developing a credible tool for measuring it (Mayer-Salovey-Caruso Emotional Intelligence Test, or MSCEIT, 2002). Daniel Goleman, a journalist specializing in the area of the brain and psychology, worked from the writings of Mayer and Salovey to popularize the concept of emotional intelligence in his international bestseller, *Emotional Intelligence* (Goleman, 1995).

Rather than seeing emotions as some sort of a primitive aberration in people that leads them to make mistakes and experience regrets, instead the findings show "that emotion is not just important but absolutely necessary for us to make good decisions, take optimal action to solve problems, cope with change, and succeed" (Caruso & Salovey, 2004). It is not hard to see, then, that emotional strengths play an important part in the discovery of a life purpose.

The basis for emotional intelligence is made up of four skills or strengths:

1. **Identify and express emotions**. This is the fundamental ability to recognize feelings and emotions by (a) being aware of emotional clues in yourself and in people around you, (b) being able to discern between different types of emotion, (c) being able to identify the level of intensity to which the emotion is present, and (d) being able to identify what these emotional clues mean.

People with strength in this ability are better pilots of their lives because they have a surer sense of how they really feel about personal decisions from whom to marry to what job to take. They are also tuned in to the emotions of others and as a result have healthier and stronger relationships.

As you look at the hands shown on this page, what do you see? Did you notice the hands formed a heart?

2. **Use or generate emotions**. This is the ability to know which emotions or moods are best for different situations and to get yourself into the "right mood."

   People with strength in this ability employ their feelings to enhance their thinking and endeavors. They realize that emotions, when rightly used, can help them solve problems, make better decisions, reason out situations, and be more creative. They will be more self-motivated and will prioritize their thinking process based on emotional input.

3. **Understand emotions**. This is the ability to recognize and grasp emotional information. This starts by gaining an emotional vocabulary—knowledge of simple and complex emotional terms. It then adds emotional comprehension—understanding how emotions combine to form another emotion, progress or intensify, or transition from one emotion to another. Finally, emotional analysis occurs—being able to understand possible causes of emotions and predict what kind of emotions people will have in different situations.

   People with strength in this ability have a solid grasp of emotional intelligence. They will tend to be more accurate in their interpretation of moods and emotional situations, and as a result will be more likely to deal correctly with such situations.

4. **Manage emotions**. This is the ability to regulate emotions in yourself and in other people. This involves monitoring, observing and distinguishing differences, and accurately labeling emotions as they are encountered. This ability is based on the belief that feelings and moods can be improved or modified, with strategies being developed to accomplish this. This does not mean, however, the denial or suppression of your emotions or the emotions of others.

© Brian Tan, 2012. Under license from Shutterstock, Inc.

People with strength in this ability can bounce back quickly from life's setbacks and upsets. They are also able to assess the effectiveness of how they recognize and handle emotions in various situations.

SUMMARY

Ironically, emotional strengths may be confused in our modern society with weakness, and society responds by not placing as great a value on this strength domain. As a result, we end up with a culture where relationships are confused and people try to hide from each other. This inner turmoil often leads to feelings of inferiority and self-doubt and causes confusion in the search for a life purpose.

Emotional strengths are harder to detect than physical strengths. Once again, one of the most effective ways is listening to what others who know us well say about us. Another way is to complete exercises and assessments of our emotional strengths. We will look more closely at some examples of how to do this in the exercise section of this chapter.

Remember, each of the strength dimensions provides a bridge among the other dimensions. Emotional strengths provide the bridge of feelings among the other strengths. What do we mean by this? It is through our emotions that we actually sense and feel what is going on with the other strengths. This adds color and vitality to our lives.

REFERENCES

Caruso, D., Kornacki, S., & Brackett, M. (2006). *Teaching emotional intelligence skills*. Stamford, CT: EI Skills Group.

Caruso, D., & Salovey, P. (2004). *The emotionally intelligent manager*. San Francisco: Jossey-Bass.

Goleman, D. (1995). *Emotional intelligence: Why it can matter more than IQ*. New York: Bantam Books.

Mayer, J. D., & Salovey, P. (1993). The intelligence of emotional intelligence. *Intelligence, 17*, 433–442.

Salovey, P., and Mayer, J. D. (1990). Emotional intelligence. *Imagination, Cognition, and Personality, 9*, 185–211.

Weil, A. (2008). http://www.drweil.com/drw/u/id/ART00521

Name____ Class Days and Time ________________________

9.1

WRITE A LETTER

For this assignment, there are two parts that address two different questions and yet the response and format are similar; the difference lies in the focus of the question. With each question, you will be asked to write a letter to a person. Whether you send the letter or not, is entirely up to you, but this assignment is similar in outcome to writing in your journal. Sometimes the act of writing is cathartic in nature and by placing your words on the paper, you will feel better and be able to move on, other times you may actually feel the need to send the letter. This assignment is to address some of the emotional struggles, pain, or happiness you have occurred in your lifetime. (If you are uncomfortable having the faculty member read your letters, you should ask them to check off the assignment by showing them you completed but are not comfortable having them read your letters).

Letter 1

I want you to think of the one person who has made the most positive impact in your life, and I would like you to write a thank you letter to them. In the letter, I would hope you express your appreciation for what they have done during your lifetime to make you the person you are today. We often forget to say thanks and love to those who have impacted the person we have become and then they are gone. Take this opportunity to give thanks. This will hopefully be the easier of the two letters. Be open, sincere and let your emotions come forth.

Dear ,

Letter 2

This letter should be addressed to someone who has hurt you and the pain still exists in your spirital and emotional state. As we move forward in our lives, this is the kind of baggage that can impact our emotional wellness for long periods of time. The focus here is to be honest, yet not to attack as that will not solve the issue, and likely will escalate the issue. Some of you will use this idea and mail it; others will express the pain they have caused and move forward without ever sending the letter. Good luck.

To ,

Name________________________________ Class Days and Time ____________________

9.2

MANAGING STRESS

If you are experiencing high levels of stress, what can you do to keep this from overpowering you? Review the following list. Practice at least five of the techniques. Write a paragraph on how you responded to each method.

1. Monitor your emotions to gather important information about your state of emotional well-being. Use this information to make decisions in your life and adapt your behavior.
2. Apply the emotional strength of "what-if" thinking to bring direction to chaotic emotions and thoughts. This will help you gain a better understanding of all the different scenarios possible in your situation. This often also has a calming influence.
3. Attend to your spiritual well-being. It has a direct relationship to your emotional well-being and your level of stress. You will learn more about how to do this in Chapter 11. Give special attention to meditational solitude and prayer.
4. Attend to your physical well-being. It also has a strong relationship to your emotional well-being and your level of stress. Give special attention to diet, aerobic exercise, and sleep.
5. Practice breathing exercises to help calm your thoughts.

   "Practicing regular, mindful breathing can be calming and energizing and can even help with stress-related health problems ranging from panic attacks to digestive disorders" (Andrew Weil, M.D. 2008). For students, this can include test anxieties as well.

6. Practice other relaxation techniques.

- Listen to soothing music. Choose music that has a beat that is slower than your heart rate. Classical or new age music can be very relaxing.
- Take a few deep breaths.
- Focus on your breathing. If you are thinking about breathing, it is difficult to think about your worries.
- Lie down in a comfortable place and tense and relax your muscles. Start with the muscles in your head and work your way down to your toes. Tense each muscle for 5 to 10 seconds and then release the tension completely.
- Imagine yourself in a pleasant place. When you are actually in a beautiful place, take the time to make a mental photograph. Memorize each detail and then close your eyes to see if you can still recall the scene. Return to this place in your mind when you feel stressed. Some people visualize the mountains, the beach, the ocean, a mountain stream, waterfalls, a tropical garden, or a desert scene. Choose a scene that works for you.
- Use positive thinking. Look for the good things in life and take the time to appreciate them.

- Maintain a healthy diet and get enough exercise.
- Practice yoga or tai chi.
- Keep things in perspective. Ask yourself, "Will it be important in ten years?" If so, do something about it. If not, just relax.
- Discuss your feelings with a friend who is a good listener or get professional counseling.
- Keep your sense of humor. Laughter actually reduces the stress hormones.
- Maintain a support network of friends and loved ones.
- Practice meditation. It is a way of calming the mind.
- Get a massage or give one to someone else.

Chapter 10
Intellectual Wellness

Goals for This Chapter

- To be able to understand the nature and value of intellectual strengths.
- To be able to identify the discovery, process, and application disciplines associated with intellectual strengths.
- To be able to begin identifying intellectual strengths in yourself.
- To be able to identify your own preferred learning style.
- To be able to understand how to apply your own preferred learning style.

KEY TERMS

intelligence
intelligence quotient (IQ)
visual learning
auditory learning
kinesthetic/tactile learning

CONCEPTS

Probably every student arriving at college asks "Am I smart enough to be here?" SAT or ACT scores have given you one answer. Your GPA from high school has given you another. You may have even taken **intelligence** tests to find the answer to your question. The problem is that you might be asking the wrong question. Maybe

Intelligence

capacity for learning, reasoning, understanding, and similar forms of mental activity you need to focus less on "if" you're smart and more on "how" you are smart. What do we mean by that? We defined the intellectual strengths domain as the capacity in our lives that enables us to discover, understand, and apply truth in an ever-expanding manner.

Intelligence quotient (IQ)

a score derived from one or more standardized tests to determine intelligence.

Throughout recent history, intellectual capacity has been correlated to what has been termed the **intelligence quotient**, better known as **IQ**. This is determined by measuring an individual's ability to respond to visual imagery, to respond to verbal input, and to apply skills in both areas to the solution of problems. More recent studies have shown this to be too narrow a focus on the intellect. Howard Gardner has proposed the idea of multiple intelligences (1983). In other words, people might be "intelligent" or "smart" in different ways.

Visual learning

a learning style in which ideas and concepts are best assimilated through the use of images, pictures, colors or designs.

LEARNING STYLES

One of the primary reasons that the intellect needs to be looked at with a broader perspective is that people learn in different ways or styles. One simplified approach to learning styles divides people into three primary groups of visual, auditory, or kinesthetic/tactile learners.

Auditory learning

a learning style in which ideas and concepts are best assimilated by hearing and listening.

- **Visual learning** occurs primarily through looking at images, such as pictures, diagrams, demonstrations, and body language.
- **Auditory learning** occurs primarily through hearing words—both spoken and written.
- **Kinesthetic/tactile learning** occurs through hands-on doing and interacting.

People rarely, if ever, learn only in one style. The reality is much more a preference in learning styles. However, it is important to understand what style you prefer. This can help you approach classes and studying in a more effective manner.

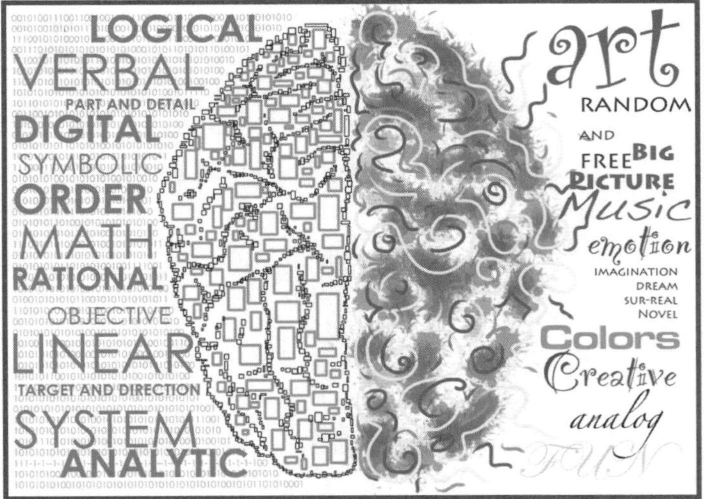

© Rakkandee, 2012. Under license from Shutterstock, Inc.

Learning Atmosphere

Another approach to learning that shows our distinctiveness as individuals was developed around our preferred atmosphere or setting for learning. This concept suggests that each person has unique strengths and preferences across a full spectrum of physiological, sociological, psychological, emotional, and environmental elements. The interaction of these elements occurs differently in everyone and will affect the way they concentrate on, process, absorb, and retain new and difficult information (Dunn & Dunn, 1992, 1998, 1999).

Learning Atmosphere

Stimuli	Elements
Environmental	Sound
	Light
	Temperature
	Design
Emotional	Motivation
	Persistence
	Responsibility
	Structure
Sociological	Self, Pair, or Team
	Feedback from Authority
	Variety vs. Routine
Physical	Perceptual
	Intake
	Time
	Mobility
Psychological	Global/Analytic
	Right/Left Hemisphere
	Impulsive/Reflective

Kinesthetic/ tactile learning

a learning style in which ideas and concepts are best assimilated through physical experiences and actions.

Knowing your own strengths and preferences in this learning atmosphere can be important to success in your college experience and in life after college.

Intellectual Disciplines

A final approach to consider in understanding intellectual strengths centers on the disciplines of the mind that help us build the ability to discover, understand, and apply truth in an ever-expanding manner. Jay Wood (1998), a philosophy professor at Wheaton College, refers to these as intellectual virtues. James Sire (2000), a professor at the University of Missouri, considers these to be habits of the mind. Assessing your strengths in these disciplines and developing them will help you in your academic pursuits in college.

Our definition of intellectual strengths identifies three categories of intellectual disciplines: (1) those we use to discover knowledge; (2) those we use to process the knowledge into an understanding of truth; and (3) those we use to apply the truth after we understand it.

Discovery Disciplines

Curiosity. A strong desire to learn more about something. People who are curious have an excitement for knowledge and eagerness to search for truth. They openly inquire about why things are the way they are. They truly are explorers in the galaxy of information and comprehension.

Teachable spirit. A willingness and eagerness to learn. People who are teachable are characterized by an absence of a "know-it-all" attitude. They are not indifferent to knowledge. They are open to diverse views and forms of knowledge.

Persistence. A firm and steadfast continual search for knowledge and truth. People who are persistent keep on pursuing truth despite obstacles, warnings, or setbacks. They do not give up their quest even when data is inconsistent, obscure, or seemingly nonexistent.

Humility. Discovery humility is a modest view of one's own importance pertaining to the possession of knowledge. People who have intellectual humility always see themselves as a learner and are always willing to be taught by others.

Process Disciplines

Integrity. The quality or condition of interpreting information collected with honesty. People who have intellectual integrity do not make data fit their preconceived ideas. Instead they collect data with an open mind and then allow this data to inform the conclusions they make.

Critical thinking. The mental process of actively and skillfully conceptualizing, applying, analyzing, synthesizing, and evaluating information to reach an answer or conclusion. People who think critically ask "why" questions constantly. They rarely accept things at face value.

Patience. The capability of calmly awaiting an outcome or result even in the face of obstacles or challenges. People who are intellectually patient do not come to hasty conclusions and are not impulsive in their interpretations.

Humility. Process humility is a modest view of one's own importance pertaining to the possession of understanding. People who have intellectual humility do not see themselves as omniscient and hold very few "truths" as absolute. To them, the search for meaning and understanding is a lifelong adventure.

Application Disciplines

Courage. The quality of spirit that enables a person to face the unknown or new ideas without fear of implications or repercussions. People who are intellectually courageous avoid being dogmatic. They are willing to take risks in proposing new ideas or relinquishing old ideas that no longer appear to be valid.

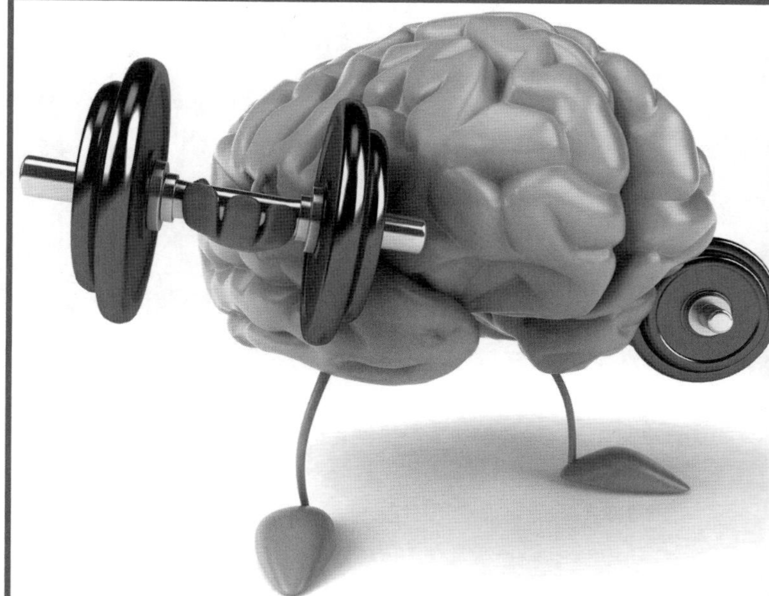

© Julien Tromeur, 2012. Under license from Shutterstock, Inc.

Systematic thinking. The mental process of formulating concepts into an organized set of interrelated ideas or principles that can be applied to life. People who think systematically realize that knowledge and understanding are useful only if others can see how to interact with and use them.

Advancement. The application of an understanding of knowledge to improve on what was already known. People who advance intellectually take forward steps in acquiring and understanding knowledge. Their desire is to see intellectual activity as a developmental process that leads to progress. They are not satisfied with the status quo.

Humility. Application humility is a modest view of one's own importance pertaining to thrusting one's own understanding on others. People who have intellectual humility do not see themselves as a dogmatist whose duty it is to tell others how they should live. People with intellectual humility instead see their role as inspiring others to join the journey of discovering, understanding, and applying truth.

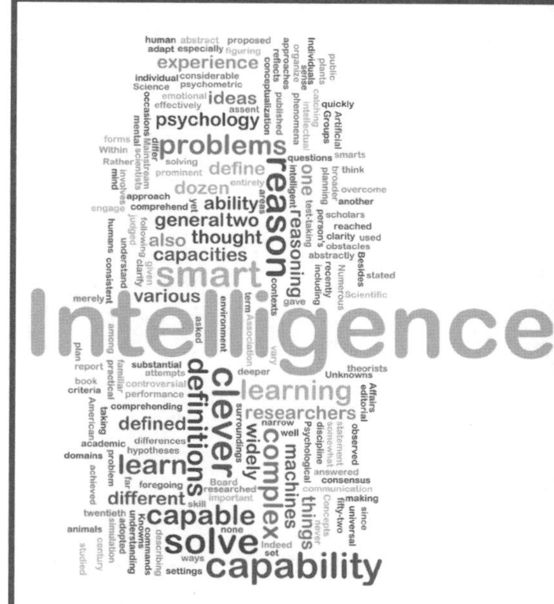

© Kheng Guan Toh, 2012. Under license from Shutterstock, Inc.

SUMMARY

For the most part, when people talk about intellectual strengths, they are referring primarily to IQ. As a result of this, we end up with a culture where people think they are smart when they really aren't. This confusion often leads to feelings of inferiority and self-doubt related to IQ and causes uncertainty in the search for a life purpose.

From our discussion we see that your true intellectual strengths are affected by your learning style and your preferred learning atmosphere. Further, we found that intellectual strengths are made up of disciplines that encompass a far greater spectrum than just IQ. This complexity, as with the other strengths, makes it harder to see when we have these strengths. Again, one of the most effective ways is listening to what others who know us well say about us.

Remember, each of the strength dimensions provides a bridge among the other dimensions. Intellectual strengths provide the bridge of information among the other strengths. What do we mean by this? It is through our intellect that we learn about what is going on with the other strengths. This adds the knowledge and understanding required to live our lives.

REFERENCES

Aguilar, L. S., Hopper, S. J., & Kuzlik, T. M. (2001). *The community college: a new beginning*, (3rd ed.). Dubuque, IA: Kendall/Hunt Publishing Company.

Dunn, R. S., & Dunn, K. J. (1998). *The complete guide to the learning styles inservice system*. Boston: Allyn & Bacon.

Fralick, M. F. (2006). *College & career success*, (3rd ed.) Dubuque, IA: Kendall Hunt Publishing Company.

Sire, J. W. (2000). *Habits of the mind*. Downers Grove, IL: InterVarsityPress.

Wood, J. W. (1998). *Epistemology: Becoming intellectually virtuous*. Downers Grove, IL: InterVarsityPress.

Name_______________________ Class Days and Time _______________________

10.1

LEARNING STYLE QUIZ

Why does learning new skills and information seem to come so easily for some people, while others struggle? Is there one right way to learn something? Is there anything you can do to increase your personal learning power? The answers to these questions come from understanding how people learn, and especially how you learn.

But what happens if you figure out your preferred learning style and your teacher's instructional style and find they don't match? Should you drop the class in despair? No, you are going to need to develop strategies to match your learning style with a teacher's differing instructional style.

Read the following questions and circle the letter of the best answer in your opinion. There are no right or wrong answers in this quiz. Just circle what you usually prefer.

1. When learning how to use my computer, I prefer to
   a. read the manual first.
   b. have someone explain how to do it first.
   c. just start using the computer and get help if I need it.
2. When getting directions to a new location, it is easier to
   a. look at a map.
   b. have someone tell me how to get there.
   c. follow someone or have him or her take me there.
3. To remember a phone number, I
   a. look at the number and dial it several times.
   b. repeat it silently or out loud to myself several times.
   c. remember the number by the pattern pressed on the keypad, the tones of each number, or writing it down.
4. For relaxation, I prefer to
   a. read a book or magazine.
   b. listen to or play music.
   c. go for a walk or do something physical.
5. I am better at
   a. reading.
   b talking.
   c. physical activities.

6. In school, I learn best by
   a. reading.
   b. listening.
   c. hands-on activities.

7. I tend to be a
   a. thinker.
   b. talker.
   c. doer.

8. When I study for a test, it works best when I
   a. read and picture the information in my head.
   b. read and say the ideas out loud or silently.
   c. highlight, write notes, and outlines.

9. It is easier for me to remember
   a. faces.
   b. names.
   c. events.

10. On a Saturday, I would prefer to
    a. see a movie.
    b. go to a concert.
    c. participate in athletics or be outside.

11. In a college class, it is most important to have
    a. a good textbook with pictures, graphs, and diagrams.
    b. a good teacher who gives interesting lectures.
    c. hands-on activities.

12. It is easier for me to study by
    a. reading and reviewing the material.
    b. discussing the subject with others.
    c. writing notes or outlines.

13. When I get lost, I prefer to
    a. look at the map.
    b. call or ask for directions.
    c. drive around the area until I recognize familiar landmarks.

14. When cooking, I often
    a. look for new recipes.
    b. talk to others to get new ideas.
    c. just put things together and it generally comes out okay.

15. When assembling a new toy or piece of furniture, I usually
    a. read the instructions first.
    b. talk myself through each step.
    c. start putting it together and read the directions if I get stuck.

16. When solving a problem, it is more useful to
    a. read a best-selling book on the topic.
    b. talk over the options with a trusted friend.
    c. do something about it.

17. Which statement do you like the best?
    a. A picture is worth a thousand words.
    b Talk to me and I can understand.
    c. Just do it.

18. When I was a child, my mother said I
    a. spent a lot of time reading, taking photos, or drawing.
    b. had lots of friends and was always talking to someone on the phone.
    c. was always taking things apart to see how they worked.

Score your quiz:

Number of a answers 5 Visual Learner

Number of b answers 6 Auditory Learner

Number of c answers 7 Kinesthetic/Tactile Learner

What did you discover as a result of taking this quiz about your preferred style of learning?

____

____

____

____

____

____

How can you use your preferred learning style to help you with classes in college?

Kinesthetic/tactile learners will find these strategies helpful:
• Sit in the middle of the class where you can be involved in whatever is going on in class. • Ask well-thought-out questions in class. • Participate in class discussions; don't just sit passively. • Take notes and highlight important information as you read the textbook. • Have plenty of paper for taking notes in class to help you concentrate. • Get physically involved as much as possible. Volunteer to assist in a lab demonstration, collect samples, or go to the board to work a problem.

- Make charts, models, etc. to bring the content to life.
- Work with fellow students in learning teams or study groups.
- Use manipulatives (learning aids you can move) whenever possible.
- Use interactive computer software when available.
- Read while walking on the treadmill.

Visual learners will find these strategies helpful:

- Sit near the front so you can see the teacher and the board clearly.
- Read the chapter before class so you will be familiar with the content to be covered.
- Pay close attention to pictures, illustrations, charts, and other visual aids in the textbook.
- Take notes in class so you will have something to review later.
- Use all handouts given to you by the teacher as learning tools.
- Highlight important information, and take notes as you read.
- Create your own visual aids such as flowcharts, diagrams, sample problems, etc.
- Use flash cards to review things you need to memorize.
- Visualize the information as you read or listen to the lecture. See it in your mind's eye.

Auditory learners will find these strategies helpful:

- Sit near the middle of the class where you can hear everything that is said in lectures or class discussions.
- Ask well-thought-out questions in class.
- Go over class material with a friend or fellow student.
- Organize a study group with people from your class to talk about what you are learning.
- Tape-record your classes, then listen to the tapes at night before you go to sleep, while you're exercising, or when you're driving your car.
- As you read your textbook, stop after every section and recite out loud what you have just learned (main points, new vocabulary, important names and dates, how to do the problem, math or science formulas, etc.).
- Read your textbook out loud or into a tape recorder to play back later.
- Get the audio versions of books you have to read for literature and listen to them before you read. Be careful about movie versions because they often do not follow the story line closely enough.
- Read each chapter after you've heard the instructor explain the concepts in class.

Name______________________________ Class Days and Time ______________________

10.2

LEARNING STRATEGIES

Most college students find their lives filled with activities outside the classroom, such as work, sports, and social times. As a result, finding enough time to study seems to be a problem for many students. The recommended study ratio for college courses is a minimum of 2 hours outside class for every hour in class. When questioned about how much time they spend studying, students generally admit that the time they spend is not sufficient. Students who are serious about overcoming this challenge cannot focus on learning styles alone. There are certain, welltested strategies that most successful college students adopt. Developing these strategies will help you maximize your study efforts so that you use the time you have to the best advantage.

Characteristic	I do this	I need to do this
I arrive on time for all of my classes. Class attendance is a high priority for me.		
I sit in the front or middle of the class where I can easily see and hear and will not be distracted.		
I pay attention in class. I do not disrupt others by talking, nor do I "space out" and miss important information.		
I come prepared for class. I have read the chapter and my homework is done. I bring my book, notepaper, and pens to class so I am ready to listen and take notes.		
I participate in class discussions. I know I will learn more if I am involved, plus I am contributing to the learning process.		
I ask questions in class, especially if I don't understand or if I want to know more.		
I give the instructor and others positive feedback in class. I make eye contact when someone is talking and express appropriate body language.		
I get to know other students in each class. I have at least one other person I can ask for help or with whom I compare notes. I don't feel like a stranger.		

I contact the instructor if I know I must miss class. I get any handouts and information that I missed prior to the next class session whenever possible.		
I develop and use my own, personalized learning tools. I mark my textbooks to suit my needs. I have what I need (calculator, pocket dictionary, planner, etc.) to do my assignments.		
I turn in all assignments on time. I don't lose unnecessary points by turning in late or incomplete work.		
I follow the directions. When I'm doing an assignment, I make sure it is what I'm supposed to do.		
I seek help when I need it. I use the support services the college provides (tutoring, counseling, etc.). I don't let pride keep me from getting tutoring. I would rather pass than fail.		

Which characteristic or characteristics in the previous chart do you struggle with the most?

____

____

____

____

____

What steps can you take to move your practice from the "I need to do this" column to the "I do this" column?

____

____

____

____

____

____

Name______________________________ Class Days and Time ______________________

10.3

IDENTIFY YOUR STUDY HABITS

Check "Yes" or "No" to identify areas where your study habits could use improvement.

TRUE ABOUT ME?	YES	NO
1. I always look through my textbooks before classes start to see what the course will cover.		
2. I usually look up unfamiliar words when I'm reading my textbook, using the text glossary whenever possible.		
3. I highlight my textbooks and make margin notes when reading.		
4. I am able to pick out the topic sentence in a paragraph.		
5. I have a regular place for studying, and my study environment is free from distractions.		
6. I plan my study sessions when I know I am rested and will be able to concentrate.		
7. Before starting to read a new chapter, I look over headings, questions at the end of the chapter, and illustrations so that I have a general idea of the topics to be covered in the chapter.		
8. If I have several chapters to read, I divide the material into several reading sessions.		
9. I set specific goals for each study session (number of pages to be read, draft of English assignment to be completed, reviewing for a test, etc.).		
10. I study new material as soon as possible after class.		
11. Before studying new material, I take a few minutes to review the previous assignment.		
12. I reread highlighted, underlined, and/or boldfaced material and any margin notes I've made when I'm reviewing for a test.		
13. I am able to predict questions that are likely to be on the test.		
14. I try to find a study partner for each course.		
15. I know where the reference and periodicals sections are located in my campus library/LRC.		
16. I know where the "open" computer labs are on my campus.		
17. I already know how to use the Internet.		
18. I have already used one of the campus tutoring services.		

Which of the practices in the previous chart do you struggle with the most?

What steps can you take to move your practice from the "NO" column to the "YES" column?

Chapter 11
Spirituality and You

Goals for This Chapter

- To be able to differentiate between religion and spirituality.
- To explore individual spirituality and what impact it has in your life.

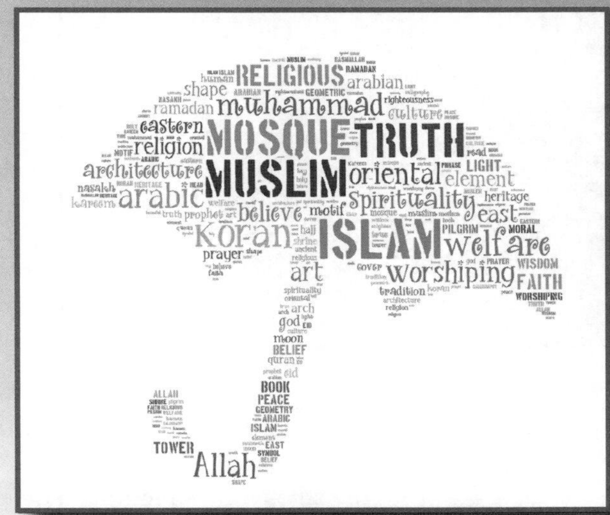

KEY TERMS

spirituality
organized religion
atheist
agnostic

INTRODUCTION TO RELIGION AND TO SPIRITUALITY

Many people assume that religion and spirituality are the same. They can be connected, even intertwined, but they can be as different as the sun and the moon. In this chapter, my hope is to scratch the surface of these two concepts by discussing my view and then sharing with you my spiritual and religious journeys. If you ever

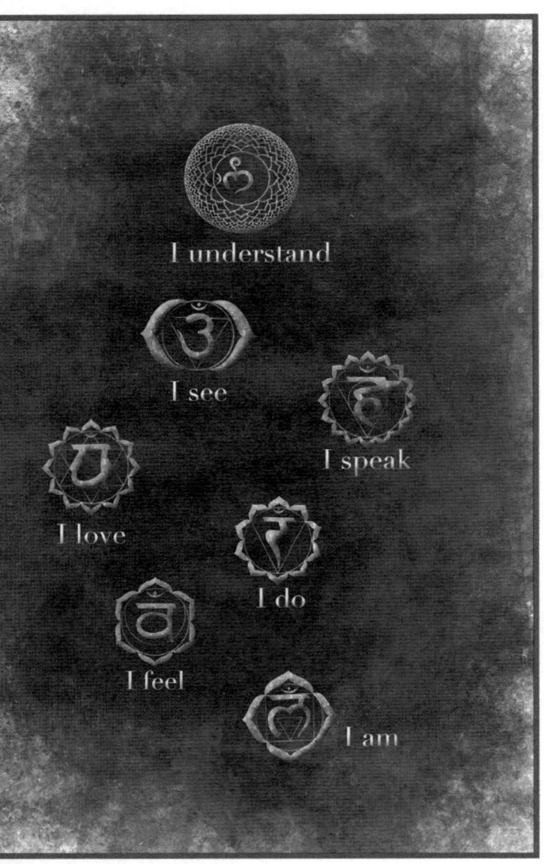

© Photosani, 2012. Under license from Shutterstock, Inc.

have some extra time on your hands (perhaps, but not likely), try to have a conversation with someone to explain either to them your religious practice and or how your spirituality is of importance to you.

The world's religions, of which there are many, have some very common themes, but each has its own specific beliefs and practices. If you review history, you will see many of the wars have been about religion with one culture or country trying to have another country practice its religion. If you think about it, the United States was founded on the pretense of escaping religious persecution in England.

There are whole courses on the world's religions at our college. If you want to explore religion at a deeper level, I would suggest taking such a course but here is a simplistic brief introduction to religion.

All religions have similarities. The followers of the religion know that when they go to church, temple, mosque, synagogue, monastery, or meeting house, they will be surrounded by others with the same beliefs, who share the sacred place housed within the building. Religious ceremonies will be consistent each time they practice them. They will listen to a religious leader or lay person, whose words will be spoken with reverence from a book, tablet, scrolls, or whatever contains the written word of their God. Each action of a ceremony will have symbolism to the followers. The service is a holy ceremony that provides comfort, faith, and support from the group who is practicing its beliefs. The ceremonies within each religious group will have its own customs, readings, and prayers. Participants will feel at home and welcomed by those of the same faith.

Spirituality

concern for the unseen and intangible, as opposed to physical or mundane; appreciation for values having to do with morality, goodness, the soul.

Organized religion

an institution founded to express belief and worship a particular divine power or divinity in an ordered manner.

Spirituality is similar and yet different. Instead of following an **organized religion**, spirituality can be based on your personal beliefs and following your inner path, still maintaining a belief in something larger than us.

Many people talk about being spiritual, but do not follow a specific religion, but that is still an integral aspect of our wellness. My spiritual connections came to me sooner than my religious faith, and I will share my travels with you shortly.

I have always felt a spiritual connection to the earth, specifically water and two different and distinct animals: wolves and dolphins. When we discuss spirituality, thoughts, and feelings, we all have some concept of what we feel connected to. Usually, many people say that their spiritual makeup occurs when they are within the natural world. Occasionally, I will have students state that they find comfort in being surrounded by people on a busy street, and the energy that exists there helps them feel connected and ready to face the day's challenges.

Do you have an inner voice that you listen to? Is this voice your guiding compass when confronted with questionable choices?

Your spirituality should be about finding yourself, demonstrating compassion to your fellowman, and becoming a better person. The question I will ask you later is to define what spirituality means to you. There are magazines, books, videos, websites, and self-help books that all discuss how, when, and where to find your spirituality. My hope and belief is that if you have a spiritual side that you will be able to address what it means to you. If you don't, not to worry, your spirituality exists at some level, and at the time you are ready, I hope you will embrace it, nurture it, and just be.

So the question you may be asking is this: Can I be religious and not spiritual? Can I be non-religious and spiritual? Can I be neither religious nor spiritual? Yes, to all three questions. During your lifetime, you may transition through each of these questions. Many teenagers leave or don't practice their faith during high school and college, but a life event happens and it may lead them back to their religion or perhaps to try another.

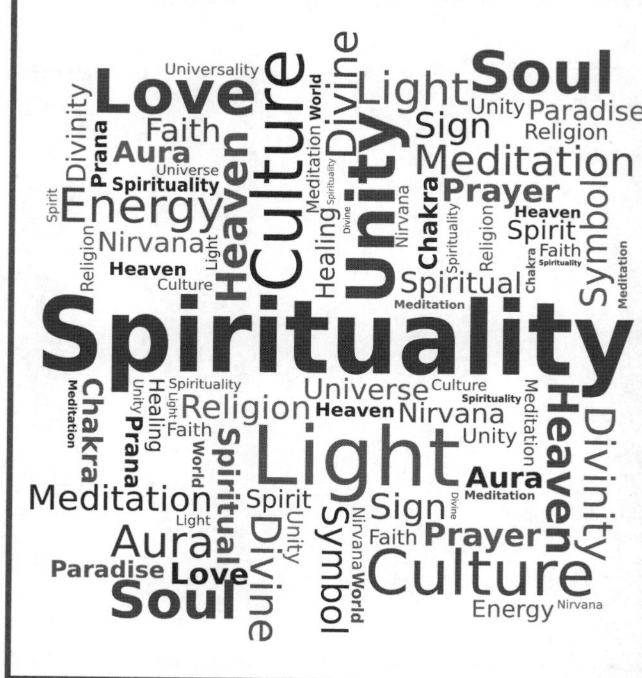

© artellia, 2012. Under license from Shutterstock, Inc.

One of the outcomes from the 9/11 terrorist attacks on the World Trade Center was the tremendous surge in people going back to churches, temples, synagogues, or mosques, and that surge lasted several years. When another tragedy occurs in this country or even in the world, you will again see an increase in participation. There is an old statement from World War II—"There are no atheists in foxholes." The underlying message is that during the horror of war, when you see death on a daily basis, perhaps in that moment when bombs are blowing up all around you, and bullets are zipping overhead, perhaps then is the time you believe in God as you pray that he keeps you alive during the battle. Perhaps a life crisis will lead us to think about a spiritual being, about guardian angels, or talk to a God to help us survive and move forward.

The journey is challenging but I believe that the outcomes, what it provides each of us, are worth the turmoil the questions we may have. The questions we may ask are directly related to something we cannot hold, touch, or visibly see.

My Personal Spiritual and Religious Journey

I was raised by parents who were ***atheists*** *(a belief in nothing related to a God; we are born to die). I went to a local church because the pastor was a friend of the family. After my grandfather died when I was thirteen, I had several things happen in my life that caused me to believe that a guardian angel was watching over me. (A gun going off next to my head. Taking a gun apart and having the bullet fire away from my body. Falling asleep at the wheel on the way to Nashville for a week-long training session while I was listening to Led Zeppelin's "Stairway to Heaven" and waking up to see green grass all around me as I calmly drove back to the road.) These events caused me to believe that I was more than lucky, so I felt someone was watching over me. It only made sense to me that it had to be my grandfather as he was the only person I had lost and I didn't have any other reference to God.*

At this point, late in my teens, I started to change from being an atheist to becoming an ***agnostic*** *(a belief in something; just not sure what). Part of the whole process of learning in a college environment is to challenge the pretenses you hold, and I began to wonder what else there might be. During this time, I also began to appreciate all my time on water, whether it was on Seneca Lake, Downey's Bay in Canada, or on a Florida beach. I found peace and joy whether I was in the water*

Atheist

a person who does not believe in the existence of God or gods.

Agnostic

a person who claims neither faith nor disbelief in God.

© LilKar , 2012. Under license from Shutterstock, Inc.

swimming, boating, or sailing. Growing up I loved sitting on the lake and watching the waves roll in, seeing the storms coming down the lake or trying to skip rocks across the water. This love for the water continued to grow and be nurtured. If I was down, hurt or sad, being near water was a sure-fire cure. I always felt better.

Also around this time, I started to feel a connection to wolves. I would go with friends in the winter to the place in Canada my grandparents owned and hear the wolves howling at night. The sounds they made on those cold and snowy evenings were hauntingly beautiful and I felt a kinship whenever I heard them. During the day we could crosscountry ski and find their paw prints.

In graduate school, I met my wife, a devout Catholic, who offered me the chance to attend Catholic masses with her every Sunday. So almost every Sunday, I would attend mass with her and her family. When I visited I always felt welcome, but I still was not sure how religion fit into my life. Often, my wife would ask if I was ready to join the Catholic Church, and my answer was always the same. I enjoy attending, liked to listen to the readings, but I still had questions.

In early January 2000, my father was diagnosed with lung cancer. At the end of March on his first day without chemo, I called him at 8:00 p.m. to see how his first day went without treatment. He was very happy talking about all he had to do, all he had to catch up on after spending so much time in the hospital receiving treatments. Ten minutes later, I received a phone call from a neighbor who said, "Get to the hospital. Your father is bleeding out." I knew he had died. My sister and I went to the hospital and my thoughts were confirmed. We took my mother home, called the people we needed to call, and then I drove the hour back home. My wife was waiting for me. It was one of those typical late winter mornings, around 3:00 a.m. There was a solid cloud cover; it was snowing, raining, and just a miserable weather-wise. It was made even worse knowing my father would no longer be there in my life. At that moment, I asked God, knowing all the good my father had done during his professional life and knowing my father didn't believe in any God, to give me a sign that he knew my father was a good man and that he would welcome him. At that moment, the rain let up, the snow stopped, a small section of the clouds opened up, and one single star shone through the night sky. That was God's answer to me. In less than a minute, the clouds closed back up, the rain and snow started to fall again, but I had an answer.

That experience led me to understand that some of my questions could never be answered in complete totality and I decided then to start the RICA process (Rite of Christian Initiation), which was almost a year of classes, conversations with others, and learning more about the Catholic faith. I was no longer a spectator; I was becoming part of the largest following in the world. At the Easter vigil, I became a Catholic, and while I may not have all the answers through my faith journey, I came to understand that I may have them someday.

I became a lector, a minister of communion, and a commentator for my church. The first time I stood in front of my congregation to do my first reading, I could feel my mother-in-law standing beside me helping and smiling the whole time. She had passed away less than six months before that time, but she was right there with me.

I continue to look forward to what my life journey will be, but for me my faith and my spirituality will help me through the tough times and it will help me appreciate the beautiful times. I enjoy and marvel at every sunrise, sunset, amazing storm, or the calming sound of water.

© Kuttelvaserova, 2012. Under license from Shutterstock, Inc.

So you may ask where the dolphins come in. (Besides the fact that I am a fan of the NFL Dolphins for most of my life.) About twenty years ago, we started to vacation in the Outer Banks. Whenever we walked the beach, one of the day's highlights was to see dolphins swim just offshore. Over the years, I began to kayak with them, and they would literally swim right along the boat; the older dolphins on the outside and the younger or juvenile dolphins swimming closed to the shoreline. They would play with the boat, dart around, and have fun. There is something amazing about hearing the dolphin's blow-hole opening up, and hearing them taking a breath as they swim by. When they surface, you can see their eyes as they look through you; to me it always feels like they are looking to the depths of my soul to see I measure up. If I don't, they won't trust me and leave. Luckily for me, they stay with me for a period of time before they are off. So these experiences of sharing the ocean, hearing their breaths, and looking into each other's souls have made dolphins a part of my spirituality.

That has been my personal journey and I hope that my story will help you further broaden your understanding and acceptance towards religion and/or spirituality. It is strongly understood that spirituality is an integral component of wellness. Our focus throughout the text has been to create an understanding of wellness and how staying well can help us manage our stress levels and the negative impacts of stress on our mind, body, and spirit.

© casejustin, 2012. Under license from Shutterstock, Inc.

Name________________________________ Class Days and Time ____________________

11.1

SPIRITUALITY

Short answer/essay questions:

1. The first question is to discuss whether you were raised in a religion and if you are still practicing your religion? If not, what changed your mind?

   What is your definition of religion?

2. How would you define spirituality?

3. Would you describe yourself as a spiritual person? If so, explain. If not, how did you come to that conclusion?

4. Do you have any spiritual connection to a place or animal? Describe.

5. What is your viewpoint of guardian angels or angels in general?

6. Has there been a time in your life when you found that either your religion or your spirituality helped you through tough times? If so, explain how.

7. What do your religion and/or spirituality mean to you?

11.2

SPIRITUALITY

Draw or sketch your answer to the following question.

1. If you were to have a tattoo depicting your religion or spirituality, what would it look like? Draw a rough version below. If you cannot imagine having a tattoo, draw or sketch a piece of art that would reflect your concepts. (Think Michelangelo's Sistine Chapel.)

Chapter 12

Diet for a Healthier You (or Not Making Your Diet a Stressor!)

Goals for This Chapter

- To develop a working understanding of how food fuels our bodies.
- To understand the types of foods we consume and what the body needs.
- To understand the change from the food pyramid to the MyPlate concept.
- To be able to read labels and determine what you are actually eating.
- To be able to look at fast food and restaurant menus to comprehend what you are eating, both calories, serving size, and kinds of food.

KEY TERMS

nutrition	food pyramid	transfats
obesity	MyPlate	
complex carbohydrates	simple carbohydrates	

INTRODUCTION

As you read the chapter title, you may be asking yourselves why we are discussing **nutrition** in a stress management book. The answers are multiple, and as you read the chapter and complete the assigned worksheets, I hope that your questions will be answered. But quickly, the reason is

> ***Nutrition***
>
> obtaining the nourishment necessary for health and growth.

that we need to see the correlation between what we eat on a daily basis and our energy level, how we feel about ourselves, to weight gain or loss, to heart disease, and early death. We need to address how many of us are emotional eaters who, when faced with stress, use food as one of our tried and true stress management tools. The problem is that when we eat as a stress reliever, we eat poorly, consuming junk foods or comfort foods, which are high in fat and sugar. If we made choices to eat broccoli, carrots, sugar snap peas, and tomatoes when dealing with our stress, then eating food would not be a bad stress management tool.

The other issue in this chapter on nutrition is that there is so much misinformation about fueling the body. I hope to at least begin the process of making you an educated consumer. It won't happen overnight, as we have to break lifelong learned behaviors. If you still live at home, you have to eat what is provided, but you can make informed choices that will make a difference. I have students tell me that they will eat better when they become parents. Not likely, since the stress and the time commitment that comes with being a parent often makes a person more apt to go for the quick fix, order in, or cooking high fat, processed foods from a box.

Obesity

a medical condition in which extreme overweight and excess body fat impacts health.

So here is the first question I have for you. Can you describe eating your favorite food?

What were the descriptor words that you used to describe eating your favorite food? As you describe this food, it should make you hungry for it, your mouth should be watering, and your taste buds should be salivating. That is what food should be. Now if you tried to describe a fast food hamburger, can you really become excited for the great flavors of that type of burger? If you answered yes, we have a lot of work to do. So let's get started.

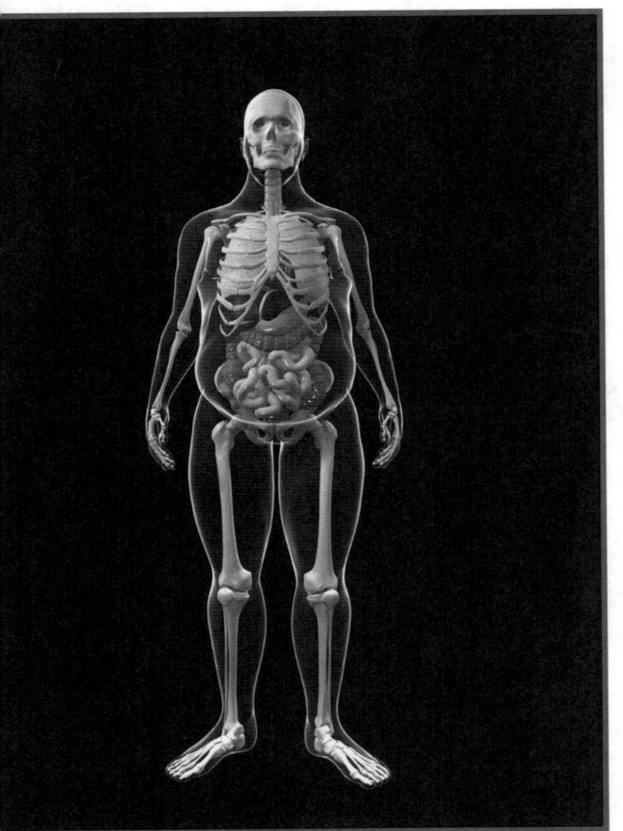

We are seeing so many issues related to our diet that we face a huge challenge. We discuss wellness as if it were an easy fix, but it is certainly not an easy or quick fix. As Americans, we remain very unaware of the nutritional needs for our bodies and how to fuel the body correctly. Countless thousands try the newest fad diet or exercise program to help lose weight. How many late nights have you stayed up to watch the latest infomercial on weight loss either product or exercise program? Think about the cost to advertise on TV and then think about how often these programs air. There must be an amazing amount of money being made and yet the results are pretty pathetic for the most part.

THE FATTENING OF AMERICA

There are two primary issues in my mind that are directly correlated to the fattening of America. I want you to consider that the **obesity** epidemic has only been an area of interest and research within the last twenty to thirty years. When I was in college, you didn't see very many people who would have been considered obese, let alone morbidly obese. Walking around my college campus in the 70s, I honestly can't remember seeing many students who would have been considered obese. Then two major things occurred that had tremendous impact on the health and wellness of the American population: the growing numbers of technological advances we have seen in the last twenty-five years and the growth and access of fast food around the country.

When I was growing up, we played active games outside all the time. Today, many of the youth of America consider playing to be their gaming systems. The issue is that they are not active, not sweating, and burning calories. The secondary issue is the types of food that we are eating while playing these gaming systems. Think about your food choices when gaming. I am willing to bet they are not often quality choices and you probably eat more than you think. We now stay connected on the computer or on our smart phones, which require very little movement. Have you ever broken a sweat texting? (I hope not, because texting is not a physical activity which counts towards exercise or play.) Additionally, we now have hundreds and hundreds of television shows that capture our attention and contribute to our coach potato society. If you love watching college football and professional football during the fall on every Saturday and Sunday, you can literally watch football from noon until midnight. Watching and not playing is impacting many of us.

The second issue that has a direct correlation to the fattening of America is the abundance of fast food within every community. There was a time (in my lifetime) when going to a fast food restaurant was a treat, something you did once in awhile. That is not the case anymore. Fast food is no longer considered a treat; it is now a contributing factor to the obesity epidemic. People eat fast food because it is convenient; they are busy and only have time for a quick bite. We know it is bad for us, but it is there, so why not eat it. The other day, one of my students, while recording her food intake for the week, indicated that on one day she had fast food for breakfast, for lunch, and for dinner. Even though she knows her choices were bad, she is likely to repeat this behavior. How can you watch "Super Size Me" and still want to eat fast food? How can we see videos like "Fast Food Nation," "Forks over Knives," and "Food Inc." and not be at least concerned about the foods we are consuming? Educated consumers will make choices on their beliefs, their concerns, and an understanding of what they consume.

For reference, refer to the five images that follow. They represent a snap shot of the last twenty-five years and the growing obesity epidemic in this country. The Center for Disease Control (www.CDC.gov.) began to track obesity numbers across the United States in the late 60s. Go to www.CDC.gov./obesity/data/adult.html for a closer view of the colors associated with the slides.

The first slide is from 1985. At that time, thirteen states reported less than 10 percent of their adult population was in the obese category. Eight states reported their adult population was between 10 to 14 percent. The other states either didn't report or didn't have concerns with obesity. When this slide was released, there was some concern that these states had a certain percentage of adults who qualified as obese. This led to concern and better tracking and research into obesity. Obesity has, in the last twenty-five years, become a new health concern. Obesity now ranks as one of the the top four health concerns of the United States behind heart disease, cancer, and metabolic syndrome. In 1996, every state was in the range of less than 14 percent or less than 19 percent. In 1997, a new color was added as three states had an adult population that now measured at 20 to 24 percent. In 2001, a new color and range was added as one state jumped into the 20 to 24 percent of adults

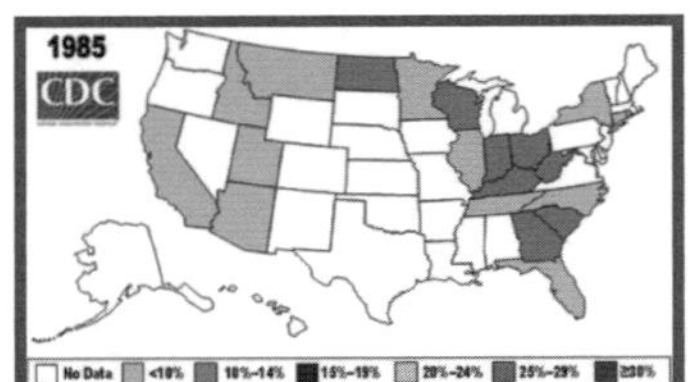

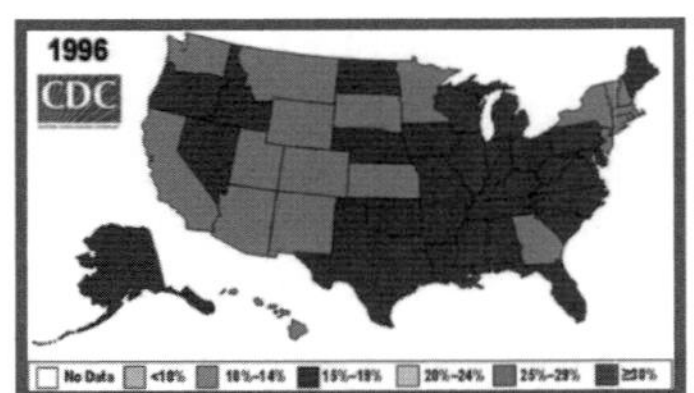

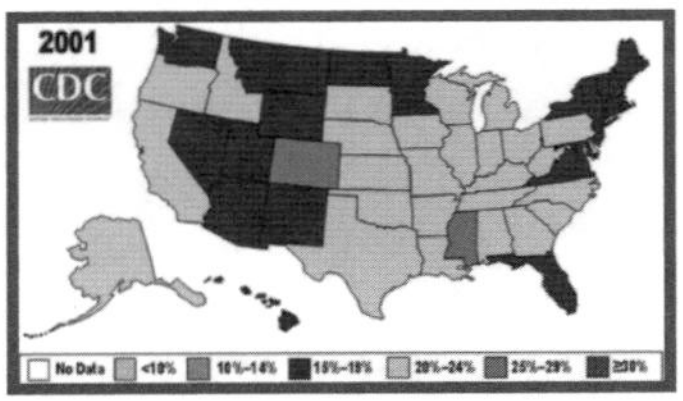

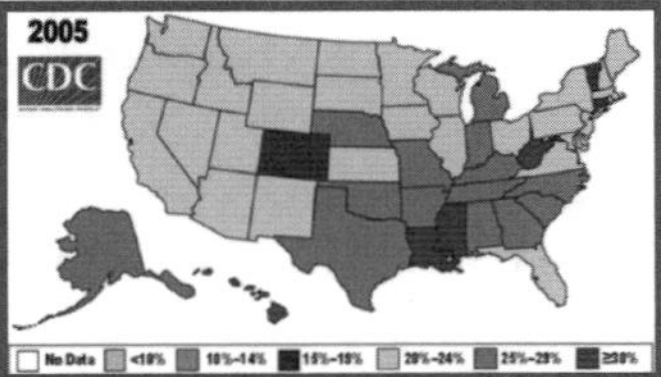

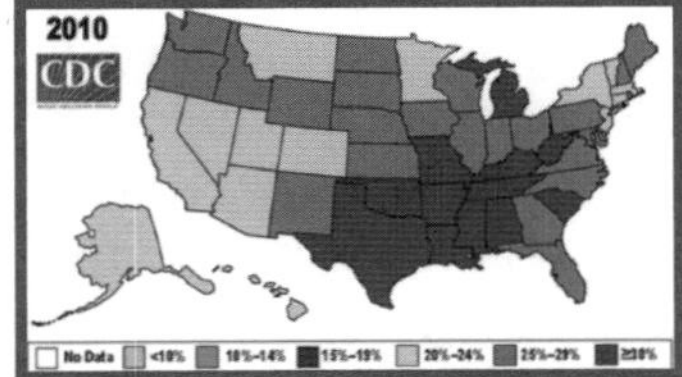

being obese. Then in just four years, two other colors were added, which indicated ranges of 25 to 29 percent, and greater than 30 percent. Considering how quickly we have grown obese, I think we have to reflect on the impact of fast food and technology has played to the fattening of our country.

One of the other scary outcome of the obesity epidemic is medical researchers are speculating that by the year 2050 that 50 percent of Americans may be diabetic. If you scroll further down the obesity slide show, you will find more images that track adult-related diabetes. It follows the same pattern of growth as obesity in the United States. So it makes sense that if we do not make drastic changes in the foods we consume and the quantity we consume, we are on the precipice of a health and wellness crisis.

CHANGING OUR THINKING, CHANGING OUR ACTIONS

Complex carbohydrates

large chains of sugar units arranged to form starches and fiber; includes grains, breads, rice, pasta, vegetables, and beans.

Food pyramid

a nutritional diagram or eating plan in the form of a pyramid with complex carbohydrates at the bottom and fats and sugars at the top.

One of my colleagues shared this quote with me and I love the message: "Eat food, not too much, mostly plants." What a great starting point for this discussion (Thanks Leanne). When discussing nutrition and fueling our bodies, we must review basic information that you probably have seen before. We need to understand the function of food and how the body utilizes what we feed it. Simply stated, our bodies are machines and the foods we consume provide energy for the engines. If the fuel is of poor quality (junk food, processed food, fast food) then the end results over time will also be poor. These poor results range from weight problems, adult related diabetes, high triglyceride levels (bad fat-LDL and total fat levels within our bloodstream), and low levels of energy.

When the fuel is of better quality, **complex carbohydrates** (fruits and vegetables), low fat protein (skinless chicken, deep-cold-water fish, nuts, soybeans and tofu), the opposite outcomes tend to occur. We have more energy, sleep better, have better control of weight management, less risk of hypokinetic disease (diseases related to having low energy and little or no movement in our lifestyle), lower blood pressure, lower pulse rate, and lower blood fat levels. Our health and wellness is maintained or significantly improved by changing our diet. We will have to take ownership of the foods with which we fuel our bodies. The choice becomes yours and yours alone.

You were likely raised on the **food pyramid** from the United States Department of Agriculture (USDA). The base of the pyramid was grains, breads, cereals, rice, and pasta. It was recommended that we consume six to eleven servings. The next level of the food pyramid was vegetables, which suggested that we consume three to five servings and the fruit group was two to three servings daily. The next level of the pyramid was two to three servings from milk, yogurt, and cheese. At that same level were two to three servings of meat, poultry, fish, beans, nuts, eggs, and legumes. The top of the pyramid consisted of foods to use sparingly. However, many Americans have inverted the food pyramid and eat many foods from the top levels of the pyramid and eat fewer fruits, vegetables, and grains (especially whole grains).

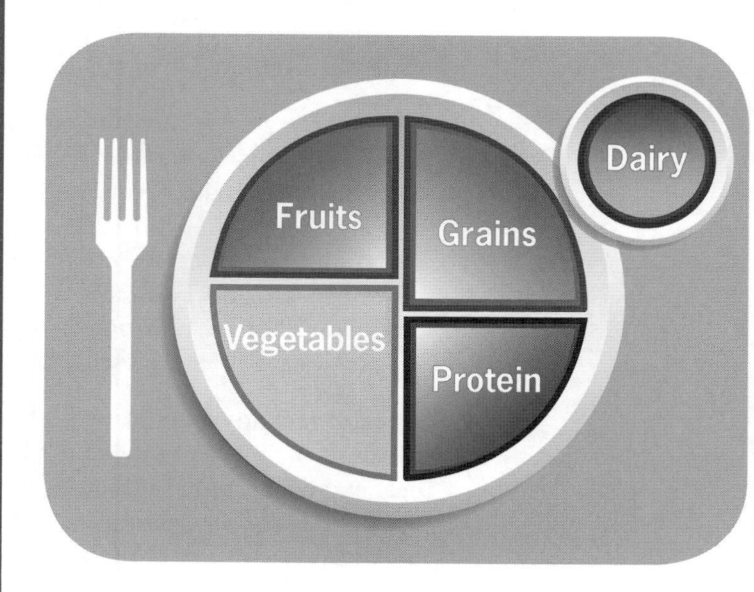

The food pyramid was recently replaced by **MyPlate**, a new strategy to educate the American population. When you have several minutes, go ahead and log into www.CDC.gov./obesity/data/adult.html for more information than I can place here within this overview chapter. The MyPlate is slowly catching on, but the focus is to teach about size proportions and what a healthy meal should consist of each time we eat.

> ***MyPlate***
> current nutrition guide published by the United States Department of Agriculture, depicting a place setting with a plate and glass divided into five food groups.

The plate is shown as having the four food groups we should eat every day. They are fruits, vegetables, protein, and grains. There is also a cup for dairy. As you review the plate, you will notice that the plate is not split into quarters as many people believe. The vegetables and grains are the two largest spaces for your food; the protein and fruit are of similar size and a little smaller than the vegetables and grains. The concept is to visualize the plate and try to make the proportions similar to the plate. Another recommendation is to add color to each meal. Try to eat a rainbow of colors throughout the day, which will help you eat healthier and fuel the body well. You will be adding healthy nutrients, fiber, and antioxidants by adding color by eating fruits and vegetables.

> ***Simple carbohydrates***
> sugars that provide calories but no nutritional value.

The foundation of a healthy diet is to increase the amount of complex carbohydrates (simple carbohydrates are sugars and white flour) we consume each day. The food from breads, cereals, and grains are the cornerstone of adding complex carbohydrates to our diets. By consuming these complex carbohydrates, we are adding fiber to our diet, which is beneficial to our digestive system. Some of the primary nutrients these foods add to our diet are riboflavin, niacin and iron. A highly recommended suggestion is that within the breads, grains, pasta, and cereals to consume whole grains or unbleached products. Simply stated, darker is always the better choice. Try to consume products that are not very processed and eat whole grains as close to the original form as you can find.

I recently read an article that makes a strong visual argument. They take a bowl of fruit and photograph it every day for three weeks. You see this beautiful fruit, which slowly starts to decay and rot and have mold grow on it. The fruit has life within it and supports new life growing from it. Another pictorial takes a McDonald's Happy Meal and records pictures over a two-year period. The results are dramatically different. Even after two years, the before and after pictures of the Happy Meal have not changed. No growth, no mold; the food is dead and doesn't support any new life growing from it. If you are interested in seeing the pictures, they were published in Shambhala, Sunday, May 2012. The focus of the issue was Embrace Change. The title of the article was "Impermanence is Buddha nature."

Fruits and vegetables are another aspect of a healthier diet. They are mostly complex carbohydrates, low in calories that help us eat a rainbow of colors in our daily intake of food. The biggest issue in today's American diet is that most of our vegetables are highly processed or we eat fast food French fries and count them as a vegetable. We cover our vegetables with butter and sauces, to add flavor. We need to rediscover the flavor palette that fruits and vegetables provide. Nutrients from fruits and vegetables are vitamins A and C, riboflavin and fiber. They are nutritionally dense and low in caloric cost. An average apple contains 80 calories and a regular candy bar has anywhere from 250 to 350 calories.

The last section of the plate is a protein, preferably a low-fat, lean protein. Here we want to consider chicken without the skin; fish, preferably deep, cold-water fish, lean cuts of beef and pork, ground turkey, or vegetable protein from soybean products (tofu), nuts, and beans. The average serving size of protein is three ounces, approximately the size of your fist or the size of a deck of cards. For nuts, it's about ten to fifteen. The nutrients found in protein are iron, niacin, vitamins B-6 and B-12, and protein.

The choices we make and the quantities we consume have a direct impact on the how efficiently the body's systems work. We can lower our fat intake by following some simple guidelines. Remove all visible fat before cooking, remove poultry skin, improve cooking techniques and styles, consume less grilled meat, eat leaner cuts of meat, eat less processed meats such as bologna, hot dogs, and pepperoni, and limit the number of times we go back for seconds.

Next on the plate is a cup for dairy. Whether you are consuming milk, cheese, or yogurt as your dairy product, you have to be aware of both size and fat content from this food group. If you drink milk, try to make the change from whole milk (about 65 percent milk fat), to 1 percent milk (about 15 percent milk fat). There is a debate as to whether skim milk is the best choice. Here is what I would suggest: if the only source of dairy within your diet is from milk, then 1 percent is the best choice. We need some milk fat to strengthen bones, bone growth, and build stronger teeth. If you eat cheese or yogurt, then you may want to drink skim milk to lower your overall fat intake. The nutrients within dairy are calcium, riboflavin, protein, fat, and Vitamins A and D.

The biggest change from the food pyramid to MyPlate is there is no place for fats, sugars, oils, or sweets and desserts. Mostly, these types of food are high in simple carbohydrates (refined sugar, butter, margarine, condiments, and salt). These foods have earned the moniker "junk food" as we consider them empty calories, which contribute high caloric cost with little or no nutritional value. An example to help you understand how the American diet has changed, it is said that the average American consumes one hundred pounds of sugar each year and at the same time consumes around twenty-five to thirty pounds from fruits and vegetables. That is approximately twenty, five-pound bags of sugar every year. That is more than one bag of sugar each month. Where is all this sugar? It is found within most processed foods, sugary drinks, soda, ice cream, cookies, donuts, and white bread among others.

There is one outcome I want you to reflect on as we move forward. Many Americans are addicted to two types of food: sugar and fat. We love them and, it seems, we cannot get enough of them, and then we wonder why the sudden increase in our waists and our body weight. As you look around the college campus, I guarantee you will see several things. First, we live on caffeine, from coffee and soda to energy drinks. Second, we choose fast, quickly available food, whether from a vending or a fast food offering. You will see classmates eating poorly. At the start of the class, they appear energetic and engaged in the class. Then in about twenty minutes, the blood sugar spike crashes and they become lethargic; they have an energy drain and are struggling to make it through the rest of the class. Then as soon as they leave the class, they look for another "fix" of sugar to balance their blood sugar levels. They go to the next class and the process is likely repeated.

Another question we are often asked is related to protein drinks and whether they are good and worth taking. Too much protein is hard on our kidneys, and for the most part we are not negligent with our protein intake. Read the labels, research them, and decide why you are considering using protein drinks as a supplement to your diet. What benefits does it provide that a well rounded nutrition plan doesn't already provide you?

We need to break our dependence on sugar and fat and make the switch to complex carbohydrates and lean protein, which the body utilizes better so blood sugar levels don't suffer the highs and lows to the extreme we see from the sugar "fix."

Here are the basic guidelines for types of food consumption within our diet. We should try to eat around 55 to 60 percent of our food (calories) as carbohydrates. The qualifier here is they should come from complex carbohydrate food sources: fruits, vegetables, whole grains. Our fat intake should be 20 to 30 percent, with only 10 percent of our fat intake coming from animal sources. This may sound high to you, but I have read the average American diet consumes approximately 45 to 47 percent of their calories from fat. I remember reading an article several years ago that suggested that if every American consumed only 30 percent of fat in their diet, we could decrease heart disease by 50 percent in this country, and if every American only consumed 20 percent of their calories from fat, we could eliminate heart disease. If we did that, each of you would be able to obtain reasonable health coverage. I don't know if we will ever be able to make this change. It is asking a lot. The last food type we should consume is protein and it is recommended that we consume between 12 to 15 percent of our calories from here. With protein, we want to consume leaner cuts, and to understand serving size and use this knowledge when we are eating.

BECOMING AN INFORMED, EDUCATED FOOD CONSUMER

The first step may be the hardest, since it involves changing your behavior. We know that to change any behavior, whether it is adding an exercise program or becoming an informed food consumer, it will take around eight weeks to make the change. So this is not an easy process, but it is one that I hope you will consider. There are countless ways to become a healthy consumer of food. First you must truly believe that eating healthier is important and making a commitment to eating better is making a long term commitment to your health and wellness. If that is not enough, then you are making a commitment to your loved ones to take care of them and to be with them for many years to come. Pick your motivation, and stay focused.

The next step is to learn how to read labels and understand what we are consuming. As we read labels, we begin by reviewing the list of ingredients, which are listed most to least. I worry when the list of ingredients begin to sound like a science experiment instead of something that tastes good. Here is the list of ingredients for an apple: apple that is all. Okay, if you are eating organically, they will state that no pesticides were used on the apple. We are also looking for hidden sugars. Fat content, types of fat, any time we see partially hydrogenated with unsaturated oil, we need to understand that the unsaturated vegetable oil has been changed to an unhealthy food. These are considered to be **transfats** (the latest concern within our diet.) We have seen a tremendous increase of transfats in food processing. They have been found to increase the risk of coronary heart disease and it is recommended that we try to avoid them or only consume it in very small amounts.

> ***Transfats***
>
> hydrogenated vegetable fats; formed when hydrogen is added to a liquid fat, so it remains solid at room temperature.

Making reading labels a part of our daily lives is actually simpler than it sounds. I am not asking you to read every label each time you go shopping. Pick an item you often purchase at the grocery store. For the example let's use cereal. We all have our favorites, but many of them are processed grains and high in sugar. So we are in the cereal aisle. We pull out a box and start to review the ingredients. If you find things like bleached whole grains, automatically put it back on the shelves. Then I look for the types and frequency of sugars within the food. The more sugar found in the top ten ingredients, the sooner it should go back on the shelves. After reviewing five or six boxes of cereal, hopefully you have found several that appear to be healthy and you would eat. From then on, each time you purchase cereal, you have several choices. Then, unless a new cereal comes out, you don't have to read every time. Then if the next item you purchase often is bread, repeat the same process to identify several brands that meet your criteria. Over the eight-week period, you can make your shopping quicker and healthier.

Nutrition Facts

Serving Size 1/4 Cup (30g)
Servings Per Container About 38

Amount Per Serving	
Calories 200 Calories from Fat 150	
	% Daily Value*
Total Fat 17g	**26%**
Saturated Fat 2.5g	**13%**
Trans Fat 0g	
Cholesterol 0mg	**0%**
Sodium 120mg	**5%**
Total Carbohydrate 7g	**2%**
Dietary Fiber 2g	**8%**
Sugars 1g	
Protein 5g	
Vitamin A 0%	Vitamin C 0%
Calcium 4%	Iron 8%

*Percent Daily Values are based on a 2,000 calorie diet.

The next step in reading labels is to look at the caloric content, the percentage of daily needs based on a 2,000-calorie diet. We can quickly calculate the calories based on grams per serving. The rule is known as the 4-4-9 rule. Every gram of carbohydrate and protein has four calories per gram and each gram of fat has nine calories. So the label tells you how many grams (gm) there are for each food type, carbohydrate, protein, and fat. Simply multiply the numbers to calculate how many calories and what type of calories they are. If a food has 50 gms of carbohydrates in a serving and 25 gms of fat, you may think it is a good food. Do the quick math; 50 × 4 indicates the food has 200 calories from carbohydrates (then you have to look at simple and complex) and the 25 × 9 indicates the caloric cost of fat within the food is 225. If the food has 425 calories per serving, then it is over 50 percent fat content. Not a good food to consume. It may taste awesome, but it is still a high fat food with a cost to our bodies and our health.

Take the time to shop, learn to understand your food choices, and slowly work on making better choices each time you shop and eat. It will be a slow process, but one that is very enlightening and very helpful in helping you eat and fuel your body better.

RULES FOR EATING

Some simple changes we can adopt or utilize will make simple and impactful changes within our diet. Some are easy to add and others take thought and action. Some will be review from this chapter and others will be new comments to implement. Let's get started.

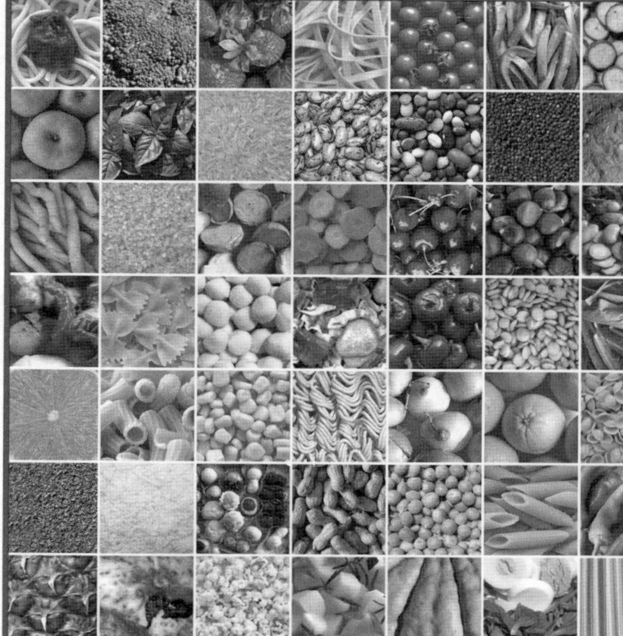

1. Eat mostly complex carbohydrates, fruits, vegetables, and whole grains.
2. Eat less fat, especially animal fat.
3. Eat a variety of colors every meal, every day.
4. Don't skip meals. It impacts and changes both your blood sugar levels as well as slows the basal metabolic rate (calories you burn at rest).
5. Drink sixty-four ounces of water each day. Your body is mostly made up of water, so this is a common sense suggestion.
6. Eat three to six small meals every day.
7. Change the size of our meals; the most important meal of the day is either breakfast or lunch. The smallest meal of the day should be dinner, as we are not very active after dinner. A tough change, but a significant addition.
8. Set a time in the evening and don't eat after that time. The calories are often empty and the digestive process is taxed while sleeping.
9. If you like to eat, then add muscle mass to your body and more activity to increase the quantity of calories you can eat every day.
10. Never deprive yourself a favorite food; use it as a reward or for a special occasion.
11. Add two meatless days into your eating plan.
12. Allow a cheat day every week; this entitles you to eat some foods you are avoiding for a specific reason.
13. Read labels. Know what you are eating.
14. Shop on the outside of your food store. Usually you will find the fruits and vegetables, bread, protein, cheeses, milk, dairy, and paper goods on most of the outside loop. When you start shopping the center aisles, you will be exposed to a wide variety of processed, boxed food that has little nutritional value.
15. Never food shop on an empty stomach or while you are hungry. Every food will call your name out and you will tend to add extra food to your cart.
16. When shopping, use a list, and only allow yourself to buy only one item that isn't on your list.
17. Stick to small proportions on your plate; use the salad plate to serve dinners on. Your plate will be fuller and it will appear that you are eating more.
18. Drink a large glass of water twenty minutes before your meals. This way you are starting with a half-full stomach instead of an empty one. This allows less food to be eaten to fill you up.
19. Only eat fast food once in awhile. Make fast food a blast from your unhealthy past. If you go to a fast food restaurant, don't order french fries, skip the dessert, and change the number of fat calories you will consume during the meal.
20. Stop drinking soda.

21. Don't rely on fads for weight loss.
22. Understand these simple statements: For weight maintenance, calories consumed have to be equal to calories burned on a daily basis. For weight loss, calories consumed have to be less than calories burned on a daily basis. Weight gain comes from consuming more calories that the body burns on a daily basis.
23. 3,500 calories equal a pound.
24. Eat less white and processed breads, grains, pasta, and rice; eat darker whole grain foods.
25. When eating out, only eat half of the meal and take the other half home for lunch or dinner the next day. Restaurant portions are getting larger and larger. Don't eat it all at once.
26. If you order a dessert at a restaurant, split it with your companion.
27. Learn the visual cues for what constitutes a serving size for all food types.
28. Try to modify your diet and follow either the Mediterranean Diet or the Harvard Healthy Eating Plan.
29. Eat food, not too much and mostly plants
30. Remember, we are what we eat.

Can you think of or add any other for rules for eating?

____

____

____

CONCLUSION

There are many college courses on just nutrition which offer a more in-depth look at foods, the biochemistry of foods, and how to make foods we consume healthier. If nutrition is an interest, then I recommend taking a course that will be more in-depth than this chapter. The focus of this chapter is to be a nutrition primer. My goal was to review material you have seen before and start the process of making you an educated consumer. I wanted to ask basic questions regarding your eating behaviors and to suggest possible ways to slowly make changes in your diet.

If you try to make changes, I must reiterate that changing a behavior is a process. Don't try to make all the changes at once. If you do, it will likely set you up for failure. Pick a behavior you have wanted to change, and focus on making that change. Remember it will take time to make the change, so allow at least eight weeks. If you fail one day, don't give up; start again the next day. I gave up all sodas and as I write this, I haven't had a soda for more than five months, but there are times I would like to taste a diet Pepsi. However, I decided to make the change and have stuck with it so far. So can you. Don't pick the hardest behavior to change. Start with something you believe you can achieve. Once you have made the change, you will have had a positive experience and feel good about yourself. This change can be the foundation of many more changes you will make in your lifetime.

Fueling your body is not a sprint; it is an activity you will do each and every day of your life. It is truly a marathon, and I hope I have introduced ideas to make you think and take ownership of your nutrition. I hope you will begin to think about your food intake, and each time you make a choice of foods to eat, will try to lean toward as many positive choices as possible. I wish you the very best and wish you good eating and good health.

REFERENCES

Center for Disease Control and Prevention. Accessed May 2004 and June 2011. www.CDC.gov./obesity/data/adult.html.

Fischer N. "Impermanence is Buddha Nature." *Shambhala* (May 2012): 53–59.

Name____ Class Days and Time ________________________

12.1

RECORDING DAILY INTAKE

This homework assignment requires you to record everything you eat and drink over seven days. I am not asking for a calorie count, but I want you to record every food you eat or drink (meals, snacks, and alcohol). Include the time of the day, how much. (Don't say a cookie or cookies, but give the total you consumed). With each day, I want you to also record any exercise you did that day to help us look at your whole week's experience. We will then use this to analyze your dietary intake for the week.

Total number of fruits and vegetable servings consumed during the week? _______

How many of your meals resembled the USDA MyPlate as discussed

in the reading? _______

Name____ Class Days and Time ______________________

12.2

READING FOOD LABELS

Read two food labels from foods that you normally eat. If at all possible, use a food label from a food that you believe is bad for you, but you enjoy the taste. Also include a food label from a food which you believe is a healthier choice. I want you to analyze the food labels and discuss the chemicals and other items listed in the ingredients list. I want you to calculate the total number of calories in the package based on calorie per serving and total servings in the package. I want you to calculate the calories of fats, carbohydrates, and protein and determine if this food is healthy or something we might consider "food porn" or food that is really bad for you. Give any additional comments as you deem necessary.

1. Food Label 1: Comments:

2. Food Label 2: Comments:

Name____ Class Days and Time ____________________________

12.3

EATING OUT

This assignment involves visiting a fast food restaurant and asking for the required restaurant nutritional guidelines. The other option is to print the information from their online website. Once you have attached the nutritional guideline to this sheet, I want you to calculate the total intake of calories for three meals of which you likely would eat at this restaurant. Try to use a restaurant that you regularly eat at; it will be more meaningful. With each meal, I want you to list the food you would eat, the total number of calories of each item, the amount of fat calories in the food, and total amount of sodium consumed. After you have completed each meal, add the total number of calories you would have consumed that day and the amount of fat and sodium you consumed. Then next to it, I want you to review the menu and make suggestions that could make eating at your restaurant better for you.

Name of restaurant: ____ and include the hard copy of the nutritional guidelines you used.

	Food Item	Calories	Fat	Sodium	Recommended Changes
1. Breakfast:					
2. Lunch:					
3. Dinner:					

Chapter 13
Are You Taking Care of Mother Earth?

Goals for This Chapter

- To understand how we damage the earth through our actions.
- To develop an understanding of your personal carbon footprint.
- To develop a plan to lessen your overall impact on the earth.
- To be able to comprehend how damaging the earth around us impacts our wellness and increases our stress.

KEY TERMS

Clean Air Act	carbon footprint	recycle	reuse
Clean Water Act	4 Rs	reduce	repair

You may have asked yourself why we include a chapter on taking care of the earth in a textbook that is bridging stress, stress management, and wellness. Well, if you recall in Chapter 1 when the components of wellness were introduced—physical, emotional, intellectual, social, spiritual, environmental, and nutritional—the focus was to delve deeper into each area of the wellness continuum and then tie it back to stress. So to frame this chapter, we have to begin with asking a few simple questions that will take some time to reflect on and develop honest answers: How do you take care of the earth? What impact do you make on it? What is truly your carbon footprint? Can you improve your impact on the environment in which you live?

HOW DO YOU TAKE CARE OF PLANET EARTH?

How often do you consider what you are doing to the earth or more importantly how often do you change your behaviors to have a lesser impact to the environment you live in? The following questions will start the process of comprehension of what we do.

1. Do you recycle your paper, cans, bottles, plastics? Do you understand what is recyclable where you live? What plastic numbers are accepted locally in your hometown? ______________________________

   ____

2. Do you have an area that you commit to walking most of the time, whether it is to your college, to work, to a restaurant, or to a store? If where you are going is less than ____ miles, will you walk? If where you are going is farther than ____ miles, will you drive?

3. If you live in the residence halls, have you ever driven to class on the other side of campus because it is too far?

   ____

4. Do you litter? The composition time of a cigarette butt, aluminum can, or a plastic water bottle can be as long as 450 years. ______________________________

5. Have you replaced your normal light bulbs in your residence with energy efficient light bulbs? ______________________________

6. When you are done using your computer, iPod, or coffee maker, do you unplug them, or do you let them to continue to draw energy, thinking it is no big deal?

   ____

7. Do you keep the thermostat at a lower temperature and wear sweatshirts or use blankets in the winter? ______________ In the summer, do you keep the air conditioner around 74 to 75 degrees to save energy? ______________

8. Do you leave the water running while you are brushing your teeth? If you do, you are wasting gallons of water each day. ______________________________

9. Are the foods (especially produce and meats) you eat, locally grown, which cuts down on smog emissions from having your food trucked in? ______________

10. How green in your lawn? Do you have a lawn service that applies pesticides two to four times each growing season? Where do the pesticides go after they green up the lawn? (The answer is it ends up in our ground water at some level.)

    ____

11. How old is your car? Do you change the oil regularly? Do you keep the air pressure at recommended pressures? Do you carpool whenever you can? ____________

____

12. Do you walk or bike instead of driving whenever possible? ____________

How far do you walk or bike on a daily basis? ____________

How long is your average shower? Five minutes, ten minutes, fifteen minutes, or longer? An average ten minute shower uses between twenty to forty gallons of water depending on your water pressure in the home. Think about those of you who take a second or even third shower in a day!

13. Do you utilize public transportation whenever possible? ____________ If not, why don't you? ____________

14. If and when you buy your next or first new car, what will your parameters be? Will you look for power, style, miles per gallon, color, how green the car is from the plant to delivery to you? Each of your answers will have an impact on the earth.

____

15. Have you ever lived or had to worry about going outside due to a smog alert, because the air was so thick with particles that it made breathing difficult?

____

(I remember once flying into Southern California. As we flew over the last mountain range, we went from this beautiful scenery of mountain vistas to a literal brown cloud hovering over the city of Los Angeles (the city of Angels). That evening at least, the angels' wings were covered in brown particulates.

This list of questions is by no means inclusive, but it is meant to be thought provoking. Are you contributing to making the earth a better place or are you contributing to using up our natural resources without a thought or care in the world? If you are not thinking about how to make a difference, then you are only left with one question: How long can the earth survive with the manner we are treating her?

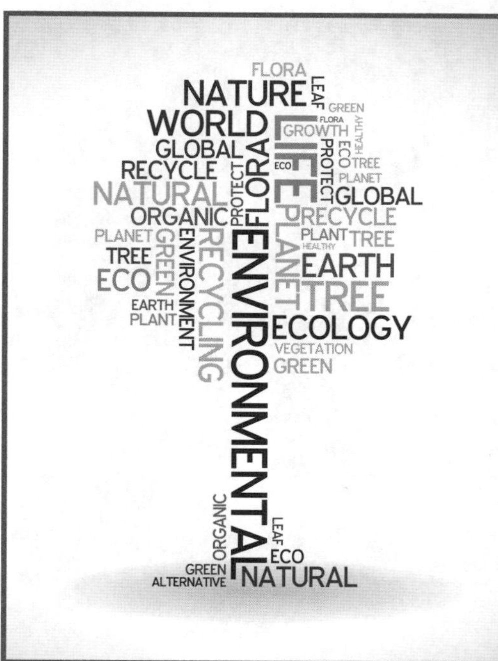

© Petr Vaclavek, 2012. Under license from Shutterstock, Inc.

WHAT IMPACT HAVE WE MADE ON THE EARTH TO THIS POINT IN THE HISTORY OF HUMANITY?

In my lifetime, I have seen and read about some of worse case examples of how we take care of the earth. Take Ohio, the state of my birth.

In the 1960s, the Cuyahoga River caught fire and actually burned. It wasn't the first time that the river had caught fire. Imagine the Genesee River (or any river near where you live) actually catching fire and burning because the chemicals, gas, and oil were so concentrated in the water that it literally ignited. The river was declared dead, and so began

Clean Air Act

federal law created to reduce chemical emissions into the air on a national level.

Clean Water Act

primary federal law that governs water pollution by setting wastewater and water quality standards.

the long, slow, arduous attempt to change the ways the factories and plants handled their waste. I remember pictures showing pipes coming straight from the plants and depositing all the chemicals and other pollutants into the river. The river fed Lake Erie and obviously impacted the quality of the water there. It took decades for the water to clear up as the factories learned and were held to a higher standard. Thus began a series of legislation, **Clean Air Act** and **Clean Water Act**, which were the first major steps in this country to change the way we handled waste and looked to the future.

Lake Erie actually was declared a dead lake, with no life at all. No fish, no frogs, no swimming as it was hazardous to your health. I remember visiting the beautiful shoreline on a hot summer day, wanting to go for a swim, only to read signs that the beach was closed.

We used to be able to actually eat the fish from Lake Ontario until the late 80s. Then it was recommended to not eat fish from the lake more than once a month. The current recommendation is to not eat fish from the lake at all due to the chemicals the fish have lived in and have been exposed to. The chemicals are actually stored in the fat of the fish.

Another example of the effect humans have on the natural world has been several studies in Sweden and Canada that actually investigated the impact of the birth control pill and fish. Although the studies are limited, the outcome is that birth control pill chemicals are actually being excreted into the waste system. Some of the chemicals are ending up in the natural world and are lessening the number of fish being born. Who would think that a major health care program could have detrimental impacts in the natural world? Obviously, these studies need to be expanded and repeated multiple times, but it should cause us to stop and think.

No doubt, you have heard, read, or researched the issue of global warming. There are multiple theories that range from it doesn't exist to we are damaging the earth so badly that the Polar Ice Caps are melting and the useable water, which is housed there, will begin to flood the coastal regions of the world. What is obvious is that we have impacted the world's water supply negatively and we must change our ways.

Here are some facts that I find amazing in regards to our wastefulness and misuse of water, a very precious resource. The average household uses around 350 gallons of water a day; Americans use greater than 400 billion gallons of water every day. When we flush a toilet, the average toilet uses five gallons. That is why one of the newer, greener trends within toilets is a two-flush system. One button is for urine and uses much less water; the other button uses more water to remove the feces. It's a great idea and we need to develop more of these ideas to protect this natural and valuable resource.

It is said that 97 percent of the earth's water is salty, 2 percent is frozen in the ice caps and glaciers, and only 1 percent of the water in the world is available for all of humanity. That includes drinking, agricultural, manufacturing, community, and personal usage. Do you waste this resource or do you limit your usage to try to make a difference?

YOUR CARBON FOOTPRINT

© 2012 Dustie. Under license from Shutterstock, Inc.

Have you ever considered your impact on the earth? If you have, I hope it has led you to change at least in small ways to try to contribute to making the environment a better place for all. If you haven't, then we will introduce the concept of your carbon footprint, which is really a method to measure your impact on the earth. Each of us every day, uses materials that create a global impact through the amount of carbon emissions given off. That is our **carbon footprint**. By measuring our carbon footprint, we can measure the impact of our choices—as we eat, work, travel, and play. By measuring our footprint, we are able to determine how much damage our individual contribution has made to the world's climate change. The impact we make is measured in carbon emissions (usually measured in pounds or tons). It's becoming an increasingly useful tool to open our eyes and help us develop a better understanding of how each of us impacts global warming.

Carbon footprint

the total amount of carbon dioxide (CO) and other greenhouse gases emitted over the full life cycle of a product or service.

The carbon footprint is the total amount of carbon dioxide (CO_2) and other greenhouse gases emitted over the full life cycle of a product or service. Every product we consume, every electronic we purchase, every smart phone we use, the food we eat at a restaurant, all have a carbon footprint (www.treehugger.com). The footprint is not limited to when we buy it; the footprint begins in the process of making the item, continues in the process of shipping it to our community, expands father in the cost of the store storing it, the cost of electricity to keep the store open, to the energy we use to go to the store and then drive it to our homes. The total carbon footprint includes all of the energy from creation to the time it ends back in our landfills. With our passion for the best and newest technology, we have become a throwaway society and are quickly filling up our landfills. We need to change our ways; we need to each make a commitment to make changes and value the precious natural resources that we have. The earth does not have an unlimited supply of natural resources; the sooner we value, protect, and recycle our natural resources, the less we will negatively impact the world.

WHAT AND HOW WE LIVE IMPACTS THE WELLNESS OF THE EARTH

Do you remember in the chapter on meditation and the variety of guided imagery that you practiced from the appendix? Now think about meditating to images of a trashed world, with garbage and pollution all around you. Not a pretty concept, but if we don't consider drastically changing our ways, the images I have created for you may be the only images we will have left. In the spirituality chapter, we discussed the connection we have with the natural world, a place where we can find peacefulness, time to ourselves, a place to recharge our batteries. What if those places become harder to find or even worse, they stop existing? The sooner we make changes, the more powerful the impact will be.

So what changes can we make? Some of the concepts are not new, but as long as they have been around us, many ignore them or think to ourselves there effort will not matter. Yes, all efforts will matter as we take on the responsibility of being better stewards to earth.

4R

ways to exercise stewardship over the earth; recycle, reduce, reuse, repairs.

The time to consider the 4 Rs is now. The **4 Rs** are recycle, reduce, reuse, and repair. You have likely seen print and TV ads urging us to reduce our waste and recycle as much as possible. The other words may be somewhat foreign to you, so let's further discuss each of the R's.

Recycling

to convert waste into reusable materials.

The first R is to continue or expand our **recycling** efforts around the globe. One of my family's favorite places to vacation is the Outer Banks, North Carolina. We have been going there over the last twenty-five years and each year I see more and more of the impact from the high volumes of traffic, not just on the beach, but in traffic to the beach and how we impact the area. I remember spotless beaches, where the only treasures we found were seashells that had washed up on the miles of beach. Each year, not only do we find fewer seashells, but we find more litter, ranging from discarded cans, cigarette butts (which take hundreds of years to decompose), bottle tops, fishing lines, and now since more people are bringing their pets to the beaches, you often see them kicking some sand over the poop and acting as if they did a good job. When we first started visiting the Outer Banks in the 80s, I was always amazed that recycling had not caught on yet. The garbage was picked up three times a week, and hardly anyone recycled anything. We always tried to make sure we did, but it was hard, as communities didn't support recycling. You would think a community that makes a living from the tourist industry would have wanted to take better care of this beautiful spot on the earth. There were no garbage dumps on the islands, so they had to truck the garbage inland, increasing the overall impact of the garbage and raising the carbon footprint. The good news is they now have recycling trailers set up at several locations around the islands and more and more people are recycling. Unfortunately, they still pick up the garbage three times a week and it is incredible to see the waste and the volume of garbage at the end of each week.

So the first question related to the Rs is: how much of the waste that you produce on a daily basis do you recycle? How much of your waste that you produced today was really recyclable?

Are you willing to change and try to recycle more than your current status? The first step has to be taken be each of us. We need to develop and sustain a grass roots effort where each of us can make a difference in our local communities, our state, our nation, and hopefully the world.

Reduce

to use less or consumer fewer products.

Reduce is based on changing the way we use our natural resources. The National Resources Defense Council discusses this as being a relatively new concept. To help the consumer understand the concept they suggest "cutting back from where you are now." It is a mindset that Americans have not fully embraced. Look at our consumption of electronics (smart phones, TV's, computers, iPods). When the newest comes out, how many of you run out for the latest model, even though the one you currently own is working fine? My father once had a T-shirt with the following motto, "He who dies with the most toys wins." What do we win by purchasing the newest, latest model of item? Even if we believe that we win, the earth loses. What do we do with the older model? Have you donated your cell phones to a battered women's shelter for women who are in abusive relationships? When your computer is no longer fast enough for you, what and how do you dispose of it? There are components within all computers that we can reuse and protect our natural resources.

The next time you have the urge to purchase the newest and latest, take a moment and ask yourself if you really need this, and consider what impact the purchase will have on the earth. Then ask if you can skip this version and hold onto an older model for another year or two. If we all could start to think like that, we can reduce our wastefulness and make a difference. So at least think about your next purchase, and hopefully your decision will impact for the earth for years to come. (Just think if we didn't gobble up the latest new version, maybe the companies would start to be greener and roll fewer new toys out. If we don't purchase their products, they are stuck and will have to at least consider changing their business model.) Thank you in advance.

The next R is **reuse**, and the concept is slowly catching on with mainstream America. Instead of throwing your items away, do you donate to need groups who would think your old computer is state of the art? Your old iPod is awesome especially when compared to their disc players. We have seen a growth of thrift stores, allowing items to be repurposed, given a new life, keeping them out of landfills, and the people who buy them are thrilled to have some clothes, electronics or toys, they could never afford when brand new.

Reuse

to repurpose or continue to use products instead of replacing with newer versions.

Reusing is something we can all add to our lifestyle. I love this recommendation I once heard while watching one of the early morning TV shows. Each time you purchase a shirt, a new pair of pants, a new suit, take something out of your closet that you no longer wear, no longer fits, or you no longer like. Try it the next time you buy an article of clothing. Remove something from your closest, donate it and make a difference. You may like it (at least I hope so).

The last R is to **repair** the item instead of automatically replacing it. Sometimes replacing works, depending on the age, the energy efficiency of the item, and how much life it still has. Sometimes we have to pay someone to estimate the cost, but often times repairing is a viable option and will positively impact the earth. The newest buzzword is green cars that are battery driven. If we drive a hybrid or battery car are we making a difference? Yes, we are, but the return on investment of the cost of the car with the savings from not purchasing gas has been calculated to be more than five years before you break even. This is based on the higher cost of the cars being fueled by batteries and the average cost based on MPG. They are a green product, but buy them because they work in your lifestyle. Don't buy one and then not like it and replace it.

Repair

to mend or fix a product instead of discarding it.

One of the methods I try to focus on within the repair concept is that whenever I buy appliances, electronics, lawn mowers, I purchase the extended warranty, which provides protection for a period of time beyond the normal warranty. This protects me as often the product is not built to last and we are a throwaway mindset society. With the protection packages, the company is required to repair the product and if they can't, then they will replace it with a new model. Even with the protection plans, I find that I at least have to hear all of my options, which slows me down from contributing quickly to our throwaway mindset society. I understand this may not work for all, but it is something to consider.

Another suggestion, which may lead us to repair instead of throwing away, is to look at the quality of the craftsmanship as well as the material. Is it a quality material or something that is flimsy and will not hold up to normal wear and tear? If you have ever purchased a base model of any generic car, you understand the lack of quality materials in the product. They offer a cheap product made from cheap materials to bring people in and then we pay more for the next model up. Cheap stuff tends to break quickly and we often replace with the next level, then it breaks and we replace again. If we purchase something of quality, we will be more likely to want to repair it. By spending more for quality items, in the long run it will be cheaper and less damaging to the environment. Research and study before you purchase a new product? Google it, look for reviews, talk to others who have purchased items similar to what you are looking at. Read consumer product reviews to see what they have to say. I always review consumer reports for current prices, recommendations at different price points, and I am usually pleased. Additionally, by using the web for our research, we can find the best price advertised instead of driving around town trying to save $40, adding to our carbon footprint.

The last recommendation beyond the 4 Rs that will help us protect the earth and the environment is stop being an impulse shopper. Do your research, watch prices, and realize that certain items go on sale at different times of the year. If possible wait until a product is on sale. Recently, we purchased a new washing machine as our fifteen-year-old machine died. (I guess having four boys wore it out.) We did our research and went shopping at a major store. The item we purchased was the floor model, which was listed as a $950 machine on sale for $599; they didn't have any more in stock, so they offered us the floor model for $500 which included a five-year extended warranty included in the price. After you deducted the cost of the warranty (which I would have bought anyway) we were able to purchase the washing machine for $260 actual cost. By being patient and having done our research, we had to replace instead of repair, but I put our old machine by the side of the road and within two days, a person collecting scrap metal picked up and took care of recycling it. At the same time as I was purchasing the new washing machine, I saw a snow blower on sale for 80 percent of original price. It was a great deal, but my current snow blower, which is around twelve years old, still does the job I need it to do. So if I had purchased because it was a good deal, I would have gone against everything we have discussed in this chapter.

It is on you to bring the 4 Rs into your lifestyle. While, you're at it, don't be afraid to bring friends and families along. Remember our goal is to make a difference within our home, our community, our state, and ultimately the world. The 4 Rs—reduce, reuse, recycle, and repair—will make a difference. Think about your actions and how they impact the world around you.

Each time we focus on the 4 Rs, we are creating a healthier earth, one that will hopefully be here for years to come.

REFERENCES

www.hugger.com/culture/yourcarbonfootprint. Accessed May 31, 2012.

www.nrdc.org. Accessed May 15, 2012.

Name________________________________ Class Days and Time ____________________

13.1

BECOMING GREENER

Answer the questions that follow and do the activity.

1. List the 4 Rs and discuss your current commitment to any of them. If you don't currently use any of them, or use them only occasionally, discuss how you can improve in your commitment to better stewardship to earth.

   a.

   b.

   c.

   d.

2. The second assignment is to keep an account of how much waste you create in one day. Make it a normal day, so record how many miles you drive, ride or walk; the amount of paper products you consume; approximate how much water you use while washing dishes, your clothes, taking a shower, using the toilet, brushing your teeth. Keep the paper products and weigh the waste you created in one day, and then try to calculate the amount of waste you might create in a year. This will require you to do some searching on the web, but it will be worth the time.

3. Try to calculate your carbon footprint. One of the best calculators I have found on the web is a free carbon footprint calculator at www.nature.org/greenliving/carboncalculator/index. After you have calculated your footprint, I would like you to discuss how you can lessen your impact of the earth in several paragraphs.

Chapter 14

Complementary and Alternative Medicine (Or Eastern Meets Western Medicine)

Goals for This Chapter

- To develop an understanding of what Complementary and Alternative Medicine (CAM) is and how it is used.
- To demonstrate base knowledge regarding the five categories of CAM and be able to give several examples of each.
- To demonstrate knowledge of Western medical practices and Eastern medical practices.
- To discuss the definition of synergy.

KEY TERMS

Complement and Alternative Medicine (CAM)
synergy
ki
qi

INTRODUCTION

I would like to start this chapter off with is this simple question: What is **Complementary and Alternative Medicine (CAM)** and how is something that has been practiced for thousands of years suddenly considered a New Age concept? The thought process of CAM treatment for

Complement and Alternative Medicine (CAM)

a group of diverse medical and health care systems, practices, and products that are not generally considered part of conventional medicine medical issues is something which just began in the last ten to twenty years cannot be further from the truth. CAM may have become more mainstream in this country over the last few years, but it has been practiced for centuries in other cultures. We need to accept and better understand it. It is time for Western medicine to accept it either as an adjunct partner, or for some folks, as the primary medical approach.

The National Center for Complementary and Alternative Medicine (NCCAM) defines CAM as a "diverse medical and health care systems, practices, and products that are not generally considered part of conventional medicine." In the chapter title, I mentioned Eastern medicine meets Western medicine for a reason; they are both acknowledged treatment paradigms. As CAM has become more mainstream in this country, some estimates suggest about "40 percent of Americans have tried some type of CAM." There has to be more conversation as well as understanding of similarities and differences between Western and Eastern medical approaches. Medical schools in this country are starting to introduce CAM into their curriculums and more doctors are learning more about CAM, so they may be better able to have a conversation with their patients. One of the largest concerns occurs when a sick person goes to a primary care physician (PCP) and the doctor prescribes medicine, tests, or surgery in cases as they deem appropriate. This is often the outcome when we see our primary doctor or the specialist to whom we were referred. As we delve into our illness or disease, many of us begin to search the Internet to find out all we can about the diagnosis. We read about alternative approaches; some that are way out there and others that report varying degrees of success. As we continue to research, we may start to hear about alternatives that we have found within the CAM areas that appear promising.

Synergy

two or more objects or entities working together to produce a result not independently obtainable.

Sometimes this next step is often confusing and overwhelming, but we may decide to try the alternatives instead of or in addition to the tests, scans, and blood work we've already started. If we don't discuss the other information we have learned with the medical team, we may make our medical treatment care plan worse instead of better. The one question medical professionals often forget to ask is: Are you taking any herbals, practicing any CAM programs, or talking to anyone else regarding a treatment plan? If the question is asked, and answered affirmatively, then the concept of a team approach should be considered. If the question is not asked, often times the patient will not bring it up and the doctor will not alter his approach. The problem occurs as the doctor follows his protocol, with the result that the Eastern practice may alter the Western approach's outcome. After the fact, you will hear doctors then ask, "Are you taking anything or trying any other approaches I should know about?"

© lenetstan, 2012. Under license from Shutterstock, Inc.

We know that certain drugs cause a **synergy** when combined with other drugs. The outcome being that the two good drugs by themselves act appropriately, but when they are combined, the drug interaction can be very harmful, perhaps even fatal. The patient must be honest with the doctor, they must be honest with the Eastern provider, and they must understand how they are being treated by both, as well as understand the outcomes and any issues from combining other treatments. This can only occur with open and honest communication between all participants.

The next paragraph is not a condemnation on our traditional doctors, but we have become a nation of individuals who have this underlying belief from doctors, friends, and from TV, radio and the Internet that popping pills will cure what ails us. We love to take medicine to try to solve every little medical problem we have. If we have a headache, take a pill; if our stomach is upset take a pill/tablet; if we have problems with our sex life, pop a little blue pill; if we want to lose weight, take a pill that promises the world; if we have high blood pressure, take medication instead of increasing activity and losing some weight. If we are at risk for heart attacks, heart disease or a stroke, take a pill. We need to consider other options. We need our doctors to talk straight to us and limit the amount of pills we are given. Yes, pills have a function, but I wonder if we jump to them way too quickly? Why don't we try other techniques and use the pill as the second or third approach, instead of the first?

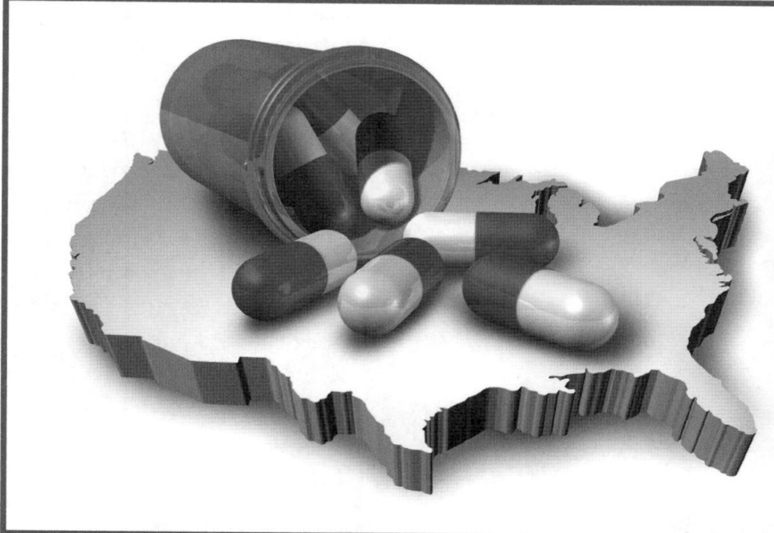

Another major difference between Western and Eastern medicine is that often users of Eastern medicine employ CAM as part of their health and wellness plan. For many users, it improves their quality of life. Think about a massage. Yes, it can be used to help loosen a muscle in contraction, but it may help removing the blood or lymphatic fluid buildup. Plus it just feels awesome.

The specific reason you are engaging in CAM therapies will also indicate your viewpoint and your willingness to try whatever is available to you to maintain or improve your overall health and wellness or as a treatment for disease and illness.

CATEGORIES OF COMPLEMENTARY AND ALTERNATIVE MEDICINE

There are five categories of CAM, which are classified as mind-body interventions, biological-based treatments, manipulative and body-based methods, energy therapies, and traditional Chinese medicine. All are alternative medical systems as classified by the National Center for Complementary and Alternative Medicine. See National Institute of Health (www.nccam.nih.gov).

1. Mind-body interventions include many of the relaxation techniques already discussed within the previous chapters. They include guided imagery, meditation, Tai Chi, hypnosis, yoga, Pilates, and prayer. Many of these are wonderful forms of

exercise and movement that are beneficial to the body and the spirit. Prayer was discussed briefly in the spirituality chapter, but is self-explanatory and you have either prayed at some time in your life or you haven't.

2. Biological-based treatments (herbals, botanicals, dietary supplements) include a variety of botanicals, vitamins, minerals, and dietary supplements. In this category we find perhaps the largest usage in this country and at the same time, this is the least controlled in regards to quality control of the biological-based products. The history of herbals is long and many of the modern drugs we take are based on botanicals (digitalis is a derivative of foxglove, for instance) found within the world healthcare systems. As stated in the article "Plant Based Drugs and Medicines," Taylor states that "Today there are at least 120 distinct chemical substances derived from plants that are considered as important drugs currently in use in one or more countries in the world."

© fotohunter, 2012. Under license from Shutterstock, Inc.

We know that herbals and botanicals are medically important; we still have much to learn from plants to help us cure illness and disease worldwide. One of the concerns with this area has been related to the clear cutting of Amazon rainforests before we have time to study and learn from the medical shamans of the indigenous tribes who have used the plants in the rainforest throughout their culture. The techniques are passed down from shaman to shaman and much has not been recorded. A fear is that we will wipe out a species that may play a significant role in solving cancer and other diseases.

Another concern within the botanicals and their prevalence and usage in this country is they are not really regulated by the Federal Drug Administration (FDA). How often have you seen an ad, an infomercial, or a product demonstration regarding a "miraculous outcome from the product" only to be duped? Without regulations from the FDA, the promises of quick cures are misleading and the consumer should be wary of quick fixes. Often times you can have an analysis of a product only to find that different batches have different compounds or the primary ingredient is at different levels. Do your research, check out multiple sites to educate yourself about the potential of a new product, and hear what other users are saying.

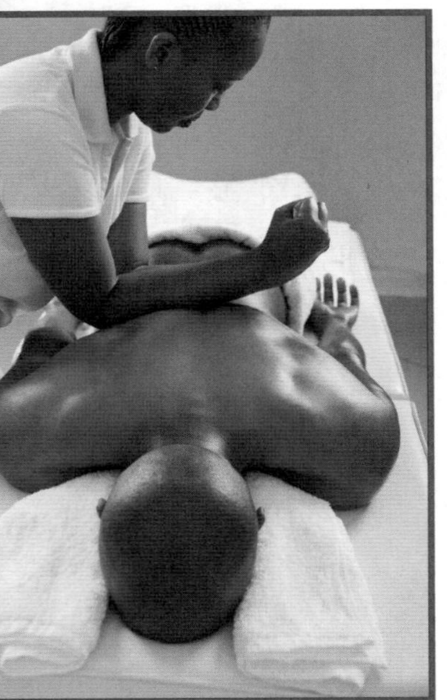
© Lucian Coman, 2012. Under license from Shutterstock, Inc.

About a decade ago, there was a new rush in the weight loss world to try a new product that promised great results. The product was known as Ma Huang, or Ephedra. Individuals started to have adverse reactions to the herbal product including rapid and irregular heartbeats, chest pain, insomnia, and death. It went from great potential to being banned in many states and pulled off shelves in other states. So the message is that the botanical world will continue to have an impact for both traditional Western medicine and Eastern medicine. As consumers, we have to be open-minded, educate ourselves to the potential and side effects, and if we use any botanical products to inform our doctors when we see them in the office.

3. Manipulative and body-based methods are techniques that focus the treatment plan on the body's major systems, musculoskeletal system (muscles and bony structures), as well as the blood supply and lymphatic component of the body.

The two most common forms practiced in this country are spinal manipulation (chiropractor care) and massage therapy. Massage therapy is a very common technique and its popularity is growing every year in this country. Within the last decade, we are beginning to see insurance companies starting to include it as reimbursable treatment under their policies. This acceptance of massage therapy as a valued treatment by the insurance companies has lead to this being a popular tool to manage our healthcare.

© Bruce Rolff, 2012. Under license from Shutterstock, Inc.

4. Energy therapies are used to balance or change the energy flow with the body. This energy is called our **ki** (Japanese term for our life-force energy within us). The most common technique that you may have heard of is Reiki. With Reiki, the hands of the practitioner will work on the energy of the body by circling with his or her hands to try to return the client to an energy balance in their body. They are attempting to balance the ki. I have observed it being performed at several labyrinth walks. Other techniques in this category include acupuncture, acupressure, electromagnetic, energy systems, and qigong.

5. Traditional Chinese medicine is growing in usage in the United States. The emphasis of a traditional Chinese medicine practitioner is to focus on returning the body's energy system to a balanced state, which is how the life force moves within us. They use a variety of techniques, but the premise is based on the **qi** (Chinese word for our life force) and the yin-yang theory, which says that two opposite forces exist within our body that impact our life energy. Practitioners use a variety of techniques, but they focus much of their time on observation of the person. Their techniques are high touch, no technology. They include observing the body, the tongue, use of smell, palpation of the body, and the pulse to diagnosis the health problem.

After their observation they will develop a treatment plan for the patient, which will likely include many of the CAM therapies already discussed. Their treatment plan will be focused on returning the qi to a balance and will likely use Chinese herbal medicine and acupuncture to treat the person.

Ki

Japanese term for the life-force energy within each of us.

Qi

Chinese word for the life-force energy within each of us.

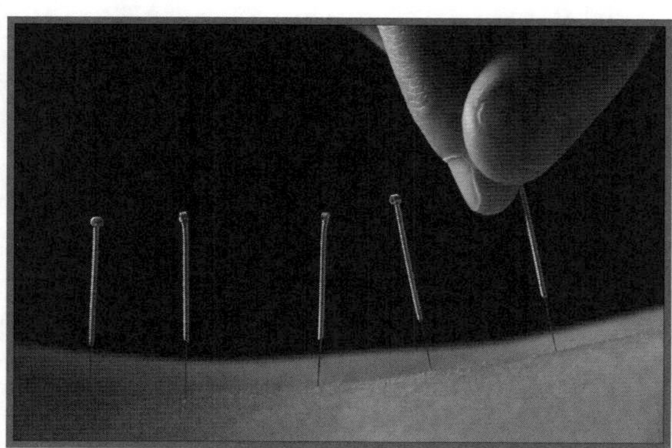

© Yanik Chauvin, 2012. Under license from Shutterstock, Inc.

© Monika Wisniewska, 2012. Under license from Shutterstock, Inc.

SUMMARY

The main area that needs to be addressed for CAM therapies to grow and become more mainstream in this country is the need for evidenced-based research which measures the outcomes of the various practices. The research has been limited over the last twenty years and often has been focused on the qualitative side of the CAM. The NIH is pursuing more quantitative research and as the research base grows, this will enable both sides to bridge the gap from Eastern and Western medicine. When this occurs, each of us will have more options to include in our and our families healthcare.

The focus of this chapter was to open the door and to introduce you to complementary and alternative medicine. After reading about the categories, I hope you have a better understanding of what each is. Perhaps some of you have already added CAM into your wellness and stress management plan.

Here is my life wellness plan: I am responsible for my overall wellness and my experiences that both have played a role in my overall health and my management of stress in my life. I constantly try to use techniques that utilize the many wonders of Western medicine, which are less than 100 years old, and combine those with the techniques of Eastern medicine, which have been in use for thousands of years. I have found both are beneficial to me.

I wish you well on your life's journey and my guess is you will read, discuss with others, and add some CAM into your life. Safe travels. My wish is for a wonderful life for each of you.

REFERENCES

www.nccam.nih.gov first accessed in June, 2005.

The Healing Power of rainforest herbs. Taylor, L. Square One Publishers, Garden City Park, NY. March 2005.

Name____ Class Days and Time ________________________

14.1

COMPLEMENTARY AND ALTERNATIVE MEDICINE

Short research questions. Feel free to use the internet to develop definitions for the following terms.

1. Complementary and alternative medicine is ________________________

____

2. Ayurveda is ____

____

3. Homeopathy is ____

____

4. Drug synergy is ____

____

5. Naturopathy is ____

____

6. Qigong is ____

____

7. Evidenced-based research ____

____

8. Quantitative research is ____

____

9. Qualitative research is ____

____

10. Reiki is ____

____

11. Chiropractor care is ____

____

12. Acupuncture is ____

____

13. Pilates is ____

____

14. Shamans are ____

____

15. Botanicals are ____

____

Name________________________________ Class Days and Time ____________________

14.2

CAM TECHNIQUES YOU HAVE TRIED OR THAT INTEREST YOU

For this assignment, I would like you to research each of the categories as presented within the chapter. For each category, I would like you to research the topic, summarize the technique, and indicate if you have ever tried it or would you ever try it.

1. Mind-body medicine

2. Botanicals or herbals

3. Manipulation and body based practices

4. Energy therapies

5. Traditional Chinese medicine

Name______________________________ Class Days and Time ______________________

14.3

BOTANICALS AD HERBALS

For this worksheet, you must visit the NCCAM website home page. In the left column is a link to Herbs at a Glance; open it. Your assignment is to summarize four different botanicals. At least two have to be something you have never heard of before. Write a short paragraph as to why it is used, potential side effects, what form it is delivered to the consumer, and any other pertinent information worth sharing. Then say whether you have ever or would ever use it. Educate you and me with your material.

1. ______________________

2. ______________________

3. ______________________

4. ______________________

Chapter 15
Walking Meditations: Experience the Labyrinth

Goals for This Chapter

- To understand the differences between a maze and a labyrinth.
- To understand the global growth for labyrinth use.
- To understand the value of walking a labyrinth and walking meditation as a stress management tool.

KEY TERMS

labyrinth
finger labyrinth
Chartres labyrinth
Cretan labyrinth

WHAT IS A LABYRINTH?

First, I would like to share with you my personal experiences with labyrinths. My first time was on a college campus. My department sponsored a labyrinth facilitator to bring her portable labyrinth and invited our students and the college community to try a walking meditation. The labyrinth was located in a large room, with rope lights on the outside, and instrumental music playing. The room was peaceful and very calm.

I was intrigued and looked forward to the experience. The facilitator had poster boards to help you understand what a labyrinth was. I also took the time to talk to her and listen to her enthusiasm for labyrinths. It was then my turn to walk the path. I walked it slowly and my spirit became calm. I became connected to the path as I focused on the turns and walking towards the center. Upon arriving in the center, I stood for several minutes and then I slowly retraced the pathway out. For me it was an instant connection; something inside of me felt at home. I was calm and very relaxed. I thoroughly enjoyed the experience and I still love to take the time for this version of a walking meditation.

I have walked labyrinths around the country, but perhaps my favorite was at a Franciscan monastery in Florida. The path was lined with ground-up shells and sand; other shells and coral lined the pathway. In the background, I could hear the wind blowing through the nearby bamboo as if chimes were playing. I could hear the nearby river and the abundance of wildlife and boat traffic, but I was at peace and felt so calm.

It is my hope as we introduce labyrinths to you, that at some point during the semester, you too will take the time to find a labyrinth and walk the path. Each walk actually has different outcomes, and you never know for sure what you will experience while walking a labyrinth. In the United States alone, there are currently over 1,000 labyrinths.

Labyrinth

one of the oldest meditative or contemplative tools; an intricate path walked for personal, psychological, and spiritual transformation.

Cretan labyrinth

ancient labyrinth said to be located on the island of Crete and associated with the myth of the Minotaur.

The **labyrinth** is likely one of the oldest meditative or contemplative tools known to humanity. A labyrinth is a walking meditation, a spiritual tool that has been used throughout history for both personal and spiritual growth. Labyrinths have been around for over 3000 years in a variety of patterns and in cultures across the world. Some of the cultures where labyrinths have been found include ancient Crete, France, Norway, India, Ireland, Hopi Native American Indian Tribes, and the British Isles. When reading, all I could about labyrinths, I have always been left with the same question and my answer is always the same as well: How did something so similar appear within so many different cultures? In our time, it is very commonplace for a major event to happen somewhere in the world and within minutes, you can find out about it from a tweet, a Facebook post, and twenty-four hour news channels. That was not true even a century ago. In the past, civilizations often had little or no interaction or even awareness that other cultures existed. How did the **Cretan labyrinth** found in early Greece also find its way into the Native American Indian cultures? To me this is an example of the spiritual nature that exists within the labyrinth.

Lauren Artress, probably the one person who has contributed the most to the resurgence of the labyrinth in this country, says that the labyrinth is a "tool to guide healing, deepen self-knowledge, and empower creativity. Walking the labyrinth clears the mind and gives insight into the spiritual journey. It urges actions. It calms people in the throes of life transitions." Helen Sands discusses walking a labyrinth as a movement toward the center, similar to our own personal journeys we take during our lifetime. She states, "If we are ill or suffering, the path of the labyrinth, therefore takes us on an inner journey of healing, toward personal well-being and newness of spirit."

The preceding photo shows a person walking a labyrinth in a wooded setting. My experience is that walking a labyrinth (whether it be full size or a finger labyrinth you can do while sitting at your desk) is truly a spiritual and meditative practice. It is a tool that can be added to your stress management toolbox and one that I hope you will enjoy.

WHAT A LABYRINTH IS NOT

© Camilo Torres, 2012. Under license from Shutterstock, Inc.

A labyrinth is not a maze, but often times you will the two interchanged as being the same. A maze is designed to be complicated and frustrate you at some levels. Likely, you have seen or participated in a corn maze, where teams take on the challenge and try to arrive at the center and back out in the shortest amount of time. Within the maze, there are blocked paths, dead ends and with each step, your frustration level may rise and leave you not enjoying the experience of not finding your way. Mazes provide multiple choices, different paths, some are right, others lead to frustration. By walking within a maze, the user has to develop plans, goals, strategies, and outcomes to solve the maze. A labyrinth, on the other hand, consists of a winding path with no dead ends or blocked areas that is used to recreate life's journey, life themes, healing, and appreciating our lives. A maze is designed to confuse and frustrate and a labyrinth is designed to calm and help us relax and be peaceful.

Some quotes that I have found and use when I introduce the meaning of walking a labyrinth to a group may prove helpful.

- "The best place for each of us is where we stand." Ralph Waldo Emerson
- "Meandering leads to perfection." Lao Tzu
- "There is nothing so wise as a circle." Rainer Maria Rilke
- "People say that walking on water is a miracle, but to me, walking peacefully on the Earth is the real miracle." Thich Nhat Hanh
- "And now we stand on asphalt, lost in a forest of skyscrapers, barraged with distractions, and harried by the pace of modern life, our cells lead us in a process of reclamation. The circle is calling. Listen." Christina Baldwin.

Each of these quotes helps bring meaning to the labyrinth experience and allows me to share the potentiality of the labyrinth. I find that walking a labyrinth addresses many of the psycho-spiritual aspects of wellness. Walking on the path is a connection to our spirituality, a connection to the earth, a peaceful and reenergizing event. Walking the path brings simplicity to our hectic lives. It helps us find a few moments of calmness before we face the rest of the day. While walking the labyrinth, we find a connection of the mind, body, and spirit. Walking helps us free our minds. During the walk, we may see clearer, we may receive answers. We just have to let our minds become calm, clearer and then listen.

HEALTH, WELLNESS, AND STRESS MANAGEMENT: OUTCOMES OF WALKING A LABYRINTH

The interest and growth of labyrinths is a worldwide phenomenon. There is a world Labyrinth Society, www.labyrinthsociety.org where you can find more information. On their website you will find additional information, including a labyrinth finder worldwide, a thorough history of labyrinths, research on labyrinths, and even download a hand labyrinth for your own use.

A relatively new activity from the society is a World Labyrinth Day. World Labyrinth Day is an event where labyrinths around the world host walks and try to send positive energy around the globe. The focus is to time the walks on the specific day (usually the first Saturday in May) and have the energy from the walks wash over the earth and spread a message of peace and love throughout the world. Other common times that you may see labyrinth walks advertised are the spring and fall equinox, during a full moon, and at the beginning of each season. Watch for these events and if given the chance, participate and feel the spirituality of these activities.

Why would you want to walk a labyrinth? Research has examined both quantifiable and qualitative aspects of labyrinth walking and there has been a tremendous growth in labyrinth research which indicates the resurgence of labyrinth use has become more main stream. Some of the quantifiable research has examined blood pressure, pulse rate, cortisol level, and other changes from the labyrinth experience. Other research has focused on the qualitative (mood changes, reporting of feelings, and lowering of stress) outcomes of walking a labyrinth.

One of the testaments to the value or healing nature of labyrinths is found within their acceptance in Western medicine. We are seeing a resurgence or growth of labyrinth usage on hospital grounds. Many new hospitals are including them on the grounds or within the building where they are seen as a spiritual and healing activity for the hospital staff, visitors, and families of the patients. They are placed there for the medical staff to walk and meditate to help focus before surgery, or to clear their minds from the tremendous stress of working in the hospital setting. They are also being used by the families of patients while loved ones are in surgery or are facing death from an incurable disease. The walk is a reflection and a connection to their loved ones, just as the families of Knights of the Crusades in medieval times used the labyrinth. During the Holy Wars, knights and their families were separated for years at a time. So many of the cathedrals in France had labyrinths built on the grounds (the most recognized labyrinth in the world is the Chartres Cathedral) and families of the knights would walk the labyrinth and feel connected to their loved ones.

I have been practicing walking labyrinths for the last ten years and I have always introduced my students to the labyrinth. Whenever possible we visit a traditional labyrinth and enjoy the experience, but at other times, I have only been able to use finger labyrinths. As with any of the new material, some students love the experience and others are very unsure. The point is to try something new and perhaps you will be like me and find the opportunity to be worthwhile.

1. Walking a labyrinth helps us quiet the distractions around us and specifically helps us quiet our minds. When we quiet our minds, often the issues we are facing become clearer.

2. Whenever I am stressed and when I walk the labyrinth my stress levels at the end of the walk are lower. The walk is my personal time and whether I am walking by myself or with a group, I always leave feeling better.
3. I see walking the labyrinth as a spiritual activity, a time for spiritual growth. I was fortunate to find funding to have a labyrinth installed at my college. One of the recommendations when building a labyrinth is to have an energy dowser find the energy of the space you will be placing the labyrinth on. If you were to walk the labyrinth at my college, you would notice that the entrance is facing north. That was a conscious decision which took in the energy of the space, but mostly I choose a north facing entrance to represent the Genesee River, which is one of the few rivers in the world that flows to the north.
4. When walking the labyrinth or using the finger labyrinths, the activity promotes the interaction of the mind, body and spirit. Any stress management text or article I have ever read discussed the connection of the mind, body, and spirit. My experience and those of my students have supported this connection after discussing their personal experiences of the walk. One of my favorite activities with the finger labyrinths is to have users use their non-dominant hands the first couple of times to increase the connection of the brain and the hand. I have asked students to use two-finger labyrinths and walk both at the same time. It is challenging, but certain calmness comes over them from the focus and satisfaction of being successful.
5. There is the physical aspect of following the path both in and out; I have actually walked wearing a pedometer to see how many steps I have taken to complete the walk. Walking the labyrinth is a spiritual activity, and sometimes a social activity because often you will share the space with others, and you will connect with them, often without talking. It is an emotional experience as people often compare the walk with their lives or with the struggles they are experiencing. The labyrinth is seen as an intellectual activity as it promotes both right- and left-brained activity. We have to focus on the walk to follow the path, especially the curves on the path. The labyrinth is truly an activity which supports many of the components of wellness.
6. The journey of the labyrinth is often seen as a way to open your heart to the joys of life or to the pain bottled up within our spirit and soul. If you listen, you may be surprised to what you hear.
7. A labyrinth is a form of meditation; the difference is this is a walking meditation that is often shared with others. Movement is a key core value to being healthy and a walking meditation appears to bring both movement and calmness into our crazy and hectic lives.
8. Robert Ferre discusses the labyrinth as being very effective in dealing with grief. The labyrinth is often described in the feminine, possessing nurturing qualities. While dealing with grief, people say they feel supported within the labyrinth. It gives users the opportunity to recharge before coming out to face their realities. They are often refreshed, reenergized, and ready to move forward.
9. In her published study entitled "Exploring the Effect of Walking the Labyrinth," M. Kay Sandor made the following comments related to the health aspects of walking a labyrinth. Their low demand, low cost nature holds promise for individuals with a variety of chronic conditions such as hypertension, multiple sclerosis, ADHD, and stroke rehabilitation. She suggests further research be done, but feels that the labyrinth maybe a valuable complementary tool for both health promotion and prevention of disease.

In summary of the benefits of walking a labyrinth, it crosses over many of the wellness strands we have presented within the book. They address our emotional, mental, physical, and spiritual aspects. They help us heal and we need them.

HOW TO WALK A LABYRINTH

The labyrinth is seen as a purposeful walk that takes a single path to the center of the labyrinth. Within the center, individuals often pause, meditate, and then when they are ready, follow the same path out. It is indeed a walking meditation and often represents our life's journey. When walking a labyrinth, we discuss the experience as the three Rs: releasing, receiving, and returning or reflection.

Before you begin the walk, pause and take several moments to quiet your mind. Sit on the outside of the labyrinth and focus on quieting your mind and focusing on your breath. If music is playing, listen to the melody and allow yourself to let go of the outside influences and focus on yourself while walking the labyrinth.

1. **Releasing.** As you enter the labyrinth, follow the path to the center. Focus on the turns within the path. Focus on quieting your mind. This is the time to open your heart and quiet the mind. Listen to your body and your spirit; do not rush the walk.
2. **Receiving.** Each labyrinth has a different center spot. The most common version of the labyrinth is the **Chartres labyrinth**, where the center is called the rose. The rose symbolizes the beauty, love, and enlightenment of the feminine. Each petal symbolizes the aspects of creation: mineral, vegetable, animal, human, the spirit world (angelic), and the mystery of the unknown. The center of all labyrinths is a place of rest, a place for meditation or prayer. This is the time of openness and peacefulness. You experience or receive what the moment provides you. Stay in the center as long as you need. Walking a labyrinth is never a timed event; walkers will experience it in the version they need.
3. **Returning or reflection.** You choose when to leave the center and start the journey outward, following the same path. This is a time to review and appreciate the healing forces at work and how they may apply to your life. When leaving the labyrinth, take a few minutes sitting on the outside of the labyrinth and feel the energy around you.

Chartes labyrinth

world-famous thirteenth century labyrinth located in the cathedral in Chartres, France.

Labyrinth Walk Suggestions

The first rule of walking a labyrinth is that there is no right or wrong way to do it. That being said, there are some general rules to help make the experience a worthwhile activity. I have seen young children run into the labyrinth. Sometimes they follow the path, other times they run in a beeline to the center, and then they skip out. They are experiencing the labyrinth the way they want and it is actually fun to watch young kids experiencing the labyrinth for the first time. (Some commonsense rules which we need to mention: turn your cell phone off, leave your keys with your other stuff, no headphones on during the walk. If walking indoors, take your shoes off. If the labyrinth is outside, consider walking without shoes to connect with nature.)

1. Take a few moments on the outside of the labyrinth, sitting on the floor or the ground. During this time, begin to focus inwardly, open your mind to the activity and begin to become aware of your breath. Cleansing breath is not mandatory, but I find it helps settle the mind and the body before I begin to walk.
2. When walking a labyrinth, you will be walking a two-way path (in and out), so it is likely you will encounter others on the path. If you meet another person on the path, step aside and allow the other traveler to pass. Then return on the path and continue the journey. Do what feels natural to you.
3. Walking a labyrinth is not a timed activity; some may finish the walk in fifteen minutes or so, while others may take thirty minutes or longer. Some will stay in the center to sit and meditate; some will feel a connection to one of the petals within a Chartres version of the labyrinth and stand or sit there and meditate or reflect. The time is yours; the experience is yours; enjoy and listen.
4. Walk at the pace that feels comfortable to you. I have walked the labyrinth and been very mindful of each step, so my pace is slow and the walk is deliberate. I have witnessed others who walk slightly quicker at the beginning, and as they continue the walk, their pace slows. Some may even follow the pathway in, and then just walk straight out. As stated earlier, the walk is yours, so don't worry so much about the how to and focus more on the experience.
5. If there are more than seven or eight walkers on the labyrinth, then wait until someone finishes before you start your walk. When someone comes off, pause to allow them to leave the entrance before your begin your journey.
6. Maintain silence throughout your walk. This allows for your own reflection as well as the others who are sharing the experience with you.
7. Many of the labyrinth walks I have participated in often have a chime before you enter. If one is present, gently ring it as a welcome to the labyrinth and again as you leave the space.
8. Don't be surprised if many labyrinth walks have music to help set both a calmer environment, but also to add to the overall experience.
9. Be open-minded and try a labyrinth walk. It may not be for you, but you will never know until you try.

FINGER LABYRINTHS

Finally, I would like to discuss the concept of **finger labyrinths**. Walking a finger labyrinth is the same experience, but in a format you can do in your office or your home. You can even download a screen saver for your computer and walk the labyrinth on your computer. I have a variety of hand labyrinths in my office or within the department. What I love about finger labyrinths is they often add another sense during the experience. One of my labyrinths is made out of corian material, and when you first touch the labyrinth the material will feel cool to the touch, but as you follow the path, the material warms to your touch, to your energy. Another labyrinth I have is made from cedar, so as you walk you can smell the cedar, which I find to be relaxing and helps me focus on the walk. I also have a variety of labyrinths which are painted in the colors of the chakras. If you understand the

Finger labyrinths

small, portable labyrinth that is "walked" by tracing a finger over the design.

©EcOasis, 2012. Under license from Shutterstock, Inc.

chakra energy flow of the human body, you may be aware of a blockage within the flow, so if you use the color that represents your blocked chakra, it enables you to focus on the blockage and free the energy flow of your body.

Whenever I introduce finger labyrinths to my students, I always ask them to use their non-dominant hand on the walk and to keep their eyes closed for the time. If they miss a turn, or jump a pathway, then just continue the walk. Remember the path in and the path out is the same. Using your non-dominant hand is often awkward for most of us. It slows us down, so we don't speed through the experience. I also have the users walk for a length of time; some students will continue the walk in and out, until I stop them. Others will stop after one trip, so they are limiting the experience. If you walk a hand labyrinth, set a time and continue to follow the path for the allotted time. If you need a little more in-depth experience, take two finger labyrinths of the same style, and have each hand follow the path. Your focus will be intense, but often students who walk two labyrinths at the same time discuss how much they enjoyed the experience.

Whenever I use finger labyrinths, I dim the lights in the room, play acoustical music to help center and calm down the energy of the room. As with many of the activities within this book, I believe that you may truly enjoy walking a labyrinth and you will see a difference in your mood, your energy will be better and most importantly you will feel calmer and more at peace.

REFERENCES

Artress, Lauren. *Walking a Sacred Path, Rediscovering the Labyrinth as a Spiritual Practice.* New York City: Riverhead Books of the Berkley Publishing Group, 2006.

Sands, Helen Raphael. *The Healing Labyrinth, Finding Your Path to Inner Peace.* New York City: Barron's Education Series, 2001.

Sandor, Kay, and Robin Froman. "Exploring the Effects of Walking the Labyrinth." *Journal of Holistic Nursing* Volume 24, Number 2 (June 2006): 103–110.

Westbury, Virginia. *Labyrinths, Ancient Paths of Wisdom and Peace.* Cambridge: De Capo Press, 2001.

Wass, Cassandra Camille. *Meditative Mazes and Labyrinths.* New York City: Sterling Innovation, 2009.

Labyrinth Enterprises. "12 Reasons to Have a Church Labyrinth." Accessed April 7, 2005. www.labyrinth-enterprises.com/12reasons.html.

Name______________________________________ Class Days and Time ________________________

15.1

EXPERIENCING A LABYRINTH WALK

1. Attend a labyrinth walk in the community or during any open hours of the college's labyrinth. I would like you to share your experience from the walk.

2. After walking a labyrinth, would you agree that it is a spiritual activity? YES or NO. Explain your response.

3. During class you will have the opportunity to use the finger labyrinths. Compare and contrast the two types of labyrinth walks. What was similar and what differences did you notice or experience?

4. Did you feel that the labyrinth was a spiritual activity? Would you consider walking a labyrinth again? Do you feel that this could be a useful tool in your stress management toolbox? Explain each of your answers to these questions.

Name____ Class Days and Time ________________________

15.2

DRAWING YOUR OWN LABYRINTH

One activity I often do is to draw a labyrinth on the beach when I am on vacation. It is not that hard to complete. I would like you to draw a labyrinth of your own design or create either a Chartres or Cretan labyrinth (if you Google, you can find simple steps to create them). Use color and if you create your own labyrinth, explain the meaning and your concept of your labyrinth.

Chapter 16
Next Steps to Wellness: Lowering the Impact of Stress on Your Body

Goals for This Chapter

- To assess the integration of wellness into your life.
- To authenticate the major themes of stress in our life.
- To reassess all new techniques added to your stress management tool kit.
- To have a great life and make the most of it.

© Robert Spriggs, 2012. Under license from Shutterstock, Inc.

KEY TERMS

tool kit

OTHER TOOLS TO CONSIDER FOR YOUR STRESS MANAGEMENT TOOL KIT

Remember back in Chapter 1 when I asked you to write a list of things you currently do to handle your stress? We further divided that list into good stress management tools and poor stress management tools. The next focus of the text was to introduce you to other positive ways to manage your stress and to improve your health and wellness. Although no book can be inclusive as to all of the positive or negative techniques for stress management, I would like to spend a moment to add other thoughts, which may be of interest to you as possibilities for your **tool kit**.

> ***Tool kit***
>
> set of strategies, coping mechanisms, and techniques that allows you to manage and reduce the stressors in your daily life.

Communication. I hope within your cohort of family, friends, clergy, or counselor you have a person with whom you can talk and share the issues that are bothering you or more importantly, hurting you. Sometimes all we need is someone to listen to us. Other times we need someone to guide us, and occasionally we need someone to give us options or advice. If, at the present time, you don't have someone you can trust, then continue to find such a relationship, but also use your journal to write down your feelings, your pain, and your frustration. Sometimes writing is enough to see what steps you need to take.

Family. Whether you come from the closest family you have ever known or you were raised in a dysfunctional family, family will always be part of who you are. Families can be the hardest relationship you have in your life, they can be effortless, or for some they do not really exist. My hope for you is that you are lucky enough to have a good family dynamic and your family makes a difference in your life. If you come from a dysfunctional family, continue to grow, nurture your spirit, and don't let your family continue to make a negative difference in your life. If family is harming your spirit, turn to friends for support.

© Morphart Creations inc., 2012. Under license from Shutterstock, Inc.

Friends and friendship. Friends are a continuation of communication. They add warmth, joy, happiness, and companionship. Remember that all friends need nurturing and when they are there for you, remember to be there for them when needed. Friendships are like relationships; they take work. Some are short lived (as we all change and grow differently), and some have been there since elementary school and will be there until you are older, wiser, and grayer.

Humor. Brian Luke Seaward, one of the experts on stress management in this country, includes humor as a great stress management tool. I agree with him. He suggests developing a tickler folder where you keep things that make you laugh. They may be comics, cartoons, jokes, short stories, anything that makes you happy. I have laugh folders (my term) on my PC, both at work, and at home, and on my laptop. Anything that makes me smile or laugh is added. Then on a bad day, I can access my laugh folders. The contents always bring a smile to my face and to my spirit. I can move forward for the rest of the day. Perhaps your generation's best example of a laugh folder is YouTube, where you can find a wide variety of activities and stupid stunts, which you are able to download and watch almost anytime, anywhere. Remember that humor is about laughter, hopefully gut-busting laughter. Enjoy your laughter and make it contagious by sharing with others around you.

Massage. If you have ever had a professional massage, then the mention of full body massages probably brings vivid memories and a gentle relaxation response. Massage therapy has become more commonplace in today's healthcare, and if you ever have the chance to receive a professional massage, I would highly recommend it. Many people have made massage therapy as part of their wellness program and have them fairly regularly (weekly or bi-weekly). They can be pricey; a good rate is one dollar a minute plus a tip. If you are concerned with the cost, or uncomfortable with a whole body massage, consider starting with a chair massage. Usually these last for fifteen to twenty minutes and they focus on the neck, head, and shoulders which are the main areas where our body tenses up and demonstrates a negative response to stress in our lives.

© Stephen Coburn, 2012. Under license from Shutterstock, Inc.

Money management. A consistent stressor in our lifetimes will be our financial independence. With the economy performing poorly now, we never know how long a job will last, what new bills will arise, or what changes in our lives will occur. How many of you have a monthly/weekly budget? How many of you have enough in your savings to cover up to six months of bills if a significant life event occurred? (I don't have that, but I do have several months set aside). Stress from money management issues can be lessened by developing a budget, adhering to the budget, working with your life partner so both have an understanding of the money coming in and the money going out. It should be an activity that is shared whenever possible.

Music. Each of us has different music choices, but with stress management I would recommend developing several play lists on your iPod, iPad, or smart phone. When you are sad, you probably will want music that is uplifting, makes you sing, brings energy into your soul, and changes your mood. (Yes, I know someone is saying, "When I am sad, I listen to sad music like melancholy country songs." It wouldn't be my choice, but if it works for you, then go for it.) That is why music is such a perfect addition into our stress management tool kit; we can all find music that matches our mood, makes us feel better, or creates energy. Just as we suggested with humor, develop folders with music for happiness, exercising, sadness, meditation, calming, whatever you need. Access them often and enjoy the melody.

Nature. Take the time to connect with Mother Earth as often as possible. Find a park, water, woods, a flower garden, a labyrinth, any place where you can find peacefulness, silence, a place to be still and recharge your batteries. Being in nature has the ability to calm our spirits and make us feel reconnected to the world around us. There are studies that measure the importance of being connected to nature and our overall health. Your wellness prescription is the following: Go outside and search for this place. Once found, use often. Become healthier.

Time for you. The last and perhaps most important tool I want you to consider and adopt is this: Each and every day take time for yourself. If you are not taking care of yourself on a daily basis, how can you take care of those around you who need your help? The most important person is you, and even if it is only ten to fifteen minutes each day, build the time into your calendar. Nurture your spirit, your soul. Do something each and every day of your life to take care of yourself. After that, my hope is the rest will come easier for you.

© Redshinestudio, 2012. Under license from Shutterstock, Inc.

© mrfiza, 2012. Under license from Shutterstock, Inc.

FINAL THOUGHTS

Take a few seconds and review the yoga graphic and text. It encapsulates all that we have discussed through the semester and is a great summation of our journey. Throughout the semester you have been actively engaged in actions and discussion with incorporating wellness into your life and as a tool to help you manage your stress. No matter what happens when you close this book, this much I can guarantee you: You will encounter stress throughout your lifetime. If you understand that simple statement, then you can truly develop a variety of strategies to incorporate or add to your stress management tool kit.

Within this text, I have tried to introduce you to what stress is, how it impacts your overall health and wellness, and ways to take care of yourself. We introduced the following six components of wellness: physical, social, spiritual, emotional, intellectual, and occupational. Additionally we added the concept of nutrition and the environment into the mix as seventh and eighth components. Each of these contributes to our overall wellness.

One of the best visual explanations I have ever heard regarding wellness was a lecture in my doctoral program in May 2004. Dr. Janet Bezner introduced the components of wellness and succinctly stated that wellness in each of us is very similar to being in a tornado. The Tornado Model describes how we are all over the place, being tossed around with each of the components as if in the center of the tornado. On great days, we are high within each component; on bad days, we are low within each. The emotions, the wear and tear of stress on the bodies, only makes these days harder. We each have to take control of our health and wellness and by doing so we develop great tools to help each of us manage the stress in our lives.

Some days we have complete control of our lives and we think we have the world by its tail. Then a major life event happens and we are challenged to stay in control, or we can spiral out of control. When these major life events happen to you, and they will, use your stress management techniques, use the techniques you have developed to maintain your health and wellness. Fight back, stay strong, and always protect the person you are; protect your mind, body, and spirit.

One of our local hospitals has posters all around stating the following message, "Shhhh, quiet hospitals help us heal." I love the message and it should not just be in hospitals, but in our daily lives. Find quiet and savor it; it will refresh you and help you get ready for the day's challenges. So whether it be starting your day with five minutes of Sun Salutations, or sitting by a pond, embrace the quiet (it helps if you turn off all of your technology). Nurture your soul, your spirit, each and every day.

I wish you well on your life's journey. Remember to utilize your tool kit and strengthen your resolve to lower stress in your life. Don't be afraid to continue to add other techniques and approaches into your tool kit. Be adventuresome.

I wish you a long, healthy, mostly stress free (at least from major stress) life. Be happy, be joyful, and make the most of everyday. Surround yourself with good friends, family, and make a difference in someone else's life.

Find your center and love life.

Be well, safe travels, and a long and healthy life to you and yours,

Craig M. Rand

Name________________________________ Class Days and Time ____________________

16.1

CREATING YOUR OWN TOTEM OR TABLE OF CONTENTS OF YOUR LIFE STORY

This assignment has a choice. You may do whichever one strikes a chord with you.

Choice one is to create a totem pole that reflects your strengths, likes, passions; the things that make you the wonderful person you are. If you Google pictures of totem poles, you will see a vast array, which may help you design yours. Let's see your creative side come out and develop something that represents you.

Choice two is to create a Table of Contents for your life story: A new bestseller about your life from birth through your death. The future chapters will be based on your dreams and expectations, but look at your life and give titles to periods of your life. Put some thought into this and develop a Table of Contents that is reflective of your life through today and what your goals, dreams, and expectations will be.

(If you have energy left as the semester winds down, try both.)

Appendix A
Guided Imagery Meditations for Your Practice

This section of the book is focused on sharing some of my favorite guided visualizations to read, practice, and develop into your meditation experience. These are very similar to the ones that we will be using during our practice time in class. The goal of these types of guided imagery is to help you add guided imagery meditations into your stress management tool kit in order to help you develop and create a balance in your life. My ultimate goal by sharing these is to encourage the practice of taking time each and every day for you.

If there is one message that I hope you have found from reading this book, and/or taking the class it would be this: the most important person in the world to take care of is YOU. Once you have taken time to take care of yourself, whether it is the physical, the emotional, or the spiritual, then and only then will you be able to move forward to face the stressors of your life. Then you will have the strength, the joy, the desire to help take care of those you love and who need your help. If you are focusing on your wellness, then it will be easier to take care of your family, your friends, and your colleagues.

I hope by using the framework of these guided visualizations you will enjoy practicing meditation, and with time you will be able to create your own meaningful images to help you manage your stress and take time for you. The mind is limitless and I hope your life experiences will enable you to add or develop your own meaningful meditations.

A BEACH MEDITATION

Begin with your deep cleansing breaths. Fill the lungs completely. Slowly exhale all breath through the nose. Begin to quiet your mind. Turn it off. Disconnect from the outside world for the next fifteen minutes. Focus on your heartbeat. Feel the warmth of your breath. Feel the connection of your breath and your heartbeat; combined they are your life force. Become still, both in mind and body. Feel emptiness. Begin to relax and let yourself take this mental trip. Make this image come to life in your mind. Begin to focus within your mind on the color of the sky. After you have the color in your mind's eye, look further to see that you are laying on this beautiful sandy beach in Florida or the Caribbean. The beach is quiet as you are the only one there. Feel the warm of the sun as it caresses your body. Feel the warm tropic breezes blow across your body. Hear the palm trees rustle in the wind and feel the warmth of the sun as it penetrates your soul. As you sit on the beach, look over the water. See the variety of colors in the water: deep blue, green blue, aquamarine. Hear the waves as they come ashore. As your body becomes warmer, you decide to go for a swim. Feel yourself walking on the warm sand. As you come closer to the water, feel the water come over your feet as you walk in it. It is refreshing and calming. Take another step. The water is at your calves; another couple of steps and the water is at your knees. Several more steps and the water is at your mid-thighs. Dive head first into the water. Feel the bubbles as they surround your body. Feel the joy as you float effortlessly in the salt water. How relaxed do you feel as you swim in water that is crystal clear, warm, and not very deep? You can see the bottom. You see a beautiful seashell. Dive down and pick it up. Bring it to the surface. Feel the roughness of the outer shell and then and feel the beauty of the inner shell. See the colors: pinks, purples; all so beautiful and so smooth.

Swim back to shore. Enjoy the time in the water. As you leave the water, go back to the towel and sit in the peace and quiet of this beautiful beach. Now as you sit there on the beach, the sun begins to set in front of you. The sun is a beautiful bright red orange. It looks as if the water will swallow the sun. The clouds are on both sides of the sun and the colors are beautiful, the prettiest sunset you have seen. As the sun sinks into the horizon, the colors become deeper and more intense and lead to darkness. As you look up, you see the first star of the night and you make a wish, "I wish I may, I wish I might", on the star you see tonight. The stars begin to blossom, from tens, to hundreds, to thousands. The evening sky is just as beautiful as the day has been. When you are ready, begin to close the picture down in your mind and as you make the transition back to this moment in time, this place, and end with deep cleansing breaths for a minute or two. Then roll onto to your right side. Take another deep breath, and then sit up and open your eyes.

SUMMER PICNIC

Begin with your deep cleansing breaths. Fill the lungs completely. Slowly exhale all breath through the nose. Begin to quiet your mind. Turn it off. Disconnect from the outside world for the next fifteen minutes. Focus on your heartbeat. Feel the warmth of your breath. Feel the connection of your breath and your heartbeat; combined they are your life force. Become still, both in mind and body. Feel emptiness. Begin to relax, and let yourself take this mental trip. Make this image come to life in your mind. Now, within your mind, I want you to imagine a summer day, a beautiful summer day, with a blue sky, warm breezes, and a little humidity in the air. You are at your favorite park at an open-air lodge. You are with friends and family enjoying the day playing games like ladder golf, volleyball, or tossing a Frisbee. See people barbequing. Smell the great aromas of the food that is on the grill: hamburgers, hot dogs, sausage, and corn on the cob. Hear the laughter. See the smiles, and experience the fun that everyone is having on this summer day. See the faces of your friends or family. Hear the laughter. Let the joy of everyone together fill your heart and spirit. As you look to the west, you see big, dark thunder clouds billowing up and rolling your way. Off in the distance, you can hear the thunder, and see the clouds move quicker towards your area. You can see the lightening dance across the sky. It is beautiful to watch; some is coming straight down to the earth; some is literally going sideways. Then the rain starts to fall. As everyone goes into the shelter, you can hear the melody of the raindrops on the tin roof. The clouds are darker. The lightening lights up the sky and the rain comes harder. The melody is intense, but calming at the same time. Just as quickly as the storm blows in, the storm leaves. The rain lets up. The sound of the rain on the roof becomes ever so soft, and as you leave the shelter, you can still see the lightening as the storm moves away. The sun comes out, and a beautiful rainbow appears. See the depth of the colors of the rainbow. You wonder if there is a pot of gold at the end of the rainbow. People start to come out, and the sun quickly dries up the rain. TA mist is rising from the ground as the sun dries the earth out. Look around at the rain that has covered the plants and the grass. See them shimmer in the sunlight. Go back to playing the games, eating the food, and enjoying this beautiful summer day.

When you are ready, say goodbye to everyone, and close down this picture. As you began, end with deep cleansing breaths for one or two minutes. When you are ready, roll to your right side. Take another breath, and then slowly sit up. Welcome back.

© karamysh, 2012. Under license from Shutterstock, Inc.

AN EVENING SKY

Start with deep cleansing breaths for a minute, and then begin to focus with your mind on the color black. Visualize this color in your mind. Don't let any thoughts or other colors come into your mind. Now that you have focused on the color black, imagine that it is late evening and you are lying outside under the night sky. There is no other light around, and all you see as you look above is more stars than you have seen in a long time. So continue to focus on the night sky. See the thousands of stars, the moon, a planet (Mars), perhaps even a quick moving satellite speeding across the skyline. What time of year is it that you are laying outside watching the evening sky? Are you lying on the grass, a blanket, a lounge chair? What else is a part of this experience of watching the evening sky and focusing on the stars? Is it warm out? Is there a breeze? Is it cool out? Bring everything into play with this experience. Are you sharing this evening with someone? Can you find the Big Dipper which leads to the North Star? Can you find the Little Dipper or Orion's Belt? Do you see any other constellations in the sky or just a bejeweled evening sky? As you watch, feel connected to the universe. What other life exists in the galaxies?

Did you see the falling star that went from one side of the sky to the other? It was beautiful. Continue to breathe and watch the stars twinkle. Watch the steady light of the planets and relax and feel connected to the evening, to the earth, and to the magnificence of nature that you are observing. When you are ready, begin to close the picture down in your mind as you make the transition back to this moment in time, this place. As we began, we also end, with deep cleansing breaths for a minute or two. Then roll onto to your right side. Take another deep breath, and then sit up and slowly open your eyes.

A SUMMER DAY

Begin with your deep cleansing breaths. Fill the lungs completely. Slowly exhale all breath through the nose. Begin to quiet your mind. Turn it off. Disconnect from the outside world for the next fifteen minutes. Focus on your heartbeat. Feel the warmth of your breath. Feel the connection of your breath and your heartbeat; combined they are your life force. Become still, both in mind and body. Feel emptiness. Begin to relax and let yourself take this mental trip. Make this image come to life in your mind. I want you to imagine a beautiful summer day, with a beautiful blue sky, and a warm sun basking the earth. You are lying in a big, old, comfortable hammock. The hammock is hung between two big trees. The trees are covered with leaves, but the sun is sending shafts of sunbeams through the leaves. You can feel the warmth of the sun on your body. There is a warm breeze blowing through the yard. It gently rocks the hammock. Between the warmth of the sun on your face and the gentle rocking of the hammock, you are at peace with no cares in the world. Life today is calm, peaceful, and you are just embracing this moment of summer.

Perhaps on the table next to you is a cold glass of lemonade or ice tea. See yourself taking a drink and feel how refreshing the drink is. Enjoy the simple pleasures of this summer day. Focus on being in the hammock. Focus on the warmth of the summer day, and the shafts of sunbeams cascading through the leaves of the trees that are holding the hammock up. Focus on the way the sunbeams play on the leaves. It is almost if the sunlight is a waterfall tumbling over the leaves as it arrives where you are lying. When you are ready, focus on the trees, and close this picture down. Save it for another day, and as you make the transition back to this moment, where we are today, as we begin we end, focus on your deep cleansing breath. Completely fill your lungs with new air, new life force. Remove the stagnant air, and refresh your body with your breath. When you are ready, roll over to your right side. Take another deep breath, and then when you are ready to come back to this moment, sit up, and open your eyes.

© KellyNelson, 2012. Under license from Shutterstock, Inc.

THE WHITE BOX

First, make sure that your body is comfortable. Lie flat. Make sure your head, shoulders, and legs are in a straight line. Let your legs drop open a little to relax the hips. Focus on your deep cleansing breaths. Fill the lungs completely. Slowly exhale all breath through the nose. Begin to quiet your mind. Turn it off from what is going on outside of this room. Focus on your heartbeat. Breathe. Feel the connection of your breath and your heartbeat; combined they are your life force. Become still, both in mind and body.

Today, we are going to try something a little different, so within your mind's eye, I want you to imagine that you are walking down a long, cool, stone corridor. The path is lit by torches on the wall spaced out every twenty yards on so. As you are walking down the hallway, you can feel the coolness of the space. The ground is hard and well worn, and up ahead you see a big, old door. The door is made from hand-hewn lumber. It is very heavy, and has big, old hinges and a lock. As you wonder how you will enter the doorway, you place your hand in your pocket and you find a skeleton key. It looks like a perfect fit for the door. You place the key into the lock, and with some effort, the lock finally turns. You start to open the door, and then you see a bright white light. As your eyes become used to the light, you see a room that is empty except for a table in the middle that has a box on it. You close the door. You go to the table, and you see that the box is yours. It has your initials on it. What is your box made from—wood, metal, plastic? See your box. It has other markings that represent your life experiences, so you know the box is yours. As you open the box, you see that it is filled with paper and a writing tool. You take out the first piece of paper. Now

© Sipos Andras, 2012. Under license from Shutterstock, Inc.

you identify the biggest stressor in your life at this moment. Write it down on the paper and then write down what you need to do to address this stressor. Sign your name to the paper, fold it over in half, and write a big number "1" on the outside of the paper. Place it in the box. This is your action plan, what you will do after you take this time for yourself. Take out the second piece of paper, and identify the second biggest stressor in your life at this moment. Write it down on the paper, and then write down what you need to do to address this stressor. Sign your name to the paper, fold it over in half, write a big number "2" on the outside of the paper, and place in the box. Take out the third piece of paper. Identify the next biggest stressor in your life at this moment. Write it down on the paper, and then write down what you need to do to address this stressor. Sign your name to the paper, fold it over in half, write a big number "3" on the outside of the paper, and place in the box. Now you have made a list of the major stressors in your life. You have identified them and are leaving them in the box.

Walk out of the room and back down the hallway. Feel the stones of the floor and the coolness of the hallway. As you walk, you feel lighter because you have left your stressors back in the box.

You are walking out of the hallway to your favorite place, a place you enjoy, feel safe, and relaxed. See this place in your mind. Create the place and enjoy your time there. See everything there. Why does this place make you feel better? Be there. See everything about this place: the space, the weather, the people, and the food. Make it come alive in your mind. Enjoy your time in this safe place.

Now it is time to go back to the room. See the hallway. Feel the stones as you walk down the hallway. The hallway is warmer this time. The air is lighter. You are at the door. Place your key in the lock, turn, and pull the door open. Walk to the center where your box is. See the box. Open the box and pull out the first piece of paper. Reread the stressor, recommit to the action plan you will be working on today. Tear up the paper and toss the paper into the air where it is consumed by the bright light. Now pull out the second piece of paper, reread, commit to the action plan, and make sure that you address this today. Tear up the paper and toss it into the air where it is consumed by the bright light. Then take out the third piece of paper, reread the stressor, recommit to the action plan and to working on this today. Tear up the paper and toss it into the air where it is consumed by the bright light. You know what your stressors are today. You have identified an action plan to address these stressors. Now go forth and make your day a better day.

As we always end, close the picture down in your mind and as you make the transition back to this moment in time, this place, and end with deep cleansing breaths for a minute or two. Roll onto to your right side. Take another deep breath, and then slowly sit up and open your eyes.

YOUR FAVORITE PLACE IN THE GREAT OUTDOORS

Begin with your deep cleansing breaths. Fill your lungs completely. Slowly exhale all breath through the nose. Begin to quiet your mind. Turn it off from what is going on outside of this room. Focus on your heartbeat. Breathe. Feel the connection of your breath and your heartbeat; combined they are your life force. Become still, both in mind and body.

Today, I want you each to go to a place you have always wanted to visit but have never been; some place in the outdoors. Think about a place on this earth that you want to visit; perhaps this place is on your bucket list. It is a place that holds a fascination for you. You feel connected or have a longing to spend time there.

Now, once you have that place picked, begin to see it in your mind. Make the place come alive. See all aspects of this place. What is the terrain--beach, canyons, mountains, snow, or water? Are you sailing on the ocean, hiking in the wild, or walking through a forest? Imagine this place and make it come alive in your mind. What is the weather like? The temperature? See the trees, flowers, and the color of the sky. Is there any wildlife? Any birds in this place? Why did you choose this place? What attracts you here? What makes this place somewhere you want to visit? Identify the reasons. Are you sharing this trip with someone or is this just for you? Enjoy the beauty, the peacefulness, and the connection this image has to you. Enjoy your time here. As you close down the image in your mind and begin to make the transition back to the present moment, place this image in your mind. You can always visit again as it has significance to you. As you come back, end with deep cleansing breaths. Take a long, slow inhalation and a long, slow, exhalation. Take one or two minutes of deep cleansing breaths, and then roll to your right side. Take another breath and begin to become aware of your surroundings. Slowly sit up. Welcome back. Keep the energy from this meditation with you all throughout the day.

A CONVERSATION WITH EITHER YOUR GOD OR SOMEONE WHOM YOU HAVE LOST AND TRUSTED

Today, our meditation will be a little different. Begin with your deep cleansing breaths. Fill the lungs completely. Slowly exhale all breath through the nose. Begin to quiet your mind. Turn it off. Disconnect from the outside world for the next fifteen minutes. Focus on your heartbeat. Feel the warmth of your breath. Feel the connection of your breath and your heartbeat; combined they are your life force. Become still, both in mind and body. Feel emptiness. Begin to relax and let yourself take this mental trip. Make this image come to life in your mind.

I want you to decide with whom you will be having a conversation. If you have a God that you believe in, then I want you to start to imagine your vision of your God. See God sitting in a big, comfortable chair opposite you. If you don't have a God whom you believe in, but you have lost a friend or family member, then you can have the conversation with that person. I want you to imagine that person as you remember him or her. Again see that person sitting in a big, comfortable chair opposite you. Once you have either God or a person pictured in your mind, have a conversation with them. Discuss with them the person you have become. Talk to them about your strengths and weaknesses, your dreams, your failures, your goals. Listen to their responses and be fully engaged with this conversation. Then as always, I want you to close down the conversation. Review what you talked about, and as you make the transition to here and now, end with deep cleansing breaths for a couple of minutes. Roll over to your right side. Continue with one or two deep breaths, then slowly sit up and become aware of where you are.

OCEAN KAYAKING

Begin by centering your body. Make sure that you are in a straight line; with legs open slightly, arms to your side, palms up. Begin with your deep cleansing breaths. Fill your lungs completely. Slowly exhale all breath through the nose. Begin to quiet your mind. Turn it off from what is going on outside of this room. Focus on your heartbeat. Breathe. Feel the connection of your breath and your heartbeat; combined they are your life force. Become still, both in mind and body.

Now that you are still, in your mind, I want you to create the following picture: you are on a beach with an ocean kayak, somewhere around the Outer Banks of North Carolina. What is the color of your boat? Is it a bright blue, orange, yellow, or green to be easily seen on the water? Feel the life jacket that you are wearing. See yourself standing at the water's edge, watching the waves, checking the temperature of the warm water. Now see yourself walking into the water, pulling the kayak with you. When the water is up to your knees and after the next wave rolls in, jump on the kayak and start paddling before the next wave comes ashore. As the next wave comes in, feel the boat bounce up in the air. Feel and taste the salt water as it sprays your face and body. Keep paddling until you are past the wave break. Now start paddling parallel to the shore. Feel the boat as it glides over the waves. You are never far from the shoreline. Feel the peacefulness of being on the water. See the pelicans as they glide along the water looking for fish. The water is a deep blue green. You can see the bottom. The water is crystal clear. What other things do you see as you kayak? As you look down the water, you see a pod of dolphins heading towards you. They are so graceful. As they get nearer, the younger ones swim right next to your boat. You can hear them breathe. You can see their eyes. They actually look into your soul. You feel a strong connection to them. They even give you a tail fluke splash as they swim by. It is so amazing to have this experience. It makes for a great day. Embrace the warmth of the day, the beautiful sun, the warm water, riding the waves, and connecting with nature. Make it your own.

When you are ready, begin to close the picture down in your mind and as you make the transition back to this moment in time, end with deep cleansing breaths for a minute or two. Roll onto to your right side, take another deep breath, and then sit up and open your eyes.

© Pichugin Dmitry, 2012. Under license from Shutterstock, Inc.

A SUMMER CARNIVAL

Begin with your deep cleansing breaths. Fill the lungs completely. Slowly exhale all breath through the nose. Begin to quiet your mind. Turn it off. Disconnect from the outside world for the next fifteen minutes. Focus on your heartbeat. Feel the warmth of your breath. Feel the connection of your breath and your heartbeat; combined they are your life force. Become still, both in mind and body. Feel emptiness. Begin to relax and let yourself take this mental trip. Make this image come to life in your mind. Now, within your mind, I want you to bring to life a visit to a summer carnival. See yourself on a summer day or evening. Hear the sounds of the carnival. See the rides, the lights of the rides, the smell of the foods, the laughter, and screams of delights from the children running around taking it all in. Now in front of you, see the merry-go-round. Imagine yourself in line watching it go round and round. It stops and it is your turn. See the horse that you want to ride. Get on the merry-go-round

© Alan49, 2012. Under license from Shutterstock, Inc.

and sit on your horse. What color is your horse? What color mane does the horse have? Does it have a feather headdress? If so, what color is that? Now the merry-go-round goes around and around, up and down. You see the scenes on the inside of the merry-go-round, which are pictures of the countryside. You see the people waving to you as you go around and around. What a simple joy. Feel the smile on your face. Feel the memories of riding coming back to you.

As the ride ends, you walk around the carnival taking in all of the sights: the games that people play to win stuffed animals, the smells of the food that make your mouth water. You see friends who are enjoying the carnival. Watch the children run from ride to ride, laughing. See the joy on their faces. Embrace the simple joy of this evening. As the sun sets, see the bright colors on each of the rides. See the Ferris wheel lighting up and walk over and get in that line. As you get on the ride, feel yourself going up. See the moon and stars and the whole carnival from the air. Enjoy the ride, going round and round. Take the simple joy of this day and keep it with you the rest of the day.

When you are ready, begin to close the picture down in your mind and as you make the transition back to this moment in time, this place, as we began we also end with deep cleansing breaths for a minute or two. Then roll onto to your right side. Take another deep breath, and then slowly sit up and open your eyes.

A RIDE IN A HOT AIR BALLOON

Begin by centering your body. Make sure that you are in a straight line with your legs open slightly, arms to your side, palms up. Begin with your deep cleansing breaths. Fill your lungs completely. Slowly exhale all breath through the nose. Begin to quiet your mind. Turn it off from what is going on outside of the room. Focus on your heartbeat. Breathe. Feel the connection of your breath and your heartbeat; combined they are your life force. Become still, both in mind and body.

Now that you are still, today in your mind I want you to create the following picture: you are driving down a country road with a good friend or a family member on a beautiful fall afternoon. The car pulls into a field and in the middle of the field you see a hot air balloon being set up. The wicker basket is already on the ground, and the balloon is starting to fill with the hot air. You walk up to the crew to ask how they are doing. The balloon is getting larger. What colors and patterns are on this hot air balloon? When the balloon is fully inflated, the captain asks if you both are ready to go for a ride. What a great surprise! You readily agree and step on the stairs and climb into the basket. With that, the pilot gets in and calls the crew to let go of the ropes. He hits heater and a rush of flames helps the balloon to rise into the sky. Look up and see the beautiful colors of the balloon. The colors are so bright and brilliant against the backdrop of this beautiful fall sky.

The balloon rises slowly. You are just above the trees, and each of the trees is in full autumn colors. The balloon rises slowly and you look around in a 360 degree panoramic view of the countryside. It is so peaceful up here in the air. The only sounds are from the propane tank heating the air and from your conversations with your friend and the pilot. The world almost appears still. The fall foliage is ablaze with reds, yellows, maroons. Below you can actually see the balloon's shadow as it rolls gently across the fields. You can see fields with cows, goats, and some deer playing. Up ahead you see a farmer's market with a corn maze and a huge field filled with pumpkins. You can see lots of people at the market, and they are all pointing up in the sky at you. You can see their smiles, their happiness for the fun they know you are having. You keep drifting and eventually the farmer's market is behind you. You float over some ponds and can see the reflection of the sun and the balloon on the surface of the water. A little further you see a river rolling through the countryside, surrounded by the beauty of the trees in full fall foliage. As you get closer to the river, the pilot starts to let some air out of the balloon and you start to slowly lower down towards the river. You are just above the tree line. The leaves are beautiful, reds, yellows, oranges against the beautiful blue sky as you sink closer to the river. You start to think that you are going to land in the water. You can see the reflection of the balloon in the water, but at the last minute, the pilot fires up the flame and the hot air balloon begins to rise. Up, up, and away, and you are floating back over the countryside. What an amazing ride. As you look around, the countryside looks like a painted post card. The colors are so beautiful. The view is amazing. You are calm, so relaxed.

© gary718, 2012. Under license from Shutterstock, Inc.

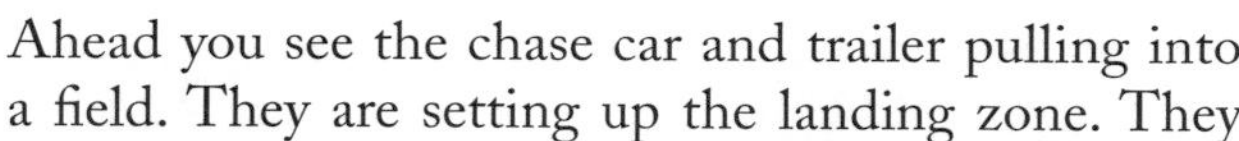
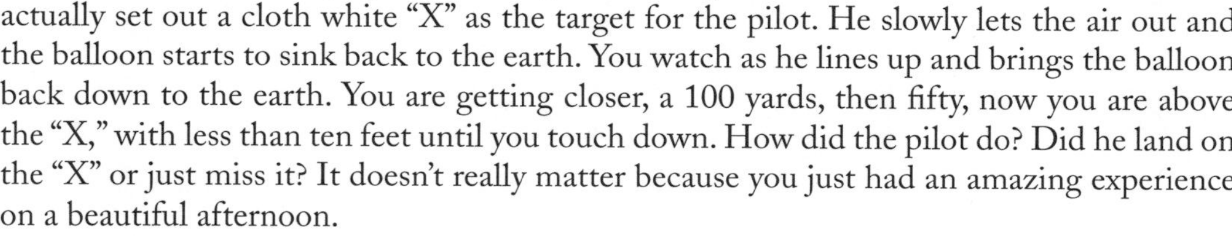

Ahead you see the chase car and trailer pulling into a field. They are setting up the landing zone. They actually set out a cloth white "X" as the target for the pilot. He slowly lets the air out and the balloon starts to sink back to the earth. You watch as he lines up and brings the balloon back down to the earth. You are getting closer, a 100 yards, then fifty, now you are above the "X," with less than ten feet until you touch down. How did the pilot do? Did he land on the "X" or just miss it? It doesn't really matter because you just had an amazing experience on a beautiful afternoon.

The crew grabs the ropes and anchors the balloon. They put the stairs up and help you and your friend out of the balloon. They release the hot air, and you watch as balloon sinks back to the earth. As the tradition goes, the pilot and crew bring out a bottle of sparkling grape juice (or stronger if you are of age), to celebrate a wonderful flight and to make a toast to good memories and to new and old friends. When you are ready, begin to close the picture down in your mind and as you make the transition back to this moment in time, this place, and end with deep cleansing breaths for a minute or two. Roll onto to your right side. Take another deep breath, and then sit up and open your eyes.

Appendix B
Recommended Websites and Other Resources

This list could never be comprehensive, but I have listed some of the current websites that I utilize for my personal information as well as preparing my lectures in any of my health and wellness related courses. I hope you find the list useful, and I hope that you will add some of these into the bookmark section on your PC. Use them to help you stay healthy and well.

1. www.realage.com. One of the assignments to help you determine your age based on lifestyle compared to chronological age. You can sign up for web newsletter that often has useful material.
2. www.labyrinthsociety.com. A good webpage for labyrinths and related articles as well as information. It includes a labyrinth finder for anywhere in the world.
3. www.withinsight.com. A good website that has a variety of meditations available to you.
4. www.journalforyou.com. An electronic journaling site with tips and suggestions to make your journaling assignment a good and valuable experience.
5. www.nccam.nih.gov. A website sponsored by the National Institute of Health, a leading source for information on Complementary and Alternative Medicine.
6. www.nationalwellness.org. The leading site for information on health and wellness.

7. www.welcoa.org. Link to Wellness Council of America with some useful information available.
8. www.webmd.com. The leading and most trusted website for health or disease information. Well designed and maintained by doctors, so the information is current and trustworthy.
9. www.mayoclinic.com. Another leading medical website that has information on illnesses and diseases and maintained by the Mayo Clinic.
10. www.nata.org. Website for the National Athletic Trainer's Association, useful for health issues related to being active and or involved with sports.
11. www.aahperd.org. National Association for Health, Physical Education, Recreation and Dance, a good reference for being active. A place to find out information on new games, rules, places for guidance, information to keep our youth moving.
12. www.drweil.com. A popular health advisor who has his own newsletter and website with material on staying healthy.
13. www.beinggreen. A good beginning website on environmental issues, sustainability, and living green.
14. www.heart.org. The American Heart Association's webpage, a good site with helpful information as related to staying healthy and taking care of our hearts.
15. www.usda.gov. The Department of Agriculture's website, a wealth of knowledge on food safety, dietary guidelines, climate, and environment among many others.
16. www.spiritualityhealth.com. The website for the magazine called *Spirituality and Health* that explores the health of body, mind, and spirit using a science, psychology, sociology and/or medical perspective.
17. www.cspiinet.org. The webpage for the Center for Science in the public interest, a great source for current information. Their focus is to educate the consumer regarding safer and healthier foods, honest food labeling, and research regarding foods we all eat. I love their Nutrition Action Newsletter for current and useful information relevant to our lives.
18. www.apta.org. The National Association for Physical Therapy, a good resource for information on staying active after an injury, and information related to improving or maintaining your wellness.
19. www.gracecathedral.org. Dr. Lauren Artress, the leading pioneer of folks who have helped bring labyrinths back into the mainstream. This is her current church and the heart of the labyrinth movement.
20. www.nutrition.gov. A great resource for dietary guidelines, MyPlate, and nutrition education.
21. www.cdc.gov. The webpage for the Center for Disease Control, which has a wealth of quality information related to healthy living, multimedia material, diseases and conditions, and much more.

22. www.kripalu.org. A center for yoga and other stress techniques. It is a retreat with weekend or week long events. If you need a place to get away, refresh your mind or body, I would recommend what they offer. If you are willing to work while attending a program, you can significantly lower your costs.

23. www.healthypeople.gov. The government's site for developing a plan for improving the health of the United States. A good framework for the focus of the health experts in this country for the next ten years.

24. www.brianlukeseaward.net. A world-leading expert on stress and wellness who is a consultant, motivational speaker, author, videographer, and an awesome individual. Check out his books, videos, and meditations.

Another reference source that is available on our smart phones and iPads is a wealth of apps that have been developed with a stress management and/or wellness information. The obvious concern I have with listing them is that we talk about technology increasing our stress, but at the same time I have to admit that I find some of these useful and are loaded onto my current iPad. Check them out and make use of them whenever possible. My list is in no way inclusive, as so many new apps come out monthly, but it is a starting point.

I-PAD AND SMART PHONE APPS

With the numbers that are added weekly, I am unable to state that each will be available. What I do know with apps is that you must use key words related to wellness, meditation, yoga, fitness programs. The technology is there for us to use and add to our tool kit.

WebMD: same access to quality health information as listed in the website area.

HDYoga: provides useful information and demonstrations related to a variety of Yoga poses.

I-Chi, Power HD: engages the useful in a variety of chi energy exercises and activities.

Yoga: another yoga that provides information to the top one hundred yoga poses.

Zen Garden Sands: allows the user the chance to make a meditation sand garden, which you can rake, add rocks to it, and wipe it clean and start again. I enjoy this one often.

Nature Sound and Naturespace: both apps bring small snippets of sounds of nature. Just helps set the stage to relax, assuming that sounds of nature help you relax.

Anti-stress: a catalog of quotes related to dealing with or improving your stress response.

Tomorrow: an app that allows you to develop a "to do" list that will help you stay organized and on task. Think time management meets better organization. Of course it only helps if you make use of it.

BikemapHD: allows you to access a variety of bike routes to help you get moving. Remember exercise and play are great tools in your toolkit and having a quick access to safe routes is awesome.

FitnessTracker: allows you to check out exercise programs, access to fitness magazines, food and body tracker, and a selection of videos demonstrating a variety of exercise.

Each of the game apps can involve a social connection, although you have to not just play the machine, but you have to enter the games that you interact with others. My family plays Words with Friends, Hangman, and a version of Pictionary. It helps keep family and friends connected and involved.

For the iPhone there is actually an app that keeps track of steps taken, shows the route and elevation of your walks, so make use of the technology and integrate technology as a part of your wellness programming. Your technology can become your back-up training partner.

MUSICAL SELECTIONS THAT I HAVE USED IN CLASS FOR MEDITATIONS

As I developed this list, I will include some of my favorite artists that I use within my stress management class. The one recommendation I have is to find a variety of musical selections that work for you. If you like New Age, then use it. If you like soft jazz and it works for you, continue to build the library. With the advent of smart phones and other technology, you can add a folder of music for meditation. Keep it simple and use before exams, a job interview, stuck in a traffic jam, or whenever you need help to lessen the stress response. I hope you enjoy some of my selections. Many of these recommendations are often in play whenever I am in my office. I have found that by listening to this music, I set the mood for when students come in visit. I try to walk the talk and it relaxes the mood when a frustrated student comes to visit me. Not to say, I don't listen to other musicians (Bruce Springsteen), but these albums are intended to calm and they do.

William Ackerman can be found on the Windham Hill Record label.

Best of Hearts of Space, music from the National Radio Series.

David Lanz, a wide variety of music that I use often.

Mia Jang, CD called "Water Circles."

I have never been disappointed from any of the New Age music from Windham Hill. I would recommend checking them out as a good starting point for your music selections for meditation and relaxing.

Another company I have had success with is called Narada. They have a wide variety and I enjoy their product.

China Meditations of the Orient, from Inside Sounds, incorporates a variety of traditional Chinese instruments along with other contemporary music.

Two Worlds One, Lisa Lynne and Aryeh Frankfurter, produced by New Earth Records.

Another artist whom I love to listen to is Jim Brickman. His music is mostly piano as he was a classically trained pianist, but his hit songs have words with them. As you build a relaxation folder, I would include his music.

Glossary

4 Rs: ways to exercise stewardship over the earth; recycle, reduce, reuse, repairs.

A

Aerobic activity: physical activity that uses oxygen, increasing the heart rate and breathing.

Agnostic: a person who claims neither faith nor disbelief in God.

Atheist: a person who does not believe in the existence of God or gods.

Auditory learning: a score derived from one or more standardized tests to determine intelligence.

B

Basal metabolic rate: the rate at which your body uses energy while at rest to maintain vital functions such as breathing and body temperature.

Breath: exhalation and inhalation of air from the lungs.

Burnout: completely overwhelming stress that causes a person to shut down both personally and professionally.

C

Carbon footprint: the total amount of carbon dioxide (CO) and other greenhouse gases emitted over the full life cycle of a product or service.

Cardiovascular: pertaining to the heart and blood vessels; often referred to as a type of exercise that strengthens the heart and lungs.

Chartres labyrinth: world-famous thirteenth century labyrinth located in the cathedral in Chartres, France.

Clean Air Act: federal law created to reduce chemical emissions into the air on a national level.

Clean Water Act: primary federal law that governs water pollution by setting wastewater and water quality standards.

Complement and Alternative Medicine (CAM): a group of diverse medical and health care systems, practices, and products that are not generally considered part of conventional medicine.

Complex carbohydrates: large chains of sugar units arranged to form starches and fiber; includes grains, breads, rice, pasta, vegetables, and beans.

Cretan labyrinth: ancient labyrinth said to be located on the island of Crete and associated with the myth of the Minotaur.

D

Depression: a sense of despondency and dejection, often accompanied by feelings of hopelessness and inadequacy.

Diaphragmatic breath (cleansing breath): a deep breathing technique that draws air deep in the lungs by using the diaphragm rather than by flexing the rib cage.

Distress: bad stress; negative stress that has harmful consequences on our body both mentally and physically.

E

Emotions: that part of the consciousness that involves feeling and the capacity to detect and respond to sensory stimuli.

Environment: the totality of surrounding things, conditions, or influences.

Environmental stressors: any external factors such as weather conditions, noise, and crowds that create stress.

Eustress: good stress; a stress that brings joy and happiness such as the birth of a baby.

Exclusive meditation: a type of meditation in which you focus on one thought, slowing the mind, concentrating on the breath and often using a mantra such as the word "OM."

Exercise metabolic rate: the rate at which your body uses energy while exercising.

F

Feelings/sensitivity: nonrational, internal sensation not connected with sight, hearing, taste, smell, or what is classically correlated to touch.

Fight or flight response: the first stage of GAS in which the sympathetic nervous system automatically prepares a person to either confront (fight) or escape (flee) from a threat.

Finger labyrinth: small, portable labyrinth that is "walked" by tracing a finger over the design.

FITT Formula: a way to design an exercise program based on Frequency, Intensity, Time, and Type of exercise.

Food pyramid: a nutritional diagram or eating plan in the form of a pyramid with complex carbohydrates at the bottom and fats and sugars at the top.

G

General Adaptation Syndrome (GAS): a term used to describe the body's short-term and long-term reactions to stress. It consists of three stages: alarm, resistance, and exhaustion.

Guided imagery meditation: a type of meditation in which you use hypnosis-like suggestions to create images in the mind, which elicit positive emotions such as joy, love, happiness, and calmness.

H

Happiness: state of positive emotions.

Helplessness: the feeling that you have no control over a situation or action and can see no possible positive outcome.

I

Inclusive meditation: a type of meditation in which you focus on the range of emotions you have experienced throughout the day without passing judgment on your thoughts or feelings.

Intelligence: capacity for learning, reasoning, understanding, and similar forms of mental activity

Intelligence quotient (IQ): a score derived from one or more standardized tests to determine intelligence.

J

Journaling: private writing for either record-keeping or thought-processing, often used as a stress reduction technique.

K

Ki: Japanese term for the life-force energy within each of us.

Kinesthetic/tactile learning: a learning style in which ideas and concepts are best assimilated through physical experiences and actions.

L

Labyrinth: one of the oldest meditative or contemplative tools; an intricate path walked for personal, psychological, and spiritual transformation.

Lotus position: a cross-legged meditation position for meditation, with the left foot resting on the right thigh, and the right foot resting on the left thigh.

M

Meditation: contemplation; a quiet, alert, yet focused state of mind often used as a relaxation technique.

Mindfulness meditation: a type of meditation in which you are engaged with and focused on a single activity, without letting your thoughts wander.

MyPlate: current nutrition guide published by the United States Department of Agriculture, depicting a place setting with a plate and glass divided into five food groups.

N

Nutrition: obtaining the nourishment necessary for health and growth.

O

Obesity: a medical condition in which extreme overweight and excess body fat impacts health.

Organized religion: an institution founded to express belief and worship a particular divine power or divinity in an ordered manner.

P

Physical Activity Readiness Questionnaire (PAR-Q): a questionnaire to help you determine if it is safe to begin an exercise program in your current physical condition.

Physical fitness: having enough physical energy to go through a normal work and leisure day as well as maintaining sufficient reserves to handle emergencies.

Physiological stressors: factors that are damaging to emotional or psychological health such as injury, serious disease, depression, or serious drug and alcohol use. These generally are long-term stressors.

Plan of action: the means by which you focus your thoughts and decide what steps are needed to take to achieve your goals.

Presentism: the act of being physically present in a workplace, but either not working or being inefficient at work by doing non-work related activities such as checking personal email, going on Facebook, or playing games.

Psycho-social stressors: the ordinary stresses of daily life such as losing your job, moving, ending a friendship, divorce, getting a speeding ticket, car accident, starting or stopping school, illness etc. These tend to be of shorter duration and/or are self-limiting.

Q

Qi: Chinese word for the life-force energy within each of us

R

Rate of perceived exertion (RPE): a method of determining exercise intensity by using a scale of 1 to 10 to estimate how much energy you feel you are exerting during a workout.

Recycle: to convert waste into reusable materials.

Reduce: to use less or consume fewer products.

Repair: to mend or fix a product instead of discarding it.

Resilence: the ability to adapt quickly to the situation and move forward positively.

Resiliency: the ability to bounce back from obstacles and/or adversity in daily life; the ability to cope with life stressors in a positive way.

Reuse: to repurpose or continue to use products instead of replacing with newer versions.

S

Second-hand smoke: inhalation of smoke in the environment from tobacco products used by others.

Self-efficacy: the confidence in yourself to make positive things happen; a belief in your ability to succeed in all or most life situations.

Self-esteem: a feeling of self-worth; the ability to meet life's challenges with confidence.

Simple carbohydrates: sugars that provide calories but no nutritional value.

Social health: the economic and social conditions under which a person lives or a society functions.

Spirituality: concern for the unseen and intangible, as opposed to physical or mundane; appreciation for values having to do with morality, goodness, the soul.

Stress: an absence of inner peace; emotional and physical wear and tear on the body; emotional and/or physical turmoil.

Synergy: two or more objects or entities working together to produce a result not independently obtainable.

T

Talk test: a method of determining exercise intensity based on your ability to carry on a conversation during the exercise.

Target heart rate (THR): a guideline for safe cardiovascular exercise based on age and workload on the heart.

Third-hand smoke: inhalation of lingering chemicals within upholstery, bedding, curtains, and other material resulting from the use of tobacco products.

Time management: the act of organizing the way you spend your time so that the most important and/or the most necessary activities are prioritized and accomplished first.

Time management strategies: the skills, tools, and techniques used to manage time when approaching specific tasks, projects, and goals.

To do list: a list of things you want to accomplish within a given time period.

Tool kit: set of strategies, coping mechanisms, and techniques that allows you to manage and reduce the stressors in your daily life.

Transfats: hydrogenated vegetable fats; formed when hydrogen is added to a liquid fat, so it remains solid at room temperature.

V

Visual learning: a learning style in which ideas and concepts are best assimilated through the use of images, pictures, colors or designs.

W

Weight training: exercise using your own body weight as resistance, a form of stack weight equipment, or free weights.

Wellness: the state of being in good mental, emotional, physical, and spiritual health.

Index

D

E

F

T

U

V

W

Y

Z